Boy on the Bridge

AMERICAN WARRIORS

Throughout the nation's history, numerous men and women of all ranks and branches of the US military have served their country with honor and distinction. During times of war and peace, there are individuals whose exemplary achievements embody the highest standards of the US armed forces. The aim of the American Warriors series is to examine the unique historical contributions of these individuals, whose legacies serve as enduring examples for soldiers and citizens alike. The series will promote a deeper and more comprehensive understanding of the US armed forces.

SERIES EDITOR: Joseph Craig

An AUSA Book

Boy on the Bridge

*The Story of
John Shalikashvili's
American Success*

Andrew Marble

UNIVERSITY PRESS OF KENTUCKY

Published by the University Press of Kentucky,
scholarly publisher for the Commonwealth,
serving Bellarmine University, Berea College, Centre
College of Kentucky, Eastern Kentucky University,
The Filson Historical Society, Georgetown College,
Kentucky Historical Society, Kentucky State University,
Morehead State University, Murray State University,
Northern Kentucky University, Transylvania University,
University of Kentucky, University of Louisville,
and Western Kentucky University.

Editorial and Sales Offices: The University Press of Kentucky
663 South Limestone Street, Lexington, Kentucky 40508–4008
www.kentuckypress.com

Unless otherwise noted, photographs are courtesy of the John Shalikashvili family.

Library of Congress Cataloging-in-Publication Data

Names: Marble, Andrew, author.
Title: Boy on the bridge : the story of John Shalikashvili's American
    success / Andrew Marble.
Other titles: Story of John Shalikashvili's American success
Description: Lexington, Kentucky : University Press of Kentucky, 2019. |
    Series: American warriors | Includes bibliographical references and index.
Identifiers: LCCN 2019023227 | ISBN 9780813178028 (hardcover) | ISBN
    9780813178042 (pdf) | ISBN 9780813178059 (epub)
Subjects: LCSH: Shalikashvili, John M.—Military leadership. |
    Generals—United States—Biography. | United States—History,
    Military—20th century. | United States. Army—Biography. | United
    States. Joint Chiefs of Staff—Chairmen—Biography. | United
    States—Foreign relations—1883–2001. | Georgian Americans—Biography.
Classification: LCC E840.5.S473 M37 2019 | DDC 355.0092 [B]—dc23
LC record available at https://lccn.loc.gov/2019023227

This book is printed on acid-free paper meeting
the requirements of the American National Standard
for Permanence in Paper for Printed Library Materials.

∞

Manufactured in the United States of America.

Member of the Association
of University Presses

To RRM, ELF, and SKW

Contents

List of Illustrations   ix
Preface   xi
List of Abbreviations   xvi
Prologue: The Boy on the Bridge   1

Part I. The Nomination of John Shalikashvili

1. Only in America   9
2. How Many Shalikashvilis Can There Be in the World?!   22

Part II. Old World Roots

3. Will It Play in Peoria?   27
4. Missy and Wartime Warsaw   35
5. Countess Julie Pappenheim   49
6. Oma and the Passing of the Old World   62
7. Betrayal   74

Part III. New World Opportunities

8. To Become an Officer?   87
9. Dimitri, Prisoner of War   98
10. A Strategic Yes   112
11. The Crucible of OCS   116

Part IV. Paying It Forward: Operation Provide Comfort

12. Savior of the Kurds?   133
13. Mushroom Cloud   151
14. Huddled Masses   169
15. Warning the Iraqis   190
16. A World Figure?   211
17. Briefing Congress   227

Part V. To Confirm a Chairman

18. Getting to Yes   241
19. The Ghost of Dimitri   255
20. Blondi and the Boy on the Bridge   272

Part VI. The Twilight of an American Dream

21. Retirement Day   291
22. The Final Inheritance   304
Epilogue: The Meaning of a Life   311

Acknowledgments   323
Appendix A. Timeline: Old World   328
Appendix B. Timeline: New World   331
Notes   337
Select Bibliography   371
Index   375

Illustrations

Maps and Figures

World War II Europe   48
Provide Comfort Theater of Operations   174
Operation Provide Comfort Organizational Structure   194

Photographs

Altmühlbrücke, the Altmühl Bridge, view from the south   2
Altmühlbrücke, the Altmühl Bridge, view from the north   3
John Shalikashvili's nomination ceremony   20
A happy Colin Powell and ecstatic Bill Clinton   21
John Shalikashvili, the year of his departure for the United States   29
Dimitri, Missy, John, and Alexandra Shalikashvili   37
Great Aunt Countess Julie Pappenheim   50
The Bavarian village of Pappenheim, Germany   51
The *Altes Schloss* (Old Schloss)   53
Dimitri Shalikashvili watching sons John and Othar play Indians   55
Line drawings by a young John Shalikashvili   56
Adam Johann von Krusenstern   64
The Rudiger family estate in Bialystok, Poland   65
John Shalikashvili's maternal grandparents   67
The SS *America*   70
Donna Bechtold   75
Robinson Barracks, home of the Field Artillery Officer Candidate School,
   mid-1950s   86
Paternal great-grandfather Major General Jean Osipovich Shalikashvili
   "The Brave"   91
Dimitri Shalikashvili, 1923   104
David Shalikashvili, John Shalikashvili's uncle   111
OCS candidates suffering through a Jark March   122
John Shalikashvili at Field Artillery Officer Candidate School   125
Kurdish refugee camp in northern Iraq, spring 1991   134
Lieutenant John Shalikashvili in Fairbanks, Alaska   141

Black Hawk helicopter flying past CH-47 Chinook helicopters, Diyarbakir, Turkey   152
Operation Provide Comfort headquarters at Incirlik Air Base   155
Commander Shalikashvili visiting Isikveren   176
John Shalikashvili and first wife Gunhild Bartsch   178
Shalikashvili meeting with Iraq's Brigadier General Nashwan Thanoon   192
The Operation Provide Comfort commander under media scrutiny   210
Kurdish refugees being repatriated by truck to Iraqi lowlands   229
Shalikashvili visiting with Kurdish refugee children   233
Major John Shalikashvili during the Vietnam War   236
Les Aspin and Bill Clinton   240
Dimitri Shalikashvili and "close family friend" Walter Schellenberg   257
Donna Bechtold in nursing school   275
General John Shalikashvili's retirement ceremony   294
John Shalikashvili and wife Joan at his retirement ceremony   302
John Shalikashvili on visit to Georgia   305
John Shalikashvili undergoing physical therapy   308
Gravesite of John Shalikashvili   310
John Shalikashvili wearing 3D glasses   312

Preface

March 6, 2011—Du Pont, Washington

John Shalikashvili sat in his living room, immobile and inscrutable. He was strapped into a wheelchair, torso leaning right to compensate for his paralyzed left side, a heavy sweater warding off the constant chill he'd felt since the stroke.

Then the unexpected happened. "Is that a death mask?" he blurted out, his thick accent failing to mute the shock in his gravelly voice. "Is that the devil?" his eyes, wide now, locking onto a spot in the distant nowhere.

Sitting off to one side, I shifted in my chair. I recalled the retired four-star army general recently telling me, voice more hopeful than authoritative: "One sin that can't be forgiven is not to believe. You can murder someone and still be forgiven."

Though having logged appreciably more time preventing armed conflict than commanding troops in battle, the graybeard was still responsible for people's deaths. Depending on how one counted, thousands, hundreds of thousands, or perhaps even millions of lives saved or ended could be tallied up in his personal ledger. Was there a magic ratio? When the time came, how would the scales of St. Peter tip?

We continued sitting there in silence, the stroke-damaged brain of the thirteenth chairman of the US Joint Chiefs of Staff wrestling with fearful images of his unknown future, and my biographer's brow furrowing as I quietly pondered how best to discern the man's past.

I was serving as editor at an Asia policy think tank when I first heard of John Shalikashvili, our newest and most prominent board member. Though unfamiliar with the US military, I was soon intrigued by three aspects of the general's life.

First was his highly improbable American success story. How in the world had he done it? How had a stateless, penniless World War II refugee who'd emigrated from Europe to the New World as a teenager gone on to become the highest-ranking officer in the US military?

Then there was his dramatic backstory: Not only had Shalikashvili had a front-row seat as a child to some of the bloodiest carnage of the war, but he was also actually the scion of two long and prestigious European aristocratic bloodlines. Did the eyebrow-raising facts that he'd been born a prince and survived the destruction of Warsaw have anything to do with his improbable rise to national security decision-maker?

Third was his curious reputation. "He's a quiet, decent man and a very hard worker," judged Joint Chiefs chairman General Colin Powell, who'd urged President Bill Clinton to appoint Shalikashvili as his successor. "There is a mistaken notion that you have to have Pattonesque qualities to be a great general. You don't need to rant and rave or be an arrogant jerk to be successful. 'Shali' showed that." Many other civilian and defense officials agreed, labeling him humble, caring, thoughtful, both a team player and a consensus builder. Someone with "no ego need."

This perplexed me. It's the Alpha males, not the nice guys, who finish first, right? Consider Steve Jobs, the controlling and manipulative CEO who led Apple to dominance in the tech industry. Or the irascible General Norman Schwarzkopf, who'd bulldogged an international coalition to quick victory in the first Gulf War. Then there's former CIA director General David Petraeus, a man whose stellar career was coupled with a reputation for deep-seated ambition and unflagging self-promotion.

Shalikashvili's character bedeviled for another reason. Asked once to name his greatest weakness, he replied: "I don't like confrontation." Seriously? Here was a man with a successful career in armed conflict, a man who shepherded the querulous European defense chiefs to consensus as NATO's top military leader during the tumultuous security environment of the early 1990s, and a man who as chairman of the Joint Chiefs from 1993 to 1997 not only oversaw the squabbling branches of the US armed forces but also represented them on the fractious battlefield of American politics. Could Shalikashvili really feel weakened by an aversion to conflict? And what kind of leader would make such an admission in the first place? Did his unusual character and reputation, then, also contribute to his unlikely American success?

So I decided to understand Shalikashvili better. That's why I was visiting the general on the day of his macabre visions. I was returning borrowed family photo albums because, with my full-time job behind me, belongings in storage, and car packed, I was leaving the next day on an open-ended cross-country research trip to delve deeper into the reasons for his success.

I was particularly interested in sounding out his character. If I discovered that he did indeed live up to his reputation, I'd need to explain not just how much his softer leadership approach aided his career rise but, more to the point, why the downsides of this style never put a brake on his upward climb.

Or what if I discovered Shalikashvili's public image was wrong? What if avoiding the spotlight had been a strategy to cloak substantial ambition and self-interest in shadow? If so, I'd need to answer different questions: How far short did the real Shalikashvili fall from his public image? And why were others so convinced his character was sterling?

My research has been extensive. All told, I've traveled more than thirty thousand miles, visiting over thirty cities, twelve states, three countries, and two continents. I've interviewed well over three hundred people, including relatives and classmates as well as both military and civilian bosses, subordinates, and colleagues, ranging from VIPs like Bill Clinton, Madeleine Albright, and Colin Powell, who worked with him in the 1990s, down to fellow privates in the 1950s. I've scoured, among other archives, one hundred-plus linear feet of restricted materials split between two coasts, uncovering such gems as his classified "201 File" containing the performance reviews and other evaluations from his thirty-nine-year career, personal notebooks covering his last eight years in uniform, fifteen thousand sets of correspondence from his time as both SACEUR and chairman, and a thick compendium of domestic and foreign media stories published during his chairmanship.

This broad array of sources has enabled me to catalogue the recollections and opinions of a wide cross section of people who collectively knew him for nigh his entire life. I've ascertained that his performance review as a young lieutenant in 1961—having "established a reputation that has placed him in the enviable position of being respected and liked by privates, generals, and contemporaries"—did indeed echo up through his retirement in 1997. Even those who crossed paths with him at different points in his career, including bosses who became subordinates, felt Shalikashvili remained the same regardless of his rank or the widening gap between their respective ranks.

It was almost unsettling. Given his reputation and especially his post-stroke condition, I was confident Shalikashvili wasn't trying to influence my findings behind the scenes. So why did so many people have such similarly positive evaluations?

Unfortunately, for quite some time my extensive research uncovered precious little insight into how "Shalikashvili the man" differed from "Shalikashvili the reputation." What motivated him to act in the glowing ways everyone described? What internal forces, whether benevolent or malevolent, could drive someone to behave so consistently across the decades?

It was hard to discern. Shalikashvili was known for being "tight-lipped, like WWII heroes." Even those closest to him were often unaware of basic facts or major events of his life. Astonishingly, the 150 letters he wrote to his parents from 1950 to 1991 rarely contained sentiment deeper than a greeting card. To date, I've identified only one instance when Shalikashvili in adulthood wrote down private inner thoughts: his reflections on the major stroke that upended his life in 2004. At the end of that essay he'd scrawled "Further respondent sayeth not," an arcane phrase used in legal proceedings to protect oneself from charges of perjury.

Tight-lipped indeed.

But then, in the wake of Shalikashvili's death in July 2011, a woman reached out to me.

"Blondie" had met Shalikashvili at a pivotal juncture: when, as a newly arrived teenage refugee in the mid-1950s, he was straddling a rupturing fault line, with the weight of his Old World experiences on one side and the uncertainty of New World promise on the other. And when he was young enough, lonely enough, and lost enough to be uncharacteristically open, especially with another wayward soul.

When she first contacted me, she was dealing not only with her husband's cancer and then subsequent death but also the first of three types of cancer that would strike her own body, the last of which ended her life in 2013. Not only did recounting their time together seem to provide her much comfort during these dark days, but more importantly, as I came to learn, by helping the world better understand this person whom she clearly loved and admired, she seemed to be striving to make up for past sins and to assuage old guilt. Seeking atonement, especially at life's end, is strong motivation to open up.

The things Blondie shared made me realize that his European roots were absolutely key to understanding John Shalikashvili as a human being. So much so that I'd soon board a plane to Europe to better understand the storied accomplishments of his ancestors, the mettle of four close relatives, and the full weight of his Old World childhood experiences. Most of all I needed to look into secrets Blondie had confided in me.

The fascinating story I've since pieced together is laid out here in what is an unusual biography, particularly for a senior military figure.

The primary purpose of this book is not to explain how a "great man of history" shaped the events of his day. Nor is it a cradle-to-grave overview of a person's life. Some major aspects of his life and career—like the intricacies of policy battles he fought as a general officer or the details of his family life as a husband or father—are merely summarized or left for other biographers or students of history.

Instead the emphasis is on understanding his chairmanship as a journey, not a destination. It's an investigation into how an unlikely American success story was made, how an unconventional and complex man came to be.

Also unusual is that the book seeks to "show" who he was, not "tell." And given that Shalikashvili has said so little about himself, I've relied heavily on others to do the showing—including Blondie in the New World and four key relatives in the Old. By portraying the beliefs and actions of his parents, his grandmother, and great aunt, for instance, the book encourages readers themselves to make vivid connections about how genes, upbringing, and childhood experiences influenced Shalikashvili's rise up the ranks.

The structure of the book is also atypical, relying heavily on flashbacks and jumpforwards to make important causal connections. These temporal shifts are signaled by triple asterisks, as are the occasional sections where exposition by the biographer supplements this largely character-driven biography.

These multiple story lines that appear at different places throughout the book—from Old World people, places, and events to New World opportunities and challenges—are then drawn inexorably together at book's end. There, through a series of unexpected revelations, readers will discover the deepest motivators, both benevolent and malevolent, that spurred General John Shalikashvili's improbable American success.

Abbreviations

32nd AADCOM	32nd Army Air Defense Command, Kaiserslautern, Germany
AIT	Advanced Individual Training
C-130	large military transport plane
CINC	Commander in Chief (discontinued term for certain command positions)
CTF	Combined Task Force (multinational)
DCINC	Deputy Commander in Chief
DIVARTY	Division Artillery
EUCOM	US European Command
JTF	Joint Task Force (multiservice)
MACV	Military Assistance Command, Vietnam
NATO	North Atlantic Treaty Organization
NCO	noncommissioned officer
NGO	nongovernmental organization
OCS	Officer Candidate School
PVO	private voluntary organization
ROTC	Reserve Officers' Training Corps
SACEUR	Supreme Allied Commander Europe (military head of NATO)
SETAF	Southern European Task Force, Vicenza, Italy
SHAPE	Supreme Headquarters Allied Powers Europe, Mons, Belgium (NATO operational HQ)
UNHCR	United Nations High Commissioner for Refugees
USAREUR	US Army Europe, Heidelberg, Germany
VC	Vietcong
X.O.	Executive officer

Prologue

The Boy on the Bridge

April 1945—Pappenheim, Germany

Pappenheim. It's a place deeply connected to the past. Families have resided here for generations. Villagers ply the traditional trades, like baker, butcher, innkeeper, and tailor. A mosaic of houses dating from this century all the way back to the 1600s imbues the Bavarian village with charm. The buildings nestle together, pitched roof scraping pitched roof, hugging the base of a steep hill wedged into the center of the village.

Atop that hill towers the Burg. This stone castle, complete with ramparts, battlements, and at one point a working drawbridge, has stood guard since the early eleventh century. Yet this is not Pappenheim's oldest landmark, as the castle was constructed around a preexisting stone tower, one of a network the Romans erected hundreds of years earlier to mark the border of their ancient empire.

The Burg was built for the aristocratic German family that, centuries ago, endowed the village with its name. The Pappenheims were forged into the chain of history itself. As far back as at least 1145 the counts of Pappenheim held the hereditary title of *Reichserbmarschall*, Imperial Marshal of the Holy Roman Empire. A main duty of the office was to oversee the gathering of retinues from the various states of the realm for the periodic elections of the Imperial Diet or the coronation of a new emperor. In 1521, Imperial Marshal Ulrich von Pappenheim brought Martin Luther to the Heylshof Garden in Worms to either confirm or renounce his views to Emperor Charles V and the Diet. At the 1792 coronation of the last emperor, Francis II, it was Count Carl Theodor Friedrich Pappenheim, the empire's final marshal, who served as master of ceremonies.

Though the Roman tower remains intact, much of the Burg lies in ruins. Some hold it was destroyed by either the Swedes in the Thirty Years' War or the French during the War of the Spanish Succession. Others whisper it was blown up by an eccentric Pappenheim ancestor. What-

1

Altmühlbrücke, the Altmühl Bridge, view from the south, circa early 1900s. (Courtesy of Tom Karl.)

ever the reason, after the castle became unlivable, the family moved down the hill to a *schloss* (a manor or estate) that they constructed during the late sixteenth century. In the early 1800s this estate became known as the *Altes Schloss,* the Old Schloss, once the *Neues Schloss* was built for the Pappenheim family a vigorous stone's throw away.

Just to the side of the New Schloss stands the *Altmühlbrücke.* Built in 1878 by a local master craftsman, the bridge was a thing of beauty, sporting angled pilings, boardwalk-style transversed planking, and comely iron latticework railings accented with matching angled supports. Spanning the one hundred-foot width of the Altmühl River, a tributary of the Danube, the *Altmühlbrücke* allowed foot, hoof, and wheel to cross the gap between the town center and the areas to the north.

It was on this wooden bridge that citizens of Pappenheim would unexpectedly come to gather late one evening in April 1945.

The end of the war was approaching. The village was aiding the war by serving as a depot for railroad cars, small boats, uniforms, mattresses,

Altmühlbrücke, the Altmühl Bridge, view from the north, circa early 1900s. The back of the New Schloss is visible to the right. (Courtesy of Tom Karl.)

and other military supplies. One wing of the New Schloss's ground floor had been requisitioned by the German army to serve as a *Wehrersatzinspektion*, headquartering one hundred or so recruiters for the Fuhrer's war effort. Unsurprisingly, almost all able-bodied males in the village had long since been sent off to fight. Those who remained were mostly the elderly, women, and children.

One youngster was eight-year-old John Shalikashvili. Though endowed with a mop of tousled blond hair and a set of piercing crystal-blue eyes, he was not German. The boy was a refugee. A stateless refugee, in fact, because he'd been born in Warsaw to parents who were not Polish. Having escaped Poland months ago following the end of the bloody Warsaw Uprising, his family had come to Pappenheim because his grandmother, who'd fled with them, was sister to Countess Julie Pappenheim. The countess had unexpectedly become matriarch of this aristocratic German family in 1905 when her husband, Count Ludwig Magnus Heinrich Carl Pappenheim, died prematurely in a hunting accident at the age of forty-three. The extended Shalikashvili family had arrived here in October 1944 all but destitute. Whatever family resources not destroyed by war or left behind in Poland had been squeezed into a few battered suitcases. The countess had, as was proper, opened rooms for them in the New Schloss.

Despite having reached the sanctuary of Pappenheim, the refugee boy had yet to find final respite from war. Recent intelligence reports warned that Allied troops had begun advancing southward into Bavaria. This news prompted the *Wehrersatzinspektion* commander, accompanied by the mayor, to survey the village by jeep. Mounting a defense of Pappenheim, the general concluded, would be too difficult.

As soldiers began evacuating southward into the Alps, a small contingent set about breaking down the headquarters. Stacks of military documents were brought out from the New Schloss, dumped into a makeshift burn pit in the back courtyard, and set ablaze. Soon after, John's older brother Othar was asked to help move some boards. Having just returned from escorting escaping German officers to the train station in a nearby town, he hadn't known of the burn pit. Turning the corner while maneuvering one end of the load, Othar stepped squarely into the red-hot embers. The burn was severe enough to require days of recuperation.

Would the Allies bomb the village before invading? Pappenheimers were worried. And with the *Wehrersatzinspektion* on the first floor, the residents of the New Schloss were particularly concerned. Thus the Pappenheims, Shalikashvilis, and other guests soon settled into a new nightly routine. Abandoning their antique-appointed rooms on the schloss's upper floors, they would made their way along extended corridors and down sweeping spiral stairways crowded with stately oil paintings of Pappenheim ancestors. They'd pass by cabinets displaying the colorful tin soldiers collected by the countess's son and arranged in mock battle against scenery painted by the countess's own hand. Hustling by the converted offices of the German military, they'd then descend the cellar stairs to the protection of the basement.

But as the days passed, no bombs or artillery shells landed. With sufficient amenities and companionship, fear diminished. In its place settled a kind of monotony—sometimes even boredom.

Until the evening of April 23.

That's when a thunderous explosion rent the night air, causing everyone in the New Schloss to freeze in fear. It had been close by, because immediately after came the sound of objects clattering against the back of the building and the tinkling of shattering glass.

And then, silence.

Those in the basement listened intently, ears straining for clues as to what was happening outside. Strangely, what followed was not the sound of continued explosions or the follow-up of gunfire. As the seconds turned to minutes, what finally pierced the air were voices. German voices. Angry German voices.

Outside the Pappenheim estate a heated debate had arisen. Lured outside to investigate, villagers had discovered something so egregious as to make them stand up to the remaining Nazi authorities in town.

Earlier, SS officers had cast about for a strategy to buy time for the escaping German military. They'd intently studied the town's topography. Pappenheim proper was bounded on three sides by the Altmühl River, which flowed along the east, north, and west sides of town, tracing a wider contour line around the village's main hill. At the northern tip was the *Altmühlbrücke*. Flanking that bridge, about fifty yards to the west, was a narrow wooden footbridge connecting the New Schloss's rear courtyard to a small park on the north side of the river.

The noise that had just shattered the quiet Pappenheim night was the SS blowing up the footbridge. The explosion had sent pieces of planking hurtling toward the Pappenheim estate, shattering some of the schloss's windows.

But that detonation, the villagers quickly learned, had been but a trial run. For there on the southern end of the *Altmühlbrücke* was a chilling sight: a stack of almost two hundred pounds of dynamite. If those explosives were set off, the New Schloss would suffer much more than broken windows. The handsome three-story neoclassical building, a structure designed by a court architect to the king of Bavaria and completed in 1822, would suffer substantial damage. And there, across from the New Schloss, just off the southeast corner of the bridge, sat the Hotel Krone. Constructed in the late 1500s, that landmark was a mainstay of the village economy. Much of Pappenheim's commercial and social life, in fact, pulsed through this *Marktplatz* intersection—the bridge, the public marketplace just south of the bridge, and the network of roads that came together in between. The villagers simply could not let the soon-to-be-departing SS officers trigger that second stack of dynamite.

Something had to be done.

So the mayor stepped in with a compromise. He activated the *Volkssturm,* a ragtag militia composed of members of the Hitler Youth, the elderly, invalids, and other males aged sixteen to sixty found unfit for military service. The militia fanned out across Pappenheim, pressing all able-bodied villagers to muster at the *Altmühlbrücke*. "Dismantle the bridge," the militia ordered. Render it impassable to whatever machinery and equipment the Allies might bring.

Wielding picks, shovels, and even their bare hands, the Pappenheimers were now toiling in the darkness. And working alongside, thin arms of youth set against thick decking planks of old, was John Shalikashvili.

He could not have felt more alone. His father was off fighting for the Germans in Italy, and the family had since lost contact with him. His mother, also absent, had likely left Pappenheim on yet another of her searches, hoping beyond hope to learn her husband had been captured by the Allies rather than killed. The burns to Othar's leg had kept him from reporting. The third Shalikashvili sibling, Alexandra, was too young to be of help; their elderly grandmother, too frail.

Hours passed. The villagers worked anxiously, caught between the dark skies above and the cold depths of the Altmühl below, between the watchful eyes of the SS officers on the riverbank behind and their fear that Allied bombs or artillery might rain down from the skies in front.

Yet as the morning drew near, the skeletal substructure of the *Altmühlbrücke* lay only partially exposed. Not long after dawn's first glimmer, John paused his efforts. He glanced across the river.

And that's when he saw them—there on the opposing bank, rifles at the ready, the lead scouts of the 86th US Infantry Division.

"These," he would recall one late September day more than five decades hence, "were my first Americans."

Part I

The Nomination of John Shalikashvili

1

Only in America

August 11, 1993—Washington, D.C.

It was late afternoon, and a brief ceremony was about to kick off on the grounds of the White House. Though hastily arranged, the event would start early enough to be assured airtime on the evening's newscast. On the Rose Garden lawn a sweep of video crews, photographers, and reporters were jostling for a good angle on the vacant podium at the base of the veranda steps. Any moment now the president of the United States was going to appear behind that grand seal of his office, lean into the twin microphones, and introduce to the world the person he was nominating to serve as the thirteenth chairman of the US Joint Chiefs of Staff.

This was no small thing. During four years in office a commander in chief makes no nomination for a military post that matters more. Among the 1.7 million active-duty personnel currently serving as the building blocks of the US armed forces, the chairman of the Joint Chiefs is capstone. As the apex of that grand pyramid, he outranks them all.

Today's nomination held extra gravitas. This next chairman would be only the second in history to begin his term with the expanded powers granted by the 1986 Goldwater-Nichols Act. The chairman, despite his title, had previously been just one of five equal voices on the Joint Staff; by law he and the four service chiefs—one each for the army, navy, air force, and marines—had provided collective advice to the civilian leadership. But now, among other new privileges, the chairman serves as *the* principal military advisor to the president, secretary of defense, and National Security Council. This was far from a minor tweak of the job description. Viewers, readers, and listeners in national capitals and defense sectors around the world would thus be itching for a first impression of the man who might soon wield such influence.

Yet no one assembling had an inkling that a curious thing was going to occur during the evening's ceremony. Lasting no longer than a heartbeat or two, it would involve not the nominee, but two other men. One was the president himself, William Jefferson Clinton, the charismatic post–Cold War leader of the world's only remaining superpower. The other was arguably the most popular and politically astute US military officer to don the uniform since World War II: the current chairman of the Joint Chiefs, General Colin Powell.

What would pass between these two men would occur in full view of the phalanx of media gathered here on the White House lawn. Yet few watching would likely notice—and even fewer would understand its significance.

At 5:30 p.m. one side of the French double doors just off the Oval Office swung open. To loud and energetic applause, the president stepped onto the veranda, with the much-anticipated nominee one pace behind. Tracking next came a solemn Vice President Al Gore, followed by an impassive Powell. Last to emerge was Secretary of Defense Les Aspin, ever-avuncular with his signature rumpled appearance.

"Good afternoon, ladies and gentlemen," Clinton began from the podium once the nation's top political and military leadership had lined up by his side.

A hush settled over the media. The nation was wrestling with a host of bruising security challenges, many stemming from the question of how to redefine the mission of the US military given the end of American-Soviet bipolarity. How should the US armed forces maintain readiness now that the country was implementing steep troop reductions and even steeper defense budget cuts? How involved should the military be in the hybrid "not quite peace, not quite war" forms of conflict, the Somalias and the Bosnia-Herzegovinas, that seemed part and parcel of this new post–Cold War world? On the domestic front, should homosexuals be allowed to serve openly in the military? And what of the role of women in the armed forces? The president of the United States now stood before the bristling array of lenses and microphones, ready to introduce to the world the man he desired to be his primary military advisor on these and other seemingly intractable issues.

"It's a great honor for me to be here today," intoned Clinton, his pale blue suit, off-white shirt, and muted red tie capturing both the patriotism and gravitas of the occasion, "to introduce to you and to our nation the person whom I have selected to replace Colin Powell as the chairman of the Joint Chiefs of Staff: General John Shalikashvili."

Shall-he—what? Hearing the president introduce his nominee, many tuning in to the ceremony were surely at a loss. Few Americans had ever heard that jawbreaker of a surname, let alone had a clue who this particular Sha-kash-whatever was. Even a Joint Staff spokesman would embarrassingly admit to the media: "I'm saying it the way the other people on my staff are saying it: '*Shah-lee-KASH-villy*,' with the emphasis on the '*kash*,'" only to follow up hours later with the clarifying mea culpa: "It's '*Sholly-kosh-VEE-lee*,'" which was the European pronunciation preferred by the general, who was currently serving in Mons, Belgium, as Supreme Allied Commander Europe (SACEUR), the military head of the North Atlantic Treaty Organization (NATO).

Greater puzzlement, even bewilderment, would follow from those hearing the four star speak from the podium later in the ceremony. This is America! How could the nominee for the country's top military post speak in such heavily accented English?!

If the name and voice were odd, did the chairman-designate at least look the part? Even here, many viewers were underwhelmed. As the nominee stood, hands folded behind his back, quietly taking in the president's remarks, anyone could see this was not the chiseled warrior who towers down at you from an army recruitment poster. For one, Shalikashvili stood just five-foot-nine. In this lineup of recognizable leaders, most of whom outstripped the six-foot mark by a good two inches, the nominee looked downright diminutive. True, he was endowed with a square jaw, jutting chin, barrel chest, and ramrod posture. One could imagine such features might have lent him a Pattonesque air in younger days. But fifty-seven years of living had saddled this army general with the trademarks of advanced middle age—thick bifocals, thinning hair, a slight paunch. "Physically unimposing" summed up one reporter. "More like a businessman than a soldier," another would sniff. There was no outward spark, no apparent dynamism, no clear mover-and-shaker persona. "He does not ooze charisma," summed up a third.

Who *was* this guy the president was nominating for such a key post?

Though the former governor of Arkansas knew relatively little about the nation's top generals and admirals before capturing the presidency, his choice to lead the Joint Chiefs resonated across his team of advisors. At the Pentagon, Aspin had put Shalikashvili's name atop the list of viable candidates he'd sent the president in early August, a move supported by Deputy Secretary William Perry. The key figures in the White House were similarly on board. National Security Advisor Anthony Lake had given the thumbs up, as had the president's most trusted counselor on foreign affairs, Sandy Berger. Ditto for George Stephanopoulos, Clinton's all-purpose adviser, and for the nation's secretary of state, Warren Christopher.

Increasing the nominee's attractiveness, Shalikashvili was also well received at the other end of Pennsylvania Avenue. This was key. While it was the president's prerogative to nominate a candidate, only a majority vote of the Senate could confirm the appointment. Boding well for the general's upcoming confirmation hearing was that he was well liked among the Senate Armed Services Committee, which would do the initial vetting of the nominee, and also had broad appeal in the larger Senate body, which would do the final voting. For good measure, the general was similarly held in high regard in the House of Representatives, including its Armed Services Committee.

Such unanimity among the national political gatekeepers was a rarity. Rarer still, the nominee also enjoyed a solid reputation among those who knew him in the military, from the top brass down through the rank and file, not only within the army but also across the other service branches.

Despite this unusual wellspring of respect for the general, the White House still faced challenges. For one, Shalikashvili was all but unknown outside key parts of both the defense establishment and the even narrower world of foreign and security policy elite. Second, among the fifteen candidates the president had considered for the position, the nominee hadn't actually been viewed as the obvious front-runner. Shalikashvili was, as some media covering today's nomination would report, a "dark horse candidate."

Many out there were going to need a convincing introduction to the president's unusual choice for chairman. These next few minutes were critical.

"He's widely known to his friends as General 'Shali,'" Clinton continued helpfully. "And since we're going to be seeing a lot of each other," the commander in chief grinned to the chair-designate, "and you're going to have to write a lot about him," this now directed at the media, "I think I'll just start using the shortened version of his name."

Over the next six and a half minutes the president would pontificate before the Rose Garden crowd. With increasing verve, he'd wax eloquent and enthusiastic on the life, career, and capabilities of this General Shali.

"He is a soldier's soldier, a proven warrior, a creative and flexible visionary," Clinton began, outlining three overarching virtues he felt distinguished his nominee.

In the first, "a soldier's soldier," the president was clearly invoking the spirit of the first chairman of the Joint Staff, General Omar Bradley, the World War II commander known as the "GI's general" in recognition of the concern he showed for the ordinary soldier. Shalikashvili, Clinton testified to the Rose Garden assembly, "has shown me a real concern for the ordinary men and women who have enlisted in our armed services and who are living through this difficult and challenging period of downsizing." This care for service members, the president continued, was helping the much leaner US military machine continue to pack a powerful a punch. "He understands how to downsize the armed forces, and still maintain the strongest military in the world, with the equipment and, most important, the trained force with the morale we need to always fight and win when we have to."

Next was "proven warrior." The general, a decorated Vietnam veteran, had commanded every unit from platoon to division. He was also a consummate warrior-diplomat, as demonstrated in his last three assignments. This included command of Operation Provide Comfort, the post–Gulf War multinational effort to rescue at-risk Kurdish refugees. Next, as assistant to the chairman of the Joint Staff, Shalikashvili had served as Colin Powell's representative to Secretary of State James Baker. Now as SACEUR he not only commanded all US forces in Europe, presently the most prestigious and important of the military's five geographical combatant commands, but concurrently served as the military head of NATO, putting him in charge of a mind-boggling 2 million troops, 2,300 tanks, and 5,200 warplanes.

Finally there was "flexible visionary." Here was a military leader, Clinton explained, who not only "clearly understands the myriad of conflicts—ethnic, religious, and political—gripping the world, as well as the immense possibilities for the United States and for the cause of freedom that are out there before us," but also "has shown a proven ability to work with our allies in complex and challenging circumstances."

The president pointed out two critical examples of the general's knack for translating such vision into multinational reality. First was Shalikashvili's leadership in creating "a NATO rapid-reaction corps to undertake peacekeeping missions that are significantly different from our Cold War challenges." Second was his skill in "persuading NATO members to consider missions outside traditional alliance boundaries"—which, Clinton emphasized, was "a very, very important step" in NATO's recently announced willingness to finally use airstrikes against the Serbian forces besieging Sarajevo.

For these and other reasons, the president affirmed, Shalikashvili has "the deep respect of both the troops who have served under him and the military leaders who have worked with him," thereby putting the army general in a "unique position to be an advocate for the men and women in the armed services and for the national security of the United States," one who could advocate broadly and effectively "to the Congress, to the country, and to our military allies throughout the world."

"I selected him," the president finally stated outright, "because I believe he has the ability to lead and to win any military action our nation might ask of him." And then Clinton brought up the candidate's reputation for honesty: "Above all, I am confident that in every instance he will give me his absolutely candid and professional military advice, which, as president, I must have."

At this point, halfway through his remarks, the commander in chief shifted his sales pitch.

"There is much more to his life than most Americans now know," Clinton pivoted, raised eyebrow and widening smile hinting at revelations to come. "It is a great American story," amazement now tingeing his voice. "It began as so many American stories do: in another land."

The Warsaw-born Shalikashvili, Clinton explained, was the son of a Georgian army officer. "That's the Georgia over there," clarified the president with a playful tilt of the head and wag of the finger, "not over here." He spoke of how the nominee's family had become "caught in the crossfire of ethnic and national rivalries" and, in a slight mischaracterization, how in 1944 when Shalikashvili was eight years old "his family had fled in a cattle car westward to Germany in front of the Soviet advance."

"He came to the United States at the age of sixteen," the president continued, glossing over how this highly improbable event had come to pass. Also unmentioned were the storybook details of the trip itself. Like how in 1952 Shalikashvili bade goodbye to the Old World from the deck of the SS *America,* a majestic red-white-and-blue-colored ocean liner. During the November transatlantic voyage the teenager had delighted in his first Thanksgiving meal—replete with white linen tablecloth, fresh roasted turkey, and piles of sweet potato. And his first few days on US soil had been spent in wide-eyed wonderment among the skyscrapers of New York City, that famed landing point for so many immigrants to the New World.

Shalikashvili's American dream began in earnest when he arrived soon thereafter in his adopted hometown of Peoria, Illinois—a quintessentially American city located deep in the nation's heartland. Picking up the narrative now, Clinton boasted to the nation how Shalikashvili had shouldered a full course-load on his first day of high school. He repeated the exaggerated truth that his nominee mastered English while sitting in the darkened seats of a local theater mesmerized by that most American of icons, John Wayne. And how in a Peoria courtroom in 1958 John Shalikashvili raised his right hand and swore to support and defend the Constitution of the United States of America—the first and only citizenship he'd ever be granted.

It was a storybook beginning. And its dénouement seemed at hand. If in the days ahead Shalikashvili's appointment were indeed confirmed by the Senate, it would be the first time in US history that a foreign-born officer occupied the post.

This, though, was just one of three milestones now within his grasp. Obtaining his certificate of naturalization was what seemed to have jumpstarted his military career in the first place. "The very first piece of mail I ever got as a U.S. citizen," he'd recount with a wry chuckle, "was my draft notice." Yet never before had a lowly draftee ever gone on to reach the top spot in the US military machine—the second milestone now in his sights.

Finally, if confirmed Shalikashvili, would become the first chairman to have earned his lieutenant's bars by way of Officer Candidate School. Prestige-wise, this in effect was the army's "community college" route to being commissioned an officer, one less glamorous than the equivalent "ivy league" path of West Point or the next-best "state school" avenue of ROTC.

"Now," the forty-second president of the United States continued from the podium with vigor, "I intend to nominate this first-generation American to the highest military office in our land on the strength of his ability, his character, and his enormous potential to lead our armed forces."

Then, after a dramatic pause, the president, pride and awe resonating in his voice, offered up three powerful words:

"Only in America."

Only here in this land of opportunity, Clinton was implying, could such an improbable success story occur: a stateless, penniless war refugee—one caught in the waning days of World War II on a bridge between advancing US soldiers and a fleeing German war machine—had come, almost fifty years later in life, to be standing here at the White House today, about to accept the president's nomination to become the highest-ranking officer in the world's most powerful military.

"I now invite him to the podium for whatever remarks he might wish to make." At last, Shalikashvili's cue. Polite applause filled the air as the general, pausing to toe into place a small stool, stepped up to the microphones.

He stood silently for a moment, this man who might soon occupy the top spot in the armed forces of a country that spent more on defense than the next ten top countries combined. Then, small hands grasping the slanted sides of the lectern, the general began to speak.

"Thank you very much, Mr. President, for your trust and confidence in me"—as he uttered these first words, his accent, a Germanic-Slavic mix, was unmistakable. In contrast to the president's lengthy remarks, the general would offer only a few lines. The first was long, almost rambling. "For someone who at the age of sixteen came from Europe to the United States and who has in all those years since then benefited so richly as I have from the boundless opportunities that our country offers . . ."

To those listening, it was apparent that his voice, despite being gravelly, had a pitch oddly higher than one might expect. And perhaps because his short, barrel-chested frame was similarly mismatched by slender legs and arms, he gave off a slight dwarfish or even elfish air.

His sentence continued: ". . . it's extraordinarily gratifying to me to be given this opportunity in a small way to repay my country through service in such a position of such high responsibility."

"Boundless opportunities." "Benefited richly." "Repay my country." These words carried across the lawn with particular resonance, the timbre of his accented English driving home, even more surely than could the president's animated storytelling, that the nation's chairman-elect was indeed a first-generation American.

According to the traditional Horatio Alger plotline, American success stories like Shalikashvili's are a special kind of "rags to riches" tale. The United States, the belief goes, is the land of opportunity. It's that famed place where through hard work, determination, and pluck anyone can rise as high as their talents allow.

What abilities had propelled John Shalikashvili to the podium here today, a hair's breadth from reaching the highest possible station in his chosen career? Putting aside factors beyond his control, what characteristics had propelled him upward, without fatal stumble, over the many hurdles that surely crowded his thirty-year path to the Rose Garden lawn?

Many today were wondering this very question. And encouraged by the president's glowing remarks, some were surely turning their gaze back on the nominee for a closer look.

Yet for most of the ceremony Shalikashvili's countenance conveyed little but polite respect. Those watching carefully, however, might have detected occasional flashes—a quick sparkle of his eyes, a faint rise in the corners of his lips, a slight tucking in of that square chin when Clinton's remarks turned humorous or brushed on the personal. In those briefest of moments the four star had seemed almost bashful, mischievous, even bemused.

What those watching the nomination ceremony could not possibly pick up on, however, was this: as he stood there at the base of the veranda steps, the eyes of the world on him, John Shalikashvili was also looking back.

Behind thick lenses of wire-rimmed spectacles, penetrating blue eyes were peering out at the assembled crowd. And these were eyes that not only had seen much, but saw much.

That's because, unbeknownst to many who engaged with him, what entered his field of vision was interpreted by a mind as scalpel sharp, and as singular, as that of the four other men—Aspin, Gore, and even Powell and Clinton—standing shoulder to shoulder with him.

It was a mind shaped in large part by the Old World.

President Clinton's enthusiastic thumbnail sketch had in fact left out some of the most dramatic elements of Shalikashvili's European roots. Some of this omission, as would later be revealed, was intentional. Yet many details about this man's past were unknown to almost all.

For instance, few watching the ceremony had any clue that the nominee actually came from royalty.

Yes, royalty. He was born Prince John Malchase David Shalikashvili. Records trace the earliest Shalikashvili prince back to Georgia in the year 1400. Who'd have believed that Shalikashvili, clad here today in US Army dress greens, had his own illustrious family crest? Or that his mother, a countess, had been born in the Winter Palace in St. Petersburg, where his maternal grandmother had served as lady-in-waiting to the last tsarina of the Russian Empire?

Equally astounding, and just as equally unknown, was his family's distinguished history of military service. Shalikashvili princes had served as Chamberlain of the Royal Georgian Court, a key civil-military position, as far back as 1611. The last to hold the title was the nominee's great-grandfather and namesake, a decorated general. And who'd have guessed the pedigree of the maternal side of the family sparkled even more brightly? Like how his mother descended from the first admiral in the Imperial Russian navy to circumnavigate the world.

Of all his Old World ancestors, four had shaped him most. There was his *Oma,* or his maternal grandmother, Countess Marie Rudiger-Bielaieff. And her sister, Countess Julie Pappenheim. Then there were his parents, Dimitri and Maria or "Missy" Shalikashvili. Based on who they were, not just as aristocrats but also as human beings, these four relatives had, particularly during the pressure cooker of World War II, helped infuse in him a rare set of abilities, values, and motivations.

And it was this Old World legacy—not just the positive aspects but unexpectedly the negative ones as well—that had enabled John Shalikashvili to take such effective advantage of the golden opportunities, and to overcome so many of the punishing obstacles, that the New World had in store. The obstacles, moreover, had arisen not just in his professional career but in his personal life as well. In fact, so intertwined were these two dimensions of his life, the public and the private, that it would be impossible to understand why Shalikashvili was being nominated to the nation's highest military post without insight into both.

Take Clinton's admission that he'd chosen Shalikashvili because "above all" he knew the general would always provide absolutely candid advice. That's because in the course of drawing on the old to assimilate to the new John Shalikashvili had built for himself a highly unusual reputation. It wasn't just that he was judged honest and "straightforward." More generally, he was widely viewed—by bosses, colleagues, and subordinates; by both civilians and those in uniform; by those both at home and abroad; and by those at almost every stage of his career—as being the polar opposite of the stereotypical Alpha Male leader. According to recent news reports, he was said to be "low-key," "self-effacing," and "informal." A consensus builder who "understands teamwork" and "is willing to examine options and adjust to political realities." Someone "extraordinarily sensitive in terms of caring for people" and whose humility was "bone deep." One who balances "firmness" with "compassion." A man with a voice "seldom raised but always heard." Someone, all told, who was "enormously loved and respected."

This unique reputation—which seemed almost too sterling to be real—was why Shalikashvili was here today. Without it, he never would have been Clinton's choice for chairman. Without it, the White House,

Department of Defense, and the US military wouldn't now be lining up so solidly behind his nomination.

Yet all this curious backstory to how Shalikashvili's American success had come about had largely escaped the myriad executive and congressional staffers charged with vetting the candidate in preparation for the president's final greenlight today.

Were there any hints of this story-within-a-story discernable to those casting an appraising eye on Shalikashvili here at the podium this evening?

Perhaps yes. So critical a role had those four ancestors played in the general's career success that their ghosts could almost be seen on the steps of the Rose Garden veranda: faintly, Countess Julie Pappenheim; sharper yet, Countess Marie Rudiger-Bielaieff; and—almost corporeal—Dimitri and Missy Shalikashvili. Here were the echoes of Europe that reverberated in this immigrant's American success story.

But specters are not always a welcome presence. In the days ahead, one of these four ghosts would again materialize—and threaten to derail John Shalikashvili's full attainment of the American dream.

Today, however, was a time to appreciate the honor being given to him. "I look forward with great enthusiasm, Mr. President," Shalikashvili continued, head swiveling briefly—and quite intentionally—to face the president, "to helping you keep America's armed forces the very best that we have ever had, and soldiers, sailors, airmen, and marines that have no match."

The nominee then ended his brief remarks this way: "And I must tell you that I am also deeply grateful to the man who has carried on that task with such singular distinction up to now: my friend, General Colin Powell." After thanking the president one last time, Shalikashvili stepped back from the lectern.

It was done. John Shalikashvili had accepted the president's nomination to become the thirteenth chairman of the US Joint Chiefs of Staff.

As cameras rolled and flashbulbs popped, the general turned to his right to accept a handshake of congratulations first from a positively beaming president and then from a smiling Colin Powell. The chairman-elect then pivoted to his left, extending a hand across the back of the lectern toward the vice president . . .

And that's when the curious thing happened.

At this instant something flashed between the nation's top political

John Shalikashvili's nomination ceremony, White House Rose Garden, August 11, 1993. From left to right: General Colin Powell, President William J. Clinton, Shalikashvili, Vice President Al Gore, and Defense Secretary Les Aspin. (DoD photograph. Courtesy of the NBR Gen. John Shalikashvili Archives.)

leader and its highest-ranking military officer. In the brief seconds the nominee was being congratulated by Gore and Aspin, the clearly joyful president, catching the eye of the current chairman, let loose an emphatic fist pump of victory with his left hand. Powell volleyed back almost instantaneously with a widening of his grin and a smart nod of his chin.

It was an odd exchange for these two men—one the first Democratic president to hold office in twelve years and the other a general who'd been appointed to the chairmanship by Republican president George Bush Sr., who years prior had served as Ronald Reagan's national security advisor, and who years hence would be appointed secretary of state by George Bush Jr.

The commander in chief and his foremost military advisor had, in fact, been known for not seeing eye-to-eye ever since Clinton took office in January. The two titans had squared off from the opposite ends of almost every major issue. If it wasn't the service of gays in the military, it was the use of force in Bosnia. If not the extent of defense budget cuts, then it was the depth of troop level reductions. Some administration officials had gone so far as to suggest that on the issue of allowing homo-

A happy Colin Powell and ecstatic Bill Clinton. (Reuters / Gary Cameron - stock.adobe.com.)

sexuals to serve openly in the military, Powell's behavior had bordered on insubordination—a charge the chairman couldn't have denied more vehemently.

Many thought such sharp differences in policy preferences helped explain why Powell, at the start of the Clinton administration, had unsuccessfully approached Aspin about stepping down months before his term's September expiration. That was a significant request: only three of the eleven chairmen preceding Powell had left office shy of a full term.

But here on this mid-August evening things were different. Tonight there was nothing but complete agreement between these two larger than life figures. For whatever reasons, for whatever mix of the public good and personal self-interest, the president of the United States and the current chairman of the Joint Chiefs both keenly wanted John Shalikashvili, more than all other candidates, for the job.

"We got him!" was what Clinton's elated fist pump was signaling on this nomination day. "Yes indeed we did," confirmed Powell's nod.

For a while there had been serious doubt they would.

2

How Many Shalikashvilis Can There Be in the World?!

August 11, 1993—Fallbrook, California

In a house tucked away among avocado groves and strawberry fields, a fifty-seven-year-old woman lay settled in bed. The bedside radio was on, volume turned low, the perfect sleep inducer for someone whose unquiet mind often kept slumber at bay. The voice of a news announcer recapping the day's events murmured from the speakers.

As she lay finally just on the edge of sleep, one news story penetrated Donna Kurtz's fading consciousness—*President Clinton today nominated four-star army general John Shalikashvili to serve as the next chairman of the Joint Chiefs of Staff.* "No, that can't be true!" her drowsy mind protested. "Yet how many Shalikashvilis can there be in the world? And how many, god damn it, are named John?" Sleep then overtook her.

Awakening the next morning, she bolted out of bed. With a quick snap the television set was on. In minutes she saw it—the image being broadcast for the world to see.

"Oh my god!" she gasped, the shock of recognition forcing her to steady herself against the bed. "The decades had certainly changed him," she thought, "but that cowlick of hair, that grinning smile, and, oh, that darling jutting chin." This *was* the John Shalikashvili she knew!

Then, amid joyous laughter, came a sequence of realizations. How proud she was of him, how so very happy she was for his success. Oh Christ, came the thought that had come occasionally over the years, "I am still so in love with this little idiot!" "That clever, complicated idiot, the one with so many different sides to him that so few got to see, the one who'd drawn me in by his love of bedevilment, of twists and turns, by a mind that was mysterious, not straight-forward as many had assumed." Yes, he was a consummate diplomat even back in high school. Beguiled by the image he cultivated, so few classmates understood what a tactician he was, how what he thought and what he said could be miles apart.

"You always had it in you John!" she actually blurted out loud. Never willing to fight a losing fight, he instead kept his temper and, as he'd always say, "live to fight another day." "Oh my God, look at you now!" she exclaimed. "It looks like you have fought patiently—and won!"

Before bringing herself to shut off the television that morning, one last thought came to her. It was a wistful imagining she'd indulged in occasionally through the years and, given yesterday's turn of events, was now more poignant: how different both their lives would've been if she hadn't betrayed him that summer almost forty years ago.

Part II

Old World Roots

_3_

Will It Play in Peoria?

June 2, 1954—Peoria, Illinois

They'd driven up Grandview Drive that evening, the two golden-haired teenagers, to celebrate their completion of an important rite of passage. Graduation had finally come and gone, leaving them and their classmates feeling some mix of joy, fear, and numbness. This was the rich part of town, with its forested estates and high bluffs offering spectacular vistas of the Peoria River. They'd been granted their diplomas today in a city located famously in the heart of Illinois and, even more famously, in the heartland of the nation. "Will it play in Peoria?" was the phrase popularized during the vaudeville era because the city's population was almost a perfect representation of the country as whole.

Peoria High School, founded in 1856, was one of America's oldest. Commencement exercises had been held in the school's auditorium. Speaking to over two thousand graduating seniors, family members, and friends, two honor students cited the importance of the four freedoms—freedom of speech and of religion, freedom from want and from fear—that President Roosevelt had famously stressed in his message to Congress back in 1941. For the graduating class of PHS '54, extending such values was part of what it meant to be American.

All that pomp and circumstance, all that patriotism and excitement, were now behind them. They were here alone, having stolen a darkened patch of lawn on the fringes of someone's fancy estate. The teenagers were lying in each other's arms, absently taking in the twinkling of lights along the riverside far below.

Graduation was a time of endings and beginnings. And not just for them as individuals but for them as a couple. It was agonizing for Donna to think about what was soon going to happen.

Much more pleasant was to appreciate how far they'd come.

* * *

They first met at the start of senior year. "Hi. I'm John Shalikashvili," he introduced himself. "Well, that's a mouthful!" she countered. "What's so hard about that?" he volleyed back. Taking a stab at it, she'd gotten it right.

She had just returned to Peoria after spending a year away. John had started classes midway junior year, the year she was gone. Her friends judged she'd come back changed—quieter, sarcastic, no longer a jokester.

Donna immediately fell for his handsome looks. John was a natural athlete, with a runner's legs, a slight waist, and a lean yet muscular chest and pair of arms. He had no flaws in his slightly tanned skin, except that it could turn reddish when he was stressed.

This sly devil, she felt, well understood the effect he had on women. He'd purposefully talk in low tones, compelling you to take a step closer in order to hear. And once you responded, he'd pretend not to have quite made out your words, politeness then pushing you to draw even nearer. And then, when he had you where he wanted, he'd begin conversing with you. Calmly. Attentively. Not only was his accent alluring but he had that way of purposefully screwing up his English phrasing just enough to be absolutely charming.

"Transformingly beautiful" was how she summed him up.

So what drew John to her? The answer was complex, but her physical appearance was surely one reason. After they became close, he'd often tell her how German she looked, how much he admired her hourglass figure, pale skin, blonde hair, blue eyes, and Teutonic facial features. She would, he assured her, fit right in in Europe. If she were riding a train and were stopped for any reason, there'd be no need for a passport to prove her identity. "When I study your face and body," he once said to her in an almost whisper, "it's like I never left there."

That's why during their early months together she thought it quite odd how he'd react whenever friends called her "Blondie." "Don't *ever* call her that," he would demand in a rare public display of anger. "Call her Donna."

Others told her that before they even met, he'd asked who she was. "Donna Bechtold," was the reply. "Ahh . . . Bachtold," John had said. During World War II her paternal grandfather, an Amish man of German ancestry, had indeed swapped that vowel in their last name so the family would blend in better here in the States.

Like many others who first met John, she asked if he was German. "No, I'm not. I'm not a Pole either. Actually I'm from a place you've never heard of. A place called Georgia." Then, pride unmistakable: "I'm Georgian." She, like many of their classmates, had no idea where or

John Shalikashvili, circa 1952, the year of his departure for the United States. Donna, his high school sweetheart in Peoria, described him as "a natural athlete, with a runner's legs, a slight waist, and a lean yet muscular chest and pair of arms. He had no flaws in his slightly tanned skin, except that it could turn reddish when he was stressed." (Courtesy of Anita Ziegler Hollweck.)

even what Georgia really was. "Oh, you're from Georgia . . . like down south?" she teased. Though turning a bit red and stiffening slightly, he laughed and explained again. She would later often hear people say to him "you must be German because of your accent," and John would just go along with it. Other times he would even volunteer he was from Germany. It was easier that way.

No matter his ethnicity, John certainly had a worldly, sophisticated air about him. Like how he'd hold his cigarette not the American way, between forefinger and middle finger, but instead use four fingers on top and place his thumb underneath, often elevating his little finger. Unlike the macho, aggressive attitude common among the guys she knew, he instead was unfailingly polite, whether to adults or to people their own age. He never told dirty jokes, swore in front of her friends, or got plastered. He knew what women liked and disliked, what embarrassed them. Understanding where the line lay, he knew exactly how far he could push.

Though she didn't know why, elegance and class saturated his every mispronounced word.

Such airs, however, weren't always appropriate here in the heartland of America. Sometimes when he'd take her out for a meal, he'd rap the side of a knife against his water glass to call the waiter. He'd knock loudly, chin held high, and then lower his head to lock eyes back on her.

"Don't do that shithead!" she once hissed. "This isn't Germany!"

"I just want service," he defended.

"That's so rude!"

"No it's not, that is how you ask for service."

"That's *not* how we do things here, John. And your chin, drop it a little. It makes you look arrogant."

"What does that have to do with anything?" came the confused reply.

She vowed to teach him how to be American, and the best place to start was with his English. Others would be nice when he misspoke, never repeating a correction more than twice. But she was his biggest critic: "John, with that accent you sound like you're really pissed!" She was also his biggest teacher, working to snap into shape not just his accent but also his use of pronouns, verbs, and the like.

Because John loved the movies, they often went to the cinema together. As they sat in the balcony watching whatever was playing, she'd often hear him mumbling the dialogue softly in hopes of sharpening his English. Once, during one heartbreaking scene, he made a sound that caused her to turn and look. What she saw shocked her—John, that boy who always had such iron control over his emotions, was shedding tears.

This sensitive side came out in other ways. Luring him once into a punching match, her fist hit him forcefully in the gut. When he belatedly dropped an arm to protect himself, a slip of his elbow knocked her in the eye. It immediately began swelling up. He instantly grabbed her and began apologizing. She told him it didn't hurt; she was just stunned. She tried to continue their tussle. "Come on you chicken, let's go!" But John, tears forming, continued to hold her tight. As her eye began to swell shut, he finally broke off to get some ice. After that incident, John refused to play fight with her again.

It was bewildering. "This boy could actually feel my pain, maybe even more acutely than I myself did." She couldn't understand such a great apology, certainly something no man in her own family would offer. In her family there were women, yes, but certainly no "ladies." A family in which female relatives—imitating starlets like Joan Crawford and Bette Davis—would readily slap each other whenever blood boiled.

How wonderful, it dawned on her that day, to finally be treated like a lady.

Donna never felt like a normal teenager, let alone a lady. John picked up on that—and more. One day early on he extended himself in a way she hadn't expected. "I think you have been hurt very badly," he posed. "Everyone says so. Is it true? They say you used to be light-hearted, but that you have a crazy mother." Her family must be mistreating her, he accused. "They must resent your looks. Just look at how they dress you! Even your shoes are lined with cardboard. And you've never seen a dentist." Yet Donna denied anything was wrong.

Later John kept pressing. "Some guy has hurt you, I can tell. I just reach for the salt and you wince like you expect to be hit. You stare into space. You're often angry over nothing." But she offered up only a hint: "I dated a man who was cruel. That's all you need to know." She ended the subject by saying that if John loved her, he should forget it; otherwise, she'd leave him if he kept bringing it up.

What was it Donna was hiding?

One big thing was the long dark shadow cast by her mother. Bitter and controlling, Donna's mother was expert at inflicting ridicule and pain. She'd rant on and on about how she never wanted Donna, how she'd also gotten saddled with two more brats, both boys. She'd perversely volunteer to others that she had never touched Donna as a baby except to bathe and dress her or change her diapers—chores she'd left to Donna's aunts whenever possible. Never nursed, Donna had sometimes been fed watered down Karo syrup, causing her baby teeth to fall out prematurely. As Donna grew into a teenager, her mother—just as John accused—had indeed seemed to increasingly resent her beauty, rarely buying her clothes or other beauty supplies. At one point Donna resorted to stealing shampoo, just a dollop at a time, from a home where she babysat.

Her father, an illiterate man, never displayed her much love. Though not mean, he was certainly passive—like when her mother was inflicting corporal punishment on the kids. Her grandmother too did little to defend her; her aunts certainly never did. Everyone would melt into silence in the presence of her overbearing mother.

Why was her mother so horrible? Donna would never find out all the reasons, but the roots were perhaps laid even before Donna was born. Her mother had grown up on a farm in Indiana during the most brutal years of the Depression. Donna's grandmother had been a nurse, a job that had taken her riding horseback all over the county for long stretches at a time. That meant Donna's mother had stayed at home, cooking, cleaning, and watching over five younger sisters—a fate she'd only escaped by leaving home at the age of twenty-four. From such experiences resentments can build.

It wouldn't be until much later in life that Donna would learn perhaps the biggest reason for her mother's hatred. It was a long-kept family secret, one that her mother would finally hurl at her one day in a moment of anger: Donna was the child of rape. (Her biological father was, unbeknownst to Donna, a neighbor.) Her mother had tried, but failed, in several homemade attempts to abort her. The two brothers were legitimate—that's why they got better treatment.

With such a background and upbringing, how could Donna have become a normal teenager? Not wanting to reveal this twisted homelife, she kept people at a distance. This coldness weighed heavily on her relationships with the guys she dated.

Her junior year of high school, her family had moved to Pittsburgh. With Donna's looks, attracting men was easy. Yet, saddled with such low self-esteem, she'd gone with some real losers. One was a popular athlete. After they started going out, he began treating her rough. So she broke up with him. Then one night he called to say he wanted to apologize. When he came to pick her up she got into his car. Inside was a gang of his friends. They brought her to a park. By the time they'd dropped her off, hours later, a few blocks from home, she was covered in bruises, cuts, and bite marks. Pieces of her hair had been ripped out of her head.

Not long after, when she found out she was pregnant, she'd had no choice but to confess. Her mother, wrongly fearing that Donna's stepfather was the culprit, paid a neighbor to throw her down the stairs in hopes of inducing a miscarriage.

That didn't work.

So at four months of pregnancy, Donna went to an abortionist. She'd spent the night there at the doctor's office, along with three other girls. The next morning, upon hearing the chiming of distant church bells, she offered up a simple prayer asking for forgiveness. Asking for a new beginning for them all.

Her family returned to Peoria for the start of her senior year. And that's when John Shalikashvili entered her life. With him, a new beginning was actually possible.

She eventually opened up to him, revealing at least some of what her life was like. "In return, John soon began to do things to buck me up. He'd do my homework, cover my ass at school with teachers who adored him but disliked me. He'd brag on and on about my Germanic good looks. He'd tell me, over and over again, that I was already a great artist, a great writer—my two main passions in life."

Weekdays, they often sat on the grass during noon break and he'd open his lunch sack to show her the cheeses he'd brought, the apricot preserves baked into *kuchen,* a German-style cake. Donna would have two slices of stale white bread spread with margarine and sugar. John, exchanging sacks with her, would pretend he loved her lunch—though what he was surely enjoying was watching her take her first heavenly taste of brie.

And then came the next careful step.

One day, from out of nowhere, John pulled out a red cashmere sweater. It was gorgeous. Seeing it unwrapped and unboxed, she asked whose it was. "It's my mother's sweater," he replied. But then he paused a moment, for this was the first time he'd brought her up in conversation. "Just try it on," he continued.

Donna could not recall ever in her life having owned a single new sweater, unless it was some nylon thing both gaudy and cheap. Yet she refused at first, feeling it was humiliating to accept what seemed like charity. But John wanted her to have the chance to wear beautiful clothes; she could tell because for a boy who was hard to read otherwise, his eyes were where his emotions showed.

She soon took to regularly wearing his mother's things. There were many cashmere cardigans in a range of tasteful muted colors, suede shoes, a white silk blouse still wafting the elegant fragrance of his mother's perfume, and occasionally even a piece of jewelry. Every aspect of her wardrobe—color, texture, cut, even fragrance—suggested impeccable breeding. After Donna had worn an item for more than a day or two, John would need to smuggle it back. But the shoes, oh it made her almost purr that she could keep those a bit longer.

For the first time in her life Donna Bechtold dressed beautifully—just like the many moneyed classmates who lived in the imposing estates on Grandview Drive.

* * *

They were lying on the grass in that very neighborhood this graduation evening.

Donna once again looked up at him. He was such an insightful boy. He'd been able to sense when someone mentally scarred was doing her damnedest to fake she wasn't. He'd figured out that her sarcasm and razor-tongued wit were largely a defense mechanism against the effects of her dysfunctional homelife. With his empathy, caring, patience, and even strategy, John had become her caretaker, something she'd never had.

But where the heck did these traits come from? Donna's horrible family background was such a large part of why she was so messed up. So was John's personality similarly rooted in his upbringing?

Based on his behavior, Donna intuited that John had been raised by women both loving and lovely. Yet he rarely spoke of his family. At first she'd barely noticed or even cared. Anxious to hide her own miserable homelife, she'd just been glad the subject never came up. Later, after she finally began sharing her story with him, she'd figured his continued silence was out of respect for her: "He knew my parents could not have been more different on a social scale from his own."

Graduation had actually been the first time Donna had met the Shalikashvilis. Eager to celebrate his achievement, John's parents and sister had come to the school auditorium. Nobody from Donna's family had bothered.

How strange it had been to finally come face to face with Mrs. Shalikashvili, the woman whose clothes Donna had so often worn. While trying on her silky navy raincoat one day, Donna had actually slipped into the fantasy that she too had such a wonderful mother. As happiness washed over her, she actually felt love toward Mrs. Shalikashvili—love for a mother who so obviously loved her children.

John, Donna thus surmised, "was like a Kennedy son, the golden child upon whom a smart and loving mother places her dreams." Surely it had been some combination of Old World good breeding and family upbringing that had produced such a charming boy?

4

Missy and Wartime Warsaw

October 1, 1944—Warsaw, Poland

Missy Shalikashvili was relieved. Despite the chaos, she, her three children, and her mother had finally arrived at the train station. The Warsaw Uprising, launched two months earlier, was finally ending. The Poles had lost their bid to end what had now been five years of German occupation. The cease-fire was set to be announced tomorrow. Although Germany and Communist Russia had signed a nonaggression pact just prior to Hitler's 1939 land grab in Poland, the Nazis pulled an about-face two years later and invaded the Soviet Union. The two sides were now at war. With Russian troops now gathering ominously outside of Warsaw on the eastern side of the Vistula River, many in the city wanted to flee before more violence broke out.

Both Missy and her mother, Countess Marie Rudiger-Bielaieff, had particular reason to fear the Soviets. Missy's late father, Brigadier General Alexandre Bielaieff, had served on the staff of the Supreme Headquarters of the tsarist Russian military. His brother, General Mikhael Bielaieff, had been minister of war in the empire's final year. If captured by the Russian communists, Missy's entire family would assuredly be deported to Russian labor camps or even killed outright. That's why Missy's group had made their way here to the station, a trip made extra nerve-racking because her mother, who was fighting pneumonia, had to be brought by stretcher.

Thankfully, it didn't take long for Missy and her charges to be cleared to board one of the freight trains arranged by the Germans for Polish wounded. Although not really German, all she needed to do was inform the administrators in their tongue, which she spoke fluently, given her mother's Baltic-German ancestry, that her husband was an officer in the German army. The train cars had been outfitted with bunked hospital beds, a stove, and red crosses painted on the boxcar sides. The uninjured either sat on the floor or on their bundles of belongings. Shortly thereafter the train departed westward toward Germany.

Visible from the train windows was the ghostly landscape of Warsaw. The city now lay half in ruins, grim testament to the unprecedented violence visited on Poland's capital not just during the Uprising but also back in 1939 when Hitler's troops originally invaded the city. And more punishment was in store: by war's end Warsaw would become the most destroyed city of World War II.

In thirty-eight years of life Missy had seen her share of inhumanity. Perhaps that's why she felt her spirits lifted later when the train arrived in Litzmannstadt (the Polish city of Lodz).

Many of the city's inhabitants brought food to the station. They passed these precious gifts—bowls of soup, fruit, and bread—through the barbed wire fence to the grateful refugees. The refugees then continued on to Poznań, a Polish town near the German border, and were taken by truck to a temporary holding camp arranged for German evacuees from Warsaw.

The camp at Poznań was a welcome haven. Everyone was allowed a bath and then assigned quarters. After being carried to a bed, Missy's mother was attended to by a doctor and given hot cereal and milk by a nurse. Then, and only then, did Missy bring her children to the crowded dining hall for a long-overdue meal.

Missy was a beautiful woman—blessed with smooth skin and high cheekbones. She dressed in attire elegant enough to complement her slender frame but not enough to be immediately eye-catching. Though she was not humorous or outgoing, her smile could lubricate a social interaction or, as when holding her youngest child in her arms, radiate her joy. But those thin lips were also known to tighten. Her face could take on an undertone of tenseness, a warning signal that things were not to her liking. Her children knew not to trifle with her.

All three of her lifeblood were now seated by her at the table, blind to all but the bounty before them: soup seasoned with meat, bread and butter, and coffee with milk.

The oldest of her children was Prince Othar Joseph, whose given and middle names honored distinguished Shalikashvili ancestors. Othar was big and strong—he'd weighed eight pounds at birth to John's six and a half, a differential that had continued as the boy matured. Perhaps that was why the eleven-year-old liked physical challenges and could exhibit such bravery. With his father away at war, he'd automatically stepped up to shoulder family responsibilities. His disposition, however, had become increasingly serious. Missy perhaps worried about him the most.

The youngest was her four-year-old daughter, Princess Nina-Alex-

(*Left to right*) John, Missy, Alexandra, and Dimitri Shalikashvili, Warsaw, 1943.

andra, who was named after her paternal grandmother, Nina, and her maternal grandfather, Alexander. Tiny for her age, she had curly blonde hair and bold blue eyes. Because Alexandra was so young, hopefully she'd emerge largely unscathed from these horrors of war.

Then there was John. The doctor whose hands delivered the young prince into this world on July 27, 1936, was a military man. Colonel Slivinsky, the owner of an exclusive private clinic in Warsaw, had been the personal physician to the late Marshal Jozef Pilsudski, the great patriot who'd played a significant role in Poland regaining its independence in 1918. Though her husband, Dimitri, was now fighting for the Germans, at the time of John's birth he'd been serving as a foreign contract officer in Pilsudski's Polish cavalry unit, the famed Chevau-Legers, or 1st Light Horse Regiment.

Upon seeing his baby's gray eyes and dark brown hair, Dimitri had all but cooed with pride at these obvious Georgian features. The baby was named after Dimitri's grandfather, Jean Shalikashvili, a distinguished Georgian general. He was baptized by a Georgian priest at a ceremony held in their spacious apartment in the officers' quarters of the Chevau-Legers, part of the Polish Cavalry barracks in Warsaw. Like brother Othar before him, at christening John was given a small golden cross on a golden chain.

It was engraved with the emblem of the original Saint Nino's cross, which Nino is said to have used to bring Christianity to Georgia.

Legally, however, all three children were citizens of no country. As a condition imposed on all foreign contract officers in the Polish army, Dimitri had signed away the right to apply for Polish citizenship. And because Missy also wasn't a Pole, their children, despite having all been born in Poland, had not been granted citizenship. And because both parents had themselves become stateless following the dissolution of the Russian Empire, their children had no other citizenship to which to lay claim.

Since birth John had generally been happy and sociable by nature, a smile often gracing his face. Thankfully, he seemed to have maintained this disposition despite the trying circumstances of war. At three years Othar's junior, John probably did not comprehend as much of the violence of these past five years.

Hopefully he would remember even less.

* * *

The long and trying road that brought the Shalikashvilis to Poznań began on September 1, 1939, the day Hitler's troops attacked Poland. Under the blare of emergency sirens, Dimitri's cavalry unit was mobilized to resist the invaders. After saying quick goodbyes in Warsaw, Missy boarded a train back to her parents' rented villa in the suburb of Skolimow. That's where the children—only the two boys then—had earlier been sent to safety.

When Missy arrived she found her family in a nervous state. Polish and German fighter planes skirmished in the skies. Though Skolimow had so far remained free from fighting, war victims were pouring into town, many shot at as they'd fled the capital city. With each passing day, her parent's sizable villa became increasingly crowded with friends and relatives fleeing the bombardment of the capital. Missy's mother worked shoulder-to-shoulder with the housekeeper, rising at 5 a.m. each day to prepare food for their growing number of houseguests.

Missy did not sit idle while her husband was off fighting and people around her were suffering. Having completed first aid courses earlier in the year when Polish-German relations began deteriorating, Missy joined other regimental wives as a Red Cross volunteer. The organization was using vacant villas in Skolimow as makeshift field hospitals for the injured and wounded. Missy scrubbed rooms, sterilized medical equipment, comforted patients, and occasionally helped out in surgery. She once assisted in amputating the arm of a woman who'd been shot in her right shoulder—a seamstress who'd likely never thread a needle again.

Another patient was an eleven-year-old girl with nine bullet wounds in her back. By encouraging her to think about how wonderful it would be to lie in a clean, white bed once the surgery was finished, Missy managed to comfort the screaming child long enough for the doctor to place the ether mask over her face.

On September 8, German tanks rumbled into town. Suspicious that the big tower at her mother's villa was a scouting post for the Polish military, German soldiers came to search the house. They warned the family at the outset to turn over any weapons. Though not finding the gun Missy had hidden under a flowerpot, they became agitated upon discovering a Polish cavalry uniform of Dimitri's. Missy pacified them, however, by speaking in German. The soldiers eventually departed, taking only a few bottles of wine.

Under the blanket of their 1939 nonaggression pact, Moscow and Berlin had effectively divided Poland up into respective spheres of influence. Taking advantage of the chaos created by Hitler's invasion, the Soviets too had marched into Poland, intent on reclaiming lands viewed as part of the Russian motherland. Caught between the two armies, the Polish military clearly could not hold out. The war to defend Warsaw would last little more than one month.

One day before the fighting concluded, Missy was surprised by a letter from Aunt Julie, her mother's sister, who lived in Bavaria. Dimitri had sent word to Julie, asking her to let Missy know he was now a prisoner of war (POW) of the Germans.

This was chilling news. Given her husband's past service to the tsar, Missy had no illusions about what would happen if the Germans turned her husband over to the Soviets. At great expense, Missy and a neighbor hired a horse-drawn wagon to take them to Warsaw as soon as the roads opened.

When Missy arrived at the barracks of the Chevau-Legers, her heart sank—it was now occupied by a German regiment. Her inquiries yielded no news of Dimitri's whereabouts. Thankfully she was allowed to visit the family's quarters. The three-story brick building, she discovered, had been badly damaged by artillery fire. After climbing the stairs to their apartment, she was shocked at the sight of their living room, bedroom, and nursery all lying in shambles. Pausing to offer up thanks to God that they'd fled Warsaw before the attack, she set about salvaging what she could. Soon their former housekeeper appeared. This kind soul, who'd been hiding on the ground floor of the building since the bombing, had rescued many of the family's valuables, even saving photos and a civilian suit in case Dimitri should have need.

A wagon, hired at even greater expense, then brought Missy, the housekeeper, and the remnants of the Shalikashvilis' belongings back to Skolimow.

Missy eventually received welcome word from an officer from Dimitri's regiment: her husband was being held at a Polish military hospital in Kraków. Heart singing at the news, she donned her Red Cross uniform and pin, grabbed her Red Cross certificates, and left Skolimow. With the rails not working, she hitchhiked on whatever vehicle could take her closer to Kraków. Along the way she busied herself attending to any sick passengers. At each transfer point her heart would skip. She never knew if the Germans would allow her to continue.

When Missy finally arrived at the hospital three days later, it was a shock to her husband. Wasting no time, he explained the good luck that had brought him here: the hospital had been set up by a Red Cross volunteer, a Jewish woman dedicated to saving lives by visiting German POW camps and identifying so-called "sick" prisoners to bring back with her.

Any joyous feelings of being reunited quickly faded, however, as Dimitri related how tenuous his situation was. With each passing day, prisoners at the hospital were either being handed over to the Russians, which for Dimitri would mean a death sentence, or sent to POW camps in Germany.

But luck was with them. The physician in charge of the hospital, himself a POW from the Ukraine, put Missy on the hospital staff, allowing the couple to remain together and work out a strategy.

First priority was to get a certificate from the medical authorities attesting to Dimitri's poor health. In a piece of ironic good fortune, his health was indeed declining: he'd developed a bleeding stomach ulcer and his heart had begun giving him problems.

Missy next sought help from another of her mother's sisters: Aunt Sophie, who had married into the aristocratic Prussian family of the Manteuffels. Her husband, Baron Henry von Manteuffel, was a colonel in the German army and a relative to Hasso von Manteuffel, a well-regarded officer who later in the war would command the famed 5th Panzer Army during the Battle of the Bulge. Missy got word to have her uncle place a call from Berlin to inquire about Dimitri's health, as having this Manteuffel family connection made known at the hospital might keep Dimitri from immediate transfer.

They needed that extra time. Missy struck out once more, though by now the rails had thankfully begun working again. First was a brief check on her family in Skolimow and then on to Lublin, her mother's birthplace, to implore the local authorities to sign papers certifying that Dimitri would take over the flour mill her parents owned there. Next stop was Warsaw to secure more signatures from yet higher-level German authorities.

Missy returned to Kraków in triumph. Thanks to her family's resources and her own courage and fortitude, she'd gathered all the necessary documents and signatures before the Germans had seen fit to transfer Dimitri elsewhere.

Now came the excruciating wait for his release to be approved.

On December 28, 1939—the very day all remaining POWs left the hospital for camps in Germany—her husband's papers arrived. Dimitri was no longer a war prisoner.

But this good news was soon overshadowed by bad. Back in Warsaw that evening they learned from friends that Missy's father had just passed away. Missy was now the closest family member her mother had left.

In 1940, with their third child due in December and no hospital in Skolimow, the Shalikashvilis, together with Missy's mother, moved back to Warsaw in October. They'd live in one of the spacious apartments in a three-building complex Missy's mother owned on Bratska Street. Because the property included some twenty apartments, the rental fees, together with the income from the Lublin flour mill, gave Missy's mother the wherewithal to support herself and her daughter's family. This was a godsend. Neither Dimitri nor Missy expected immediate employment.

Though the Shalikashvilis strove to maintain a low profile, ethnic tension ran rife. They took to wearing a pin of the flag of Georgia, a signal to the Germans that they were not Polish. Knowing the ill-will between the Russians and the Poles living in Warsaw, Missy's mother often helped her Russian friends by inviting them over for a decent meal. Such loyalty sprung from many sources: the part of her bloodline that was Russian, her service at court in St. Petersburg, and the fact that her late husband was a tsarist Russian general.

This affinity, however, could cause tension within the family. One day Missy's mother came across a news story published by the Germans. The article listed the names of thousands of Polish officers killed by the Russians in the Katyn Forest massacre of 1940. "That's not possible!" Marie exclaimed. Dimitri emphatically protested. He knew the story to be true: he and others in his unit had purposefully surrendered to the German military. "Because the Soviets would have killed him for being a traitor," Othar would later explain. Some of Dimitri's closest fellow officers hadn't been so lucky: captured by Russian troops, they'd been tortured, killed, then left to rot in Katyn.

Yet Missy's mother could define her nationality as suited her. Born in an ethnically Polish part of the Russian Empire, she would sometimes state unequivocally that she was Polish. Missy too had spent time living in Lublin, her mother's birthplace, and as blood will be blood sometimes also identified herself as a Pole. Missy hated to see their Polish friends suffer under German occupation, especially those who were Jewish.

Eventually Dimitri was given a job on the committee of the Georgian Colony, an expatriate organization for Georgians. By early 1941 he was serving as colony president.

Missy too served the Georgian cause. She aided in the colony's efforts to locate and provide food and medicine for Georgians held in German POW camps and hospitals. She would return home from such trips to the field and, eyes filled with tears, relate to Dimitri how painful it was to see these Georgians in such deplorable conditions, how skinny they looked, how they shivered as they reached out for the care packages she'd brought.

One particularly cold winter day, Missy set out with two Georgians for a remote POW camp. Lugging suitcases full of food and medicine, they boarded a train in Warsaw. On the way, they steamed past a grim site: frozen bodies, surely of Polish partisans, hanging from wooden gallows. After disembarking, the group trudged a good distance through deep snowdrifts before finally arriving at the camp.

At the gates, Missy, the translator, spoke to the guard. "We are representatives from the Georgian Red Cross. We are here to provide assistance to Georgian prisoners." The guard escorted them to see the commander of the camp, who expressed his regrets. A typhoid outbreak in the prison meant they could not meet any of the prisoners. He did offer, however, to distribute the food to the Georgian POWs.

This prompted Missy to ask if the sick were getting medical attention. "Well this is not a hospital!" the commander snapped. "The stronger men will survive." But Missy pressed on, opening the suitcases and asking him to make sure the food was distributed evenly and also pointing out the medicines and vitamins they'd brought.

Taken aback, the commander demanded to know where the supplies had come from. With strict rationing in place, such things could not be purchased legally.

Though trembling with fear, Missy looked the commander in the eye.

"We members of the Georgian Colony," she declared, "all pitched in to buy these items on the black market for our men suffering in POW camps."

To her great relief, the commander's sharp edge faded. He actually smiled at her. What she'd done was highly illegal, he warned. And yes she could be severely punished. But he could see she did it for a worthy cause.

The commander then brought the group to meet the senior officer of the Georgian POWs. Because of the danger of typhoid, the Red Cross representatives were forced to talk to him across an open field. At one point the officer spoke to Missy in Georgian. Missy apologized in Russian for being unable to speak to him in his own language. "But I am the wife of a Georgian," she assured him, "and certainly consider myself a Georgian."

In January 1943 Dimitri once again went off to a war. This time it was in a German uniform. Over Missy's protests, he'd joined the Georgian Legion, one of the ethnic military groups Germany had formed to aid their flagging war effort.

With his departure, Missy returned to the role of sole protector of the family. Life in Warsaw was becoming increasingly difficult. Though their rations had improved now that her husband served the German military, there still was never enough food to go around.

A reprieve came, however, when by the fall of 1943 Dimitri was posted to France, where supplies were more readily available. He began sending home care packages containing useful items, such as a couple pounds of butter and some knitting wool, or extravagances, including dresses and French perfume, that Missy could easily trade on the black market for more pressing staples. Once there was even a gift for Alexandra: a handmade rag doll with black buttons for eyes, a luxury at a time when all German factories had switched to war production.

Yet Warsaw was growing increasingly dangerous. Resistance to the German occupation would break out sporadically. One day when Missy and her youngest were out walking, a hand grenade exploded, knocking Alexandra to the ground and causing Missy to tremble in fear and anger.

As a result of such acts of defiance, the Gestapo was constantly on the lookout for saboteurs of the Third Reich. Suspicious of everyone, they seemed always to be searching homes, always to be making arrests. One afternoon there was a knock on the Shalikashvili's door. Two men were calling. One wore a Gestapo uniform, the other was a Pole in civilian clothes. They both carried guns. They also held a search order. Missy had no choice but to let them in.

The men began searching the apartment. They soon uncovered some gold rubles, a forbidden item—all gold was supposed to be turned over to the German authorities. The uniformed man immediately began screaming, brandishing his gun and threatening to shoot everyone for harboring gold. He angrily demanded *all* their valuables. When Missy's mother went to her bedroom to get her jewelry box, the man in civilian clothes followed. While the Gestapo officer raged on, Missy managed to whisper instructions to Othar—sneak upstairs to a neighbor's apartment and call the office of the Georgian Colony. Her son managed to leave without being observed, and upon his return left the front door ajar to allow rescuers to slip in quietly.

Within minutes almost two dozen German *Uberfall-Kommando* arrived, accompanied by old General Koniashvili from the Georgian Legion. With a sharp *"Haande hoch,"* the police disarmed and handcuffed the two men. And then, there in the dining room right in front of Missy, her mother, and the children, the German police proceeded to beat the intruders bloody. "What do you mean, breaking into the house of a German countess?" they screamed as their blows rained down.

The bandits were hauled away, and Missy was brought to police headquarters to testify. The uniformed man had indeed once served in the Gestapo—but, after being kicked out, had joined with his accomplice to commit robberies. The German was given life imprisonment; the Pole was ordered executed. All valuables, save for the gold pieces, were returned to Missy.

Once Missy returned home, however, a neighbor implored her to go back and ask the Gestapo to spare the life of the Polish man. Missy obliged, only to have the judge tell her that she was very naive, that these criminals would have killed her family, and that she should be grateful she wasn't being punished for hiding gold rubles from the authorities.

Reports eventually filtered in that the Soviet army was drawing nearer to the city. This news raised hopes—and rumors: the Poles in Warsaw, emboldened by the possibility of Soviet assistance, might soon launch an uprising to take back control of their city.

Fearful for her family's safety, in July 1944 Missy gathered up the family's valuables and stored them in a place she hoped would remain safe. Then she departed for the railway station, bringing only her three children. Her mother had refused to leave. "I am Polish, and Poland is my home."

Arriving at the station, Missy found a German troop train set to depart for Germany. "Come on in, we'll make room," the soldiers cheerfully offered once she identified herself as the wife of a German military officer. But Missy couldn't do it. Unable to abandon her mother, Missy turned her charges around and headed back to their apartment. It was an emotional decision, one that even Othar knew put the entire family at risk: "If we'd been caught by the Bolsheviks, we all would have been killed. Even grandmother."

On August 1, 1944, eager to establish a government before the hoped-for arrival of the advancing Soviet army, the Polish Underground finally launched the uprising. The Germans responded immediately. The fighting was bitter; the shelling, indiscriminate. The Shalikashvilis could only hunker down inside their apartment—and pray. From time to time they spotted German dive-bombers in the sky or heard partisans and German soldiers locked in gun battles on neighboring streets.

During breaks in the fighting the children would, on rare occasions, be allowed outside to play in the courtyards. Their apartment complex offered a triangular patch of grass that, wedged in between two of the apartment buildings, offered enough shelter to serve as playground.

Yet during wartime enjoyment is evanescent. At one point Missy was accused by Polish partisans of being a spy for the Germans. She was put under house arrest. The charge was serious. As son John later recalled: "Our backs were against the garden wall and they were going to shoot us all."

But that's when the resistance commander of the military sector in which their apartment was located arrived. Luck was again with the Shalikashvilis: the captain, who'd graduated with Dimitri from the Polish School of Cavalry, had been one of Dimitri's closest friends. He cleared her name and spared the family from death.

While luck was intermittent, danger was ever-present. One day, right after the Germans captured the part of Warsaw known as Old Town, escaping fighters of the Polish Underground emerged from the sewers right outside the Shalikashvili's apartment. Missy's children looked on wide-eyed as exhausted partisans spilled out from the bowels of the earth, hoisting their war dead up with them.

The partisans took the Shalikashvili's building as their base. That triangular patch of grass where the children played soon became a crowded cemetery: adult bodies were buried in the middle, the corpses of the children were interred in the corners. Othar was impressed by how humane the Polish fighters remained under the stress of war.

That the Polish Underground was now living in their house probably made it inevitable that violence would come directly to the Shalikashvi-lis. One day intense street fighting came terrorizingly close to their house. Whether the Germans soldiers would have attacked the apartment is unknowable, because at that moment a deafening roar was heard. The house began shaking violently, pieces of the apartment complex crumbled and fell, and the Shalikashvili's ceiling began filling up with smoke. Their building had been hit by a German dive-bomber.

A quick search calmed Missy's worst fears—none in her family was hurt. Others in the complex had most certainly been killed or injured. The family rushed to the safety of the cellar.

And so Missy, her mother, and her three children began living underground. For a while they stayed in their own basement. They then took shelter in a series of cellars in an attempt to avoid the fighting. "Most often the only way to get anyplace was through the sewer lines," John later recalled. As they moved about, Othar, the strongest, took charge of the heaviest suitcases. The family had to pay others to carry the stretcher bearing Missy's mother.

The family spent weeks underground. Conditions were harsh. At no time was there electricity or running water. There were no bathrooms, no ready way to cook food. Not that food was often available. "A piece of bread during this period," John later remembered, "was like a holiday meal."

Othar and John occasionally would muster the courage to emerge from the cellar. Dashing behind makeshift barricades of overturned wagons or pieces of broken concrete, they'd bolt for a temporary soup kitchen set up by the Polish resistance. Taking such risks, though, could all too easily result in a life cut short by bullet or explosion. Yet Missy had no choice but to suppress her maternal instinct; she had to let her children do it so the family could survive.

And her children both held up and helped out under these trying circumstances. Once, when some Poles asked for volunteers to go gather up corn husks they'd discovered above ground, Othar automatically raised his hand. The most dangerous missions—such as fetching water or gathering firewood from destroyed homes—fell to him. He'd run about his tasks hunched over, clutching whatever supplies he'd found, sometimes being shot at as he darted about.

And John? If he wasn't helping to look after his sister, he was striving to comfort his sick grandmother. Was he tending to others because that was all a boy his age could do, particularly with his older brother shouldering the heavier responsibilities? Or was this simply the boy's natural predilection?

Though the Polish Underground fought tenaciously, they were out-manned and underequipped. Their hope—that the Soviet army gathered outside the city would support the uprising—never materialized. The Soviets had no interest in having a Polish government to negotiate with if and when the Germans lost the larger war. The day thus eventually came when the Polish fighters were forced to surrender.

When word reached the Shalikashvilis that the Uprising was ending, Missy could not but acquiesce to Othar's eager request to venture out to see what the Germans were up to. He'd already proven himself; he was no longer a child. Othar soon reported back that yes the fighting had stopped, the Underground was surrendering, and—because the Allies had warned Germany to treat the Poles according to the Geneva Convention—those who laid down arms were not being mistreated.

The Warsaw Uprising, for all practical purposes, was over, allowing the Shalikashvilis to scramble out of the cellar and back into the light of day.

* * *

It was hard to believe that the dangers of Warsaw were really behind them, that they'd all somehow managed to escape alive. Yet here they were, seated in the dining hall of the refugee camp in Poznań, finishing up the last bites of their first real meal in weeks.

As Missy leaned forward to get up from the table, a pouch hanging from her neck by a string swung forward under her clothes. Inside was Dimitri's most precious possession: the journal of his service on the only diplomatic mission of free Georgia, the 1920 mission to Ankara, Turkey. Though unable to bring much with her, she knew not to leave this behind in Warsaw.

Tomorrow Missy would ask the officer in charge of the camp to send a telegram to the Georgian Liaison Office in Berlin. The last she knew her husband had been posted there. Hopefully he'd remained safe in Berlin, would thus receive her telegram, and could come escort them on the next leg of their journey.

Despite the danger of allied bombings, Missy and her charges were on their way to Pappenheim, Germany. There in that beautiful Bavarian village, Aunt Julie—John's godmother, in fact—was preparing to take them in.

Seeing her family safely through to their destination was Missy's sole focus right now. The larger struggle—how to find real stability for her family—would have to come later.

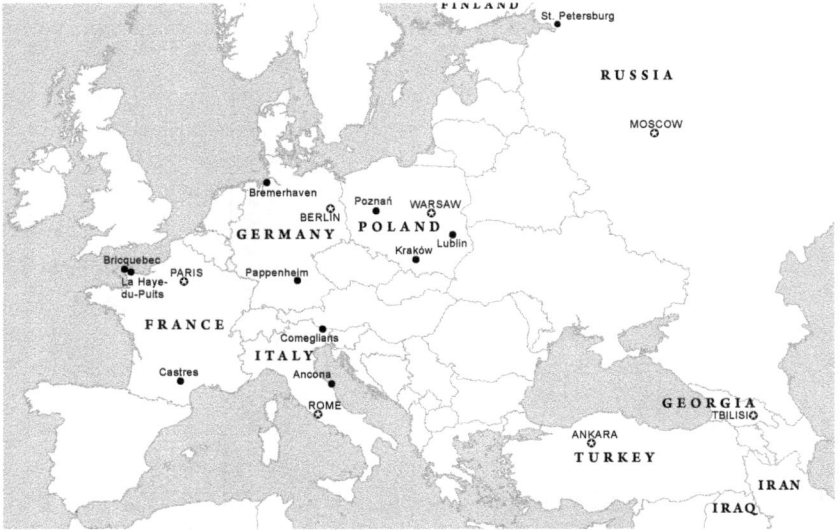

World War II Europe

5

Countess Julie Pappenheim

Spring 1947—Pappenheim, Germany

Countess Julie Pappenheim stood under the portico that framed the towering double-doored entrance to her stately residence, the *Neues Schloss*. Though approaching her eighth decade of life and no longer graced with the porcelain skin, full lips, and smoky eyes of her youth, she was still a striking figure. Despite her husband's passing when she was only thirty-seven years old, Julie had not remarried. She would remain forever attired in black, the color of mourning, a public symbol of her loyalty and commitment not only to her departed husband but also to something larger—the estate of the noble Pappenheim lineage—and, by extension, to something more narrow—her own financial security and social position.

The countess emerged from between the portico's arched columns and turned left onto the main thoroughfare. Ahead of her, just past the edge of the Pappenheim estate, the road branched.

Off to the left was the entrance to the *Altmühlbrücke*. Almost two years had passed since American troops appeared on the other side of that bridge, signaling war's end for Pappenheim. In the tumult that followed, US soldiers had installed their headquarters in the first floor of the New Schloss, the very space vacated hours earlier by remnants of the fleeing German military. The occupation government took shape soon thereafter, bringing in US and other Allied administrators, who remained in Pappenheim even after the bulk of the Allied troops eventually cycled out. The walls of the village train station became a checkerboard of flyers, some displaying the names and pictures of wanted political criminals, others tacked up by civilians desperate for information on missing loved ones.

Reaching the intersection, Julie turned right down *Graf Carl Strasse*, a thoroughfare honoring the Pappenheim count who served as the Holy Roman Empire's final imperial marshal. How time had a way of changing things. For hundreds of years the family had wielded the right to

Countess Julie Pappenheim,
John Shalikashvili's great
aunt and godmother, circa
mid-1880s.

extend political asylum to anyone who crossed into Pappenheim land.
That was just one of the privileges they'd lost with the fall of the Holy
Roman Empire in 1806. Since then even minor perks had been stripped
away, including the exclusive right to order trains to stop at the village's
railroad station, which ended in 1917.

The reputation of the village and its people too had fallen. *"Ich
kenne meine Pappenheimer"*—"That's how I know my Pappenheimer"—
was an expression coined by Count Gottfried Heinrich Pappenheim,
field marshal of the Holy Roman Empire in the early 1600s. During the
Thirty Years' War, he'd uttered that line upon learning his men's performance in battle had more than fulfilled their reputation for courage
and loyalty. The phrase then spread far and wide after being adapted in
Friedrich Schiller's famed Wallenstein trilogy in the late 1700s. Pappenheimers, everyone knew, were people easily identified by their admira-
ble actions. But no longer. Having gotten twisted somewhere along the
way, the phrase was now actually a rebuke, a way to express disappoint-
ment—at someone who'd screwed up yet again or was once more proving a liar and cheat.

The Bavarian village of Pappenheim, Germany. The Burg sits atop the village's hill. Visible in the lower left corner is the back of the Old Schloss, and just visible on the lower right, the Altmühl Bridge running between the New Schloss (background) and Hotel Krone (foreground). (Courtesy of Frank Dietrich.)

World War II was the latest historical force to bring change to the Pappenheims. Foremost was that Julie's only grandson, Count Joachim-Ludwig, had been killed in the fighting at Normandy, thereby terminating the line of male inheritors to the Pappenheim estate. What the future held for this aristocratic family was now much less certain.

The countess continued down the cobblestoned street, the beautiful architecture of Pappenheim surrounding her. To the left were the Hotel Krone and the towering Evangelical Church. On the right, a row of two- and three-story buildings hosting shops at street level and residences above.

Few village folk had been left untouched by the war. Well before the fighting stopped, millions of refugees had flooded into Germany—including Germans expelled from places like Poland and Czechoslovakia as well as many non-Germans, especially Poles, dislocated during the violence. Pappenheim, originally with a population of thirty-five hundred, absorbed close to two thousand refugees between 1943 and 1945.

The influx strained village resources. Locals were forced to open up their homes to the refugees, with the mayor even confiscating space in one of the village's two main churches. Many Pappenheimers resented these interlopers, unhappy with the competition they posed for the limited housing, goods, services, and jobs available following the war. The refugees, for their part, were grateful for having survived the war and for a new chance to pursue a livelihood, yet many felt the injustice of having lost everything while others still had so much.

The Pappenheims, by far the richest and most prominent family in the area, had the greatest responsibility to help the village cope with the disruption. Noblesse oblige all but demanded it. Yet the family would not destitute itself trying to meet what was an overwhelming humanitarian need. What they did do was offer up rooms to needy refugees first in the New Schloss and then, after renovations were complete, in the Old Schloss. Julie's daughter-in-law, Liutta, who eventually had taken over stewardship of the family from Julie, also served as head of the district's Red Cross. And Julie herself visited the sick in the hospital or helped out by word or deed wherever else she could. For this and other reasons, the villagers were fond of her.

This notion—that one's manner of treating others is at least as important as what you actually do for them—was embodied by Julie's only son, Ludwig. Casual and easygoing, he remained on a first-name basis with classmates and was not afraid to share in manual labor. Then there was his youngest daughter, Ursula. Cheerful, straightforward, and unconventional for a countess, she'd help with chores whenever home on break from her agricultural studies. Both father and daughter were also well liked in the village.

Julie continued making her way down *Graf Carl Strasse*. Just ahead, off to the left, stood the Old Schloss. Part late German Gothic but mostly German Renaissance, the building, though a bit run down, was impressive. Four stories of white facade rose up from the street, ending in a pitched red roof bristling with gables and chimneys. At each corner of the main building rounded towers capped by steep spires jutted skyward.

Although a magnificent courtyard overlooked the river on the far side of the schloss, this street side was more subdued. The first story of the building was marked only by small round windows and a modest entryway. Framing the entryway were twin columns supporting a small balcony above. That balcony was part of the two-room apartment that housed Julie's sister Marie and her daughter's family, the Shalikashvilis.

That was Julie's destination today. Passing through the entryway, the countess made her way toward the stairs. The Pappenheims had done what they could to help Marie's family. Though their apartment was not

The *Altes Schloss* (Old Schloss), built to house the Pappenheim family in the early 1800s after the Burg became unlivable. For most of their stay in Germany (1944–1952), the Shalikashvili family lived in a two-bedroom apartment over the front entryway.

expansive, the architecture was beautiful, the woodwork intricate, the two rooms not small in size. That balcony was also her sister's favorite spot, a perch from which Marie would idle away the hours watching the villagers go about their daily rituals.

Once her old legs carried her up to the second floor, Julie would knock. She'd wait for someone to come to the door, which due to a quirk could only be opened by lifting the doorknob up before turning. Hopefully Marie was feeling well today. And how wonderful if Dimitri and Missy were home—the Pappenheim family found them as well mannered as they were educated. They were the kind of people that could converse pleasantly on a wide range of subjects—in French, of course, the language of cultured society.

* * *

The Shalikashvilis arrived in Pappenheim in October 1944, having braved aerial bombings along the way. Because the trains weren't running to Pappenheim that night, Julie's daughter-in-law, Liutta, drove the village's ambulance to the nearby station in Treuchtlingen to fetch them.

They arrived with precious few possessions. The Pappenheims provided the rudiments: a roof over their heads, heat to keep out the winter cold, and a few basic supplies. Yet at night, among the sea of illuminated houses in town, the Old Schloss, their home after war's end, stood in conspicuous darkness—electricity was not part of the Pappenheim's charity.

Needing to return to his post in Berlin, Dimitri did not linger. Missy thus once again became sole caretaker for three children and a frail mother. Not one to be defined by circumstances, she took pains to ensure that none of her children ever felt like a "displaced person," the terminology in vogue for a war refugee. Neither shyness nor language barrier would be allowed to delay their assimilation.

She immediately enrolled all three in school. Othar, who'd attended German-language grade school and passed the German high school entrance exam back in Poland, was sent off to boarding school, freeing up space in the family's cramped living quarters.

Alexandra and John faced a tougher adjustment. Neither had spoken a word of German before arriving in Bavaria. Alexandra entered Pappenheim's kindergarten, where the five-year-old quickly picked up the new language and customs—though she never could get used to how the women in the village curtsied to her, an honor afforded to all female Pappenheim relatives.

John faced bigger challenges. Already eight years old, the chaos in Warsaw had kept him from any formal schooling. He nevertheless plunged straight into the village's elementary school program. "And it was up to me to sink or swim," he later recalled.

But academics did not come easily to John—whether it was the one year of grade school in Pappenheim, six years commuting to secondary school in Ansbach and Weissenberg, or one final year spent at boarding school in Dinkelsbuhl. Having flunked one year of high school Latin, he'd been required to repeat the entire grade the following year. Many of his marks hovered south of average, including for English, history, and biology.

His attention was often elsewhere.

In class, John would do leisure reading, including translated comic books starring Tom Mix, the Western movie legend, or books by Karl May, a popular German writer of adventure novels set in the Old West. Like many boys his age, the American Wild West was John's passion.

Dimitri Shalikashvili watching sons, John and Othar, playing Indians, Warsaw, 1941.

Back in Poland, he and friends would dress up as Indians. In Germany, he'd sketch lifelike figures of cowboys and Indians.

On one occasion, a particularly stern English teacher spotted him indulging in a comic book. "Shalikoff, stand up!" the teacher roared, using the Russian version of his last name. Paying no heed, Shalikashvili continued reading. Again came the command, only in a more exasperated voice. Finally, looking up through a mask of innocence, John pushed himself up from his desk and announced: "Excuse me professor, but my name is Shalikashvili and that's why I didn't respond immediately." The class howled with laughter, prompting the teacher to give him an immediate black mark in the class log. The refugee boy's demeanor made it clear to the class that the punishment didn't faze him a bit.

PAGLIACCI

MADAME BUTTERFLY

OPERATIC CHARACTERS

by

TANNHÄUSER

Line drawings exhibiting John Shalikashvili's childhood creative skills.

Little wonder an old Georgian family friend would later sum up John's personality as a child this way: "He was a creative, outgoing, and naughty boy who could always cute-talk his way out of trouble."

He was indeed creative. Later in life his sister, who would go on to be a commercial designer, judged him one of the most creative people she knew. In grade school, his line drawings—of plants, flowers, operatic figures—were jaw-droppingly impressive. The art teacher, reading the situation incorrectly, once sent a note home warning Missy to stop doing her son's assignments.

John was also outgoing. Of all three children, he seemed to connect most naturally with others, no matter the environment, not least with other refugees. "John was well-liked, not shy, and fit in easily wherever he went," Othar later recalled. "He had lots of friends. I sometimes envied him." Personality-wise, the older brother was much more serious, even severe. Alexandra would liken talking with Othar to exchanging information in a Q&A session. "With John, there was this easy flow." Asked later in life to characterize Othar's personality, John would reply: "In a word? Ruthless." Then, after a pause: "He chased me with an axe once."

And naughty? Yes, John was naughty. Maybe it was youthful enthusiasm finally freed from the restrictions of war. Or his behavior might have been encouraged by his father. Once, while in Pappenheim on leave, Dimitri introduced John to both smoking and drinking. As a chain-smoker, an occasional boisterous drinker, and a soldier about to return to a war from which he might not return, perhaps the father had wanted his son to know what the world had to offer.

Whatever the reason, John was a handful. One of his tricks was to get his sister to beg American soldiers for chocolate. How could even battle-hardened GIs resist the sweet smile of this young girl with golden locks? John, though, would then go sell the spoils on the black market. He blossomed into a full-scale opportunist, buying up American-made cigarettes from GIs at 20 marks per pack and selling them to villagers for 25 or even 30 marks. Rumor went he also sold gas he siphoned out of American jeeps. Not only did John not shy from fisticuffs but once, after an argument with an adult over John and other kids playing soccer on the man's property, he later returned with a slingshot and broke all the windows in the man's house. With glass difficult to procure in the postwar period, the owner could do little but board up the windows.

When asked later in life why he'd been sent away to boarding school, John blamed his childhood experience selling marked-up cigarettes in Pappenheim. But at boarding school in Dinkelsbuhl "I found out that the wife of the principal smoked," he chuckled, "so I was back in business."

But John was never long outside of people's good graces. For he was a charmer. His missives home from Dinkelsbuhl, despite poor penmanship and numerous spelling mistakes, were endearingly convivial. "Dear Mother: You can't imagine how much I have enjoyed the pullover, and the socks are super! I'm doing well." He'd inquire about his grandmother's health, promising to make drawings to send her soon. He'd also ask after his brother and sister. Especially his sister.

John was very caring toward Alexandra. He'd carry her books during the walks along the extended tree-lined footpath to and from the train station, part of their daily commute to high school in Ansbach and Weissenberg. He'd even let her tag along when he struck out on boyish adventures with friends. Once, while the two were exploring in the village, John slipped and impaled himself on a spike of the iron fence they were trespassing over. "Don't tell mother!" he implored. It was important to stay in their mother's good graces.

Yes their mother was strict, Othar would later offer, but she had so many responsibilities heaped onto her shoulders during their war-torn childhood, what with a husband away at war, a sick and immobile elder to care for, and three children to raise. "The hero of this entire period was my mother. She was such a strong person, she found ways to overcome so many obstacles."

Later in life Alexandra would credit John for perceiving the great stress their mother was under. Even at that young age, she judged, her brother knew to help his mother out by taking care of his baby sister and Oma. "He was very good at connecting with girls, good at relationships with girls, including mother," Othar later reflected. "And he was very helpful to grandmother."

Perhaps it wasn't just empathy that shaped his behavior. Growing up in a family of strong personalities, he would have benefited from playing up his natural charm; a forceful approach would have gained him little. And especially with a father away at war and a brother off at boarding school, it made sense that John would become adept at charming women, for the power holders during his childhood—whether his mother and grandmother at home or Aunt Julie and her daughter-in-law, Liutta, in the village—were all female.

As the children settled into their new life in Pappenheim, Missy continued worrying over the family's separation from Dimitri. Her concern only increased when, in the spring of 1945, he was called away from Germany to take part in a mission to Italy. Before he left, she actually met up with him in Salzburg to discuss the whole family accompanying him, but in the end Dimitri left on his own. Soon thereafter, all contact with him ended.

About that time it became obvious that, Nazi propaganda notwithstanding, Germany would soon lose the war. With each passing day the wait for the post became harder to bear. Though desperate for news of her husband, Missy was terrified that any letter she received might contain condolences for his death.

Unable to bear the uncertainty, she sometimes left her children in the care of a local teacher and took to the road. She visited many POW camps, beseeched many Allied authorities, implored many German government officials. At the start of one trip, her daughter spotted her leaving Pappenheim on the back of a flatbed truck. This time Alexandra had not known she was leaving. Decades later she'd surmise that mother simply hadn't had the heart to tell her children that she was once again going off in search of their father.

Then one day it finally arrived. The note was short, informing Missy that her husband was, for the second time in his life, a POW. This time he was in Italy and it was the Allies who were holding him.

Yet Missy's joy would soon be replaced by frustration. The British began shuttling him from one POW camp to the next, often with no warning. Eventually Dimitri sent welcome word that he was permanently assigned to a camp in the Italian city of Ancona.

Missy, just as she'd done back in Poland after Dimitri's capture by the Germans, bravely struck out to find him. Short on money, she borrowed from a friend. Lacking the proper paperwork, she still took to road and rail, braving checkpoint after checkpoint, risking arrest every step of the way.

Upon reaching the Italian border, however, she was stopped. Her entry was categorically denied. All Missy could do was go back and await his release.

In December 1946 Dimitri finally returned to Bavaria. It had taken almost half a year since being freed from the POW camp to secure passage home. While certainly a joyous reunion for the family, some in the village might have wondered how much his arrival lightened Missy's load.

Dimitri was quite a presence. Despite the stress of imprisonment and his sharp decline in fortunes, he still comported himself as an aristocrat. He was always impeccably dressed, his attire conservative in both style and color. He tended a luxuriant mustache. His manners were excellent—habitually holding doors open for others, always taking great care in choosing his words. He was gentle. He loved reading French poetry. Harboring a deep love of animals, he held appreciation for the steeds that had served the cavalry officer "with patience and dignity" and proved "faithful companions" during "long marches and bloody battles."

Dimitri tended to leave domestic concerns to the women. He'd never set foot in the kitchen or help carry groceries and was much less involved in the children's upbringing. Yet he insisted on reading his children bedtime stories, delighting them with his creative flair for mimicking character voices.

Dimitri had returned to a struggling postwar German economy. Prices were stable thanks to government rationing, but supplies were limited. It was impossible to buy most items—such as shoes, milk, eggs, meat, or fish—without a permit. The loopholes were few and far between: a fish caught in the river, a cow that died from swallowing a nail, apples that fell from a farmer's tree onto the ground. Nobody went hungry and everyone had clothes to wear, but those who wanted additional or higher quality items had to turn to the black market.

Few in Pappenheim had that kind of money because work was not easy to find. Except for one small furniture factory, the town held no industry. Those lucky enough to secure jobs often commuted long distances by train to earn even a minimal wage.

Little wonder Dimitri found it difficult to secure work. As a former cavalry officer, his skill set was narrow. Also, his German was poor and there were plenty of skilled locals seeking employment. The Pappenheims did give him work in the New Schloss library organizing the several thousand books in their collection, but that job lasted only a few months. Dimitri eventually secured a higher-paying job as a bookkeeper in a factory in a nearby town that made military insignias. But when the US military left the area, the factory closed down.

For most of his stay in Pappenheim the former military officer remained unemployed. He wouldn't take any work—such as manual labor in the field—that he considered below his station.

But Missy did. Though the pay was small and the work laborious, she accepted employment in the *Hofgarten,* the gardens of the Pappenheim estate. "Let's be thankful," Missy instructed her family, "because the job allows us to buy fruits and vegetables at low prices, and there is joy to be found in being out in the fresh air." Still lacking enough income to support the family, Missy would go door to door throughout the village hawking soap and other small items.

Should the Shalikashvilis stay in Pappenheim or try for a new life elsewhere? It was a question Missy and her husband discussed countless times. They would debate. They would argue. She and Dimitri did not see eye to eye.

"The Pappenheims," Dimitri inveighed years after leaving Germany, "were indeed rather businesslike and hard, calculating people. They received us as refugees, as a family that needed help and shelter in times of war. They extended their hospitality toward us and we are greatly thankful for that. However, they did not believe in giving anything for nothing in return and showed it to us very clearly." Not surprisingly, Dimitri was of the mind the Shalikashvilis should not remain.

For Missy, however, the question was not straightforward. Life in Pappenheim meant many things. It was a place of both sanctuary and struggle, of family ties and community, of hope and diminishing hope. There were reasons both to stay and to go.

Both Missy and Dimitri would occasionally travel to Munich and other bigger cities to job hunt. Yet they'd been unable to find employment that both paid enough and was permanent.

With no clearly better option, the family thus remained in Pappenheim. The Bavarian village offered many benefits: relatives, a free apartment, good schools in the area, and a circle of friends—including Georgian compatriots, which gave Dimitri joy. It was a place where they could safely await the next change in their family fortunes.

6

Oma and the Passing of the Old World

November 1952—Pappenheim, Germany

In a small room of a small hospital in the quiet village of Pappenheim, Countess Marie Rudiger-Bielaieff was spending her final moments with her only child.

Two forces were pulling them apart. One was that Marie was dying. At eighty-eight years of age, she'd managed to outlast most of her contemporaries. Thirteen years earlier she'd buried her husband back in Warsaw. Of the three Rudiger sisters who'd served together as ladies-in-waiting at the court of Tsar Nicholas so many decades ago, only Marie remained. Sophie had passed three years ago, and Julie—who'd done so much for Marie and Missy's family over the decades—had departed a year later. Both sisters had married German aristocrats, a Manteuffel and a Pappenheim, and both were buried here in this village, just as Marie would be.

In a way, their collective passing would be a reverberation of the collapse of both the Russian Empire more than thirty years ago and the aristocratic way of life it had engendered. Though a different culture was now developing in this postwar era, the opinion Marie held of this change didn't matter. She would not live to be part of it.

The second force pulling mother and daughter apart was the desire of the daughter's family to make a new life abroad. Soon Missy, Dimitri, and their two youngest, John and Alexandra, would extend their final goodbyes, walk out of this hospital, and make their way onward to America. The New World held opportunities that did not exist here in the Old. The eldest, Othar, had already been sent ahead to arrive in time for his first semester of college.

Parting would be hard. For the past thirteen years, Marie and the Shalikashvilis had survived German-occupied Poland and then made a new life here in Germany since late 1944.

Because the destructive power of World War II had taken away Marie's wealth, she'd had no recourse but to live off the charity of her younger sister. There'd been a loss of pride, yes. The Shalikashvilis, having earlier relied on Marie for support, had felt similarly; decades later Othar would take pains to emphasize that his grandmother, a fiercely independent woman, had made clear that they'd lived in *her* house in Warsaw.

But there is also a comforting sense of place that comes from being with family. Here in Pappenheim, Julie and Sophie had regularly visited the second-floor apartment in the Old Schloss. All highly educated, the three sisters spoke French together. The Shalikashvili children addressed their grandmother's sisters as *Tante Julie* and *Tante Sophie*. And Marie was *Oma,* the German word for grandmother.

Oma could seem formidable to her grandchildren. At six o'clock every evening they were allowed to approach her for one hard sugar cookie each. Yet beware any child who already had candy in his or her possession—there would be no treat for anyone Oma knew did not need it.

Underneath that strict demeanor, though, lay a dedication to her grandchildren's upbringing. Oma, they would later voice in appreciation, had introduced them as best she could to the interesting things Pappenheim, and German culture more broadly, had to offer—just as she'd looked out for their welfare, cultural acclimation, and self-image back in Poland. That was how Oma had been raised, and that was what she'd passed on.

In the United States there would be a new culture for Othar, John, and Alexandra to adjust to. This time, though, grandmother would not aid them in the transition. She'd draw her last breath ten days from now—the very day the Shalikashvilis would descend the gangway onto New York City's Pier 86 to be swallowed up by the crowds of West 46th Street.

Oma didn't know exactly what awaited her grandchildren in the New World. Yet her life experiences did provide insight into the Old World legacy that they'd be bringing with them.

* * *

Throughout its long history, the city of Lublin, Marie's birthplace, had flown the flag of Austria, Russia, Germany, Sweden, and an independent Polish state. On November 21, 1864, the day Marie was born, Lublin was part of the Russian Empire. Her own identity was similarly a mat-

Adam Johann von Krusenstern, John Shalikashvili's
maternal ancestor, who was the first Russian admiral
to circumnavigate the globe (1803–1806). (Wikimedia
Commons.)

ter of perspective. Hers was a mix of Swedish, Estonian, German, Baltic-
German, and Russian blood. What Marie often claimed to be, however,
was Polish, given she'd spent much of her childhood in both Lublin and
Bialystok, two areas with large concentrations of ethnic Poles.

Perhaps best was to simply consider her to be European aristocracy.

Marie's father, Count Johann Friedrich Rudiger, came from an elite
Russian family that emigrated from Germany most likely in the eigh-
teenth century; he was the first general summoned to St. Petersburg by
the newly enthroned Tsar Nicholas. But it was Marie's mother, the former Sophie Krusenstern, who boasted the more impressive lineage. The

The family estate in Bialystok, Poland, was built in 1856 by Marie's grandfather Baron Alexander Krusenstern, the son of Admiral Adam Johann and a senator and secret councilor at the tsarist court.

Krusensterns originally hailed from Sweden, where they'd served in the Royal Government, as Philippe de Krusen had done in the mid-1600s, as well as in the military, as Lieutenant Colonel Evert-Phillippe Krusenstern had done in the early 1700s. Through migration and marriage, however, the Krusensterns eventually became part of a loose ethnic group known as Baltic Germans. Comprised mostly of ethnically German inhabitants of the eastern shore of the Baltic Sea, this group constituted the region's elite, often taking high positions in the Russian Empire, particularly in Saint Petersburg.

One of Marie's most accomplished ancestors—the explorer Adam Johann Ritter von Krusenstern—was Baltic German. An admiral in the Russian Imperial Navy, the Estonian-born officer was the first commandant of the Russian Naval Academy. His greatest claim to fame was leading the first Russian circumnavigation of the earth in 1803–1806.

Marie's siblings—sisters Julie, Sophie, and Helene, as well brother Theodor—spent much of their early years just outside Bialystok in Dojlidy, a village named after a Baltic tribe that lived there for centuries.

Their family estate was a haven of privilege—a palatial structure of blazing white ringed by emerald green gardens, shimmering ponds, and dark forestland. The residence itself was constructed in 1856 under the watchful eye of her grandfather, Baron Alexander Krusenstern, a senator and secret councilor at the tsarist court. Part of Marie's mother's dowry, the magnificent estate was styled after the villas of the Italian Neo-Renaissance yet complemented by classical elements. Only the finest furniture, paintings, and other appointments had been allowed in through its doors.

Such was the Dojlidy estate's opulence that Tsar Nicholas II chose to reside there while inspecting military maneuvers in Bialystok in 1897. And such was the family's standing that as young girls Marie and her sisters Julie and Sophie were called to the Winter Palace in the capital city to serve as ladies-in-waiting to royal personages of court, including the grand duchess and Tsarina Alix of Hesse herself.

While serving the imperial family, Marie came to establish her own nuclear family. In St. Petersburg she met, and eventually married, Count Alexandre Bielaieff.

Born in St. Petersburg in 1867, Alexandre descended from a Russian military family that had enjoyed nobility for a couple of generations. During his early career, the cavalry officer served as adjutant to members of the royal family, including the brother and then the nephew of Emperor Alexander III.

On April 8, 1906, the cries of a newborn echoed through the halls of the Winter Palace. Marie had given birth to a girl—Maria, who'd later be known as Missy. The tsarina honored the family by agreeing to be godmother. As a young girl, Missy occasionally met Rasputin on his visits to court.

The fortunes of the Bielaieffs would be buffeted by many grand political events across the decades. The first struck while they were living in Marie's birthplace. Alexandre, by now a captain in the Russian cavalry, was serving there as Seigneur de Lublin. Missy adapted well, thanks in part to the Polish language and history lessons as well as the Polish nanny her parents had provided for her back in St. Petersburg.

Then the "Great War" broke out. The German army began advancing eastward, reaching the gates of Warsaw by June 1915. Fearful for their safety, Alexandre, Marie, and Missy took flight. With great relief, the family managed to scramble aboard one of the last trains leaving Warsaw headed back east to St. Petersburg. It was a plotline that, thirty

Shalikashvili's maternal grandmother and grandfather, Count Alexandre Bielaieff, who'd serve as
a brigadier general on Russia's imperial high command in the final days of the empire. They are
attired in costume for the opulent seventeenth-cen-
tury-themed national costume ball thrown for 390
guests by Tsar Nicholas II at the Winter Palace, St.
Petersburg, in 1903. Their daughter and Shalikashvili's mother, "Missy," was born at the Winter Palace, where Marie was serving as a lady-in-waiting.
(Courtesy of the John Shalikashvili family.)

years later, would be turned on its head when Marie, her daughter, and her grandchildren would flee westward to Pappenheim ahead of the Soviet advance.

Marie's husband was promoted to brigadier general in December 1916 and assigned to Supreme Headquarters. His brother, General Mikhael Bielaieff, who'd been serving as chief of staff at the Ministry of War, was elevated to minister of war.

Soon thereafter a second political upheaval—the Russian Revolution of 1917—sent tremors across Europe. Given their close association with the tsarist government, the Bielaieffs were in constant danger. They spent part of the revolution in hiding, sometimes in rat-infested apartments and often without adequate food. Then terror struck: the family was caught, and Marie and her husband were jailed.

It was only luck—and connections—that kept them from being killed or sent to labor camps. A commissar who'd previously worked as a palace guard knew her husband from his time as adjutant; the man stepped in, securing their freedom.

After their release, the family maintained a low profile. Missy attended a Soviet school, marched with her class in parades, memorized revolutionary anniversaries. Understanding the dangers of staying in this new Soviet Russia, the family eventually located smugglers who, for a price, helped them flee.

Their escape in October 1920 was harrowing. First was a furtive train ride to the coast, followed by a long walk to a sleepy seaside town, then temporary sanctuary crouching on the floor of a fisherman's hut waiting for darkness. Then, on a stormy night with churning seas, they braved an eight-hour passage in a small open wooden boat, first dodging coast guard spotlights and then struggling against waves that repeatedly came close to swamping the vessel. Yet the shores of Finland were finally reached and, a cold sleigh ride later, the family found safe haven. A letter to Marie's sister Julie eventually secured their safe passage to Bavaria.

For the next few years, mother, father, and daughter lived in a variety of European cities—Pappenheim, Munich, Nice, and others. Their goal, though, was to secure the needed papers to settle in Poland. At the end of World War I, a new Polish government had been established. Because the Rudigers had fled Poland during the war, the authorities, doubting the family would return, had confiscated their holdings.

Marie's family finally received permission to move to Poland in summer 1924. The battle to reclaim their holdings would be an uphill one.

Sadly, the lovely Dojlidy estate had been sold off to a private buyer in 1922, in part because of a scandal initiated when Marie's mother, wanting to remain in Germany, had refused the Polish government's offer to become a Polish citizen. Lacking the financial means to fight for the family's land, Marie and her husband once again got lucky—a lawyer friend offered help in exchange for a portion of whatever was returned. After a two-year legal battle that required Marie to change her name from Bielaieff to the hyphenated Rudiger-Bielaieff, she finally managed to win back part of the family holdings, including the flour mill in Lublin.

With her mother's passing in September 1926 and with her father long since dead, Marie received her share of the inheritance. Finances now partially restored, the Rudiger-Bielaieffs often spent time abroad, traveling to Nice and other European metropolises. They did maintain a residence in Warsaw, and often rented a villa in the suburbs—a charming place to relax and entertain.

It was while visiting friends in those suburbs one day in 1931 that Missy first met Dimitri. That had been the start of a union that had gone on to enrich Marie's life, providing her three grandchildren and a sense of family during many difficult years.

Now, at the end of her life, there were no majestic estates or precious possessions for Oma to pass on in return. She'd been robbed of all that by the chaos of war.

But what she had provided was more substantial: good breeding. Aristocracy, in its most ideal state, strives for the virtues of dignity, self-discipline, resilience in the face of adversity, and, perhaps most importantly, living up to one's privilege through service to others. Though this inheritance could be given up voluntarily, it couldn't be taken away by force.

These principles had helped Marie sustain and guide her family through many waves of upheaval since the Russian Revolution. And her daughter dutifully drew on this example to similarly keep her own family together through the difficult times of World War II.

Now this inheritance in turn would help Marie's grandchildren appreciate the power of new beginnings. Their world might turn upside down; they may suffer deep and painful loss. Such things cannot be controlled. But if they hold fast to their particular family values, they could still survive, start fresh, and maybe even prosper.

* * *

On November 24, 1952—two days after departing Pappenheim—the

The SS *America,* upon which John Shalikashvili ate his first Thanksgiving meal during his transatlantic voyage to the New World. (Courtesy of Jane Schuling and the SS *United States* Conservancy.)

Shalikashvilis were in the port of Bremerhaven, Germany, standing on the deck of the SS *America.*

The ocean liner plied a route connecting Cobh, Bremerhaven, Le Havre, and New York. Though a bridge between the Old and New Worlds, she was clearly American. The deep blue of her massive hull was framed at the waterline by a stripe of fire-engine red and a band of creamy white at the deckline and railings. Raking up from the ship's deck at a youthful, jaunty angle were twin funnels painted in matching bands of red, white, and blue. The ship's interior, one of the few of its day to be designed by women, jettisoned the conventional stuffy ostentation so characteristic of stately British ocean liners. What the SS *America* sported instead was a look emanating light, cheer, and warmth—a promise of the opportunities that awaited in the New World.

What a dramatic way for a poor family to make the voyage: At 723 feet long, 93.5 feet wide, and 33,961 gross tons, the SS *America* had long been the largest ship in the US merchant marine. She carried 1,049 passengers and 675 crew in style, offering ten decks and accommodating more First Class passengers than Cabin and Tourist Classes combined. The most talked about luxuries were the ship's circular First Class smoking room, galleried main lounge, and a mosaicked swimming pool. There'd be no huddled masses shivering in creaky holds on this voyage.

How in the world had such an improbable opportunity come about?

The Shalikashvilis owed their good fortunes to the unexpected compassion of one person: Winifred Lutny, a woman neither Missy nor Dimitri had ever met.

Winifred was as distant as a relative could get. Her tenuous connection to the Shalikashvilis came through Dimitri's cousin, Dmitry Starosselsky. During World War I the two cousins had occasionally bunked together in St. Petersburg.

At the end of the fighting, Starosselsky left Russia, eventually landing in New York City. There he often kept company with Prince Georges V. Matchabelli, the Georgian emigrant who would go on to invent the famous line of perfumes bearing his name. And it was in that bustling city that he met Winifred.

Winifred was a native of Peoria, Illinois, a midwestern city too provincial to contain her for long. Adventurous, cosmopolitan, and exquisitely beautiful, she chose not to raise children or cultivate close female friendships. Instead she filled her life with travel, regularly making her way to Europe by ocean liner, hatboxes and steamer trunks in tow.

The two fell in love, married, and eventually moved to the mountaintop Wentburg Estate that overlooked Charlotte Amalie harbor in St. Thomas. The couple later divorced, however, spurring Winifred's move back to Peoria. But she never stopped loving him, or so the story went, and before he died she promised to take care of his family.

When Winifred came to learn of the Shalikashvilis' difficulties in Pappenheim, she wrote to them. Before long, care packages followed. What a stir it created when packages all the way from the United States arrived! American coffee, chocolate bars, and cigarettes—those easily fetched high prices on the black market or could be exchanged for ample supplies of fruits, eggs, and other staples. Sometimes she sent clothes and other items the family could use directly.

These gifts had been a lifeline. Times were tough for the Shalikashvilis, something John picked up on. In letters home from boarding school, he'd offer that no, he didn't need to drink milk at school, so please don't budget any money for that, and certainly don't trouble the school director about it. Please also stop sending so much butter. And look carefully in this envelope because he's returning some of the money his parents sent. This jacket here? He's returning that too, what with the mild winter and all. Nor does he need a new shirt; just a pair of long trousers, which he could have let out as needed. And please, he implored his mother, don't work in the Pappenheim's garden. He'd prefer if she didn't labor so hard.

Just like his parents, John's taste in clothing was particular. He'd ask them to send his nice white shirts from home, as well as ties that were not too colorful. In one letter he wrote, "Several days ago, Aunt Winifred's shirts arrived. They are very good. Oh, but one of them I didn't like. That is why I sold it for 9 marks. I will buy a new shirt cloth and order someone to tailor a new shirt for me." He also asked for Winifred's address, so he could write immediately to thank her.

With the specter of a possible Soviet invasion continuing to hang over Europe in general and Germany in particular, Dimitri kept reviewing the family's options. Not wanting to be dependent on the charity of others forever, he'd considered Spain, Australia, New Zealand, and countries in South America. Argentina held particular interest because his skills as a cavalry officer might land a job as a horse breeder.

Yet all these places had problems. If it wasn't unfamiliar language or difficult working conditions, it was bad climate or primitive living conditions. There were also often unexpected restrictions or requirements for refugees.

What Dimitri wanted for the family was "a destination where we could settle down and find well-paying jobs that would provide us with a decent living." "Most important of all" was "to give our children a good education." The place where this was possible? "Naturally, the United States was everyone's dreamland."

As the months and then years slipped by, the majority of Dimitri's Georgian friends who left Bavaria indeed departed for the United States. Most refugees leaving for the New World did so via the Displaced Persons Program and with the financial support of the International Refugee Organization.

Yet Dimitri made no effort to secure passage through the IRO. Instead, he continued to wait. When he finally applied for a visa, it was only after the US consulate general in Munich began accepting regular visa applications. One requirement was a signed affidavit by a sponsor in the United States.

Winifred once again proved a godsend. She enlisted the help of her brother, George Luthy, a prominent Peorian banker. Together the Luthys signed the affidavit, covered all of the Shalikashvili's travel expenses, arranged jobs for Dimitri and Missy, and lined up the local St. Paul's Episcopal Church to serve as the family's official sponsor. It was a generosity the Shalikashvilis would never be able to repay.

The only wrinkle came when the family went for their health exams. Because Dimitri's X-ray picked up an old scar on his lung, the family had to wait for a follow-up picture to ensure he was free from tuberculosis. Anxious at the delay, Winifred persuaded them to send Othar on ahead to start college on time. Not long thereafter, Dimitri received a clean bill of health.

And now it was finally happening. The SS *America* had already steamed out of the harbor, and Dimitri, Missy, John, and Alexandra were watching the contours of Germany's shores begin to fade in the mist.

Missy, though, was trying desperately not to cry. She hadn't wanted to go to America. By staying here, or at least by remaining in Europe, she'd argued, they could rely on their considerable family ties. Elsewhere their names would open no doors.

Dimitri understood what was really motivating his wife to stay. It was exactly what had put the lives of herself and their children at risk that day at the Warsaw train station when Missy had changed her mind about boarding the train to Germany: Missy could not bear to leave her mother.

Ever dutiful, Dimitri had invited his mother-in-law to go with them. She steadfastly refused: "I am German. I will stay in Germany."

Whether for reasons of breeding or natural inclination, however, Missy was a woman who would, in the end, defer to her husband.

But that didn't make the leaving any easier. Standing beside his wife as she struggled with her emotions, Dimitri took solace. She understood why they were leaving: "It was for the children."

7

Betrayal

June 3, 1954—Peoria, Illinois

It was the day after high school graduation, not long past dawn, and Donna had just dropped John off. She knew she'd catch hell for staying out all night, but it was worth it; their night on the bluffs above the Peoria River had been almost magical. Before getting out of the car, John had said it was the most incredible time they'd spent together so far.

It was hard to believe high school was over. Yesterday, though, she'd been thrown a scare. The seniors were lined up in the hall, ready to file into the auditorium. That's when Mr. Burns, the civics class teacher, rushed up to her and began causing a fuss. The textbook she turned in, he accused, was defaced. Unless she paid for a replacement immediately, he was going to keep her from graduating. She felt Burns despised her, but this . . . this was really too much! As "Pomp and Circumstance" filled the air, Donna began protesting that the book must be someone else's.

As the two stood arguing, John jumped out of line to once again come to her rescue. Although the seniors had begun marching into the auditorium, he calmly offered to pay the fine on the spot. But Burns relented. He was willing to drop the matter, Donna believed, because John was a favorite student.

* * *

John's reputation at PHS was solid.

He had made a favorable impression from day one. "He walked ramrod-straight," had "an almost military bearing"—that was the typical first reaction. Next would come silent gasps from the girls. "He was an absolutely gorgeous young man!" one female classmate swooned in recollection decades later. "He had such blond hair and the most *beautiful* blue eyes. And he was always smiling!"

John's athleticism also helped. As a fifteen-year-old back in Germany, he'd won a multiple-event competition in the fourteen-to-sixteen age group, finishing the one thousand-meter dash in a respectable three

Donna Bechtold, John Shalikashvili's high
school girlfriend (Courtesy of Donna
Bechtold Kurtz).

minutes thirty-one seconds. Here in the New World, in addition to being
captain of a local soccer team, he competed on the high school's ping
pong, tennis, track, and cross-country teams, even becoming a state-
ranked runner.

He also had an endearing personality. One classmate, a cheerleader,
would remember how, while passing in the halls, he'd lower his head
and avert his eyes when she spoke to him, offering only a bashful smile
and quiet response. "Yes he was initially shy," others would agree, but
here was a boy who was "conscientious," "always eager to learn," and
though "never overly outgoing" was always a "steady" classmate. Other
adjectives used were "kind," "polite," and "unassuming," as well as
"honorable," a "straight shooter," "trustworthy," "calm and measured,"
"bright."

"For many of us, he was the first foreigner we had ever seen," one
classmate voiced a common refrain. Known as John, Johnnie, or Kash, he
was viewed as someone who'd suffered under great challenges in Europe
and was continuing to suffer in adapting to this new environment. "Why,
he even took a full course load from the get-go despite limited English

capabilities!" Some students even let him copy off their work—it was "for a good cause. He was such a nice, deserving guy."

Germany's high educational standards had given him a leg up too. Why, the teachers here, Shalikashvili had been shocked to learn, didn't even have a master's degree! He'd once been chosen to discuss that day's topic—how cities, counties, and the like were formed. Realizing he'd reached the limits of his teacher's knowledge, Shalikashvili continued his analysis with an almost condescending tone: "As you know, sir. . . ." Another time, while walking by a class he'd already taken, Shalikashvili was surprised it was starting the same way. "No freshness, no inspiration!" he snorted. Even the skills of the German-language teachers, he judged, weren't up to snuff.

Helped along by classmates charmed by their handsome, athletic European refugee classmate, John successfully adjusted to high school in America. Despite a self-confession of having spoken little English "beyond yes and no and what time is it" when starting at PHS, he'd graduated the day before ranked a respectable 69th in a class of 260. His senior year, he'd even been awarded an "A+" for initiative by a faculty panel.

Decades later Shalikashvili would recall his surprise at "how friendly everyone was and how excited everyone was that they had this foreign kid there." His classmates had been "unfailingly kind," taking him to basketball games, football games, to the local malt shop, and the like. "It was a great adventure," he awed, "I received attention I had never received before."

"More than one said to me: 'How did you become what you became, because we always thought you were a quiet child?'" But John Shalikashvili didn't remember himself that way. Any shyness, he countered, would've been due to the language barrier or just because "the whole atmosphere in an American school is very different than in a German school."

Consider the day he'd arrived in Peoria and first met the Luthy family: John and his siblings had "walked into the room, clicked their heels, bowed, and then left the room." Or that his brother had arrived with gloves and a regimental swagger stick, Old World affectations that had raised eyebrows here in the low-key Midwest.

"Did you make friends easily?" he'd be asked. "I always thought I did," was the reply. "But again when you're different you make friends in a different sort of way."

Different? Well, Donna knew exactly how different John Shalikashvili was. And the disparity between how their classmates saw him and how he viewed them could sometimes make her eyes roll.

The storyline—of the deserving, plucky immigrant finding a comforting and comfortable new home—while not in and of itself incorrect, was but a two-dimensional image John cultivated, or at least did not dispel. It was useful. Such a reputation allowed him to be popular—or better said, to be accepted and to fit in, things Donna knew he valued. It was not lost on her that John dressed exactly like the other guys, in an oversized white or light-blue shirt and faded jeans with a tiny roll at the bottom.

But underneath that veneer of social harmonizing there was much more going on in that lively, mature mind of his. John held more opinions on life at PHS—and life in general—than he let on.

Like how he was a quiet protector of the underdog. Donna observed how he'd occasionally invite those who didn't belong to any specific group to join them in playing a game or just hang out. It was John's low-key effort to boost their reputation through association with him, or at least signal he saw value in them.

He was also extremely wary of certain people, of certain groups, especially the heavy partiers and the jocks. With them he'd refrain from talking about serious things. A careful observer would note he was always agreeable, always letting them do the talking. John seemed so interested in other people's lives, had this quiet charisma, that when needed he could easily flip people's attitudes toward him from negative to positive. That's how he managed to maintain his distance from those he disliked, those he didn't agree with, while still making it seem like they were buddies.

For John was a master actor. As soon as they were alone together, he'd often tell Donna what he really thought of some classmates. His readings were often cynical. "I hate that phony S.O.B." he once muttered through the polite mask that still hung on his face as he walked away from an interaction with one classmate. "Oh yeah," Donna jibed, "aren't you yourself being phony right now with that grin?" causing John to laugh at the comparison. This ability—to separate the thoughts and emotions in his head from how he interacted with those around him—was why so many people misunderstood him, underestimated him.

When there was open confrontation, she'd see him tense up, wait, say very little, and then quietly disengage. One of the first times this happened Donna had said: "Well, that's over." "No," John replied, "that's not over at all." He was *very* much into strategy.

Like with that boy Donna had known since grade school. The kid once boasted to John that he'd "made it" with Donna on the couch at her house. John later tested him—and it was surely no coincidence she was there to witness it. In the halls one day John asked the boy where she lived. He guessed wrong. John, smile now gone, backed him up against the lockers. Putting a hand on his shoulder, John whispered something into his ear. The next day the boy came to apologize to her, adding how afraid he was. When Donna laughed, the boy pleaded: "No, Donna, I'm scared. I did a dumb thing and I think he's not through with me. Will you talk to him?"

Of all the groups in the school's social hierarchy, the one John disliked most was the cliques. They were akin to an informal college sorority or fraternity. For a member of one clique to be seen even speaking to someone who did not belong would be noted by others members and discussed at meetings or "spreads." Freshman year girls bought a pin made of gemstone, a thing small in size but critical for popularity. John would make fun of these tokens, warning Donna, "If I catch you with one, I'll. . . ." As to the cliques themselves, "Those people are children," he would sneer. "It's just to show some kind of aristocracy."

Probably because of his European background, Donna guessed, John understood aristocracy. He would often say: "Rich people don't pay their bills on time, Donna. They return to the store gowns they've worn the night before that have lipstick and sweat on them. Some never even go inside the store. Instead they demand that dresses and shoes be brought to them. Yet the store waits and waits for the account to be paid."

If John disliked the cliques at PHS, then he hated even more the spoiled rich girls that seemed the mainstay of their ranks. "What's the matter, did poor little so-and-so lose her bobby pin on the floor?" he'd mock a classmate's latest petty problem. Once when Donna's friend was left stranded after school when her ride didn't show, John sneered: "Oh my! Oh me! Daddy is ten minutes late picking me up in his Rolls Royce, and now I'm stomping and furious!" "These girls," he'd sneer, "are beyond brats. They are selfish pigs." His steam once built up to a point where he blurted out, with a fierceness that at first shocked Donna, "If only they could be drafted into war, made to sleep in the filth of the sewers, made to take in the stench of human waste and vomit until they no longer smell it."

Over time Donna eventually came to understand where such anger came from. For John eventually began to reveal to her some glimpses of his dark past.

It first happened while parked up on Grandview Drive. He'd captivate her with tales of his time in the cellars and sewers of wartime Warsaw. He'd sound out the clack-clack-clack of gunfire and the blasting of bombs going off on the street above. He'd replay for her the Russian melody his mother hummed to them, he'd recall the stories she spun of roosters and rabbits, anything to soothe her children's fears and make them think she herself was unafraid. Those nights in the car Donna could almost smell the dust from the bombings, almost choke on the filth and stench of a people forced to live underground during war. He would get so animated, using filthy words, spittle flying from his mouth, tears tracking down his cheeks.

So vivid was his storytelling that Donna actually felt she was huddled together with the Shalikashvilis. One time she all but sensed the weight of his mother's loving arm around her own shoulder, her eyes almost made out the other arm reaching to comfort John by gently twisting the curls of his blond hair. Listening to another story, Donna could vividly imagine the stooped form of his mother sewing jewels into the hem of her coat, the cloth one with the fur trim, in preparation for their flight to safety.

She doubted he ever shared such things with others. At first she'd been puzzled why. But later she'd guess: "It was because John and I were kindred spirits, fellow sufferers wrestling with the consequences of our disruptive pasts."

What's more, his war experiences had given him a maturity that Donna felt "was way, way beyond his years." What amazed Donna most was he never talked of suffering. "It took a lot to make him feel oppressed, to make him submit, to admit defeat."

Tough, yet tender. From John she came to learn that wartime is a curious experience—it can also heighten one's sensitivities. One day he offhandedly explained his absolute love for fruit: "The taste of an orange can be delicious beyond words when it's so hard to come by."

No wonder he could exude class and appreciate the finer things in life while at that same time despising high school cliques and self-entitled girls. No wonder, upon seeing how insecure Donna felt around her moneyed classmates, he'd given her explicit advice: "Donna, if you act like you are shy, they'll dismiss you. People only know what you tell them. If you keep your mouth shut, they won't know what it is you don't know." Above all, John impressed upon her, "look like the person you want to be."

Such sentiments were revelatory. They helped Donna understand why this teenage boy was routinely smuggling out his mother's clothes for her to wear. Or why, for a formal dance they'd gone to, John ordered a bouquet of white orchids flown in from Hawaii. Though crazily expensive for a high school senior to do, he wanted hers to be the longest, most beautiful corsage at the dance. It was because he was mentoring her. *Look like the person you want to be, because, even if you are not, it is a way to survive and live to fight another day.*

War, though, produces demons that can haunt for a lifetime. But because of John's iron self-control and strong sense of privacy, his struggles were not immediately obvious. An involuntary slip on his part one day provided Donna's first glimpse into how strong his demons were.

She and John shared Mr. Burns's civics class. On the first day the students introduced themselves one by one. "When John's turn came, he put on the perfect show, mimicking the military falderal he'd been taught in Germany. Exaggerating his ramrod straight posture, he clicked his heels together, and, using every muscle in his face, spat out that crazy-assed name of his, announced where he was from, and ran through a brief bio that just about knocked Burns off his tilt."

John played the part perfectly. He certainly had that military bearing—slim figure, hair cropped close on the sides, erect torso, and, quite often, a gait one might see in a Prussian parade. "How come you walk that way you do," she once asked, "with your shoulders back, your body stiff?" "Do you think that I've never seen an officer before?" he replied.

John would occasionally get called to the blackboard to demonstrate something to the class. Playing the act to the hilt, he'd snap to his feet, click his heels, and all but goose-step to the front of the class, where Burns would sometimes hand him a five-foot pointer. With his German accent ratcheted up a notch, John would step stiffly up to the board and drive home his points with exaggerated military precision by smacking the pointer on the board. Finding the show quite funny, the class would hoot and egg him on.

One day, after his performance ended John swirled around, clicked his heels, and began marching back to his seat. In a heartbeat Donna knew something was wrong. His head was pulled back too far, his chest was thrust out unusually far, and his entire face was set in a strange rigid stare.

Donna was horrified. After class finally ended, she led him to a quiet place to talk.

"John, what happened?"

"What do you mean, 'What happened?'"

"Back in class, you were in a trance."

"Huh? No, I was just doing my act, you know to be funny."

"But when you got to the board you changed. It was like you were in a trance."

"I did not!" he said, his eyes swelling up, "I just wasn't feeling well. . . . Give me some time, okay Donna?"

Days later, John finally brought the issue up. "I want to know more, Donna. It scares me when you mention the word 'trance.' I don't remember leaving the front of the room and coming back to my seat. I don't remember that at all." That's when Donna knew there actually was some nut or bolt seriously loose somewhere in that lovely and complex machine that was his brain. "I went to another place a long time ago," he confessed. "I don't really remember much of it now, just the noises . . . and the fierceness of it all." He then joked about maybe needing to see a shrink. "This is serious, John," Donna pleaded, "after all you have been through, talking to a psychiatrist might help." No, John replied, he'd work it out by himself, but if she ever saw him act like he was in a trance again, she was to shake him, touch him, somehow get his attention. After that he would not repeat his imitation of a German officer. "No," he'd say, "it's getting old."

This incident made Donna realize "there were things lurking under the surface of him that still haunted him" and that "he had baggage worse . . . and so much deeper than mine."

The second time John revealed his inner depths, however, Donna could not have felt more deeply fulfilled.

She'd finally worked up the courage to invite John to visit her home. The house wasn't much, a little one-bedroom house with a sun porch that somehow accommodated herself, her two brothers, and her parents. Though the house was poorly built, the hilltop view was nice. Yet she was nervous—this would be the first time any boyfriend of hers met her mother.

Looking back, she felt John must have planned out the entire scenario in advance. Though he didn't call her house often, he did so this time before setting out—that little strategist surely wanted to make sure Donna's mother would be there. No doubt John had reviewed what he knew of the long list of selfish, cruel, and perverted injustices her mother had visited upon her. Just as he certainly must have worked out exactly what he'd say once he arrived.

That day her mother and brothers were sitting at the picnic table at the end of the driveway. Donna, watching from a nearby overpass, first spotted John at the bottom of the hill. Balanced on his shoulder was a watermelon, a gift for her family. Her eyes tracked his long walk up to her house, that green orb looming larger and larger the closer he came.

Cresting the hill, John strode over and, after setting the melon down upon the table, stood there without saying a word. He was waiting for the reaction that would surely come. And after Donna's introduction, it did.

"Oh yes, I know who you are," her mother sneered. "You're that little Nazi bastard Donna has been seeing." Donna immediately tried to intervene, but John silenced her.

Then he immediately let loose. The clash exploded so quickly, so fiercely, that Donna was numbed. He was spitting mad—chin jutting out, brow reddening, sweat forming on his forehead.

After a few moments of back and forth, John moved to within inches of where her mother sat. Standing there with veins popping in his forehead, John slammed his fist down on the picnic table. Glaring at this woman who so unfathomably lacked the compassion to even to hold her own infant daughter in her arms, John delivered the searing line: "Madame, even a regime as tyrannical as Nazi Germany would never allow children to be under the care of someone as despicable as you!"

That encounter was the only time Donna saw how John behaved with someone he had reason to hate. There was no suaveness, no gamesmanship, no diplomacy. He didn't back down and, at first, neither did her mother, accustomed as she was to railroading others with her cursing and physical intimidation. But after he delivered that last line, her mother, looking up at John from the picnic table, actually relented.

She got up and walked away, although not before stopping midway to look back. When she did, Donna was flabbergasted. There was a strange emotion reflected in her mother's eyes. She was afraid.

John and Donna then went off to the caves not far from her house. "She's everything you said, and worse," came his first words. When Donna turned apologetic, John comforted: "Honey, there's nothing to be ashamed of. You are nothing like that woman. Don't compare yourself to her ever."

How was Donna to respond? It was the first time anyone had stood up for her in such a big way.

That was his character. John was always working to boost her ego, to keep her from being dragged down under the weight of her family.

"These aren't your real parents, Donna. Are you sure you weren't adopted?" he'd often say. Or "your genes are from past generations. Genes sometimes skip generations, don't you know?" Other times he'd describe for her a tiny purple flower that could sprout from the cracks of rocks, the kind that, despite seemingly having no nutrients at all, still grew both strong and beautiful. "See Donna," he reassured, "you're just like that." He reminded her how, in the midst of her own isolation, she'd still been able to begin developing her skills as an artist and writer. That's why she should never give up. She should always live to fight another day. What's more, he added, she needed to understand that these bitter experiences would help her better understand the lives of others who suffer.

***

The morning after graduation Donna dropped John off not right at his house, but at a corner near where he lived. She felt it odd he always wanted to get out there. Surely he wasn't embarrassed by his house, which sat among a row of respectable two-story frame homes on a pleasant street bordering the Bradley University campus. Much more respectable than where she lived, certainly. Could it be the car? No. Though old, it was certainly not an eyesore.

Well, John had his secrets, and Donna had some of her own.

For one, her mother had recently chosen to lash out. Perhaps it was the clash with John that had set her off, or maybe it was because Donna was graduating. Something had prompted her mother to take Donna for a ride one day. As the car pulled into the parking lot of a surplus store, her mother, all smiles, announced she was getting something. It was going to be Donna's "new home."

The purchase was an army tent, which would be pitched in the backyard. Donna was now to mostly fend for herself. She'd drink and wash up from an outside water fountain and eat leftovers from the waxed paper pouches her brothers would bring out after the family finished dinner. Hiding spoons, glasses, and the like about the backyard became her way of feeling semi-civilized.

Yet Donna did not dare breathe a word to John. He already hated her mother, was always pressuring her to move out. This would be the last straw.

Donna just couldn't let him set her up to live somewhere else. For she had another secret, one that had kept her from fully enjoying last night. She was going to inflict a deep wound on John, the first person to ever give her a sense of being protected and cared for.

Donna was leaving Peoria. If she loved him and cared about his future, did she have a choice?

Part III

New World Opportunities

Robinson Barracks, home of the Field Artillery Officer Candidate School (OCS), mid-1950s. (Courtesy of Randy Dunham, Artillery OCS Alumni.)

8

To Become an Officer?

January 24, 1959—Lawton, Oklahoma

Not long after lights out, once the other candidates had collapsed into their bunks for a few precious hours of sleep, John Shalikashvili slipped from the two-story wooden World War II barracks into the darkness of Robinson Barracks, home of Field Artillery Officer Candidate School.

The OCS cantonment area was an austere grid. Each school mainstay—brigade headquarters, mess hall, service center, gymnasium, candidate barracks, classroom buildings, quad area, and parade field—squared off within a checkerboard of cement walkways reinforced with gravel trim. Not a fallen leaf or stray twig marred the grounds. No blade of grass stood taller than another. A rigid black and white metal banner identifying the school spanned the main entrance. Bookending the sign were two small, brightly polished brass cannons, twin ostentatious exceptions to the school's asceticism.

Enlistees, by mastering specialties within a military unit, serve as the backbone of the armed forces. Yet it's commissioned officers who provide the top-level leadership, a position requiring not just mastery of a military occupational specialty but also the development of substantial leadership and management skills. Being a commissioned officer is better—pay-wise, responsibility-wise, and certainly prestige-wise. That's why the ratio of enlistees to officers in the US military, standing about eight to one in 1959, is always high. Robinson Barracks was opened at Fort Sill, Oklahoma, in 1942 for enlisted men like Shalikashvili who wished to jump this divide by achieving a commission as a field artillery officer.

The temperature this January evening hovered in the thirties. Yet Shalikashvili's mind was not on the cold. Earlier today, each member of cycle 4-59, the school's newest wave of students, had received a copy of the *OCS Standard Operating Procedure*. The pocket-sized manual—which laid out the school's expectations for the conduct, appearance, knowledge, punctuality, and personal area of candidates—warned:

Newly arrived candidates always have two left feet. No matter how hard you try, the chances are nine out of ten that neither the middleclass, the redbirds, nor the tactical staff will like either your methods or your results. You will be "chewed" unmercifully at the slightest provocation, the physical training will be rough, and the disciplinary tours will be hard. The whole system will often appear ludicrous, ridiculous, and without guidance or purpose to some candidates in their early weeks. You are being tested. OCS insists on testing you as a soldier and a man before it will endorse you as a man qualified to lead American troops in combat.

"Ludicrous, ridiculous, and without guidance or purpose"—that was their first day in spades. Entering brigade headquarters to register this morning, many hesitated at the doorway, temporarily awed by wooden floors buffed to a blinding sheen. Once they'd crossed the threshold, the haranguing began. Tear off any stripes or ribbons from your uniform, the duty officer barked. For OCS was a netherworld. Within the confines of Robinson Barracks there were no enlisted men. Until you either flunked out or were finally deemed worthy of donning an officer's uniform, you were nothing but a "candidate." After being issued a bewildering array of uniforms, hats, and boots, the lucky were ordered to double-time to the holding barracks; the unfortunate, to crawl, pushing their duffel bags forward with their heads.

Lined up in formation shortly thereafter, the class met the cadre in charge of orientation week. That's when the screaming began. Salute inappropriately and you were chewed out. Respond to a question less than immediately and you were blasted. Wide-eyed candidates stood at attention, frozen in place between two tactical officers each screaming a different command in one ear.

One tradition at OCS was to end the first day with a run—a long, punishing run designed to make candidates regret thinking they were officer material. Decades later, one graduate from this period would relate the shock of his first night at OCS. The cadre announced the candidates would not stop the test of endurance until ten of them quit—not just stopped running but, as a result, were ejected outright from the program. He remembered the trial lasting three hours, with twelve candidates departing the school that evening.

In the craziness that was Field Artillery OCS, the best chance of surviving lay in keeping your head down. Graduate James McGary would later recount an event from his first week. Tac officers asked who in the class held a military driver's license. Despite having one, he kept silent. Those whose hands eagerly shot up? Those poor saps were put to work, first loading heavy footlockers onto "Cadillacs," military slang for wheeled transport bins, and then "driving"—which meant pushing— them around the cantonment area for hours.

By maintaining a low profile, McGary managed to reach graduation without having to complete a "Jark March," the school's most dreaded punishment. "I have the uncanny ability," he boasted, "to get lost in a crowd of two."

If there ever was a candidate who could not get lost in a crowd, it was John Shalikashvili. One big problem, of course, was his name.

"His name was outstanding!" one fellow private later exclaimed. "It took up his whole uniform!" bug-eyed another. It was so unpronounceable that both Shalikashvili brothers would jokingly be called "Lieutenant Alphabet" as young officers.

His name had drawn undue attention the very first night of his military career. Six months earlier he'd reported to Fort Leonard Wood, Missouri, for basic training. He stood shoulder to shoulder with his newly assembled company while the field first sergeant took roll. Attempting to call out Shalikashvili's surname, the sergeant butchered it badly. "I don't know how that god-damn name will ever fit on a god-damn name tag!" he sputtered. "From now on I'm going to call you . . . 'Shali'!"

Here at OCS John Shalikashvili's name had indeed proven too long to fit on the plastic nametag handed out today. Forced to wait for the school to make a specially sized one, John spent the day without.

And boy had he drawn extra attention. "Shashkaveelee?" seniorclassmen would deride after pouncing on the infraction and demanding he identify himself. "What kind of god-damned name is that?!" Then, upon hearing his accent, "Are you some kind of German?" "We can't put a rifle in your hands! How can we trust a German?" Push-ups invariably followed. For the ease of others—and certainly for himself—Shalikashvili began immediately dropping into a brace and replying: "Sir, Candidate Shali, sir!"

This was just day one at OCS! Why would anyone want to suffer through half a year of such abuse? So he'd snuck out from his bunk this evening. Somewhere within Robinson Barracks was a tactical officer he knew, a fraternity brother a couple years ahead of him at university. Shalikashvili was going to find him. And when he did, he'd tender his resignation from OCS.

* * *

Why had Shalikashvili wanted to become an officer in the first place? It wasn't an easy question to answer.

"He fudges rarely, and laughs often, sometimes at the ironies of his life story." That's a description of Shalikashvili in an in-depth profile decades later at the height of his power. It's a characterization that's belied, however, by one glaring exception. In recalling one particular part of his life—how and why he entered the military and decided to become an officer—John Shalikashvili was evasive, misleading, and sometimes downright untruthful.

He remained in Peoria after high school to study at Bradley University. "I had a four-year academic scholarship that George Luthy, the president of the university's board of trustees at the time, helped me secure," he later recalled.

Spurred by an interest in building model airplanes and a pre-enrollment aptitude test that pegged him as an engineer, Shalikashvili entered the School of Engineering. He was interested in aeronautics—a line of work, he noted gleefully to one friend, that paid a decent salary. Still, he admitted to another, given his family history, he wasn't ruling out a career in the military.

The motto of the Shalikashvili lineage was "without change." Many ancestors, both paternal and maternal, had distinguished careers as military officers. This heritage was reflected in the very names Dimitri and Missy had chosen for their sons. Prince O'tar Shalikashvili had been instrumental in restoring the Jaqeli dynasty, distant relations of the Shalikashvilis, to the principate of Samtskhe in 1547 after they'd been driven out by the western Georgina kings of Imerteti twelve years earlier. John's namesake, his great-grandfather Prince Jean Osipovich Shalikashvili, so distinguished himself as a lieutenant colonel fighting in the Crimean War that Emperor Alexander II himself reputedly awarded him a gold saber, with an inscription on the blade recognizing Jean's bravery and courage in battle against the Turks. Appending the title "The Brave" to his name, the Georgian prince continued his service to the empire, finally retiring at the rank of major general.

Here in America, Othar, who'd since been going by his more Amer-

John Shalikashvili's paternal great-grandfather and namesake, Major General Jean Osipovich Shalikash-vili. He appended "the Brave" to his name following the Crimean War, after Emperor Alexander II reput-edly awarded Jean a gold saber with an inscription on the blade recognizing Jean's bravery and courage in battle against the Turks. (Courtesy of the New York Public Library's Slavic and East European Collections.)

ican-friendly middle name of Joe, was first to take up the family pro-fession. George Luthy had also secured him a scholarship to Bradley, but in the spring of 1953, less than one year into his studies, Joe quit school and volunteered with the army. The bigger, stronger, more aggres-sive brother—the one who John described as "ruthless," the one who as a child had braved the dangerous streets of war-torn Warsaw to scavenge for food and water to bring back to his family below ground—joined the infantry and then the special forces.

"My father was disappointed that I'd entered as an enlisted man,"

Joe recalled. "He figured I should have gone in directly as an officer. But given his own experiences in Europe, he probably just didn't realize how difficult that was" here in the United States.

Joe, who'd always felt like an outsider—in Poland, Germany, and even Peoria—finally "found an anchor" in the US Army. He soon attended Infantry OCS, graduating in the top three of his cycle.

One of his first assignments was to teach at West Point. Yet there Joe was dealt a setback. Y. King Liu, John's classmate, stopped by the Shalikashvili home the day the news arrived. "The family was crying," Liu recalled. "Joe had been instructing how to throw a grenade when it exploded prematurely in his hand." And "because the older brother was supposed to take over the family military tradition, following the accident there was some pressure being put on Johnny to carry on." Luckily, Joe did recover from his injury—thereby reducing whatever expectations the family had for John to pursue the family profession.

Because Bradley was a land-grant institution, all incoming male students were required to take the two-year Air Force Reserve Officers' Training Corps basic course. Looking to cultivate tech-savvy young men, the air force first set up ROTC programs at engineering schools in the 1920s. Here at Bradley the training was exemplary. In 1958, the year John Shalikashvili graduated, the program would be the best of fifty-five regional programs examined by the national Air Force ROTC headquarters and, at nine hundred cadets strong, in the top 20 percent for class size in the nation.

With his exemplary military bearing, the younger Shalikashvili brother looked the model cadet. Decked out in woolen uniform, overseas cap, shirt, and tie, he wowed his classmates. With regulation shoes highly spit-shined, he'd make a show of clicking his heels together. "Shalikashvili liked marching!" one classmate recalled. "He could snap out those commands," wowed another, "just like a Prussian drill sergeant!" "He loved kidding everyone with how he could kickstep like a European," put in a third. Little wonder that Theta Chi, Shalikashvili's fraternity, appointed him pledge marshal—how marvelously his German accent, ROTC uniform, and military comportment worked to intimidate new pledges.

After two years in the basic course, cadets could sign on for another two. Those successfully completing the advanced course could then enter the air force as a second lieutenant, the lowest rank of commissioned officer. For many young men set on military service, flying planes in the air force was the dream career.

"I enrolled in Air Force ROTC," Shalikashvili explained decades later, "and then lo and behold, I found that my eyesight was not good enough to be a pilot." "If I can't fly," he decided, "I'm not going to go in the Air Force." So after two years "I dropped out of ROTC, convinced that I had severed whatever links I might have had with the military."

But this was not altogether true. The requirements at the time restricted the ROTC advanced course to US citizens. Though Shalikashvili's eyesight might have deteriorated right at the two-year mark, he would have been barred from continuing the program anyway.

Nor did he turn his back completely on the military. Toward the end of his junior year, ROTC introduced the Sabre Air Command Squadron, a ceremonial color guard team that performed with swords. Because the squad was open to cadets in the basic class, there were no citizenship requirements. Shalikashvili was chosen Sabres president his senior year. Clearly, the military life continued to exert some tug on this senior classman.

On May 13, 1958, one month before graduation, John Shalikashvili's family made their way to Peoria's courthouse. There, together with a host of other immigrants, the Shalikashvilis raised their hands and were sworn in as American citizens. The ceremony was simple, with no bands, VIPs, or long-winded speeches.

But for him the occasion was momentous. After having lived in Poland, Germany, and now the United States, John Shalikashvili was no longer stateless. One line uttered by the presiding judge would burn into his memory: "In our great land, it doesn't matter what boat you came in, for as of now we are all in the same boat."

As graduation loomed, so did the draft. It was a "peacetime draft" designed to bolster US military strength in the face of military tension short of war. Worried by Nazi Germany's conquest of France in June 1940, Franklin D. Roosevelt launched the first such draft that October. Eight years later Harry Truman instituted the second when another threat reared its head in Europe: the Soviet Union's blockading of land traffic to the US-British-French zones of occupation in West Berlin. Because this new "Cold War" tension would have such staying power, Truman's peacetime draft would remain in place for a quarter of a century, ending only as the Vietnam War began winding down.

All eighteen- to twenty-six-year-old males, citizens and noncitizens alike, were required to register. In October of his freshman year, Shalikashvili filled out his registration card. He told one friend of his worry that he'd be called up before graduation. He was safe during his freshman and sophomore years at least, because ROTC cadets were exempt from the draft. But being barred from the advanced class put him at risk during his junior and senior years. Thankfully, the second half of his college career passed uneventfully.

But with a college diploma now almost in hand, he needed to think through his next steps. To improve National Guard and Federal Reserve Component readiness, Congress passed the Reserve Forces Act of 1955. The act bound volunteers and draftees alike to six years of combined active duty and reserve time. And, in an unprecedented change, volunteers were now being rewarded though preferential placement.

This meant, however, that those who waited for the government to order them to report were now at a huge disadvantage. So effective were these new rules that General Lewis Blaine Hershey, the head of the Selective Service System, would brag that for every man now being drafted, three or four more were being scared into volunteering.

Little wonder Shalikashvili's classmates began urging him to reconsider. Six years was a long commitment to the wrong branch. Even if he couldn't become a pilot, the air force was still by far the most glamorous branch. Two years of air force ROTC would also surely give him a leg up in getting a decent first assignment. Heck, even volunteering for the navy would be preferable to, god forbid, getting drafted into the army.

But Shalikashvili wasn't swayed. "I'll take my chances," he reassured. "Who in their right mind is going to draft an immigrant college graduate?"

Graduation came in June, with Bradley awarding him a bachelor's of science in mechanical engineering. It was a difficult time for young men seeking work. Companies were hesitant to employ someone who might soon be called away to wear the uniform. But Shalikashvili had both luck and connections: he had a full-time job waiting as an engineer at Hyster, the lift truck company at which George Luthy's own son worked.

Life was looking good. Two documents in as many months—his May naturalization certificate and June college diploma—had gifted this former stateless war refugee with a measure of belonging and security that, for the first time in his life, promised to have staying power.

When June turned to July, a third document arrived. This one, though, was from Uncle Sam. The immigrant college graduate had lost his roll of the dice after all.

As he stood there reading the notice, shock coursed through his system. No, he thought, this couldn't be happening. Why, the monthly salary he would draw as an army private wouldn't even cover the payments on the dream car he'd just bought—a snazzy new green Chevy Impala convertible.

But of course it did happen. On July 30, 1958, John Shalikashvili reported to the Armed Forces Examining Station in Chicago. It was a day of long lines and too many needles. A physical and mental examination found him fit for duty—save for "compound myopic astigmatism, needs eye glasses." His hair was shorn high and tight; his right hand fingerprinted. By signing the Acknowledgment of Service Obligation he committed himself to two years of active duty.

"I must admit that when I was drafted I did not have any great longing of making the military a career," he later admitted. "I was going to serve my two years and that was going to be the last of it."

Yet "I felt an obligation," Shalikashvili clarified. "The nation had offered me some tremendous opportunities already and I was more than willing to now offer my service in return." Actually, "I was very, very, very proud to serve, and I can still remember the tingles on the back of my neck when I took the oath of service."

The peacetime draft, then, had turned John Shalikashvili into an involuntary enlistee. But what then prompted this young man who professed zero interest in a military career to aspire to officer rank?

Here is where John Shalikashvili obfuscated the most. "It is kind of a humorous thing," Shalikashvili would offer when asked why he'd applied for OCS. "My battery commander at Advanced Individual Training (AIT) had me stop by the orderly room almost daily and he talked to me about joining OCS. Now I know that what he was doing was he had a quota he had to fill. In those days however he got to my ego so I applied."

Though amusing, the story is not quite accurate. One day in the summer of 1958, before Shalikashvili had even left for the induction station, a friend from the Old World dropped by. Zurab Kobiashvili, a fellow Georgian immigrant, was accompanying his father on a visit to see Dimitri Shalikashvili. On such occasions, the two old soldiers would sit together for hours reminiscing over their World War II experiences; their stories could turn horrific. On this particular day John handed Zurab some suits, saying: "I won't be needing these any longer. I'm joining the army, and I'll be going to OCS."

And it was only four weeks into basic training—not at his next assignment at AIT—that Shalikashvili jumpstarted his OCS application. Eagerness was required because getting accepted was far from guaranteed. It required support from a commander. It demanded sheaves of paperwork, including proof of academic qualifications and character references. There were written tests and round after round of oral interviews, with tough questions to answer from panels of stern commanders and imperious OCS graduates.

Throwing himself hell-bent into basic training, Shalikashvili earned an envied spot as trainee platoon sergeant and, at the end of the eight-week program, graduated third in a cycle of almost nine hundred privates.

It was an excellent start. Yet effort could not slacken, for the application process continued during AIT. This was eight weeks of "branch training," where enlisted men got their first taste of their specialty. For Shalikashvili this meant artillery training at Fort Chaffee, Arkansas.

"As far as OCS is concerned," he wrote home from Chaffee, "we were told the other day that out of 369 people who applied last year from this post, they accepted only 69." "It's almost impossible to get into Artillery OCS without four years of university." Then, as his time at Chaffee was winding down: "There are surprisingly few of us left. In my battery only one other man outside of me survived the final battery of questions and tests."

It was not until late January 1959, after AIT ended, that Shalikashvili finally received the green light from the school's board. "As far as my fears about completing OCS are concerned," he wrote his parents, "don't let that worry. Even so I can't help feeling that I will have more trouble finishing that school than anything else. But we shall see."

John Shalikashvili, then, didn't apply to OCS because he'd been goaded into it by a battery commander. Rather, he purposefully and enthusiastically threw himself into what was known far and wide as a gut-wrenching test to become an officer.

Why had he done so?

Perhaps brotherly competition was partly responsible. "You asked me about my plans after graduation," John wrote a friend back in Germany not long after Joe joined the military. "At first I wanted to become a professional officer in the Army, but my brother is already pursuing this career. I would not want to be his superior one day."

Was John's cheek here hiding something? The younger and physically smaller brother, the one who stayed behind in the cellars of Warsaw, might have actually been hesitant to join the military out of fear his performance would pale in comparison to his more macho brother. Joe was the one, their sister would admit decades later, the family thought might make general some day, not John. Why would the younger brother volunteer himself into a competition he'd likely lose?

Being drafted into the army, however, had upset the equation, effectively forcing him to compete. The younger Shalikashvili clearly didn't like looking weak in front of his older brother. Though John was severely claustrophobic from birth, back in Pappenheim he would accompany his brother both winding their way through dark medieval tunnels in the area or wiggling their way through stacked bales of greasy sticky material used by the German navy to seal ships hit by ordinance. That's why, when the subject of how he joined the military came up, John told his brother a lie: "I enlisted voluntarily."

Becoming an officer, even if he had no plans for a military career, was thus a way the younger brother could prove he was equal to the older. So, like Joe before him, John set his sights on OCS. At the time artillery and infantry were the only two branches offering such programs. "I chose artillery OCS," he later explained, "because I did not want to compete against my brother."

But if John Shalikashvili applied to OCS to show that he could match his brother in doing their ancestors proud, why not just admit it?

Perhaps part of the answer lies in his penchant, as he'd displayed at PHS, for showing the world a likeable image. Who wouldn't be taken by the story of a plucky young immigrant whose eyesight keeps him from realizing his dream of being a pilot, but then gets drafted into the army anyway and still manages to go on and achieve great career success? Admitting to either brotherly rivalry or getting barred from continuing ROTC because of a lack of US citizenship would distract from this "American dream" narrative.

But Shalikashvili perhaps had a deeper, darker reason for avoiding mention of either his family's long history of military service or his own equivocation about a military career. There was a second close relative who likely influenced his decision to brave OCS in pursuit of becoming an officer. It was someone he much desired to be like, yet simultaneously feared he shared too much in common with. It was someone who John Shalikashvili had cause to love—and to despise.

9

Dimitri, Prisoner of War

Summer, 1946—Ancona, Italy

The lean body of Dimitri Shalikashvili lay soaking in the waters of the Adriatic Sea. For a man allowed only hard ground to sleep on and three brief showers over the course of the past year, the feeling was luxurious. As the British sergeant who brought the captured Georgian Legionnaires to the beach today had also wanted to swim, he'd simply left his rifle ashore with a sunbathing prisoner. With the POWs to be freed soon, there seemed no reason to stand guard.

To finally walk out of the POW camp—how could one simple act conjure up such deep and diametrically opposed feelings? Dimitri was eager, of course, for his captivity to end; the way the British treated their prisoners of war was, to his mind, appalling. And he longed to return to his family. Over sixteen months had passed since he last laid eyes on Missy, even longer for his children.

But Dimitri's pending freedom surely also weighed heavily. Walking out of this camp would bring to the fore a bitter truth about his life.

June 7, 1916. It had been a Wednesday. That was when Dimitri first donned a military uniform. How thrilled he'd been to wear the colors of the Regiment of the Horse Guards, that famed defender of the Russian Empire. To have seen Dimitri even as a young cavalry officer was to behold a professional. His feet rested naturally in the stirrups, long black riding boots polished to a sheen. He sat lightly in the saddle, his slight torso held erect and slender legs contoured to the horse's girth, suggesting he used a sensitive touch rather than raw physicality to direct his steed. His officer's uniform was precisely tailored. The stiff collar of his immaculate jacket rose high on his neck, ending in the trim of a white dress shirt collar. One could easily visualize the rows of buttons, insignias, and ribbons that the years ahead would surely bring. And though his hair had begun thinning at a young age, he kept it trimmed and oiled back. A small, neat moustache completed the ensemble of this dignified cavalryman.

But that Dimitri Shalikashvili of youth and promise no longer existed. Physically, he now looked older than his fifty years. His dome was more than half bald, his frame, always slight, now gaunt. And wrinkles, prominent now these past few years, lent him an almost wizened appearance.

Yet the biggest difference in Dimitri was internal. It was a diminishing of his spirit. Dimitri knew, without prejudice, that he was a skilled military man. Over the years he'd proven himself dedicated, passionate, capable. Yet his career had been frustrated at many a turn by forces beyond his control. He'd worn the uniforms of four different militaries—of tsarist Russia (1916–17), Free Georgia (1918–21), Poland (1925–1939), and finally Germany (1943–45). The first two no longer existed; while fighting in the service of each of the latter two, he'd been taken prisoner. For the bulk of his career Dimitri had been constrained by the rank limitations inherent when fighting for a country that was not your own. That's why, despite three decades of exceptional service, he'd only really earned the rank of major.

Now, just days before his release from this POW camp, Dimitri held no illusions. Never again would he fight in service of any country. His military career was ending, and he'd not risen above middling field-grade officer.

Given his proud family heritage, it was heartbreaking.

* * *

Prince Dimitri Shalikashvili was, by his own declaration, a Georgian "who loved his native land above everything in the world." He was born in 1896 when Georgia was part of the Russian Empire. Because his family "more of a habit" spoke Russian at home, however, he knew only a smattering of Georgian.

His upbringing had been privileged. The family had many estates, including their main residence in Gurjaani, his birthplace. Parents Iossif and Nina would shuttle him and his older siblings, David and Tamara, between Georgia and the family's favorite seaside resort in northern France. Often accompanying them were the German doctor and British governess the family held in employ. On one return trip from Paris, the Shalikashvilis brought back the first automobile ever to rumble down a Tbilisi street. Their fortunes did decline a bit with Iossif's death in 1904 and then in 1905 when unrest in Baku put many of the family's oil wells out of commission.

Despite these setbacks, the children received the best education. Dimitri graduated from an elite Tbilisi high school in 1914, finishing second in a class of sixty-three. That next fall he passed the demanding entrance exams to the Russian Lyceum in St. Petersburg. Founded in 1811 during the reign of Emperor Alexander I, the school educated students of elite families from across the empire. One of its earliest graduates was the Russian writer and poet Alexander Pushkin. In three grueling years, the Lyceum—in a setting of polished wood floors, Persian carpets, and fine pianos—prepared students for careers at the highest levels of government. Emphasizing the diplomatic service, the school offered courses in the history, language, and customs of many countries. For Dimitri, language instruction included French and English. Throughout the course of study for a bachelor's degree in liberal arts, students were required to maintain excellent manners. This resonated with Dimitri, because "Georgians," he firmly believed, "were by nature considerate to others, smooth mannered, kind to their fellow men, and took pride in being acknowledged as gentlemen."

Dimitri threw himself heart and soul into his studies. The Lyceum would serve as the foundation of what he knew lay next: a lifelong military career. A proud military heritage extended far back on both sides of the family tree, and he intended to do the ancestors proud.

The Shalikashvili lineage was one of the oldest of Georgian nobility. Records trace the line back more than five centuries—to two brothers, Princes Elisbar and Joatham, in 1400. The family became nobility in 1611 when Tsar Luarsab of Georgia bestowed the title of prince on Jevanchir Shalikashvili, also awarding him tracts of land.

The family boasted its own crest, a symbol of the Shalikashvili's dedication to protecting their homeland through both military and government service. It included the figure of Saint George and the lamb of god, as well as a sword, symbolizing war, crossed over a key, representing the position of "Grand-Maitre de la Cour de Georgie," chamberlain of the Royal Georgian Court—a position held by many Shalikashvili princes. Rostom Ier Shalikashvili was the first to serve as chamberlain in the mid-1700s. The last to do so was Dimitri's grandfather, who was the namesake of Dimitri's youngest son, John.

Dimitri's mother was a Starosselsky. Her father, Dmitry, served as governor of Baku, reached the rank of general, and served the vice-roy of Tsar Alexander II. Her mother was the Georgian princess Ekaterina Guramishvili. And her brother Vesevold served as a White Russian general and, in the early 1920s, would command the Persian Cossack Brigade.

With such distinguished ancestry, little wonder Dimitri and his siblings took the opportunity to serve, and serve well, in World War I. David went to the front with the Tatar Regiment of the Caucasian Native Division, serving under their Uncle Vesevold. Severely wounded in fierce fighting in the spring of 1915, David eventually returned to Georgia to recover.

Tamara volunteered as a nurse. She first served on a hospital train transporting war casualties back to St. Petersburg, and later braved enemy fire while tending the wounded on the front lines. For this service she became one of the few women to receive the Cross of Saint George. She returned to Georgia in the fall of 1915.

Dimitri was one of a wave of students who, under encouragement from the Russian government, took leave from school to support the war effort. In June 1916 he volunteered with the elite Regiment of the Horse Guards, brother David's former unit and the regiment once commanded by another uncle, Prince Alexander Bagrationi.

From that first day of basic training, Dimitri knew he'd found his life's calling. Dimitri would later recall the exhilaration of practicing a set of particularly difficult horseback military exercises: "This was a cherished tradition of the Horse Guards. . . . What speed and swiftness of motion! For a young man such moments when we were all galloping at unbelievable speed, then reorganizing while in full gallop, were exhilarating! It was beautiful—complete harmony between horse and rider. We, the riders, had only one desire: to cut into the enemy's lines!"

In November 1916 Dimitri went to the front lines to fight against the Turks, who were allied with the Germans. Though he was technically just an officer-in-training, he was given a lieutenant's responsibility of commanding a platoon, and was awarded the Medal of St. George for "bravery behind enemy lines." In August 1917 he was invited to join a select group of volunteers for a dangerous mission: going to St. Petersburg to create a diversion for a general loyal to the tsar who was planning on overthrowing the provisional government established by the February Revolution. Unfortunately, the coup never occurred.

Toward the end of his assignment with the Horse Guards, the officers in his regiment unanimously agreed to promote Dimitri to officer. Dimitri returned soon thereafter to St. Petersburg. He passed his final exams at the Lyceum and began preparing for the formal written officer examination.

Much later in life, Dimitri would write of the start of his military career as a time "when I was so young and so happy. I was full of enthusiasm and desire to prove myself in life. I wanted my life to be full of significance, rich in achievements, and above all, I wanted to be loved and respected."

But life so often does not proceed as planned.

The first major upheaval turned out to be a blessing. The Bolshevik revolution of October 1917 brought increasing chaos to Russia. With the subsequent cancelling of the cavalry officer exams, Dimitri fled St. Petersburg for the safety of Georgia, arriving home in February 1918. Yet luckily he held a document from the commander of the Regiment of the Horse Guards authorizing Dimitri to take the officer exams in Tbilisi.

With the tsar's empire being torn apart by the Russian Revolution, Georgia seized the opportunity and declared independence on May 26, 1918. Less than two weeks later Dimitri realized his childhood dream: he became a cavalry officer. In a bit of good fortune, his battlefield service during World War I was recognized and he was promoted directly to first lieutenant.

His first assignment was with Georgia's newly forming 3rd Cavalry Regiment, which was led by a commander Dimitri found honest, straightforward, dependable. Based in part on a shared commitment to seeing things done properly, it was not long before Dimitri—one of the youngest officers in the regiment—became the commander's adjutant. He later reflected on this promotion: In "all the years that I served in the military, I always happened to have much work to do—and I enjoyed it. In fact the more work I was given the better I enjoyed it."

Brother David, having recovered from his wounds, also joined the Georgian military. By 1920 he'd risen to full colonel. He used his influence to transfer Dimitri from the field to a few choice positions with the Liaison Office of the Department of Defense. Here Dimitri's language skills would come into play. His first assignment was to serve as liaison to a French and then Italian mission.

The second posting was a jewel of an assignment: as Defense Department representative on the very first diplomatic mission of Free Georgia.

He'd be going to Turkey, to liaise with the same Ottoman Empire he'd fought against in the service of the tsar. Offering goodbyes to his mother and sister, he left Tbilisi in December 1920. He felt intense pride that day: he was traveling on a passport that spelled his name Schalikaschvili, the Georgian way, not Shalikoff, as had appeared in all his prior Russian documents.

Dimitri's idyll was abruptly halted by yet another geopolitical upheaval: in February 1921 Georgia was forcibly annexed by the Communist Russian government. The return of Russian rule to his homeland would disrupt the careers of both Shalikashvili brothers and eventually leave their mother and sister all but destitute.

David was in Georgia when annexation occurred. After being imprisoned for a time, he was released by the Soviet government on the condition he leave his homeland forever. At that time Georgian exiles could choose from three Georgian Colonies abroad: one in Paris; a second, smaller one in Germany; a third in Warsaw. David left Georgia and eventually landed in Paris, where he served briefly as colony president. Military service, though, was his true calling, and in 1924 David left the comfort of the French capital to go off to Africa to serve with the French Foreign Legion.

For Dimitri, Georgia's annexation by Russia left him stranded in Turkey, a member of a diplomatic mission of a government that no longer existed. Yet during his posting to Ankara he'd kept a detailed journal on the workings of the mission. There will come a day, Dimitri vowed, that these historical recordings will be published for the benefit of all his Georgian brethren.

But where should he go next? Constantinople, where he and other Georgians had fled in the immediate wake of their country's fall, offered no long-term possibilities for employment. His thoughts turned farther westward. In sore need of trained officers, the newly reconstituted state of Poland was eagerly welcoming men with Dimitri's skills. Many incentives beckoned: foreign contract officers would receive the same pay, privileges, and duties as equivalently ranked Polish officers but would not be required to fight against any of Poland's enemies other than the Soviet Union.

Poland, to Dimitri's reckoning, seemed an excellent place to await—and perhaps help bring about—the hoped-for liberation of his Georgian homeland. On November 12, 1922, Dimitri boarded a ship in Constan-

Dimitri Shalikashvili, 1923, about the time he began formal officer training at Poland's Central Cavalry School. Dimitri served in the militaries of tsarist Russia (1916–1917), Free Georgia (1918–1921), Poland (1925–1939), and finally Germany (1943–1945).

tinople, part of the third group of Georgian officers to be welcomed to serve in Poland's military.

Fate, Dimitri knew, had been very kind in providing this opportunity to continue his chosen profession.

The two decades that Dimitri lived in Poland, from 1922 to 1943, were the happiest of his life. For one, that's when he finally realized his desire for formal military schooling. Just as the Russian Revolution had quashed his hope of attending officer school in St. Petersburg, the demise of Free Georgia had stymied a similar opportunity: the Georgian military had been considering sending their young officers to the General Staff Academy in France.

Poland, to Dimitri's delight, was both willing and ready to train him. He was first sent to Bydgoszcz for an eight-month orientation course on Poland's language, politics, and military. Then in September 1923 Dimitri began formal officer training at the Central Cavalry School in Grudziądz. For eight intense months he received instruction from a diverse group of teachers: Polish officers of the former Russian Imperial Army, Austrian cavalry officers, and the elite officers of Pilsudski's Legion.

These instructors judged Dimitri capable, intelligent, ambitious, and dutiful. He was an officer who "takes tasks seriously," "shows great love for military service," has a "meticulous appearance." More unique, perhaps, he was found to be "quiet in character," "thoughtful," and "a good listener, someone who profits from instruction."

Among his class of Poles, Georgians, and Finns, Dimitri finished in the top ten—with instructors noting that his performance would have rated even higher if his Polish language ability had been better. At the October 1924 graduation the military history instructor called out Dimitri and one other student by name for having exhibited the best work in the field of Polish cavalry.

Soon thereafter came the chance for additional training. The newly established Polish General Staff Academy at the War College was accepting foreign contract officers. This academy, in Dimitri's opinion, was the best in Europe at the time. Lacking a sufficient pool of trained instructors within Poland, the school had invited distinguished French military men—including Charles de Gaulle himself—to run the program. For the academy's first few years, classes were taught in French.

Dimitri was one of only three foreign students and one of only two lieutenants among a sea of sixty-three captains and majors. The War College's evaluation of Dimitri hewed close to that of the Cavalry School, offering particular praise for this officer of "solid character, one of tact and modesty." Dimitri graduated with honors, finishing fourth in a class of sixty. On March 1, 1925, Dimitri was formally admitted to the Polish army.

Despite these achievements, Dimitri was unfulfilled. Unlike their Polish counterparts, foreign contract officer graduates were not promoted to general staff positions, a position Dimitri greatly coveted. Instead, after simply being given an insignia of the War College to pin to their uniform, they were returned to regular regimental duties. This bothered Dimitri greatly. Everything he'd learned at the academy, he feared, would soon be lost after returning to his position of cavalry troop commander. Dimitri's dream of becoming a general officer now seemed unreachable.

His unhappiness deepened into depression. "I was fully aware," he later recalled, "that my military career was not proceeding the right way and not following the trail it should, a trail that was set up by generations and followed to the letter."

Yet, as Dimitri would also later reflect, there is a positive side to everything. He became convinced that "easy paths in life tend to make us soft." In fact, "it was in adverse circumstances that a man's character becomes strong and capable of achieving his goal."

Not long after graduation Dimitri was assigned to the 1st Regiment of the Chevaux-Legers, Jozef Pilsudski's most prestigious regiment. "An honor in itself," Dimitri knew. Though frustrated at being held back at the junior officer level, Dimitri threw himself into becoming the best cavalryman possible.

Over the next decade, his superiors judged Dimitri Shalikashvili to be an officer who "fully represents the concept of an English Gentleman." Why? Because whether in field or staff positions, he was known for "maintaining the highest standards of behavior, appearance, and self-control." He was "a quiet man, self-controlled in words and gestures," one with "great moral values," someone who is "ever-professional, ever-capable, and behaves as a person of culture and honor." In his relationships with others, he was "outstandingly loyal and deserving trust," an officer who "knows thoroughly the needs of his soldiers and cares much for subordinates." This all made him "much loved and respected by colleagues and subordinates."

This gentleman officer thus distinguished himself among his peers: "Cavalry Captain Shalikashvili, through his general value and deep knowledge, stands high above the other contract officers."

Despite this impressive skill set, however, by 1938—after twenty years of military service, including thirteen for Poland—Dimitri had only reached the rank of major.

His progress report that year stated the situation baldly: "His status as a contract officer keeps him from advancing to the higher positions that his personal, moral, and professional capabilities would dictate." No contract officer in the Polish military could, for instance, ever command a regiment or higher.

Yet there is more to life than career. There is also love and family. And Poland was where Dimitri met his wife, Countess Maria Rudiger-Bielaieff, who he soon took to calling "Missy."

One day in June 1931 Dimitri, on a whim, decided to visit friends in a Warsaw suburb. Missy and her parents happened to be visiting. As soon as he set eyes on this "shy and reserved girl," Dimitri was smitten. Slender in figure, blessed with dark hair and green eyes, she was dressed plainly in a pink cotton dress and wide-rimmed straw hat. So charmed was he by "the comfortable and unsophisticated manner" of this twenty-six-year-old girl that only three weeks later he asked her to marry. They wed the following year in the best hotel in Warsaw, surrounded by Georgian, Russian, and Polish friends.

Fate, Dimitri believed, had united them. The couple remained devoted to each other through both good and bad—and with war spreading across Europe just years after their marriage, bad days were manifest. While defending Poland in 1939, he became a POW of the Germans. How shocked Dimitri had been that day Missy suddenly appeared at the prisoners' hospital. Without her brave actions, he likely would have been sent back to Communist Russia to face certain death.

"Life is truly full of surprises. Had I not decided to drive out that summer afternoon, I may have never learned of the existence of my future wife and our lives would have turned out in a completely different way!"

Once freed from the German POW hospital in December 1939, Dimitri found it difficult to adapt to civilian life. When Germany launched her surprise attack on Russia in June 1941, his countrymen immediately saw opportunity. Might Hitler reconstitute the Georgian Legion that had fought under the German military in World War I? A representative of the Warsaw Georgian Colony soon floated the idea to the Germans.

It would not be until late 1942, when Germany's war against Russia was floundering, that Hitler finally allowed such ethnic units to form.

Despite his wife's protests, Dimitri joined in early 1943. He was eventually dispatched to the Western Front. Wounded near Normandy, Dimitri was first sent to Paris and then back to Berlin.

While in Germany he was promoted to major and then chosen for a spot in a newly forming Georgian organization and sent to Italy. During his posting there, it became clear that the Germans were going to lose the war. It was in a small town outside of Conegliano in May 1945 that Dimitri's unit surrendered to British officers.

At Udine, the point of assembly for prisoners, Dimitri surrendered his weapon, enjoyed one last good breakfast, and was taken on a day's drive to another camp.

But from then on it was a grueling cycle. First a long blur of movement, often in an open-bed truck, followed by waiting, then marching, or if lucky being transferred again by truck to yet another camp to wait for the next round of orders to make for yet another location.

He most remembered Rimini, a sprawling holding area for thousands of POWs. Arriving tired and hungry from the long truck ride, he was given no food. Confined with others to a field of bare earth, they spent a bitterly cold night, for few had army blankets. And when the sun came up, the shadeless field began to bake. The prisoners were finally given only dried uncooked meat and beans—a very inhumane thing to do, Dimitri seethed, since they had no way to cook.

Then came more riding, more marching, more camps. Once he even traveled by train. He watched in disgust as British soldiers took advantage of the Georgian POWs, fleecing them of wristwatches or draining them of every last bit of money in exchange for cigarettes.

He stayed at one camp for an entire month. What he remembered most were the postcards they'd been allowed to send home. On the first, each prisoner had been permitted to print only ten words, including signature. Another time a sergeant had the gall to bring them postcards pre-printed this way: "I am in a British POW camp. I am a member of the defeated German Army. Am alive and well," with space reserved for a signature. "Naturally no one would sign such a card."

At one point Dimitri encountered units displaying Polish banners. What excitement! His mind leapt back to September 1939 when he'd led those wonderful Polish soldiers into battle against the invading Germans. Though the Poles marching before him now were on the conqueror's side and he was but a vanquished POW, seeing them brought Dimitri joy. He wished them well, even prayed for them. And when he spied nurses from the Polish Red Cross riding in ambulances, his thoughts flew to Missy. How she loved Poland and the Polish people. A sense of profound sadness washed over him as he realized she was the only one in the world who could understand what he was feeling at that moment.

After one last transfer by train, he arrived in Ancona, where he'd be held for the rest of his captivity. Life in the camp was Spartan. The POWs slept in tents all year round, with no beds or cots and with each man issued one blanket at the beginning of winter. Most slept on bare earth, using their blanket as cover. Dimitri luckily had an overcoat to use as well. No kind of bedding, though, was of use when the winter rains soaked the ground. The tents had no heat, no electricity. The long nights with no light cast a pall over everyone. But at least the prisoners could talk to one another, which Dimitri appreciated was no small blessing.

There were no showers, only cold water to wash up with in the morning. Once a month they were issued toothpaste, a toothbrush, a roll of toilet paper, soap, and one shaving blade. They were supposed to receive cigarettes or tobacco. What they got were hard biscuits, distributed only every second day.

From time to time a representative of the International Red Cross would arrive. The POWs would lodge complaints. The IRC representative would talk to the camp commander. Nothing would change. The British, Dimitri disdained, did not abide by the rules of the Geneva Convention.

He was proud, though, of how his fellow Georgian Legionnaires held up. He believed theirs was a culture that "somehow managed to always hope for the best, that did not know the true meaning of depression." Sometimes the Georgian POWs would gather together in one of the tents. They'd let their minds carry them to a make-believe world. A fancy restaurant would be conjured up, one where excellent food, champagne, and desserts ladened the tables.

Was there such a thing as national character? Having served as a POW of both the Germans and the British, Dimitri had opinions. The Germans, he judged, were severe and required complete cooperation with all rules. Yet they were polite and their relationship with captured officers were on an equal basis.

But Dimitri found British officers to be rude, bad mannered, even heartless. They seemed oblivious that military code requires a standard of behavior toward the defeated enemy. Dimitri and other senior POW officers of the national groups would occasionally be called to receive the newest instructions from the commander. After arriving in his office, however, it would be his aide, a mere major, that spoke to them. Meanwhile, the colonel sat behind his desk, "mouth pulling on a cigarette and fanny wiggling in his chair." It was such disdain toward fellow officers, even those of the enemy, that Dimitri found so galling.

Dimitri's situation had fortunately improved in recent months. As the senior officer of the Georgian group, he'd been asked to serve as head of two other groups from the Caucasus—responsibilities that afforded certain privileges. He'd also been chosen to serve as interpreter in a special camp for criminal POWs from Germany, Austria, and Italy. After signing a statement promising not to escape, Dimitri was allowed to make the daily one-mile walk to this second camp. Duties were light, as most prisoners spoke decent enough English. Most fortunate, though, was that the guards there were actually from a Polish cavalry regiment. They willingly shared their Polish newspapers, allowing Dimitri to learn of events outside the camp.

One officer even helped him get word to Missy. And to Dimitri's great elation a letter of reply eventually arrived. Yes, everyone was in good health. The family was even receiving food and clothing from the International Refugee Organization.

Missy began sending parcels filled with food, coffee, and cigarettes, which Dimitri shared with other prisoners. The portion he kept for himself helped restore his failing health—by this time his stomach ulcers had returned and his heart had begun playing tricks again.

While Dimitri had nothing tangible to send back to his family, his letters home, to the delight particularly of young Alexandra, would include sketches from a running saga starring a stick-figured cat without a tail, one modeled after a stray that had wandered into the camp.

* * *

Floating in the waters of the Adriatic, Dimitri no longer needed to worry about being separated from his family. He could push aside the frustration that his wife's brave attempt to rescue him yet again from a POW camp had been stopped at the Italian border. It didn't matter. He'd soon be leaving the camp for good.

When he finally walked out of those gates he'd be carrying two things of significance—gifts Missy had given him that day they'd parted so long ago in Salzburg. Take these, she insisted, pressing a gold ring and bracelet into his hands; he could barter them if necessary. Despite all the hardships he'd faced, Dimitri had managed to hold on to them. He would present them to her when they finally reunited—it would be a symbol of their mutual commitment.

His first destination, though, would be Rome. There a joyous reunion awaited. He would be staying for a spell with his Aunt Ketouna, his mother's sister. His upcoming visit would be like a taste of both home and homeland.

Thinking of his mother brought pain. More than fifteen years ago, well before the war began, the Polish Red Cross had helped him correspond in brief messages with her. Family circumstances, he learned, had sunk quite low. Following the loss of Georgia's independence, his mother and sister had been reduced to selling off the family furniture, eventually even hawking cigarettes on the street to survive. Tamara, who'd fallen into poor health, needed money for medical attention.

Dimitri's brother too faced difficulties. Signing up with the Foreign Legion had come at a price. Yes, it was a rare honor for a foreigner to be allowed in as an officer. But David, at forty years of age, had to start afresh as a second lieutenant. While serving in the Morocco cam-

David Shalikashvili, John Shalikashvili's uncle, in the service
of the French Foreign Legion.
David had earlier fought for
both tsarist Russia and Free
Georgia, and was serving as
a colonel when Georgia was
reannexed by Russia in 1921.

paign David was promoted to full lieutenant—four slots below his original rank of colonel. During fifteen years of service with the French, David
earned a reputation as a demanding commander, yet one also just and
compassionate. He accumulated medals for bravery, including the Croix
de Guerre, the highest French combat medal. But upon retiring from the
legion shortly before the outbreak of World War II, David was just a captain. When the war broke out, he was recalled to active duty, given command of a reserve battalion, and finally retired at the rank of lieutenant
colonel. From full colonel to lieutenant colonel despite decades of exemplary service—that too was heart-wrenching.

Back in November 1930, when David just happened to be visiting
Warsaw, a letter from their sister had arrived. It was more bad news:
their mother had passed away. Neither brother would hear from Tamara
again. Sadly, in the spring of 1940, David too died.

That left Dimitri Shalikashvili the last of his proud Georgian family.
His upcoming stay with Aunt Ketouna would indeed be a salve for many
deep wounds.

10

A Strategic Yes

John Shalikashvili continued making his way about Fort Sill's Robinson Barracks in the cold January darkness. Though it was just the first night of Field Artillery Officer Candidate School, the program had proven so distasteful he'd snuck out of barracks this evening prepared to quit.

But why were the fingers of doubt still clutching his gut?

* * *

At only twenty-two years of age, Shalikashvili already held a cautious approach to life. Once during college he and friend Y. King Liu were in the midst of a game of tennis. Liu found playing with John amusing. Ferociously competitive on court, the European immigrant somehow managed to remain polite to a fault. "Sorry, King," would come John's inevitable response after scoring a point. But when John lost, he hid his frustration almost perfectly. The only clue Liu could detect was a slight difference in John's gait.

While the two were batting the ball back and forth across the net this particular day, two pretty girls took the adjoining court. "Let's invite them to play doubles, Johnny," Liu encouraged with a wink. "No, let's wait," came the reply. "Once we are finished this set, we'll invite them." That way, if the women declined, the boys could depart from the court with honor intact. Shalikashvili knew not to limit his options unnecessarily—and to have an exit strategy ready when he made his move.

So if Shalikashvili did quit OCS, he'd still have to serve his full two years as an enlisted man. But then what? Attend graduate school?

Sure, he'd done well in high school. The handsome, athletic, lone immigrant had been a big fish in a small pond. College, though, had been a different kettle altogether. For one, enrollment at Bradley was four times larger than at PHS. It was also much more diverse, including both American soldiers who'd returned from the Korean War ready to take advantage of the GI Bill and such a large influx of immigrants from Europe that the school ran the Nadi El Wah'da club for international students interested in sharing their cultural heritage. There was no limelight reserved for John Shalikashvili at Bradley University.

And he'd stumbled that very first semester. The blow Donna had dealt him the previous summer was surely a big part of it. When she first disappeared, he'd guessed that there'd been some problem with her crazy family. Well, his rational side comforted, Donna would write soon. But as the days stretched to weeks and then to months, the empty mailbox spoke volumes. He began to feel disgraced—how could she have left without an explanation? Had he somehow let her down or not expressed his love clearly enough? Frustratingly, if any of Donna's friends knew where she was or why'd she'd gone, nobody was talking.

Wounded in the New World, he sought comfort in the Old. After arriving in the United States, he'd kept up sporadic correspondence with Anita Ziegler, his first love back in Germany. His early letters routinely apologized for his delays in writing, provided breezy updates, and offered light but cheeky flirtation. The tenor changed in the fall of 1954, however, when it became clear Donna would not break radio silence. "You don't need to be afraid that I will be the first one to have a family," he wrote her. "I know too much to make such a mistake. I learn day by day (and the hard way—by experience—and if you use your imagination you will know what happened to me recently)." "I have learned that life can be very good," he rued, only "if you go-with-the-flow and live from day to day."

He turned to courting her. "I think that the first love always leaves the strongest impression," he scribbled. "We were just big children then! I wish I were given the same chance now that I have so much experience." "No, I am not drunk," he promised. "It's just that I lock everything inside myself."

And then he began to brag—and do more than brag. He wrote of the new car his uncle had bought him at graduation from PHS, even though classmates who themselves had cars would later remember he'd sought them out in order to double date. He boasted he was already an engineer-in-training at a tractor factory, and though Hyster had no such branch, how upon finishing Bradley he'd probably continue working for the company in Bern, Switzerland. His next letter proffered the all-but-impossible story that he'd already secured a high-paying contract to work as an engineer with a company in Europe after graduation. What's more, though just starting his sophomore year, he'd somehow be graduating in as little as two years. "That's not long to wait, right?" was the implication. In the meantime he'd look for summer jobs in Germany.

"That is to say if you are not married yet," came the hook. "If somebody asks you for your hand in marriage, think of me and throw him out. Okay?" And then, almost pleading now: "Don't be afraid, one day I will be able to escape from this damn America and I will try my best!"

Then, in June 1957 came the news. It didn't even come in a personal letter. It was just an announcement card. Anita had gotten engaged.

John Shalikashvili's American love had betrayed him. As now had his fallback sweetheart in Europe. Were these heartbreaks the reasons why he squandered much of his four years at Bradley?

As a fraternity member, he energetically capitalized on opportunities to drink, womanize, and rabble-rouse—whether at the Highway Tap (located outside city limits and thus subject to the county's more liberal drinking laws) or the Theta Chi frat house or pledge class outings. "He wasn't quite the playboy of Peoria," his brother Joe later offered, "but he was around." Male classmates willingly offered up their cars to double date with this handsome foreigner. "I just rode on his coattails!" recalled one. Such was his reputation that when his sister, a full four years his junior, visited a popular local drinking hole years later, the bouncer—upon seeing the last name on her ID—exclaimed: "Oh god, not another one!"

Unsurprisingly, the very first semester his grades plummeted. That's why he lost the four-year academic scholarship George Luthy had helped him secure: "All I had to do was maintain a C average," he later recalled. "But I bought no books that first semester. I spent most of my time drinking beer and playing shuffleboard."

Short on tuition, he was forced to work part-time. Pressed for time, he then dropped out of track, which in turn meant forfeiting the second scholarship he'd been awarded, the one for athletics. Things deteriorated so far that Theta Chi stepped in, arranging frat brothers to help him shore up enough of a grade point average so he wouldn't be kicked out of school.

When Shalikashvili finally did earn his college diploma, his academic ranking was an uninspiring 759 out of 1,008.

Attending graduate school thus wasn't an immediately appealing idea.

What about rejoining his trade? Well, his professional chops hadn't improved while working at Hyster Lift Company after graduation. Assigned to take their smallest Caterpillar lift truck and put it on wheels, his design was a miserable failure: a tap of the brakes would tip the truck forward smack onto its radiator. Moreover, working as a civilian, Shalikashvili knew, wasn't much different than serving in the military. "The only difference," he once explained wryly, "is that in the military they can jail you for disobeying."

Then there was an off-hand comment he'd made back at the end of high school. When he told Donna he was going to be an engineer, she asked what that was, exactly. "Oh, they just build things. You know—bridges and buildings." Then he added: "People who like to do this are kind of boring, actually. Not like how you see me or how I see you."

Later in life, when asked how his adopted hometown had shaped him, his reply invoked his World War II upbringing: "I came from an environment and a world where everything was upside down. There was never a time to sit down and reflect on what life is all about, what it is that you want life to mean to you. Until I came to Peoria."

So what did the immigrant now want out of life? What did he want to be? "Sometimes I think I am crazy," he wrote to Anita his freshman year of college. "I am basically two different people in one . . . I can be very serious and talk about everything and suddenly I am a carefree boy who does not know what he wants."

"Sometimes," he confided, "it is hard to determine who I really am."

* * *

Out in the cold darkness of Robinson Barracks, John Shalikashvili stood both still and silent. He was weighing his options carefully.

Was it time for him—this former stateless refugee, mediocre college student, unpromising engineer, twice-abandoned lover, and scion of a fallen aristocratic European family with a proud military heritage—to become a serious person?

Finally, decision made, he turned back to join his sleeping classmates.

11

The Crucible of OCS

July 1959—Lawton, Oklahoma

Roger O'Dwyer was sitting in candidate battalion staff headquarters, struggling to fill out a sheaf of duty roster forms. The weather was blasting hot and dry, coating the office with a layer of unbanishable Oklahoma dust. Now an upperclassman, O'Dwyer was in his last two months of the six-month program.

The OCS program at Fort Sill, the US Army's "Home of Field Artillery," was launched following the outbreak of World War II. Given the pressing need for artillery officers, the school set a low bar, cranking out over twenty-six thousand second lieutenants between July 1941 and February 1946. When the need plummeted following the end of the war, the school closed, only to reopen in 1951 with the outbreak of hostilities in Korea. Cycles of candidates then entered every two weeks, and by 1952 OCS was training about 1,250 candidates at any given time.

Now, with the Korean conflict long since over, the school was once again bottoming out. The two mainstays—West Point and ROTC—could easily meet the nation's need for new officers. OCS had thus drastically tightened ship. The bar for admission had been raised, candidates were now entering on a more relaxed two-month rather than two-week cycle, and the school was training only 120 candidates at a time, just one-tenth the Korean War peak.

With no pressing demand for new officers, OCS dialed up the pressure. If candidates dropped out in droves, what would it matter?

So physically and mentally punishing had the program become that one graduate—with bitterness still in his voice five decades later—characterized his OCS experience as nothing less than institutionalized hazing. Another labeled it a form of indentured servitude. Going on to retire as a full colonel, he judged OCS the toughest six months of his life: "It was so bad that during my first week I seriously wondered if it would be possible to break my leg in such a way as to be excused from the program but

116

not end my military career." The OCS experience at this time, as summed up by yet another graduate, was "heart-breaking, back-breaking, mind boggling, unbearable, cruel, unjust, exhausting, overwhelming, and barbaric." And the attrition rate—at 44 percent—was "as bad as walking into machine gun fire."

Yet unlike many classmates of cycle 5-59, the fifth class of candidates entering OCS in 1959, Roger O'Dwyer had neither dropped out nor been held back a cycle. In fact, he now held the second highest slot in the program: S-3, the battalion staff's operations and training officer. Handling these vexing duty roster forms was a responsibility of the position.

As he struggled to make sense of the documents, a recent graduate from the prior cycle walked in. "Lieutenant Shali, sir!" O'Dwyer snapped to attention. "Please, call me John," the officer replied, preferring informality now he was no longer bound by the rigid OCS program. Spying what O'Dwyer was up to, Shalikashvili sat himself down to help. Having also held the S-3 spot, he was no stranger to filling out these roster forms.

The symbolism was not lost on O'Dwyer. Given his spirited personality, he should have never made it this far at OCS. He owed a huge debt of thanks to the guidance of one person—the European-accented draftee who was once again by his side, extending a helping hand.

* * *

Every OCS candidate begins at the bottom rung of a rigid and severe hierarchy.

At the top was a cadre of tactical or "tac" officers. Comprised of second lieutenants and noncommissioned officers (NCOs), they were ultimately responsible for all training—formal or informal—within Robinson Barracks.

Next were the upperclassmen. They were easy to spot. On the cusp of becoming artillery officers, they had tabs on their epaulets that were red—the color of artillery—earning them the informal title of Redbirds. Horseshoe-shaped cleats adorned the heels of their low quarter shoes, lending an air of dignity to their gait—"like an old Prussian," recalled one graduate. The cleats would snap together with a resounding "click" when upperclassmen came to attention. Only Redbirds were allowed to walk at a normal pace or roam freely around the cantonment area. They supervised most activities within Robinson Barracks, especially the wide variety of rules, traditions, and ad hoc assignments designed to test the mettle of candidates. Redbirds shared two tac officer prerogatives. One was to order physical tasks as punishment to anyone their junior who failed to meet the school's many expectations. The more awesome power, however, was to assign demerits, the accumulation of which could result in a dreaded Jark March. Junior classmen all feared the sound of the approaching footsteps of the steel-heeled Redbird.

The middleclassmen were the managers, equivalent to NCOs-in-training. Sporting green tabs on their shoulders, they were banned from certain walkways and had to walk at double-time—a pace of about 180 three-foot steps per minute. Under the watchful eye of the Redbirds, middleclassmen held both formal and informal "leadership training" positions. Though unable to assign demerits, they could give orders and harass lowerclassmen for weaknesses, real or perceived.

At the bottom of the hierarchy were the lowerclassmen—"the lower gross." The equivalent of privates, they too were banned from certain walkways and required to double-time. They performed all manual labor at Robinson Barracks and were expected to unfailingly, unflinchingly, and immediately follow the orders of everyone else.

Living quarters were designed to maximize the effectiveness of this hierarchy. Candidates were divided up into lettered "batteries," each billeted in its own two-story barracks. Middleclassmen, housed in rows of open cubicles on one side of the second floor, could easily keep watch on the lowerclassman sharing cubes across the way. For both middle- and lowerclassmen, visiting the latrine or entering or exiting the building meant passing by the Redbird area on the first floor. Each battery also had its own tac staff in the barracks area keeping watch over Redbirds, middleclassmen, and lowerclassmen alike.

Under this monitoring system, the school ratcheted up the pressure. The strategy was simple: increase responsibilities in both number and weight, and then punish candidates mercilessly when they failed.

Candidates woke at 4 a.m., and within five minutes had to be in formation. Candidate battery staff would lead each battery on a run or in a round of physical training. After PT, candidates had only fifteen minutes to shower and change into their duty uniform. At 5:15 they were back in formation, this time for reveille and then to march to breakfast.

None of the meals at OCS—breakfast, lunch, or dinner—constituted a respite from the day's pressures. Because the mess hall could seat just one battery at a time, meals were only fifteen minutes in duration.

The dining hall was thus organized chaos. Meals were eaten family style, with candidates passing bowls of food along the table. Upper-classmen would take their portions first, then the middle, and finally the lower. A lowerclassman served as "gunner" in charge of refilling the empty serving bowls.

For lowerclassmen, mealtimes were another example of how ridiculous the school's practices were. The gunner often needed to replenish the serving bowls multiple times before senior classmen had taken their share—by which time the battery's allotted fifteen minutes might have ended and lowerclassmen would be out of luck.

Lowerclassmen could not simply wolf down whatever food they managed to take. OCS tradition required a lowerclassman to sit poised on the first four inches of a chair placed exactly perpendicular to the table, and—looking straight ahead the entire meal—lift food vertically up from the plate until at chin level, and then straight into his mouth. The utensil traced the same path in reverse back to the plate for the next morsel. In the wry parlance of OCS, this was how lowerclassmen received a perfect "square meal." Eating this way was agonizingly slow.

For lowerclassmen who managed to master the art of the square meal, the system had other ways to defeat. Lowerclassmen could not speak unless spoken to; but if spoken to, they had to respond. Yet demerits loomed for anyone who, forced to talk for most of the meal, left any food on his plate by meal's end. And if in haste to eat everything a candidate dropped food on his uniform? Any upperclassman who spotted stains could assign demerits for "stealing food." Perhaps the most heartless tactic to harass, though, was when right before mealtime a senior classman would assign a task that would take at least fifteen minutes to finish.

Emerging frazzled and almost always still hungry from the mess hall, lowerclassman immediately had to run the next gauntlet: battery inspection was in fifteen minutes, and lowerclassmen were responsible for cleaning the common areas. Supervised by middleclassmen, some would wash, wax, and buff the barrack floors; others would clean the latrines.

Cleaning the common areas was an extra burden for lowerclassmen because they, like all candidates at OCS, also had to keep their personal space immaculately arranged. Beds made so tight a quarter could bounce off; boots and brass polished to a high sheen; articles of clothing hung equidistant and perpendicular to the wall; and equipment arranged neatly on the shelf above the bed or in the footlocker below. Uniforms had to be immaculate—no small feat given that clothing suffered such abuse under the rigors of OCS that the school warned applicants to budget extra for laundry.

No matter how much one prepared for inspection, though, the forces of either man or nature always seemed to conspire against the candidates. "Those god-damn Oklahoma dust storms," recalled graduate Coy Short, "would kick up and coat everything with sand—including your footlocker, which you had to leave open for inspection. So of course you'd get demerits." When a moth managed to land on his bed while morning inspection was going on, James McGary was awarded three demerits for "harboring wildlife." A piece of straw that had broken off from a broom right before the inspection and landed under Jim Slagle's bed resulted in demerits for "harboring dust on a log."

After the stress of inspection, the candidates boarded the bus for the Artillery and Guided Missile School. Classes started at 7:15. The windowless building of Snow Hall was a place where lowerclassmen could shut out, at least temporarily, the horrors of Robinson Barracks. Not part of the OCS cadre, Artillery and Missile School instructors did not subject candidates to screaming, forced physical exertion, or demerits.

While classes were a chance to nurture their minds about the fine art of tube artillery and the incipient field of missilery, time at Snow Hall was also a chance to nurture their starved bodies. Because the students were bussed back to Robinson Barracks for their chaotic lunch, the students were perpetually starving. In the breaks between classes candidates thus stormed down to the coffee shop, which made fresh doughnuts throughout the day. So food deprived were OCS students that they'd often empty Snow Hall's vending machine, earning them the nickname of "candy-dates" by the Artillery and Missile School staff.

The pace continued into the evenings. Batteries lined up at 5 p.m. for dinner. After another harrowing mess hall experience, lowerclassmen would begin contemplating the countless tasks to finish before the 10 p.m. call for lights out. Two hours of study hall, from 7:00 to 9:00 p.m., were never enough to prepare for the next day's artillery classes. But with mornings so rushed, it was also critical also to prepare for morning inspection. Frustratingly, on any given evening candidates could also be assigned a host of formal leadership tasks, such as guard duty, that further cut into time.

But it wasn't these regular duties—marching, cleaning, studying, and other leadership tasks—that made OCS unbearable. The real problem was the overdose of outright harassment, much of which happened in the evening. One night a senior classmate ordered George Krumbhaar to practice his command voice on invisible "smiley faces" he indicated were on the floor by "marching" them back and forth across the barracks. At one point the senior classman judged that his command, "Platoon of smileys, halt!" had come too late. Krumbhaar's "troops," apparently, had marched straight through the door and over the fire escape. "Go downstairs, pick them off the ground, and bring them back to the second floor."

Wilbert Sorenson was once similarly ordered to command a platoon of forty-eight invisible smileys each night for an entire week. One night, after being informed he'd marched them right out of the barracks, he was ordered to run outside and pick up one smiley, bring it into the latrine, stand at attention, salute, flush it down the toilet, and whistle taps. Sorenson had to repeat this ritual forty-seven more times that night.

With so many responsibilities and yet so many opportunities to be harassed by senior classmen, one candidate unsurprisingly received twelve demerits in less than a twelve-hour period.

It began when Guy Wilhelm showed up for fire guard duty at 2 a.m. Having reported in the wrong uniform, he was given three demerits and sent back to the barracks to change. This forced him to hang up a wrinkled uniform and stow a used pair of boots under his bed. Unable to return to barracks in time for morning inspection, Wilhelm received four demerits for his unkempt uniform and boots and two additional demerits and an ass-chewing from the battery staff for being late to formation. With no time to shave before class and worried about accumulating additional demerits for incorrect personal hygiene, he grabbed a razor and hid it in his pant leg. Attempting to dry shave during class, he cut himself. During lunch, an upperclassman noticed the dried blood and slapped him with three more demerits.

The twelve demerits he'd just earned meant Wilhelm would make at least one Jark March this weekend. But how many he'd end up making was an open question. Fourteen demerits meant two marches; anything over fourteen was a total of four.

Perhaps no aspect of OCS was as ludicrous as the Jark March. Named after Lieutenant General Carl Jark, the first commandant, it formed the basis of the school's disciplinary system. It was an oh-so-painful round-trip from Robinson Barracks to the top of Medicine Bluff

Candidates suffering through a Jark March, OCS's most dreaded punishment. (Courtesy of Randy Dunham, Artillery OCS Alumni.)

Peak #4 (MB-4) on Fort Sill's West Range. These were the bluffs that Geronimo, mounted on horseback, had widely but incorrectly been said to have jumped off during his attempt to escape from Fort Sill in the early 1900s. The 4.2-mile march was commonly done with a field pack, helmet liner, pistol, ammunition belt, canteen, and rifle. Marchers were required to take thirty-inch steps at a punishing tempo of 130 paces per minute. Because candidates were prohibited from bending their knees, each step placed enormous strain on their stomach and upper thigh muscles.

Wilhelm recalled the shock of witnessing his first Jark March: "a candidate . . . began to stagger and reel. His rifle clattered to the pavement and he fell in a heap on the tracks. Someone from the OD's [Officer of the Day's] jeep that was following the marchers dragged him to a tree just behind our formation. His face was flushed and his eyes small circles surrounded by white. His breath came in great gasps. He vomited and then went into convulsions."

Any candidate unable to complete his assigned march—or one who arrived back at Robinson Barrack's even one minute past the fifty allotted for the trek—would have to attempt the grueling march again at the next opportunity.

With four scheduled Jark Marches per weekend, opportunity was not lacking. "I had another one of those marches for too many demerits," Shalikashvili wrote home. "I am getting to be an expert at those."

Unsurprisingly, candidates took extreme measures to avoid demerits. They even turned to magic. Rags and cleaning materials used to scrub floors, polish boots, and clean equipment were thrown into a pillowcase—or "magic footlocker"—and dashed behind a "magic tree" behind the barracks before morning inspection. Candidates also employed "magic equipment," keeping one set of clothes, boots, and the like out at all times for display only.

For the common areas, a quick way to buff the floor was to have one candidate lie on a blanket and be pulled around the barracks. Because cleaning latrines was so time-intensive, all forty-plus barracks members often agreed to the ludicrous practice of using just one or two of the available toilets.

Many also studied after lights out, lying under the covers with a sock-covered flashlight clenched between their teeth. One candidate even smuggled a typewriter into the barracks so he could finish an assignment. Why not? Many students polished their boots and brass in bed as well.

Yet working after lights out held danger. Sometimes Redbirds would sneak up the fire escape. Spotting candidates at work under the blankets, they'd barge in, knock flashlights out of mouths, and liberally assign demerits. Even falling straight to sleep didn't guarantee a night's rest: some senior classmen took devilish delight in waking lowerclassmen up to run an errand, such as to fetch them a Coke at 3 a.m. Being ordered to run multiple errands per night was not unheard of.

Sleep deprivation was thus rampant. One graduate recalled averaging 4.5 hours of slumber for the entire program; another eked out 2.5 hours per night for the first six weeks. Such lack of sleep took its toll. Candidates would fall asleep during class at Snow Hall. If noticed by the instructor, they'd have to stand against the wall in the back of the classroom. "By the end of the fifty-minute period," recalled Laurence Crawford, "oftentimes half the class would be standing in the back trying to keep from nodding off." Sometimes, as once happened to Shalikashvili, candidates would fall right back to sleep even while standing up.

All these stressors took a toll. Robert Lindsay, who'd been in good physical shape before OCS, lost about thirty-five pounds over the course of the program. Larry Frye lost forty in the first few weeks.

Then there was the emotional trauma. "After being harassed for one or two months straight since we walked through the gate of Robinson Barracks, many of us would be so overwhelmed we'd stand in the shower and cry," recalled John Ruoff. "You miserable candidates!" seniorclassmen would goad during formation. "Come on, we know that many of you want to quit. Just step forward now and let's get it over with!"

Those who refused to quit sometimes pushed themselves beyond endurance. While on a Jark March one weekend, one member of cycle 4-59 fell to the ground and began pounding the ground with his fists over and over again until he was restrained. Because of this breakdown, he was restricted to supply and office work. Coy Short recalled what happened one day when seniorclassmen pushed a fellow candidate too far. The cycle mate was ordered to assume the Parachute Landing Fall position and then jump down the barrack steps, one by one, while repeating some ridiculous chant. "He flipped out. He went completely wild. They had to get him on the bed and use a blanket to pin him down until the medics came and took him to the hospital. He was still in the hospital when I graduated."

Other candidates were simply dismissed outright. "Do you remember the negro who came here with me from Chaffee?" Shalikashvili wrote home. "Well, about a week ago his arm got twisted up pretty badly in hand-to-hand combat and he got dismissed from OCS. As a matter of fact, he is being released from the Army and he will be home in another week. All that is too bad, since he was a very good soldier. However, at least his arm is not too bad and in civilian life it won't bother him at all."

"It was easy," recalled one graduate, "to get out of OCS."

When a candidate did leave the program, his space in formation was left open for the next three rotations. It was a visual reminder of the tenuous nature of OCS candidacy, one designed to increase the anxiety of the remaining candidates.

Who'd be next to leave?

* * *

That was the environment O'Dwyer had stepped into upon arriving at Robinson Barracks four months ago. But he'd been lucky. Lucky in his assignment of a "big brother."

The big brother/little brother relationship was the pairing of a middle- and lowerclassman, a system ostensibly designed to help new candidates adjust to the rigors of OCS. How senior classmen actually approached this or any other assignment, however, depended to no small extent on personality. Albert Shook recalled that he was critical when

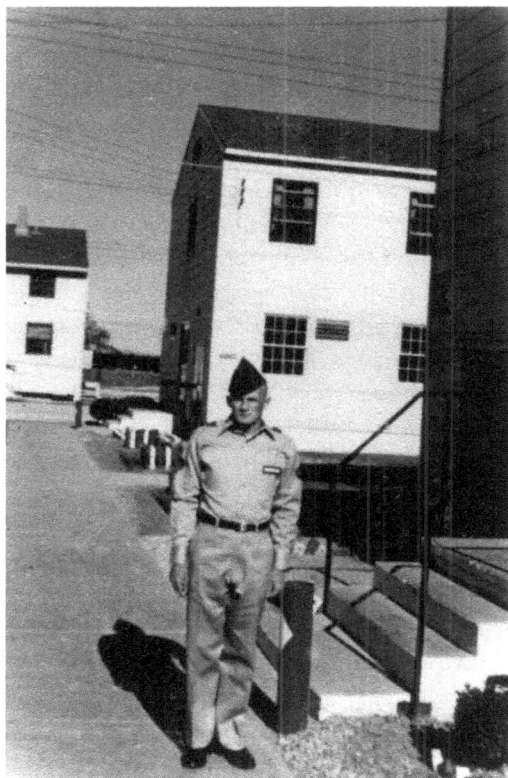

John Shalikashvili at Field Artillery Officer Candidate School (FA-OCS), 1959. (Courtesy of the NBR Gen. John Shalikashvili Archives.)

upperclassmen ragged on him and his fellow lowerclassmen. "I thought their harassment was stupid," he recalled, "but when I became an upperclassman I did the same goddamn thing." John Ruoff concurred: "When you were middle- or upperclass, you gave the lower classes the same crap that was given to you when you were at that stage." For little brothers paired with this type of candidate, explained Bobby Coggsdale, "big brother was there to harass you. Yes, he was to have some responsibility for your development—but not in a brotherly way."

Given the steep attrition rate at OCS, Shalikashvili was assigned two little brothers. One was Russell Davis. Highly professional and motivated, Davis, already a senior NCO, would graduate second in his class and eventually retire as a colonel. He recalled that Shalikashvili quickly read the situation: "He didn't need to offer any advice, and he didn't. He knew there was no need to waste both our time." Time was in short supply at OCS.

O'Dwyer, Shalikashvili's other little brother, was a different assignment. "I had an urge to be independent," he later chuckled at the memory, "and Shali made it his commitment to make sure that I would graduate in spite of this urge. He did it by pushing me physically and mentally."

O'Dwyer was once trying to lead formation. He lacked a loud command voice, however, and his older brother decided to do something about it. Ordering O'Dwyer into the big brick smokestack, some one hundred feet tall and ten feet wide, that towered over the mess hall, Shalikashvili slammed the heavy door shut. "I want you to call that smokestack to attention!" After taking a deep breath, O'Dwyer began issuing orders: "Chimney, forward march! About-face!" Every few minutes, Shalikashvili would open the door and shout: "I can't hear you!" Each time, O'Dwyer saw an ever-expanding crowd gathered around the chimney, enjoying the show. And when he was finally ordered out, everyone was laughing at him.

"I didn't think it was funny at the time, but after three weeks I understood what he was doing and we became fast friends." Shalikashvili was firm as needed, but never mean. Some senior classmen would walk away from the smokestack, leaving the poor lowerclassman to shout commands over and over until he screwed up the courage to open the door and check.

Sometimes during formation Shalikashvili would come up to O'Dwyer and quietly ask if he needed help with anything. "Middleclassman Shali, yes I need help sir!" Big brother would later seek him out. "Shali would help out if he could, but when a particularly thorny artillery problem came up, he might say, 'I don't understand it either.'"

Russell Davis observed how Shalikashvili treated O'Dwyer: "Even many of the cadres really didn't understand what Shali saw: the original intent of this big/little brother relationship was not to beat the crap out of your younger brother and get him to quit, but rather to mentor him to the best extent possible." "Shali's approach was kind of infectious," Davis added, "I was a mentor rather than a tormentor to my little brother when I became a middleclassman."

Similar sentiment came from Bob Errico. As a middleclassman he was once assigned to a dining table next to one headed by Redbird Shalikashvili. The table head set the tone for the meal; if he decided to harass lowerclassmen, then the entire table joined in, leaving the candidates with no time to eat. The upperclassman leading Errico's table had been doing just that. "I remember thinking to myself, this is wrong! An army travels on its stomach—let the poor lowerclassmen eat, why don't you?" Errico noticed Shalikashvili was instead using mealtime to answer questions junior classmen had about surviving OCS. When it came time for Errico himself to head a table, he copied Shalikashvili.

Others also noted Shalikashvili's approach. Tac officer Robert Sandla later recalled that the immigrant soldier approached his mentoring responsibilities in a more serious way than others, and that he put great effort into counseling other candidates. Robert Jenks saw how Shalikashvili, helped along by his engineering expertise, often aided other students struggling in gunnery class: "He had a quiet way of sharing his knowledge."

Certain incidents occurred during Shalikashvili's final two months that deepened O'Dwyer's respect for his former big brother.

The first involved an execution.

Some candidates in O'Dwyer's battery began suspecting that, wishing to hand out additional demerits, one tac officer was sneaking in before morning inspection to place a strand of hair inside candidate mess kits. To retaliate, one candidate captured a tarantula from the cantonment area. Before leaving for breakfast the next morning, he placed it inside a mess kit. During inspection the tac officer had indeed been scared out of his wits.

As part of their battery's inevitable punishment, the tac officer ordered O'Dwyer to conduct a formal execution of the tarantula. Redbird Shalikashvili was put in charge of supervising the proceedings. With a copy of the US Army's field manual for executions as guidance, O'Dwyer assigned battery members to appropriate positions—executioner, chaplain, physician, and the like. At the end, once the deed was done, Errico made the announcement, "That concludes our ceremony. Dismissed!" But immediately after he heard a deep accented voice boom out: "That's not right! Read that!" Following where Shalikashvili's finger was pointing in the manual, O'Dwyer saw the words: ". . . and the band will play a jaunty tune." Shalikashvili would not release the execution squad until they'd fulfilled every last required detail of the ceremony.

Yet Redbird Shalikashvili was not averse to bending the rules or speaking up to authority when necessary. One Sunday afternoon Shalikashvili was calling cadence for the first Jark March of the day. O'Dwyer, always the clown, was slotted to make both marches that day. As the procession worked its way up MB-4, O'Dwyer began to drag. Increasingly exhausted, he fell back further and further, eventually reaching the end of the line.

Now he was worried. Could it be heat stroke? Just as he was about to slump to the ground—which given his heavy load of demerits could possibly have set him back a cycle, adding two more long months to his OCS experience—his former big brother appeared. Shalikashvili, who as the leader of the march did not carry a pack or a rifle, took O'Dwyer's weapon from him, adding it to the collection slung over his own shoulder. He gave O'Dwyer a few gruff words of encouragement, and they continued on.

Upon returning to the barracks at the end of the march, Shalikashvili rushed him into the shower and snapped the cold water on full blast. Ten minutes later they heard the call—"Jark March number two, assemble!" "Stay where you are," Shalikashvili ordered. He then fixed it with the cadre that O'Dwyer wouldn't have to attempt his second slated march that day.

O'Dwyer's gift for finding trouble could also put others in jeopardy. Once, while on a timed "rapid shoot" training exercise, he was tasked with unloading rounds of ammunition and hustling them to the base of the three or four howitzers. While rushing to place one round in position, he heard an unexpected rattling noise. Looking down, he spied a snake, body curled and head held up and back.

Screaming at the top of his lungs, O'Dwyer hurled the round downward. In his panic, however, he missed the snake completely. Still not thinking clearly, O'Dwyer ran back for more shells.

When those nearest him realized what was going on, they leapt into action. O'Dwyer's actions could very well inadvertently trigger a shell's detonating mechanism, thereby incinerating everyone within the shell's one hundred-yard bursting radius, possibly even setting off a chain reaction by exploding other ordinance in the area. Luckily his classmates managed to get him under control before tragedy struck. With a flash of a knife, one candidate ended the ordeal by cutting off the snake's head.

Shalikashvili just happened to be the leader of the exercise. He could empathize with O'Dwyer. Here at OCS Shalikashvili himself made a grave error that put other lives in jeopardy. When trying to determine the length of the fuse on one shoot, he'd placed the decimal point one place shy of correct. The shell exploded much too soon. Though it was well within his prerogative to do so, and though it might have ended Shalikashvili's hope of becoming an officer, the tac officer that day did not eject him from OCS. And neither would Shalikashvili, on this day of O'Dwyer's very serious and public failure, push the matter.

It was graduation day for Shalikashvili, and he was leaving OCS having made a good impression. "He wasn't a talker, but when he did speak it was clear he knew what he was talking about," recalled one graduate. He was also neat in appearance, taking great care of his boots and brass, always looking sharp in his uniform, recalled another. "He looked like he was going to do what was asked of him, and he was going to do it right," said a third.

It was a favorable image Shalikashvili both cultivated and protected. On graduation morning middleclassman Jim Stotler was doing a last-minute commode check just before inspection. He spied Redbird Shalikashvili at the sink, wearing his new lieutenant's uniform. Stotler immediately snapped to attention, and Shalikashvili ordered him at ease.

"I couldn't believe it," Stotler later recalled his shock, "but Shalikashvili was putting in contact lenses!" The senior classman had impressed him from day one—"Shali could run anyone into the ground. He was so smart he aced tests that were never aced!" So Stotler's first reaction was: "Oh my god, he is human after all!" "If others at OCS knew about his contact lenses," Stotler later explained, "it would have been perceived as a physical weakness. He might even have had trouble staying in the top echelon of the class." Shalikashvili's resourcefulness was similarly impressive: "At that time, contact lenses were almost exclusively for movie stars and other elite. They really weren't available to the masses."

Exiting the bathroom, Shalikashvili warned Stotler: "They don't need to know about this." "Yes Sir," the middleclassman replied.

* * *

A few days had passed since Shalikashvili had helped out Redbird O'Dwyer with the duty roster forms, but the new lieutenant still hadn't left OCS. The army was fielding an increasing number of nuclear warheads, and given Shalikashvili's European upbringing—and especially since his mother was born in Russia—the military was subjecting him to a more rigorous background check.

While waiting for his clearance, Shalikashvili continued bunking in the candidate battalion staff barracks. One day O'Dwyer noticed his friend didn't look quite right. "What's the matter John?" he queried. Shalikashvili explained that his clearance was troubling him, and he was also struggling over how long he should stay in the army.

Top OCS candidates generally desired a lifelong career in the military. Yet at this point in the army's history those graduating from the program earned just reserve officer status. To stay permanently, they'd need to apply for Regular Army Commission. That's why, as a reward for those excelling in this punishing program, OCS offered this commission to the top three graduates.

Having finished second in his cycle, Shalikashvili received the offer. But even just prior to entering OCS, he hadn't planned on making a career in the army: "Mother mentioned that OCS is going to increase my tour of duty by one year," he'd written home from AIT. "That is not so. The Army has a new program now, and I am in it, under which an OCS candidate does not have to add one extra year to his service. What all this means is that I am still going to be discharged on 30 July 1960." Having since gone through six months of OCS hell, Shalikashvili now had even less interest in a military career. So he did what was unthinkable to some: he turned down the army's offer of Regular Army Commission.

So how best to approach the next few years? He planned to pursue graduate education at some point, but it was the timing he seemed unsure about. "I don't know what to do now, Roger," Shalikashvili worried aloud. "Do I stay just for the two years total or do I extend it to three? If two, the army will pay for my uniforms. If three years, I have to foot the bill myself."

This caught O'Dwyer by surprise. "John, go for three years!" he exhorted. "You look like someone who should be an officer." Then, looking squarely at his mentor and friend, O'Dwyer blurted out: "You're going to be a general some day!"

Shalikashvili said nothing, an odd expression hanging on his face. The two spoke no more on the matter. Soon thereafter his clearance came through, and Shalikashvili parted ways with Robinson Barracks.

Part IV

Paying It Forward: Operation Provide Comfort

12

Savior of the Kurds?

Thursday, April 18, 1991—Turkish-Iraqi Border

The passengers stood forward on the C-130 transport plane, crowding in behind the pilot, flight engineer, and copilot. All eyes were fixed intently beyond the windscreens. The midafternoon sun shone brightly. Visibility from the wrap-around cockpit was excellent.

Close to two hours had passed since their departure from Incirlik Air Base in south-central Turkey. The rolling brown-green slopes of eastern Turkey passing some five thousand feet below were finally about to give way to the brownish gray of taller rocky foothills just further to the east. And there in the distance, beyond those foothills, loomed a most mesmerizing sight: a glistening mountain barrier of deep purple crags and snowcapped peaks springing ten thousand to fourteen thousand feet into the sky.

Directly behind the pilot, face impassive, stood Lieutenant General John Shalikashvili. His visage, which naturally lacked the full range of flex and movement that typically reveals mood, had set further with age. At times of crisis such as this, the fifty-five-year-old commander was inscrutable.

Unless you looked at his eyes. And those piercing blues had just lit up with fierce intensity. They'd spotted a sight so unusual, so out of context for the rugged mountain terrain, that is was difficult for the brain to immediately interpret.

There in the rocky foothills just ahead and off to the right, sparkling dots were coming into view. First there were hundreds of them. And then thousands. Thousands upon thousands. The flecks lay thicker in the relative flatness of the false peaks and shallow dips, more scattered on the steeper slopes. It was as if some celebratory god had tossed a gigantic handful of glitter over that barren rocky mountainside.

The aircraft slowly banked right, providing a better view. Peering downward, Shalikashvili stared at the glimmering. What he was really seeing was darkness—the darkness of human suffering on a stupefying scale. Each sparkle was the bright sun reflecting off a tent, a tarp, a piece

Kurdish refugee camp in northern Iraq, spring 1991. (DoD photo, DN-ST-91-11693.)

of plastic sheeting. Each glimmer marked the make-do shelter of desperate Kurdish refugees. Even more precarious were those with no shelter whatsoever, no visible twinkle to catch the eye of would-be saviors in the sky.

How many were huddled down on that mountainside? Though he had only rough estimates, the numbers were staggering. This patch of terrain, which days earlier had taken on the name "Isikveren," held eighty thousand to one hundred thousand Kurds. In other circumstances, it would have constituted a thriving city.

As Shalikashvili stood processing his first glimpse of the refugee camp, a warning beep sounded. In the skies ahead the hulking shapes of two other transport planes were coming into view. The one overtaking them to the right was lumbering eastbound into the mountains. The other, flying above the distant white peaks, was headed toward them.

These two aircraft underscored the enormity of the crisis, for scattered across that expansive mountain range were more refugees.

And not just more, but hundreds of thousands more.

The eastbound aircraft was laden with tons of relief supplies it'd soon be dropping deeper into the mountains, somewhere over what would later be determined to be the forty-three separate locations, including eight major camps, where the refugees were congregating along the mountains that separated Turkey from Iraq. The westbound plane, having already released its parachutes of supplies—like food, water, blankets, baby formula—was shuttling back to a logistical base in Turkey to have its cavernous cargo hold packed for the next run.

Shalikashvili tracked the plane heading into the snowcapped mountains. While no one was certain how many refugees were out there in those mountains, the estimates—between three hundred thousand and 1 million—boggled the mind.

What would compel such multitudes—a population equivalent to a major US metropolis like Boston, Detroit, or Washington, D.C.—to take to these extreme mountains?

From the daily morning briefings he'd attended the past few weeks in Heidelberg, Germany, in his capacity as Deputy Commander in Chief, US Army Europe (DCINC, USAREUR), Shalikashvili knew the answer.

It was abject terror.

* * *

The Kurds—a largely Sunni Muslim ethnic group composed of many clans sharing a language and culture yet lacking an independent political state—live mostly throughout Turkey, Iraq, Iran, Armenia, and Syria.

After Operation Desert Storm ended in February 1991, the Kurds in northern Iraq undertook a major gamble by taking up arms against Saddam Hussein's regime. The uprising, launched on March 7, came in the wake of press statements by US president George H. W. Bush and CIA-backed radio broadcasts from Saudi Arabia that seemed to encourage them to do so.

The timing was good. The Iraqi military, weakened and dispersed by the war, was busy quelling an uprising in Shia-dominated southern Iraq. Opposed mostly by the ill-equipped Iraqi paramilitary, Kurdish forces quickly gained control over one northern Iraqi city after another.

But by March 28, Saddam, having quashed the uprising in the south, turned his attention northward. Then, in part because no US support ever materialized, the tide turned. The Kurds found themselves no match for the bullets, rockets, tanks, artillery, and particularly the helicopter gunships the elite Republican Guard, backed by the Iraqi paramilitary forces, had at its disposal.

Knowing the Iraqi government would exact revenge for this failed attempt at independence, the Kurds turned desperate. What struck terror deepest in their hearts was the fear that Saddam's wrath would reanimate the gruesome specter of Halabja.

It's not hard to imagine what a child living in that town of fifty thousand Kurds in northeastern Iraq might have experienced on March 16, 1988. Iran had just wrested control of Halabja from the Iraqis a few days prior, yet another battle in what would be the last year of an eight-year war between Iran and Iraq.

Perhaps he was outside when it happened. He'd have first heard the drone of warplanes, then felt the earth shuddering under the might of exploding shells. Moments later came billowing clouds. Young and naive, he probably stood there watching as they turned color—white to black and then to yellow—in their drift upward over 150 feet into the air. He'd be too young to understand: these clouds now dissipating across his village were lethal chemicals, likely some cocktail of mustard gas, cyanide, and the nerve agents sarin, tabun, and VK.

In shock, his ears probably didn't immediately register the screaming. Yet his eyes, widening now, would take in neighbors scurrying about. Many were stumbling, lungs having difficulty drawing breath, skin beginning to form the ugly lesions that are a telltale sign of mustard gas poisoning.

This attack was almost instantaneously killing three thousand to five thousand of his fellow Kurds. Up to 70 percent were women and children. How does one blot out the sight of a neighbor's lifeless form? Or of a child, especially one your own age, pinned down by the corpse of a parent who'd tried in vain to shield their offspring from the deadly vapors?

This horror now raining down on the boy's village would later be judged the largest chemical weapons attack ever directed against a civilian-populated area to date.

Chemical weapons terrify long after the initial attack. Survivors suffer from a range of afflictions—like tremors, atrophy, respiratory ailments, reproductive failure, skin diseases, mental illness, and blindness. Such maladies were reported in and around Halabja following the attack, and untold thousands would eventually die prematurely from these horrific complications. The terrible nature of chemical weapons was why, in the wake of the Halabja and other gassings, an estimated sixty-five thousand Kurds fled to Turkey.

The Iraqis and Iranians each accused the other of dropping the chemicals. For their part, the Kurds were adamant: the attack was part of Iraq's dreaded Anfal Campaign—a reign of terror headed by Ali Hassan al-Majid, the Iraqi general known as "Chemical Ali." The campaign dropped gas on thirty villages in 1988 alone, according to one US Senate Foreign Relations Committee investigation. Another report issued by a Kurdish doctor found that Iraq gassed 250 villages and thirty-one suspected bases of Kurdish guerillas during 1987 and 1988. Yet another analysis, by Human Rights Watch, found the campaign employed mustard and nerve gases, as well as mass executions, to kill some one hundred thousand Kurds—a clear act of genocide, the group charged.

That was three years ago. Now the Iranian ambassador to the UN was once again accusing Iraq of using chemicals against the Kurds. But was it true?

The Kurds in northern Iraq needed no proof. Why would Saddam— fresh from a humiliating defeat at the hands of the US-led coalition— refrain from once again raining chemicals on them?

So they fled.

They fled in massive numbers. And from all age groups and socioeconomic classes. They fled from small hamlets. From villages. And from the larger Kurdish cities—Duhok, Erbil, Kirkuk, and Zakho—areas recaptured stunningly quickly by Saddam's advancing military. By April 3 all resistance had melted and the Kurds were in full flight.

Early in the crisis, Barzani Massoud, head of the Kurdish Democratic Party, warned that 3 million Kurds had already fled into the mountains; international observers would later peg the number at 1–2 million. Some headed northeast to Iran, others to Turkey in the northwest.

For those fleeing toward Turkey, taking to the mountain roads and paths was a running of the gauntlet. Lines of refugees were sometimes strafed by Iraqi helicopter gunships. Kurds who started out in cars, buses, open-bed trucks, and even donkey carts became stuck in the mud and snow; they would continue on foot. For those trudging up the steep slopes, shoes were often lost to the deep mud or simply crumbled apart under the abuse of the climb; they'd continue barefoot. Many wore spring clothes suitable for the milder Iraqi lowlands; they would shiver more fiercely the higher they marched. Children clung to the necks of parents. The sick and those too old to walk were strapped to makeshift stretchers. The able-bodied staggered forward under the weight of bundles balanced on heads or laid across backs.

Yet the Kurds kept marching—over rocks, across snow and ice, and even through minefields. They continued on past fellow refugees who paused, backs bent, to scrape out shallow graves for those who perished along the way. Sorrowfully, the bodies of an estimated fifteen hundred children would be interred along these tortuous paths.

But they kept walking, sometimes more than a half-dozen abreast, forming long ragtag lines that began up to thirty miles from the border. It was a mass exodus that, from the sky, resembled a cruel marathon.

What was propelling the Kurds forward was hope. If they pushed far enough into the mountains, perhaps the Iraqis might stop chasing them. If they could just reach the border, Turkey might provide sanctuary from the bullets, shells, and especially chemicals of Saddam Hussein.

Ankara, however, had not kept the door open for long. Turkey couldn't be solely responsible for this tidal wave of refugees, no matter how desperate their circumstances. And almost nobody expected the Kurdish opposition to collapse so fast or that such massive numbers of refugees would be unleashed. For example, in advance of the ground war to liberate Kuwait, the offices of the United Nations High Commissioner for Refugees had pre-positioned enough tents and blankets in the area to sustain only twenty thousand refugees. "Because of that imposing mountainous border," explained the UNHCR desk officer for emergency planning for Turkey at the time, "we felt Turkey was the least likely of all four of Iraq's neighbors to be faced with a major refugee problem."

But they were all wrong. General Dougan Gures, chief of the General Staff of the Turkish Armed Forces, later characterized the opening days of this crisis: "The situation was really terrible. The people massed at the border. Some of them even crossed it. They plundered the stores that sold fruits and vegetables. . . . They even uprooted our apple trees in the border areas. They burned them to keep themselves warm." According to one Turkish official, 250,000 Kurds had crossed into Turkish land in the first few days alone.

The Turks, moreover, were not enamored of the Kurds. Turkey already had its own restless domestic Kurdish population, which it did not wish to augment. Ankara was also saddled with the costs of maintaining supposedly temporary camps that still housed half of the Kurdish refugees from the 1988 Halabja gassing.

So not long into the crisis Turkey made the decision to dispatch troops to shut down its border with Iraq.

* * *

From his vantage point on the C-130, Shalikashvili could discern the Turkish battalion keeping the Kurds in Isikveren at bay. Most refugees were hemmed in between two steep ridges that came together on the camp's downslope, forming the letter "V." By straining his eyes the general could perhaps just make out the thin line of green-uniformed Turkish soldiers keeping watch from the ridgelines. Additional soldiers were blockading the road that cut through the tip of the V, effectively barring the Kurds from the green valleys of eastern Turkey that lay so tantalizing below.

Barred by Ankara from crossing into the more temperate Turkish lowlands, yet too terrified to return to Iraq, the Kurds were now trapped. The refugees—hundreds of thousands of men, women, and children— had no choice but to remain clinging to the sides of these steep mountain slopes. Lacking adequate food, water, clothing, and shelter, they were in dire straits.

Appointed the new commander of this rescue mission just twenty-four hours earlier, Shalikashvili was taking today's overflight to gain a first bird's-eye view of the geographical magnitude of the crisis. From Isikveren, the plane would move on to survey the other camps strung out along the 206-mile mountain border. Their names challenged the tongue: Sinat, Yekmal, Uzumulu, Hakkari, Cukurca, Pirincken, Yesilova. Shalikashvili would be updated on each camp by US Army Brigadier General Richard Potter, whose team had been sent into the mountains early on to stabilize the situation. During the overflight Potter would reiterate that his special forces still did not know where all the refugees were located.

Looking out the cockpit, Shalikashvili could see how staggering was the task. Two hundred miles of land-mined border. Icy mountains that scraped high into the skies. Dozens of camps and many more smaller gathering sites. How would they locate the hundreds of thousands of refugees spread out across this dangerous expanse? Without a better estimate of the numbers, how could they bring in appropriate levels of manpower and supplies? One of Shalikashvili's first steps, then, would be to order up satellite pictures to supplement the gamut of methods—aerial photographs, on-the-ground patrols, and conversations with locals—already being used to locate the refugees.

He understood the critical need to find them. He had first-hand experience with how treacherous snowy mountains could be.

* * *

The 1950s were about to give way to the 1960s, and Alaska was a place of freshness and promise. "Seward's Folly" had gained statehood back in January, and America's new forty-nine-star flag had flown proudly until August, when Hawaii became the fiftieth star. The development of intercontinental ballistic missiles meant the country's air force capability was shifting away from manned bombers. With the army's efforts to expand air defense artillery, Nike missile sites were beginning to dot the state's frozen landscape. The writing was now on the wall for Fairbank's Ladd Air Field. In little over one year's time, the army would be taking control of this sizable air force base.

In July 1959, Second Lieutenant John Shalikashvili arrived at Eielson Air Force Base, Ladd's smaller nearby neighbor. Having just earned his officer's commission at OCS, he'd been posted to "the Manchus"—the 1st Battle Group of the 9th Infantry Division. It was a romantic first assignment, as he'd be on one of the US military's last ski patrols.

His battery commander, First Lieutenant Charles Glenn, picked him up at the airport. His initial impression was that Shalikashvili "looked like what one would like to think an excellent soldier looked like: trim, squared away, precise, intelligent, and with a good sense of humor."

Officer's Records Clerk Henry Phillips, on duty when Shalikashvili came into battle group headquarters to register, later recalled: "Everyone in the personnel office that day was very much impressed with the young lieutenant who was fluent in four languages and had a great sense of humor." "Some guys came in dissatisfied to be in Alaska; others were jokers, but Shali gave off the air that it was a new adventure and he was going to enjoy it." "We all said that there was a young officer that would go far."

How far would he go? With the Cold War burning hot and the base on permanent semi-alert given its proximity to Russia, maneuvers were frequent. Here was opportunity for an enterprising young man—one honed "tight as a violin string and sharp as a razor" by the crucible of OCS—to test his mettle.

One test was physical. In Alaska, Mother Nature deserved respect. There

Lieutenant John Shalikashvili serving on one of the US Army's last ski patrols in Fairbanks, Alaska, circa 1960. (Courtesy of the NBR Gen. John Shalikashvili Archives.)

was the cold: in celebration of a record low, the 9th Infantry Division would make a "72 degree-below" pin to attach to the division patch. There was danger: on one exercise, gusting sixty-mile-per-hour winds broadsided the jeep of the battle group's deputy commander; the jeep flipped, severing the general's head.

Yet Shalikashvili was drawn to the extreme conditions. Skiing was a particular passion, earning him the rare honor of a "500-mile" ski patch. He even attempted to summit the twenty thousand-foot peak of Mount McKinley, though a change in weather forced him to turn back. The bitterly cold Alaskan climate was what, decades later, Shalikashvili would blame for the broken veins in his hands and the ever-present ruddiness in his cheeks.

One time Shalikashvili agreed to accompany fellow lieutenant and OCS cycle-mate Mike McMahon on a flight to Anchorage. There they picked up McMahon's car—a shiny Morris Minor—and began the long drive back to Fairbanks.

It happened while descending one particularly steep mountainous section. With McMahon forced to ride the brakes, the tires eventually found a patch of black ice. And that's when the car began turning. Despite white-knuckle maneuvering, the vehicle kept spinning, making 360-degree circles as the car spiraled ever downward. It was only at a bend in the road, when the trunk slammed into a low snowbank, that the car was finally brought to a halt.

They jumped out to look. There'd been no guardrail. That small mound of white was all that had prevented the two young officers from plummeting some one thousand feet to their deaths.

"I was panicked," McMahon recalled. "But Shali just looked at it and said, 'Okay, Mike. Let's go.'" Had Shalikashvili too been afraid? Almost certainly. Had he remained in control of his outward demeanor? Most definitely.

The bigger test Alaska posed was mental: the challenge of being all one could be as a leader in the US military. Shalikashvili got his first real taste of command at the four-month mark when assigned to lead a mortar battery platoon.

There is a truism: "The day you get introduced to your first platoon, those are thirty or so of the biggest critics you'll ever meet." Making the artillery officer's challenge greater was that his unit was comprised of infantry soldiers. His learning curve would be steep.

But "I was very fortunate," Shalikashvili later recalled, "because I had Sergeant Grice to guide me and to teach me."

Sergeant First Class William Rudy Grice had a sterling reputation. Having grown up poor, Grice lied about his age so he could join the military as a fifteen-year-old—"Because I had to eat." That was in 1946. Sent off to Germany, he was later selected to assist General Bruce Clarke in opening up the world's first NCO academy. When he arrived in Alaska, Grice had already clocked over a decade of experience combining NCO theory and practice. He was, in the words of Shalikashvili's first battery commander in Alaska, "one hell of a fine sergeant. An extremely professional NCO."

"And teach and guide me he did," Shalikashvili decades later voiced his appreciation, but "without ever making me feel inadequate and without ever permitting me to be ill-prepared." In the mornings Grice would come into the office and—much to Shalikashvili's surprise—announce: "Just as you asked me yesterday, I've organized the inspection of the motor pool," or "I have organized a poncho inspection. If you'd just follow me."

In his diplomatic yet straightforward way, the sergeant was teaching professional competence. "Grice knew that if our platoon was going to be good at the countless things that would make us a finely honed warfighting machine," Shalikashvili intuited, "then he had to teach me and practice with me so that when I walked that gun line, the soldiers would know that I knew more than them, that if I asked them how to cut a mortar fuse there was no doubt that I would know the answer, just as I would know if there was too much play in the sight mount on that mortar."

Grice also emphasized character. "Lieutenant, quit looking *up* and worrying what the captain will tell you; look *down* and worry about what your soldiers are telling you about yourself." "If you say it is raining outside," the sergeant impressed, "people shouldn't feel the need to look out the window. Because it was *you* who said it, and because you have character, they would know it was true." Shalikashvili understood the subtext: "If you ever lose the trust of your platoon, you're through as a platoon leader—you're through as any kind of a leader."

And the last big lesson was how to treat soldiers. Five years his commander's senior, Grice had discerned that "those you lead will want to know that you sincerely care about them and will sacrifice for them, that you simply enjoy being with them."

Wasn't that why he'd prod Shalikashvili to take the extra time to get to know the members of the platoon better? As commander, he needed to know who needed extra coaching so he could fire expert on the rifle range; he needed to personally talk to Private Taylor, who'd just received a "Dear John" letter; he should visit Corporal Vencler and his wife, who had a sick child. "Every day you will have soldiers who will need your care, your concern, and your help. They expect—and I tell you they have the right to expect—150 percent of your time and best effort."

There'd be evenings in the field when the two would stand together in the cold, cup of coffee warming frozen fingers, watching the platoon go through the chow line. "Grice taught me that simple but long-standing tradition that an officer will take his or her first bite only after the last soldier has had a chance to eat." Leaders, the sergeant was telling him, place the welfare of their people above their own.

These conversations about leadership were not carried out with such directness, however. Grice, for his part, was a matter-of-fact, show-by-doing kind of guy. Asked fifty years later to recall the foreign-born second lieutenant he served under in the early 1960s, the retired sergeant was succinct: "He knew when to talk and when to shut up. He was calm. Shalikashvili was good at asking for advice—and he had the good sense to listen and learn."

What did others think of how he fared at applying these newly learned leadership lessons?

One perspective comes from First Lieutenant William Howerton, who at one point was Shalikashvili's superior but was also one of a group of young lieutenants who hung around together. "Overall he had an excellent relationship with his troops," Howerton recalled, recognizing Shalikashvili's knack for inspiring his subordinates to produce outstanding results, both in their normal duties and the extracurricular tasks they were are assigned. "But sometimes Shali would have a hard time because of his aristocratic father. He could be haughty." It wasn't just his erect bearing and sharp military dress that lent him a proud air. Shalikashvili held high standards of professionalism—or professional competence in Grice's terms.

Some viewed his high standards positively. First Lieutenant Paul Buckley, Shalikashvili's second battery commander, agreed that he was "always on duty, always looking for perfection. And people responded to this." Yet while quite demanding of his junior people to get the job done, Buckley clarified, "Shalikashvili was demanding in the proper way."

Another fellow lieutenant, John Haynes, picked up a different vibe. When among their small group of friends, Shalikashvili would offer a sharp critique when he felt standards weren't being met. "I'm not impressed with these lower grade officers," Haynes once heard Shalikashvili complain.

Clear was that Shalikashvili knew how to follow as well as lead. "At one point we had a battery commander who was very difficult," Howerton continued, "but Shali was smart enough to hold his tongue, and when necessary he could stand his ground in a polite way. He was also really good at following orders, though he might interrupt with a suggestion."

Yet Howerton found Shalikashvili far from a paragon of equanimity. Like how during off hours Shalikashvili would join in with the other lieutenants in blowing off steam by imagining creative—and even violent—ways to strike back at their commander.

Many thought him humorous, though his humor was often dry and subtle. In one letter home from AIT, Shalikashvili told of being assigned guard duty one evening: "I was never so cold in my life as I was that night marching around that stupid building with a rifle on my back. I thought at first I would die, and then, later, I was afraid I would not die. But as it turned out, I didn't even catch a cold."

And he was known for employing his humor with care. As one subordinate would later note, "Shalikashvili was funny but good with boundaries." He used humor to make him a more effective leader. As Glenn judged, he had the "ability to evidence a sense of humor under very stressful circumstances that helped him to remain calm and thus make good decisions; that helped him and others through crisis situations."

Some found him humble. Ted Hummel, a young officer who bunked with Shalikashvili and served in a security detachment supporting his unit, recalled he was always coolheaded, thoughtful, and a good diplomat who got along with guys well, adding that "in the army you meet people who say 'I'm going to be the army chief of staff or I'm going to be chairman of the Joint Staff someday.' But Shali wasn't like that."

Again, Haynes, who knew him more intimately, felt differently. He recalled Shalikashvili once saying, "I joined because my family was in the army. I'm not too crazy to be here, except to be a general." McMahon judged this consistent with the Shalikashvili he knew, recalling how his friend often jumped at the opportunity to play bridge with the more senior officers and their wives or noting that he was the only lieutenant to write a book review for a curious colonel.

The immigrant soldier, it seemed, knew how to look both down and up at the same time.

Only months into his assignment in Alaska, the newly invigorated second lieutenant had an epiphany: "If this is what army life is like, then I want in!"

But when he applied for Regular Army Commission, the army was apathetic. "Sorry, we offer you that once in a lifetime. You had your chance [at OCS] but you turned it down." Shalikashvili, though, wouldn't give up easily. "I spent the next two months on my knees going to every senior officer I could find and asking for a recommendation."

Finally, one agreed—but conditionally. Brigadier General Lester L. Wheeler, head of the army's Yukon Command, needed a temporary aide-de-camp. He agreed to give Shalikashvili the three-month position. Transferring the lieutenant from his mortar battery at Elision to command headquarters at Ladd would allow Wheeler to determine if the young reserve lieutenant in fact deserved Regular Army Commission.

Wheeler was not your stereotypical "blood and guts" general. Yes, he was rather rough looking. Undeniably brave, he enjoyed hunting bear and steadfastly believed no one should be promoted to general without having been shot at in anger. He readily made the tough decisions. Yet he was also down-to-earth, kind, plainspoken. He was, according to some under his command, a man of character and integrity, a leader who looked out for the interest of his troops. A conscientious mentor, the general both stressed the importance of showing by example and gave equal treatment to all officers—regular, reservist, and noncommissioned alike.

Importantly, the general and Shalikashvili shared a sense of humor. "Shali," noted Wheeler's daughter Helen, "was always ready with a quick joke, and had a dry sense of humor—just like my dad's."

And the lieutenant could skillfully employ this shared humor to pull his bacon out of the fire. One day Shalikashvili, who was keeping the general's schedule, strode into Wheeler's office. "Sir," he announced, "I've mistakenly booked you for two appointments at the same time." Then the twenty-three-year-old did something unexpected. Taking off his pistol, he set it on the general's desk. "Sir," the lieutenant continued, "you can shoot me now or you can shoot me later."

The general stared across the desk at his aide in contemplation. Both men, in fact, also shared a passion for outside-the-box thinking. Shalikashvili's punishment, when it came, was to accompany his boss to a fur shop. There the young officer would model different styles of coats—doing his part to help the general select the perfect gift for Mrs. Wheeler.

Murmuring a "this lad shows promise," Wheeler later penned his signature okaying Shalikashvili's application for Regular Army Commission.

As Shalikashvili's time in Alaska was winding down, he was chosen to lead a team on the northernmost fire mission yet conducted by the US Army. Here was a high-profile opportunity to apply the three leadership principles—competence, character, and concern for the welfare of soldiers—infused in Sergeant Grice's teachings.

In December 1960 Shalikashvili's crew of about thirty men flew up to Point Barrow, an indigenous village on the northernmost tip of Alaska. Striking out onto the arctic ice with members of a native scout battalion, their job was to test how both men and equipment reacted to extreme temperatures. Shalikashvili found it a seminal event: "The planning, getting supplies, doing the training, and then heading out into the vast wildness of the new state of Alaska. It was self-reliance. It was that perfect pairing of planning and leadership. We had it all right there in a microcosm."

They spent the first day in the village talking with the locals. "They are by far the friendliest people," Shalikashvili wrote home, "but live in terrible poverty and want, at least according to our standards."

The next day the team ventured onto the ice cap. Traveling over the broken dips and jagged outcrops was slow going. The young officer made his first serious command mistake that day—he allowed them to get separated from their gear, which then had to be airlifted to their stopping point. At 40 degrees below, however, tires would freeze to the ice, so supplies were dropped from L19 Cessna airplanes. When trying to erect tents at nightfall, they found it impossible to pound the stakes into the ice—forcing them to radio back for an airlift of nails. And despite the army's best arctic clothing, Shalikashvili and his men struggled to stay warm. But the locals, he noted, were operating without gloves. "It became clear that you really have to be trained and prepared to operate under those conditions."

Each day he and his native scout would venture out first on dog sleds, his team following a few hours behind by vehicle. They spent hours at a time gliding across the ice, the snow blowing across their path. The silence would be broken only by an occasional command from the scout or an answering bark from the dogs.

Trying later to articulate the almost spiritual experience, Shalikashvili struggled for the right words: "It's impossible to describe, but you feel good and strong and you kind of smile at the world, because they just don't know."

A week after returning to base, Shalikashvili's career got an unexpected boost.

Ladd Air Field was finally being redesignated the US Army's new Fort Wainwright, and Secretary of the Army Wilber M. Brucker had arrived to officiate the dedication ceremony. He'd also be appointing General Wheeler as the fort's new commanding general.

Everything was ready. The reviewing stand had been set up and covered with a tent. A battery of Herman-Nelson heaters were in place to ensure that Brucker and the other VIPs were kept warm. "And the rest of us," Shalikashvili recalled wryly even decades later, "were standing there freezing."

Here at Fairbanks, review parades were graceful, almost poetic events. The troops would don skis and deck themselves out in one-piece "over whites" with matching white vapor barrier boots. Then, to the haunting tune of the "Blue Danube Waltz," these ghostly figures would ski in formation past the tents for inspection.

To formally welcome the secretary of the army, the executive officer (X.O.) of Battery B, 2nd Howitzer Battalion, was tasked with directing the nineteen-gun salute. Brucker, upon hearing an unexpected twentieth bang, turned to Wheeler and said: "Thank the young officer for the extra round." That afternoon the X.O. was demoted to motor pool officer—and Shalikashvili was appointed as his replacement.

Later in life, when asked how it all began, Shalikashvili almost never mentioned basic training, AIT, or OCS. What was readily and warmly recalled was Alaska—for its exciting and challenging atmosphere; for the mentors, like Sergeant Grice and General Wheeler, whose teachings resonated with his growing leadership instincts; and for his growing skill set, strong job performance, and the smiling face of luck.

But Alaska meant even more. The small isolated outpost of Eielson and even the larger Ladd were "places where people quickly became important to each other, easily formed very close bonds," recalled Wheeler's daughter. Shalikashvili later admitted that General Wheeler and his wife "became my second parents when I was in Alaska." It was an expanding family—his former commander, Paul Buckley, who'd also served as Wheeler's aide-de-camp, proposed to the general's daughter, and the couple asked Shalikashvili to be best man.

"Shali warmed to this close-knit community," Helen reflected. "He was looking for the thing he was going to dedicate his life to. And he was always unabashedly proud of being a citizen and of serving his country."

Alaska, she summed up, "was an 'aha!' moment for him."

But there was still one glaring hole in his life: John Shalikashvili remained a bachelor.

There were opportunities to date of course. And not just at the officers club. Because Eielson was so small, the public school teachers ate in the officer's mess hall, making it a de facto dating pool.

But there was also competition. "Shali wanted to date the woman who'd be my first wife," McMahon later recalled with a laugh, "but I cut him off at the pass." Shalikashvili was judged "shy" or "slightly shy" depending on who you asked. "We always managed to have a good time at the officers club," recalled Colby Thresher, "but Shali was perhaps less of a party boy than some. He was more serious about his job." Unsurprisingly, some prospective dates judged him reserved.

One night a group of lieutenants had dinner at the Howertons. Wanting help with cleanup, William's wife handed Shalikashvili a dish towel. "My dad wouldn't set foot in the kitchen," was the reply. Her response was equally blunt: "No drying, no eat!" It was too cold that night for McMahon's car to start, so the crew stayed over. Shalikashvili, the only bachelor in the bunch, had to share a pullout bed with Haynes, whose wife was elsewhere. He half-joking protested that his bedmate better not mistake him for his spouse. Sure enough, a scream was heard in the middle of the night—a sleeping Haynes had thrown an arm around his bedmate.

Much of Shalikashvili's free time in Alaska was spent hunting and fishing, and, of course, skiing. When indoors, he'd play bridge, watch television, or read.

One day early on, his loneliness came to a head. Having somehow managed to track down the number, Shalikashvili had the base operator put in the call. The operator at San Antonio State Hospital tracked her down. The words "important call from Alaska" were enough to pull her out of class.

After she picked up the line, Shalikashvili said hello. She screamed, and then began crying. It had been five years since Donna had last heard his voice.

The call would last from late morning into early evening, with the hospital's operator going through a shift change. It assuredly cost Shalikashvili a small fortune.

His voice betrayed nervousness at first, even evincing a choke that Donna knew meant he was fighting back heavy emotions. The second lieutenant began by puffing himself up a bit, saying he was an army captain now stationed in Alaska and that he was learning to ski. How beautiful it was here, he enticed. If she'd come, she could see how vast, how lovely it was.

He asked her a question, one that he'd repeat over the course of their marathon conversation: Why hadn't Donna told him she was leaving Peoria that summer of 1954? Yet she kept changing the subject, like by delving into the details of her nursing program.

There was a photo of her he always kept with him, he interrupted, and he was looking at it now. Then he dropped the bombshell: he wanted Donna to marry him.

There was a moment of silence—too long of a moment.

And then demurral. "I'm an honor student, John. And now, for the first time ever, I feel accomplished." Though expressing how happy he was for her, he soon went back to reminiscing, a way of preparing her to be asked again.

When the proposal came a second time, it too was rebuffed. "I had to pull strings so I could make this phone call," he wheedled. "I know what I'm doing, Donna. This isn't puppy love." He reminded her how close they'd been: "Like one person." Why didn't she remember?

He pressed forward on another front, asking again why she'd left. "Donna, do you know what it really did to me?" Her response was to counter with a question: "Do men really cry over such things. I mean real tears like girls do?"

Despite his persistence, Donna offered no explanation of why she'd left Peoria. But she did confide one thing. About a year ago she'd gotten married to an older man who'd turned out quite crazy. He'd left in a stolen RV, taking their newborn son. She was in the midst of trying to legally end the marriage and gain legal custody of her child.

Yet John didn't waiver. He still wanted to marry her—and he was willing to help get her son back.

But Donna remained resolute. She would neither marry him nor explain her refusal.

With the conversation finally approaching its inevitable end, Shalikashvili offered up a last bit of persuading. "In answer to your question, hours ago, about if men really do cry when they are hurt . . . your answer is 'yes.'" Then, before hanging up, he told Donna how to reach him if she changed her mind.

13

Mushroom Cloud

Friday, April 19, 1991—Diyarbakir, Turkey

US Air Force colonel Eugene J. Ronsick stood scanning the skies of southeastern Turkey. The Diyarbakir airstrip, the closest improved airfield to the Iraqi border, was a busy one. Yet he was looking for one plane in particular. On board was an army lieutenant general with a long and unusual name. Today would be Ronsick's first meeting with the new boss, who was flying in from operational headquarters at Incirlik.

The powers that be had sent the army three star to supersede the original commander, an air force two star. The top brass had evidently decided more star power was needed to handle this rapidly expanding humanitarian crisis with the Kurds. Yes, it was a runaway situation in the mountains, and trying to get a handle on it, judged Ronsick, was like striving to stay seated atop a billowing mushroom cloud.

But the colonel was not at all convinced that a new commander was needed. In fact, he was downright worried this leadership change was a grave mistake.

* * *

Though the epicenter of the crisis was in the remote Turkish-Iraqi border, alarm had quickly reverberated around the globe.

On Friday, April 5, the UN Security Council passed Resolution 6888 condemning Iraq's repression of its people. That day President Bush, following telephone discussions with French and British leaders, announced: "The human tragedy unfolding in and around Iraq demands immediate action on a massive scale. At stake are not only the lives of hundreds of thousands of innocent men, women, and children, but the peace and security of the Gulf." American assistance to the Kurds, he promised, would begin Sunday.

On Saturday, four-star army general John "Jack" Galvin, who led the US military's European Command (EUCOM), issued the order establishing Operation Provide Comfort, tasking it to "execute humanitar-

A US Army UH-60A Black Hawk helicopter flies past a pair of CH-47 Chinook helicopters, Diyarbakir, Turkey. (DoD photo, DN-ST-91-09860.)

ian relief operations in Northern Iraq from Turkey." So critical was the Kurds' situation that supplies were already in the air headed to Turkey as EUCOM headquarters in Stuttgart, Germany, was writing the mission order. So critical, in fact, that the order was dispatched at the level of "flash"—a designation usually reserved for a nuclear emergency.

The operation would be a "joint task force," or JTF, involving all US service branches—army, navy, air force, and marines. Because mission priority was to airlift supplies into the mountains, Galvin appointed Major General Jim Jamerson, US Air Force Europe's deputy commander for operations, as JTF commander. Operational headquarters would be at Incirlik Air Base in south-central Turkey. The mission, Jamerson was told, would likely last ten days.

"Stop the dying." This was the simple but powerful mission statement created by Jamerson's deputy commander, Marine Corps brigadier general Anthony Zinni. And on Sunday, April 7—just forty-eight hours after Bush's announcement—the men and women of JTF-Operation Provide Comfort began doing just that. Under jet fighter escort, C-130 cargo planes that had flown straight in from US bases in Europe dropped twenty-seven tons of food, blankets, tents, medical supplies, and clothes into the mountains.

As the clock ticked through the first hours of the response, riggers and pilots worked feverishly to airlift sortie after sortie of supplies. Yet day by day, even hour by hour, the scope of the crisis kept expanding. More camps were being discovered even as the population of the known camps continued to swell.

So on April 9 a new step was taken. Special forces soldiers, initially deployed only to provide combat search and rescue support to the air elements, were organized into Sub-Task Force Express Care and dispatched into the mountains. Too many lives needed saving. Too much intelligence needed gathering.

What soon became clear was the urgent need for "more"—more manpower, more blankets, more food and water, more tents, more medical care. More of everything.

Because the scope of the crisis kept mushrooming, even the world's sole superpower couldn't handle it alone. Nor would it be given the chance. For this was the dawning of the CNN era. Even before the first JTF troops touched ground, the international media was relentlessly beaming images of the crisis across the globe. Their pictures and news stories were galvanizing the world into action, effectively turning the rescue effort into a cause célèbre.

The first to supplement the American effort were British and French cargo planes, which began delivering supplies on the 8th. That was also the day the European Union pledged $180 million in economic aid. The troops of eleven other nations—Australia, Belgium, Canada, France, Germany, Italy, Luxembourg, the Netherlands, Portugal, Spain, and the United Kingdom—would eventually be dispatched, with the first arriving on the 13th. So vigorous was the response that over twenty thousand troops—greater than a full-strength division—would eventually directly participate in this rescue operation. Countries providing boots on the ground would just as generously rush relief supplies, as would a host of other nations—including Austria, Bulgaria, Czechoslovakia, Denmark, Finland, Greece, Hungary, Iceland, Ireland, Israel, Japan, Jordan, New Zealand, Norway, Pakistan, Romania, Saudi Arabia, and Sweden.

Each new national flag joining the rescue effort seemed to be matched by the logos of two or three nongovernmental organizations (NGOs) or private volunteer organizations (PVOs). Every major humanitarian institution would eventually set up a presence in the crisis zone, like the United Nations, Red Cross, Doctors Without Borders, CARE, Save the Children, and World Vision. They'd be joined by dozens of smaller organizations, like Action Nord-SVD, HELO Mission, and Irish Concern. Close to fifty relief organizations would eventually serve in the crisis zone.

So enthusiastic was the international response that the nature of the problem soon changed. The challenge quickly became not a lack of manpower or matériel but rather the challenge of coordination. How could this overwhelming outpouring of goodwill best be translated into effective action?

On April 17, twelve days since his first announcement, Bush again spoke to the world. This rescue operation—already the largest US relief effort mounted in modern history—was being expanded further.

First, the JTF was being upgraded. With the armed forces of so many countries already in the crisis zone, it was no longer just a joint US operation. Provide Comfort had clearly morphed into a de facto, albeit loosely organized, multinational or "combined" task force. What was now needed was to formally adopt the required CTF structure.

Second, the president was also ordering a change in mission. Going forward, the men and women of this new CTF Provide Comfort would no longer simply offer "humanitarian assistance" to the Kurds. The objective now was "humanitarian intervention." This tweak of but one word would mean a fundamental reordering of the mission objective—and a substantial ratcheting up of the scope of operation.

Shalikashvili's personal whirlwind began that Wednesday, the day of Bush's second announcement. He'd started off at his post—as deputy commander at USAREUR headquarters in Heidelberg—six hours ahead of the decision-makers and thus decision-making in Washington.

Having been informed by his boss, USAREUR commander General Crosbie "Butch" Saint, that Galvin was tapping him to conduct a two-day evaluation of the situation with the Kurds, the deputy boarded a plane to Stuttgart for a briefing. At EUCOM headquarters he was updated on the dramatic changes just called for by Bush and told the upgraded operation needed a more senior commander.

That's when Shalikashvili learned that Galvin had chosen him for the job.

A flurry of in-depth briefings then brought the new commander up to speed. EUCOM staff walked him through not just the situation on the ground but also the nascent planning on how the CTF would carry out this humanitarian intervention.

Shalikashvili next boarded another plane, this one to Frankfurt, to

From April to June 1991 Lieutenant General John Shalikashvili commanded the massive international humanitarian effort Operation Provide Comfort to rescue more than 500,000 Kurdish refugees trapped along the mountainous Turkish-Iraqi border. Photo shows operational headquarters in Incirlik Air Base, south-central Turkey. (DoD photograph, courtesy of the NBR Gen. John Shalikashvili Archives.)

pick up Major General Jay Garner, deputy commander of USAREUR's V Corps. The newly expanded mission to rescue the Kurds would require his expertise.

On the last leg to Incirlik, the newly appointed CTF commander updated his notes. The past few hours had been dizzying. "I think I know what I am supposed to do," he told Garner as they moved ever closer to Incirlik, but "I am not sure what you are going to do."

When he arrived in Incirlik that evening a delicate task awaited. So quickly were things moving that headquarters had not been officially informed that Shalikashvili was the new CTF commander. It was decided that the staff of the now defunct JTF would simply take up one position lower on the chain of command—Jim Jamerson was now deputy commander, Zinni was chief of staff, and so on.

* * *

Shalikashvili would later think back on his command of Provide Comfort. One to appreciate irony, he'd recall a certain sense of bemusement at being chosen. His expertise was in defending Western Europe from a possible Soviet invasion. If he'd heard of the Kurds before, it hadn't stuck. His first thought had been to check his footlocker. Did the service schools provide a manual entitled something akin to "operations other than war"? No, because no such manual yet existed. This operation was the US military's first time heading up an international response to such a major humanitarian crisis.

Among all the three- and even four-star officers at EUCOM, why had the powers-that-be given this once-in-a-lifetime leadership opportunity to him?

There is a quotation attributed to the Roman philosopher Seneca: "Luck is what happens when preparation meets opportunity." And Shalikashvili's career in the US military had well prepared him for the exact kind of leadership opportunity Provide Comfort presented.

Most recently, he'd pulled off another devilishly complex logistical mission of high diplomatic sensitivity: USAREUR's eleventh-hour operation to move an entire corps to the Persian Gulf.

Back in November 1990, in reviewing the plans for the start of the ground war in Kuwait, Joint Chiefs chairman Colin Powell and Gulf War commander General H. Norman Schwarzkopf decided to bolster the Allied ground posture by increasing the number of US ground forces and swapping out the Gulf's outdated tanks for more modern ones. USAREUR was thus ordered to move its entire VII Corps—both personnel and equipment—to Saudi Arabia.

To call the task daunting was an understatement. The VII Corps was currently the largest in the US military, which meant transporting over seventy thousand troops plus tens of thousands of vehicles to the Gulf. As Shalikashvili later explained, "prior to the 9th of November, no one, including ourselves, thought of us as a deployment unit." The VII Corps was designed to operate from exactly where it was: from its base in Heidelberg. Moving this complex institution would take an inventing, not reinventing, of the wheel. The deadline was also a punishing thirty days, though this would be extended a couple of weeks when the launch of the ground war was delayed.

Though not officially put in charge of the operation, Shalikashvili's

USAREUR deputy commander position entailed being responsible for overseeing the receiving and moving forward of all reinforcements in the European theater. More to the point, his boss had specifically tasked him "to pick up anything that fell off the table," which meant Butch Saint was giving Shalikashvili no direct command authority but would hold him responsible for the mission's success.

One task directly assigned to Shalikashvili, though, was coordinating with the allies. For one, this meant meeting with the respective heads of Germany's southern and northern territorial commands. He'd also have to work closely with the German Federal Railway. Then there would be face time with personnel at the various ports. In Germany this meant Bremerhaven—the very place Shalikashvili had sailed from as a teenager on his way to America. As the ports in Rotterdam and Antwerp would also be used, he'd similarly visit with officials and infrastructure personnel in both the Netherlands and Belgium.

Negotiations with the German railway and other transportation officials would prove tricky. Christmas was drawing near, and the operation could not impede holiday traffic—a task exacerbated by a threatened strike by German workers.

Worried that inclement weather could increase the danger of road transport, they'd hoped to utilize just rail and barge. But complications arose. "It was one thing to deploy a corps to go somewhere," Shalikashvili came to learn, "it's another to try to provision it with all the classes of supply." That's because, in addition to troops and vehicles, USAREUR would also need to move over one hundred thousand short tons of supporting munitions by the end of February 1991. "That's a staggering number of trains," Shalikashvili explained.

There were more challenges. Scheduling rail transport was inherently complex: "You have engine men, switch men, and other details," Shalikashvili listed. The German railway was thus requiring five days heads-up and a "fairly disciplined schedule." And the army's original guestimation of twenty trains per day was quickly revised up to sixty, because you need twenty trains carrying the stuff forward, twenty trains being unloaded, and twenty trains coming back. "From a standing start, that's quite a trick." To complete the mission, they'd even beseech the French rail to lend out extra cars. Yet despite all this intense negotiation and fervent juggling to maximize rail capacity, USAREUR would still need to employ both highway convoys and river barges.

Still more adjustments were in the offing. Shalikashvili's first

thought—that the corps themselves could establish the necessary movement control cells and movement apparatus—was also proven wrong.
That's because, he explained, "the very people who needed to get out
early from VII Corps were also the people needed to establish those
mechanisms of movement control cells." And beyond the challenge of
equipment and personnel, there was also the supporting minutia, "from
security to stevedores to berthing places to port-o-potties, to whatnot—
the list just goes on and on."

Yet somehow it all came together. "It involved the combined efforts
of the Belgians, the Dutch, the Canadians, the Germans, and us," Shalikashvili recalled, "civilians, military contractors—you name it—all
working seven days a week, practically around the clock." When the
dust settled they'd somehow orchestrated 465 trains, 119 convoys, and
312 barges to transport the men and matériel of the VII Corps to an array
of aerial and seaport points of embarkation. What they'd moved was lit-
erally an army: 73,369 USAREUR-based soldiers, 48,600 vehicles, and
170,000 short tons of sustainment munitions. The bulk would depart
Europe by December 21, with pieces of resupply equipment being sent
Gulf-bound through February.

Journalist and historian David Halberstam judged it "a military tour
de force." "Up until then no one had thought of Shalikashvili as an Army
superstar. . . . In the pressure cooker of the pre–Gulf War logistical preparations, however, his star had finally shone." Impressed, Powell told Galvin "Shali is looking good, isn't he? I mean really looking good." And
Galvin—who felt no other US Army officer could likely have pulled it off
so well—agreed.

But as per Seneca's quotation, if luck is when preparation meets opportunity, what allowed the general to handle the VII Corps movement with
such aplomb? To use the term of one of Sergeant Grice's three main leadership principles, how had Shalikashvili built the "professional competencies" of both logistics mastery and high diplomacy that the US military
was now finding so valuable here in this post–Cold War world?

First, the logistical mind-set. It came in no small part from Shalikashvili's early artillery training. The US Army Artillery and Missile School
did not choose its motto, *Cedat Fortuna Peritis,* on a whim: given the
complexity and inherent danger of artillery, skill is indeed better than
luck.

Shalikashvili's first taste of artillery logistics came as a buck private
at AIT. Artillery, he wrote home, is divided into three basic groups—for-

ward observer, fire direction specialist, and cannoneer. Nearest to the fighting is the forward observer, who relates the enemy's position to fire direction control. In just thirty seconds, the fire direction center specialist computes the necessary data—exact distance, elevation, type of shell and fuse, and amount of powder—and sends that information to the cannoneers, who then fire the rounds.

Field artillery officers keep track of a multitude of variables. They must know about interior and exterior ballistics, or what happens to the projectile both inside the tube and once it leaves the firing piece. For internal dynamics, powder temperature and projectile weight are considered. Then there's tube wear: firing a weapon removes small amounts of metal from the bore, slightly increasing the diameter of the bore and thus reducing the muzzle velocity. The resultant error in range needs to be compensated for. So too do external variables, like the effects of nonstandard weather conditions and, often surprising to civilians, even the earth's rotation. If that wasn't complex enough, Shalikashvili cut his artillery teeth during the early days before computers. In manual gunnery, calculations were made with slide rules, graphical or tabular firing tables, and pencils.

The field artillery officer also worries about logistical issues, including the resupply of ammunition, fuel, and rations. The guns and the target also need to be accurately located relative to each other, and the artilleryman needs to consider the locations of friendly units in the area of operations—a whole other dimension of complication.

"This," as summed up by Jon Schreyach, operations officer when Shalikashvili was division artillery (DIVARTY) commander at the 1st Armored Division in the 1980s, "is a pretty complex management problem."

But understanding complexity is only half the battle. An effective officer must simplify that complexity in large part by setting standards and communicating them to others.

These skills are especially critical in the US Army. As the largest service branch, its core strength lies in putting boots on the ground. It's also the most diverse—in terms of education level, socioeconomic status, and ethnicity. And on average it has the youngest, and thus least experienced, members.

Standards are not only critical in the dangerous specialty of field artillery but are an absolute precondition in the exponentially deadly realm of nuclear weapons, which Shalikashvili was exposed to while serving in air defense for seven years after leaving Alaska. In 1961 he was appointed to serve as an instructor in the High Altitude Missiles Department at Fort Bliss, Texas, with a focus on the Nike Hercules guided missile system. Upon arriving, he'd been given just fourteen days to learn the general concepts and structures of this alien and complex subject and then continue that understanding all the way down to the minutiae.

Then he was thrown into the classroom. His students were US and Allied officers ranging from second lieutenants to general officers. He later judged the experience invaluable "because you learned all the tricks of the trade about teaching and how important it is that you do your homework, that you know what you are talking about."

His bosses noted: "He grasps new material quickly," is "an effective instructor without the benefit of previous schooling or experience in the Air Defense field," and is able to "conduct instruction for officer students in a clear, precise manner that ensured that the students gleaned maximum benefit." Colleague William Grubbs recalled that "it was very difficult to get up to speed quickly on missiles in order to teach it, but Shali handled it the best of them all," adding that he read "heavy stuff," like books on nuclear strategy, including the concept of massive retaliation.

Shalikashvili was soon chosen to head the missile and radar/fire control lab, and then moved into the briefing room, where in one six-month period he conducted fifty-four briefings to over two thousand personnel, including US and foreign military and civilian VIPs—further honing his craft of presenting complex material to a wide variety of people. His superiors lauded Shalikashvili for "constantly updating the subject material and the training aids that were required to make a briefing of this type and importance a success."

But how was he at the messier job of putting principles into practice—particularly when nukes were involved?

Being assigned to a nuclear weapons-capable unit was tough. Because of the inherent danger, there was no room for sloppiness, no room for mistakes. "It went beyond zero tolerance," recalled Lieutenant General Wilson "Dutch" Shoffner, who'd served as the army's deputy chief of staff for operations. The army moved nuclear weapons well over ten thousand times in one year alone, he recalled. Such efforts mandated constant vigilance, setting rigorous standards, and enforcing strict discipline. First you checked, and then you double-checked. And not just the equipment and the processes, but also the staff. The Personnel Reliability Program kept tabs on who was on medication, who was blackmailable, who might have received unexpected large sums of money. All it took was one crisis, one accident, or even one failed inspection to result in commanders all along the chain of command being relieved from duty.

"In the field of tactical nuclear weapons," added Shoffner, "when you ask an important question you expect a specific answer. And people trained this way take that attitude into other areas of their professional life."

At Fort Bliss Shalikashvili was made responsible for the maintenance of two Nike Universal and Ajax fire control systems. "His acceptance of only the highest performance standards," his boss reported, "has resulted in superior ratings on all equipment during the last command maintenance inspection."

His next assignments were nuclear weapons control officer and then commander of the headquarters and headquarters battery for the 32nd Army Air Defense Command (32nd AADCOM) in Kaiserslautern, Germany. Shalikashvili's attention to detail was noted by William Hoover, the vehicle control officer at the motor pool. Hoover recalled how in advance of one upcoming inspection the captain arrived at the motor pool with white gloves. Not even dirt or grime would escape his preinspection inspection.

While headquarters was situated in Kapaun Barracks, the command's aviation section was twenty miles distant and the Army Air Defense Command Post and Missile Control Center a full forty-five miles away. Such geographical dispersion necessitated everyone being on the same page.

Shalikashvili performed so well that he became the go-to-guy for other units looking to improve their processes. The Operations Center he organized at command headquarters was "an outstanding model of efficiency" that "has been copied, both facility-wise and procedure-wise by many other headquarters with quick-reaction missions." He developed a system of easy-to-understand instructions and booklets that a subsequent command inspection by USAREUR found so effective that its principles, artifacts, and procedures were adopted USAREUR-wide. Similarly, when the VII Corps inspector general evaluated the Headquarters Operations Center, he took copies of Shalikashvili's procedures for handling Alert, Nuclear Release, and Exercise Test messages back to the Seventh Army Operations Center for study.

"Repeatedly cited for the brilliance of his briefings and presentations to audiences ranging from lower ranking enlisted personnel, to the highest ranking military officers of all services," Shalikashvili was sent to England to present air defense briefings to all members of the Third US Air Force. The command also chose him as its representative to a Fort Bliss Air Defense School conference at which future curricula on air defense doctrine was being set.

Shalikashvili was getting noticed.

Because of his skills in all these areas—understanding complexity, setting standards, and communicating clearly—Shalikashvili could lead diverse people and groups through a range of complex, logistical endeavors. That's what the US Army wanted, and that's why he was steadily promoted upward.

There was a second reason Shalikashvili proved so effective in moving the VII Corps to the Persian Gulf: his acumen as a diplomat.

Part of it was plenty of international postings. And he was also a natural-born diplomat. But what made Shalikashvili particularly stand out was something that was hard to replicate: his mystique.

Surprisingly, it started out as a defense mechanism.

As a first lieutenant at Fort Bliss, he often whiled away off hours playing cards with friends. They'd have a few drinks, and sometimes the teasing would start. They'd call him the "Russian prince," poke fun about his dad's service in the German military. One even pulled out an old German war helmet and marched about the house.

Peter Poessinger, a fellow German immigrant who'd served as Shalikashvili's X.O. at the 32nd AADCOM, could sympathize: "I myself have never been discriminated against, though I've been made fun of. That's how I learned to have a sense of humor. It helped grow the necessary callouses."

Shalikashvili too used humor to head off barbs about his heritage. In Alaska, he participated in war games that pitted his unit, "the foreign aggressors," against troops from Washington state's Fort Lewis, who were serving as the US defenders. Dressed as a foreign military officer, he'd play the part to the hilt, shouting out commands either in accented English or some foreign language. Then there was Fort Wainwright's rededication ceremony. As the troops stood in formation reciting army songs to impress the visiting secretary of the army, Shalikashvili stood in the rear belting out the words in German, inducing guffaws from fellow officers.

At his next posting in Texas, however, a revelation awaited. "His slight accent," one commander soon noted, "proves to be an asset rather than a distracting characteristic." He drew praise for providing the much-needed service of translating instructional scripts into German and for conducting "very effectual" classes for the many air defense students who came from Germany. He was once designated as the escort officer for visiting German Defense Ministry dignitaries, and was repeatedly asked to interpret for the Fort Bliss commanding general during briefings with a variety of European visitors. He was soon promoted to chief of the entire VIP briefing section, where in one day alone he briefed the chief of staff of the Israeli army, two high-ranking generals from the Republic of China, and the head of air defense for the Pakistani army.

His European background, John Shalikashvili had come to learn, was no liability to overcome. It was a resource to be exploited.

His physical presence also lent to his mystique. But it was more than just his ramrod posture and overall military bearing. Tom Jaco, who retired as a three star, first met Shalikashvili in the late 1970s, when both were majors. "During the seminar meetings at the Naval War College, it was the way he entered the room, the way he held his head. He had very precise movements, a very precise way of speaking—it caught your eye. It commanded your attention." "It was as if," Jaco awed, "Shali had a professional military gene in him as a major."

But it was more than professionalism. "Shali had *savoir faire*," explained Lieutenant Colonel Brian Haig, who'd serve as Shalikashvili's speechwriter in the 1990s. "He had an unusual accent. People would often say 'clearly he has royal blood.'" He had a distinct walk—it was either princely or arrogant, depending on the viewer. Family friend Kyra Cheremeteff took note of his comfortable, even graceful stride: "He moved in a way that was disarming. I suspect it was cultivated." Chaplain Joe Miller stated it more directly: "Shali could strut!" Upon first meeting Shalikashvili, Lieutenant Colonel Dave Mehar thought: "Who is this little Napoleon, with his ramrod bearing, barrel chest, and funny accent, the one who walked with such an air about him? I took to thinking of him as '*il Papa*.'"—the Pope.

"Shali could be kind of imperious sometimes," agreed Colonel Tom Ross, operations officer when Shalikashvili was battalion commander in the mid-1970s. Once, after their division finished a multi-week exercise at the Yakima training center, a formal ceremony was held to mark the occasion. Shalikashvili, who was being recognized for his battalion's exceptional performance, stood at attention on the parade grounds, field coat hanging dramatically over his shoulders. "It was draped on him like a German greatcoat from World War II," recalled Ross. "And when his name was called, I asked him, 'Sir, how do we respond?' Shali replied, 'Let's salute!'"

"And then when he talked, he really got your interest," Tom Jaco continued. "In part it was because of the mystique he gave off as a World War II immigrant. In so many instances John had been there, done that, as a child." Yet Shalikashvili would never speak of his background in a group setting: "John was tightlipped like World War II heroes. All these young military guys were in awe. He became some kind of myth."

A myth often has a mythmaker.

Take his reputation as a polyglot. "The guy spoke six or eight languages" recalled Roger Casinger, DIVARTY command sergeant major when Shalikashvili was a deputy division commander in Germany, adding, "NATO brought in the people for Reforger exercises, and Shali would speak to them in their own languages. I think Shali even spoke to the Iraqi generals during Provide Comfort in their own language!" CW3 Jack Hurley, who worked for Shalikashvili in the early 1990s, hyped: "Shali not only spoke many languages, he could pick up new ones no problem—like while in the Ukraine, Germany, France, Saint Petersburg."

True, over the years he'd been exposed to many languages—English, Russian, German, and Polish. He'd also picked up at least some words in Vietnamese and, because he'd mistakenly thought it would help his tour in Vietnam, a bit of French.

But exposure doesn't equal mastery. When asked as a freshly minted second lieutenant how many languages he spoke, he answered: "Fluently? None." Of the three languages he'd ever used with any degree of comfort, his English was not perfect, he'd lived in Germany for only thirteen years and had been educated in German only to the high school level, and the Polish he absorbed as a child would be all but forgotten.

But there was, of course, no reason to dispel such favorable impressions. Once asked why he used a translator when dialoguing with German counterparts, he replied, "because I hear them twice."

For Shalikashvili, then, evincing the air of a European military aristocrat more than came naturally. It was cultivated, for it created a favorable impression.

"Look like the person you want to be," he'd encouraged Donna back in Peoria, "because, even if you are not, it is a way to survive and live to fight another day." But now his motto seemed to have evolved into something akin to "look like the person you want to be, because creating a good impression can help enhance your progress."

This worldly mystique was one critical reason why John Shalikashvili was doing well in his current position in Heidelberg. "U.S. Army Europe needed John Shalikashvili," judged Galvin, who'd both okayed Sha-likashvili for USAREUR deputy commander and then handpicked him for this unprecedented humanitarian mission to rescue the Kurds.

"Shalikashvili was lucky to have that name. Things would have been quite different if his name was 'Jones' or 'Smith.' It was because of his accent, because he was a brother, because he was a European dealing with the Europeans that he was readily embraced." "'Shalikashvili? He's great! He's like us!" Then, after a pause, the EUCOM commander added: "There was a lot of 'he's like us' in Shalikashvili's success."

David Fischer, the US consul general in Bavaria, witnessed Shalikash-vili's mystique at the level of local politics. Fischer was facing a rising tide of resentment against the US military presence in Germany. People were fed up with tanks plowing through their fields and jet airplanes making mock strafing runs during fall maneuvers. The Bavarian parliament was even threatening to pass legislation restricting US training.

When Fischer mentioned the problem to Shalikashvili, the general replied: "Set up a meeting, give me 24 hours' notice, and I'll come down to Munich."

"Now the Bavarian parliament," Fischer recalled, "must be the only one in the world with a fully functional *beerkeller* in the basement. True to his word, Shali showed up, only to face over 100 angry legislators—over several mugs of Bavaria's best." "I don't know which was more impressive, Shali's tour de force in laying out U.S. strategy in the wake of the fall of the Berlin Wall, his incredible knowledge of detail, or the fact that he managed all this in flawless, fluent German."

Shalikashvili, who'd come with only one or two aides, next dealt with practical, local issues. He responded one by one to legislators who talked about a farmer's road that was torn up, or constituents who were concerned about pollution from barracks. "It was as close to a Chicago ward heeler's meeting as I could imagine," noted Fischer. Deals were struck; compromises made. Two weeks later the Bavarian senate passed a resolution praising the US Army and requesting that their presence not be reduced locally despite the US military's Europe-wide cutbacks.

And Shalikashvili was also adept at high politics.

Consider the nail-bitingly complex and diplomatically sensitive mis-sion of Operation Steel Box. The Germans were in a state of high anxiety about this mission, undertaken in the summer of 1990, to withdraw all US chemical weapons from Europe. The operation included moving over one hundred thousand old and deteriorating nerve agent artillery shells, including sarin and VX, from storage at a US depot in western Germany to Johnston Atoll in the Pacific.

Operation Steel Box would require massive coordination and no small dose of diplomacy. US and German military personnel would need to work closely with both civilian contractors and the German police. Together they'd have to shepherd truck and train convoys carrying the dangerous cargo via Germany's public transportation system to US military ships waiting in Nordenham harbor. The great fear was either an accident or terrorist attack, the consequences of which could be catastrophic.

Compounding the mission's complexity was that two sets of trains would be routed—one containing the actual matériel and, to confuse any erstwhile terrorists, a decoy. Such a contingency required double, almost triple, the amount of personnel, equipment, transportation, and security resources and systems. The operation would ultimately involve a whopping twenty-three thousand USAREUR personnel.

Shortly before operational launch, the German transportation minister came to USAREUR headquarters to meet with Saint and Shalikashvili. After coffee and pleasantries, they got down to business.

The minister, speaking in English, expressed deep concern about the mission. "If something goes wrong," he warned gravely, "the entire government will fall."

That's when, with no prior agreement, the two American generals continued the conversation in German. Saint and Shalikashvili assured the minister that every possible detail, every possible contingency, had been thought through.

"It was like a scene from *The Godfather*," exclaimed Colonel Tom Molino, Saint's X.O. and notetaker at the meeting. "The minister suddenly and quite visibly relaxed. It was like when the godfather comes back from the restroom—but without a pistol. That's when the wave of realization hits—you aren't going to be shot after all!"

Under Shalikashvili's supervision, the chemical munitions were safely moved out between June 26 and September 22. Completed ahead of schedule, the operation offered important lessons that would later be applied to the VII Corps deployment to the Persian Gulf.

The power of Shalikashvili's unique skill set was perhaps best articulated by Major General J. B. Taylor, Shalikashvili's deputy at the 9th Infantry Division in the late 1980s: "Shali stands out and is different. People look at him and not only expect different things—but get different things."

**

Down on the tarmac in Diyarbakir, Turkey, Colonel Ronsick, who'd finally spotted the new commander's plane approaching the airstrip, was about to experience this for himself.

Earlier, upon hearing that Jamerson was being replaced as commander, the colonel's first thought had been "oh here we go." The last thing we need now is someone coming in from some desk somewhere in Germany. How could a new guy quickly get an accurate enough handle on this incredibly complex and fast-changing situation? Real lives were at stake here—hundreds of thousands of them.

Ronsick firmly believed the mission's success depended on the correct management of relations with Turkey—the only practical base for Operation Provide Comfort. The Kurdish refugees were massed on that country's southeastern border, and the immense logistical burden of quickly moving massive amounts of manpower and supplies required ports, airfields, and roads close to the crisis. That network existed only in Turkey.

What's more, during the Gulf War Ankara had allowed the international coalition to run Operation Proven Force from Incirlik Air Base, launching offensive air attacks against targets in northern Iraq. The US military thus already had both an existing headquarters in Turkey and working relationships in place with Turkish authorities. Given the massive challenge of rescuing the Kurds, there was no time to create a fresh history with anyone else.

And if Turkey was critical to the operation, then the super governor—Hayri Kozakcoglu—was the key to eastern Turkey, the region where the bulk of the humanitarian effort was based. Headquartered in Diyarbakir, the super governor ruled with an iron hand. "He was God," recalled Colonel Ken Getty, Sub-Task Force Express Care's operations officer. On April 5 Kozakcoglu had been the one who announced Turkey would support the Kurdish relief effort. He'd been the one to publicly invite the UN and private relief agencies to assist.

Ronsick was stationed in Diyarbakir because he was Provide Comfort's liaison to the super governor. He found the man to be a no-nonsense politician, a big ego, a prickly S.O.B. who operated on a "I tell you what to do, you don't tell me" basis. Dealing with him required finesse and no small dose of humility and patience.

That's partly why Ronsick believed the original commander, Jim Jamerson, was so critical. As commander of Proven Force and then JTF Provide Comfort, the air force two star had proven adept at dealing with the Turks. Gregarious and highly professional, Jamerson was also well liked by his team.

This new commander with the funny name, however, was a question mark. Would the three-star army general be perceptive enough to grasp the sensitivities of the situation and skilled enough to act accordingly?

Ronsick's gaze followed Shalikashvili's plane as it touched down on the tarmac, reduced speed, and eventually came to a halt. The colonel's first meeting with the new boss would be brief. The general was here to transfer to an MH-53J Pave Low helicopter that would shuttle him eastward toward Silopi and then onward to inspect one of the mountain camps.

Shalikashvili stepped off the C-130, followed by a small entourage. Ronsick strode over to greet his new commander. First came the obligatory salutes, and then introductions were made.

And then, in an instant, it happened.

The three-star general connected. He put his arm around the colonel's shoulders. "You are my guy," Shalikashvili said in a gravelly voice. "I need you to keep me informed both on the super governor and anything else important in Diyarbakir," he said, offering the only guidance Ronsick would get from Shalikashvili during the entire operation.

Though the general's schedule today was packed with critical inspections and high-pressure meetings, his voice was calm, his sentences unrushed. "Everything here is going to go through *you*," the general stressed. "Call me or my aide 24/7 if you need anything." Then, after asking him to set up a meeting with the super governor on the 22nd, the new commander took his leave.

Ronsick remained standing on the airstrip for a moment, nonplussed. "This is *not* your usual visiting fireman," he realized. "Right away I felt like a key part of his staff." Despite the very brief interaction, "I felt trusted. And right away I knew I could trust him in return." The new commander wasn't charismatic in the common sense of the word, yet something about his body language, about the way he communicated— or maybe just something intangible—had immediately made Ronsick feel the general was straightforward and honest, a commander who would support his liaison in Diyarbakir 100 percent. "I also somehow knew," he mused, "that I'd hurt his feelings if I myself did anything untoward."

This new commander, Ronsick almost sighed in relief that day, would surely handle both the super governor and this new combined task force expertly.

14

Huddled Masses

Isikveren was an overwhelming sight. The vast mountain camp was a jumble of tents, blankets, tarps, and other makeshift shelters of mismatched sizes, colors, and patterns. The refugees themselves wore a muddle of clashing clothing—layers of shirts, jackets, shawls, pants, and head coverings hastily grabbed before fleeing or since provided by aid workers. It was a visual farrago only intensified by the dreary browns, grays, and white of the mountain backdrop.

The camp was also noisy. Over eighty thousand refugees cooked and ate in the open, talked in the open, and—hungry, sick, stressed, and often bored from long stretches of inactivity and waiting—often argued in the open. Who could block out the incessant wail of a colicky baby? Or the shrieks of a Kurd whose loved one had succumbed to some disease or grave injury? Squabbles were particularly common in camps that, like Isikveren, were composed of multiple tribal groups. In the opening days of the crisis, the Turkish soldiers used loudspeakers and warning shots to keep the Kurds from crossing the border. The refugees sometimes threw rocks. The soldiers responded with beatings and even bullets.

Yet it was the smells that were hardest to bear. Cookfires spat acrid smoke and grease into the air, blanketing the mountainside in pungent food odors. Urine and feces covered the ground, as did assorted garbage—bones, trash, animal hides, scraps of paper. There was the stench of unwashed bodies, of clothes rank with dried sweat, and even of death and dying—gangrene and even human corpses were not a rarity here.

The walkways further added to the chaos, twisting and turning around whatever patch of ground newly arrived refugees claimed for their own. John Shalikashvili was navigating these paths today, taking in his first glimpse of what he'd later describe as "the squalor" and "absolutely harsh and grim conditions that these people were trying to survive in."

Briefed on this rescue operation multiple times over the past forty-

169

eight hours, the commander well understood how these deplorable conditions arose.

* * *

Three weeks earlier Isikveren had been a barren mountainside. But then the floodgates opened, with four or five thousand refugees on average arriving every day. By the time the influx subsided into a trickle, Isikveren teemed with a population double the threshold of an urban area in the United States.

The refugees arrived cold, hungry, bone weary. They'd walked for days, or in some cases a week or more. Media footage captured exhausted Kurds losing their footing and tumbling down the steep slopes into the camp. Many were sick or injured, with gangrenous extremities often wrapped in dirty makeshift bandages.

Yet Isikveren offered no real sanctuary. To call this or any of the other concentrations of humanity "camps" was to suggest a level of organization and supply that simply didn't exist.

Initially the only available foodstuffs were what Turks from low-lying villages hauled up to camp. Then came the hum of engines. One aid worker described what he saw at one camp. First the refugees fell uncharacteristically silent, and then, fearing Hussein's air force, began rushing for cover. A C-130 arrived, circled the camp, and then threw a toilet paper roll down to test wind direction. Soon after, billowing parachutes punctuated the skies, delivering the first pallets of humanitarian aid.

Desperate for food, the Kurds would surge forward. They'd sometimes be maimed or even crushed to death by the descending gifts, which could weigh upward of a ton. Once broken open, the relief supplies were often unevenly distributed. "The strongest were getting supplies while the weakest suffered," noted Deputy CTF Commander Jamerson. Because the Kurds prioritized maintaining a force of warriors, the first to partake were men, teenage boys, and women of childbearing age. The old and very young—those least equipped to deal with the harsh conditions—ate what was left over, if anything.

Water was a huge challenge. With no sanitation facilities, mountain streams and runoff water soon became contaminated by trash and human waste or from refugees striving to remove filth from body and clothes. One tanker truck that reached camp was surrounded, its spigot opened, and—as thirsty refugees pushed and pulled at each other—its liquid cargo gushed onto the ground.

Obtaining potable water in Isikveren thus required hiking as much as two hours back up the mountain to scrape away at packed snow. This task fell mostly to the women, who then trudged back down to camp, heavy trays or buckets of shaved ice balanced on their heads. With no cooking fuel available, snow could only be heated by firewood, a resource the tens of thousands of Kurds were stripping from the land. Frustratingly, chewing ice or drinking melted snow often made the elderly sick and infants colicky.

Malnourished and dehydrated, the refugees struggled to withstand the elements. "Even in early April, the weather was still extraordinarily severe," Shalikashvili would later recall. Nighttime temperatures could plunge, sometimes bringing freezing rain or even snow, further straining constitutions.

Little wonder the camps became incubators for afflictions—typhoid, gastroenteritis, diarrhea, dehydration, and pneumonia. With no existing medical care, the Kurds, as Doctors Without Borders warned, were facing a "medical apocalypse."

Under these primitive conditions the refugees began dying en masse. A shocking preliminary guestimate by the UN held that two thousand Kurds were dying each day. As the first responders gathered better data, however, that estimate would be cut in half. One thing, though, was absolutely clear: unless massive action was taken, the death rate could soon double or even triple. "What we are facing now is one of the greatest challenges ever in the history of refugee relief," proclaimed the president of Refugees International.

Spearheading the effort inside the camps to "stop the dying" were the uniformed soldiers of Sub-Task Force Express Care, now redesignated Joint Task Force-Alpha (JTF-A). Most were from the US Army's 10th Special Forces Group and the US Air Force's 39th Special Operations Wing, soon supplemented by troops from Britain and Luxembourg. There was also the Civil Affairs Command, staffed by reservists trained to work with local populations, which dealt most closely with the Kurds while also serving as the task force's chief liaison with the final major group in the camps: NGO and PVO aid workers.

Together these rescuers had already made a huge difference. Serving as a buffer between the refugees and the Turkish soldiers, the special forces dramatically reduced tensions, which allowed the rescue workers to organize the camps. Key was enlisting clan elders, the only credible authority figures among the refugees. With their help, the rescuers could, clan by clan, organize the manpower and enforce the civil norms needed to improve camp conditions. It wasn't just manual labor, either. Some Kurds were doctors and nurses; lawyers and teachers who spoke English, French, or German; and engineers, including one sorely needed hydrologist.

* * *

As Shalikashvili inspected the camp, JTF-A's progress was evident. Food, blankets, tents, fuel, and other supplies were now being offloaded and distributed in a more orderly and fair manner. Trash and human waste were being collected and burned, and latrines, wells, and in some cases even water pipelines were being built. The dead were now routinely gathered up and, using shovels and quicklime, buried each day on the camp outskirts. Hospital tents were being raised, the sick encouraged to wait patiently in line. There was even a word-of-mouth network to spread information, such as the news that the task force would provide hygiene and other survival courses. These efforts were critical: some three-quarters of the deaths were associated with diarrhea, nausea, and vomiting.

There was more good news. After almost two weeks of humanitarian relief, the dying had already dropped noticeably. And by April 20, the JTF-A operations officer, Colonel Ken Getty, would peg the overall death rate at only four hundred people per day. On April 26 Shalikashvili would return to Isikveren with a visiting Jack Galvin. While the two generals surveyed the camp from a hillock, a Kurdish doctor would offer welcome news: Isikveren had only three deaths. "It's the best day we've had since we got here."

But no matter how quickly the riggers loaded the planes or how many sorties the pilots flew, their efforts were not enough.

C-130 airdrops, Shalikashvili later explained, were "the most inefficient way to undertake such an operation." "If anything can go wrong on a parachute drop," Getty added, "it will." Marginal weather conditions—like low clouds, thunderstorms, snow flurries—would hamper delivery efforts, and severe conditions could turn planes back before supplies were dropped. And the parachutes, designed to drop ammo, were too small to be optimal here. "They hit like a ton of bricks," explained Jamerson. Pallets of bottled water would slam against the ground, often causing the bottles to burst. At first there were no established drop zones. Airdrops could also widely miss their mark, landing instead on the far side of a valley, a day or two's scramble away. Refugees were sometimes faced with the Cornelian dilemma of pallets that dropped into a minefield. Civil Affairs commander Brigadier General Donald Campbell would later estimate that one-third of airdropped supplies were wasted for all these reasons.

There was another supply problem. Every week tons of donated goods were being flown into airbases at Incirlik and Diyarbakir or sent by ship to Iskenderun and Mersin, Turkey's closest major ports. They'd often arrive with cargo holds stuffed willy-nilly with donations that sometimes weren't even loaded onto pallets. In the rush to push supplies to the mountain camps, the task force was often passing supplies forward regardless of the needs of the particular drop point.

The Kurds were also refusing to eat some of the donated food-stuffs. Macaroni was considered beggar's food; corn, fit only for animals. Canned foods, like sauerkraut or cranberry sauce, were completely alien. The Kurds wanted their staples: rice, flour, cooking oil, and beans—things Turkey had available in adequate quantities.

Provide Comfort was thus now organizing a better system. Two days earlier the task force had begun building a forward logistical base in Silopi, near Turkey's southeastern border. Soon, supplies from Turkey's main entry points would be sent there, inventoried, and then selectively trans-loaded to helicopters according to the needs of each camp.

Engineers would also clear mountain roads. By moving from air-lifts to bulk truck transport, the rescuers could shift from the less-than-appropriate donated foods as well as expensive MREs—the military's Meals-Ready-to-Eat—to more nutritious bulk fresh food. Improved roads would also greatly facilitate water delivery, including via the fifty Trinkwasser water trucks donated by West Germany and the construction of permanent steel storage tanks.

When operational, this new system—moving from aircraft to trucks, from push to pull—would enable relief workers to move larger amounts of supplies more quickly, cheaply, and effectively. On April 23 an operation high of 969 tons would be airlifted into the mountains; on the 24th, trucks would begin making direct deliveries.

Maintaining these mountain camps, however, was not the ultimate solution.

For one, there was no way to guarantee the sickness and death in the camps could be contained. Typhoid was already too common, and though measles had not yet appeared, the Center for Disease Control was warning of a possible epidemic. UNICEF and the Red Cross were working on a measles immunization program to help protect the camps. The threat of cholera—an infectious disease that causes a loss of fluid in the

Provide Comfort Theater of Operations

small intestine and can be fatal within twenty-four hours—loomed particularly large.

As Shalikashvili would later recall, throughout the entire operation he never stopped worrying "that a second Lebanon would occur"—that the CTF forces would be attacked. There were both weapons and agitators in the camps. One armed group was the Peshmerga: "At first we were not sure what to expect from the Kurdish fighters . . . they were variously reported to us as [numbering] around thirty thousand [men], loosely organized as a military organization." And "certainly the DEF-SOL, a Turkish terrorist organization, was a threat to us not only along Iraqi-Turkish border but even as far back as Incirlik." There were also Iraqi and Palestinian terrorists and disgruntled Kurds. The PKK, a Kurdish terror organization, was the prime threat along the border area, he'd add.

There was another concern. Thankfully none of Saddam's troops had yet been spotted in the mountains. But what if the hundreds of thousands of refugees, some of whom were armed, caught wind—accurately or not—that Iraqi troops were advancing? Or what if, simply out of frustration over the interminable waiting, the Kurds finally decided to make a rush into Turkey?

It would be impossible to stop. Here in Isikveren, they'd push past rescue workers, break through the barbed wire, and overwhelm the thin green line of Turkish guards, many of whom were young, inexperienced conscripts. There'd be deaths of refugees, Turkish soldiers, CTF forces, and international relief workers. The repercussions—for the rescue operation, for regional stability, for the Kurdish refugees themselves, and for Shalikashvili—would be disastrous.

Finally, there were cost factors. This mission was already proving exorbitant in terms of money, manpower, and equipment. In fact, the ultimate bill to the US Department of Defense alone would total $450 million. The international community could not, and would not, continue such goodwill indefinitely.

There was no other choice. The refugees—not just the over eighty thousand here in Isikveren but the other hundreds of thousands spread out along the border—had to be moved. That was what Bush had meant on April 17 when he called for a shift from "humanitarian assistance" to "humanitarian intervention."

Moving this mass of humanity, however, would be a herculean task. It would require the ability to put substantial boots on the ground plus the skills to organize multitudes of both people and supporting supplies—competencies that fell squarely in the army's wheelhouse. "As an airman," former JTF commander Jamerson later explained, "I was not a logistics king. The air force moves parts only."

That's why John Shalikashvili was here. The army three star—who'd just months earlier handled the daunting logistical nightmares of Operation Steel Box and the VII Corps deployment to the Gulf—was the logistics king Provide Comfort needed.

As Shalikashvili walked about Isikveren, it was painfully clear that moving these refugees was the humane thing to do. Most were not warriors. They were farmers, shopkeepers, doctors, and other middle-class professionals. Accustomed to life in small cities and large towns, they were withering under these cruel conditions.

The youngest were suffering most. The first special forces to enter the camps had been met with a grisly sight: strewn on trash piles were the corpses of infants. And because the Kurds preferred sons, these were most often the bodies of girls. Ominously, 70 percent of women of childbearing age were pregnant. Of the four hundred deaths that Ken Getty would estimate took place on April 20, three hundred were children. "And most," he added grimly, "were females."

Later analysis would confirm how terribly the children suffered. The

Commander Shalikashvili on the ground visiting Isikveren, one of the forty-three separate newly formed Kurdish refugee camps. Having fled Iraq after a failed uprising against Saddam Hussein, the Kurds were ill-equipped for the harsh mountain conditions. Initially, at least one thousand Kurds were dying per day, many of them children. (DoD photograph, courtesy of the NBR Gen. John Shalikashvili Archives.)

crude mortality rate for all ages would increase fifteen times during this crisis—from 0.6 to 8.9 per 1,000. Two thirds of these deaths would be children aged five years or younger, and one of every two deaths would be an infant shy of a first birthday. An estimated 12 percent of all infants— more than one out of every ten refugee babies—would perish in the first eight weeks of this crisis, mostly from diarrhea/dehydration and respiratory disease. Because 70–80 percent of the children suffered severe diarrhea, they often walked around camp naked from the waist down.

The plight of the young did not escape Shalikashvili's notice. He was known for caring about children. As a captain, "without missing a beat" he'd rush over to babysit a colleague's child when the babysitter bailed. No matter how senior he became, he'd often kneel down on the floor to play with young kids when attending informal social functions. As battalion commander, he'd "walk the floor" with his X.O.'s daughter when she was crying. Heading the 9th Infantry Division, the two star made anonymous donations to support at-risk children. "He'd have made a great high school principal," said one subordinate. When Shalikashvili ran the DIVARTY, the son of one of his battalion commanders broke a leg one weekend while the parents were away. "Shali took care of it—he took him to the hospital. He never even called us—he didn't want us to worry," recalled one subordinate. "He was like a mother hen."

But it wasn't just the refugee children who were suffering. You could hear it in the sobs of a Kurd who held a sick loved one in their arms or who stood heartbroken as a body was being taken away for burial. You could see it in the faces of too many Kurds who sat there in a stupor, blank eyes looking straight ahead, seemingly disconnected from everything around them.

To feel lost and alone. To watch helplessly as loved ones are torn from you. To have your sense of home demolished. Any observer watching Shalikashvili, three black stars adorning each collar tab of his army camouflage, might assume such weights had never touched him. But they had. And not just because he too had been a war refugee. There'd been other blows, ones dealt as he'd sought to construct a new life in America.

* * *

When you show up in the military, you are—perhaps for the very first time in your life—alone. Relatives, teachers, classmates, and friends are all left behind.

After donning the uniform, forming solid friendships can be challenging. Relationships tend to be fleeting because assignments are usually limited to one or two years, are busy while they do last, and any strong ties that form tend to trail off with new assignments. In the rise up the ladder, a defense mechanism also kicks in. You can't get too friendly because you might need to make a tough decision—to fire someone, pass them over for a key assignment, or send them off on a deadly mission. With increased responsibilities, your time also decreases, incentivizing you to guard your time, making some judge you distant or even impolite.

By the time you reach general officer, your isolation is almost complete. All new brigadier generals are sent to "B. G. Charm School," an orientation program at the Pentagon. There the message is delivered point blank: "You no longer have any friends. Be careful what you say or do. You are on parade every day." For most senior military officers, close friends are thus mostly made in childhood or through romantic relationships.

Shalikashvili had moved many times as a child—from Poland to Germany, and then to the United States. When entering the military, he had

First Lieutenant John Shalikashvili married Gunhild Bartsch, his first wife, on April 18, 1963. The subsequent two years would prove a formative period in his path to the chairmanship.

no particularly intimate friends, definitely none he regularly kept in touch with during his career rise.

In terms of a romantic partner, he'd entered the military as a bachelor. While serving with the Manchus, he'd been unable to convince Donna to come back to him, just as he'd failed to find another to dedicate his heart to. Yet Alaska itself—with its adventure, opportunity for leadership development, and strong sense of community—had helped fill the void.

But his next assignment as an instructor at Fort Bliss had paled in comparison. Somewhat disillusioned with military life, he looked into night classes at Texas Western College in preparation for a possible return to civilian life. But nothing excited him.

He ended up taking a course in Russian, which would strengthen his reputation as a polyglot. One classmate was Gunhild Bartsch. Like Donna, she was attractive. Like Donna, she was a blonde with Teutonic features. Gunhild was, in fact, an immigrant from East Germany. "You could feel the connection between John and Gunhild from across the room," recalled his sister, Alexandra, who was now going by the name Gale. Brother Joe agreed: "John was smitten. She was smitten. Yet I didn't think they should marry. She didn't come from an aristocratic background as we did."

But the two did wed. A year later she was pregnant. At twenty-eight years of age John Shalikashvili had finally done it: by starting his own nuclear family, he'd secured a firm sense of home and belonging.

However Gunhild soon developed stomach pains, pains that refused to go away. The doctor said it was just a nervous stomach. By the time they investigated further the cancer was late stage, and the tumors had spread to her liver.

There was nothing that could be done. Pushing back his upcoming tour in Vietnam, Shalikashvili secured compassionate reassignment to Germany. Gunhild would be closer to her family that way.

Christina-Maria Shalikashvili was born on May 20, 1965. She was two months premature. Her underdeveloped lungs sustained her for only three days of life.

Confined to the critical list at the army hospital, Gunhild deteriorated quickly. The doctor explained that they could increase her medication to help relieve her increasing pain, but she'd die more quickly, or they could let nature take its course. "What are they talking about?!" John vented to his sister. "Of course I want to ease her pain!" "He was extremely wrought," Gale recalled. "I have no idea how he managed to get through that." Gunhild followed their daughter in death ten weeks later.

All John Shalikashvili could do was return to his quarters, a home now in darkness despite the daylight streaming through the curtains Gunhild had made.

In large part because he rarely shared things of a personal nature, Shalikashvili would remain alone in his struggle to handle the pain. When the two brothers next met up months after Gunhild's death, their discussion wouldn't go beyond Joe offering: "Sorry to hear about Gunhild and the baby." Later, even those who came to know him best often had no idea he'd ever been married to Gunhild, let alone had lost her and their young baby so tragically.

Decades later, Shalikashvili would give a speech to the Tragedy Assistance Program for Survivors, a charity helping military families recover from the death or injury of a loved one. His remarks included these elliptic words:

> A long time ago, there was a young man whose wife died. That young man wrote home and said: "I know that tomorrow, and the next day, the sun will rise again. But for me I don't think it will shine as brightly. And I know I will laugh again, but I'm not sure there'll be as much joy in my laughter ever again."

His performance reviews from the time reveal how he responded to this, the darkest period of his career. "This officer's value can only be compared to precious jewels, rare paintings and poetry," one boss wrote. Despite being "constantly under a handicap that would cause many men to completely 'fall apart,'" "never once did this officer falter or seek special consideration or favors; he continued to march and perform in his usual outstanding manner." This included fulfilling three major jobs at once. "Normally one officer would be assigned for each task, but because of the officer drawdown Captain Shalikashvili was assigned all three."

When Gunhild was critically ill, Shalikashvili did a curious thing. He was tasked with a minor project—decorating the hallways of brigade headquarters. His boss noted how he approached this "seemingly insignificant" task with "ingenuity and attention to detail."

What Shalikashvili did was obtain photographs of air defense weapons, past and present. He hunted down unit histories, and ferreted out replicas of the various organizational insignias of all units ever assigned to the command. Gathering up all these tokens, some of which he had framed, Shalikashvili put them on permanent display.

It was a symbolic act—one that is perhaps best understood by examining, through the long lens of hindsight, the following major aspect of his reputation.

"Shali was one of those people who rose in ranks through the army based on the qualities the army is supposed to propagate: being both professional *and* caring," judged Lieutenant Colonel Brian Haig, a subordinate from Shalikashvili's final assignment.

Many officers focus on the former, especially during the critical, pressure-laden positions—like battalion, DIVARTY, and division command—that are bellwethers for one's career trajectory. Intent on proving their ability, many focus on resourcing, training, and preparing their unit for battle. In emphasizing *what* the unit needs to accomplish, they give less attention to *how* these benchmarks of performance are achieved.

Shalikashvili, however, did not see the two as trade-offs. As a two-star commander of the 9th Infantry Division in the late 1980s, he called Larry Saunders, his provost marshal, into the office one day. Saunders was getting battalion command—an officer's first real chance to lead and manage a significant amount of manpower and resources. "The army will give you a significant level of position and authority," the general advised. "It's up to you to decide what you will do with it. You will be successful if you help soldiers and their families and cut bureaucratic red tape to get the job done. Or you can stroke your ego and self-worth."

Shalikashvili showed his care for soldiers in small ways. Like when M. Shawn Malloy, realizing he was walking past the commander in the NCO mess hall one day, hastily threw up a salute that upset his food tray, dumping food and a good six glasses of milk all over Shalikashvili. People stood up and started clapping. "I thought I was in big trouble," Malloy recalled. But the commander just stood up, laughed, and said: "Soldier, it's o.k. You go back and get another tray."

And in bigger ways. Stewart Wright recalled one field exercise at rainy Fort Lewis. The call went out for a volunteer to "walk the rails"— to walk along the steel muzzle of their 155 mm howitzer to keep it continuously balanced as they moved it off the truck and set it in position. It was an unpopular duty, given the chance of slipping and falling into the muck. "I'll do it," boomed Shalikashvili's heavily accented voice. "This was the only time in my career that I'd seen an officer do it," Wright exclaimed, "and a battery commander at that! That kind of thing gets around the grapevine in a hurry—it tells a lot about a man."

And Shalikashvili was considerate even when people weren't looking. When he showed up to move into his quarters at USAREUR, Gay Van Brero, a housing intern, was inside scrambling. The previous three star had vacated late. Looking out the window, she noticed someone sitting on the curb. It was Shalikashvili. "Sir, why are you out here?" she asked. To her surprise he responded: "Because it looks like you all have your hands full. I'm trying to stay out of the way."

Shalikashvili also cared about how the military as an institution treated soldiers. When he held DIVARTY command in Germany in the late 1970s, the military was still recovering from the legacy of the Vietnam War. The overall quality of the troops was low. "Newly arrived soldiers were being overwhelmed by the demands of this overseas post," recalled Command Sergeant Major Roger Casinger. So Shalikashvili set up a two-week training program, with separate living quarters for new arrivals, providing time to handle normal check in and equipment gathering, which previously had been squeezed in during off hours. There was instruction in daily life skills, like checkbook balancing and how to drive safely given Germany's higher speed limits. There was also PT to ensure soldiers passed the requisite physical test. These steps benefited both the individual soldiers and the army as a whole.

"Then he would drop in," Casinger added. "He would go straight to the billet and start chatting with the new arrivals. 'No need to stand at attention,' he'd say. Then he'd pick out someone, like a private first class, and sit on his bed chatting for a good ten to fifteen minutes about stories from his own enlisted days. I was caught off guard that a busy general would spend so much time with the soldiers."

"Shali was very interested in helping the army adjust to changes," judged Brigadier General Rex Weaver, who oversaw the DIVARTY's nuclear facility at the time. Located at a remove from headquarters, the facility was thus difficult to manage. For one, the military police, which included females, were billeted alongside the troops in the facility's barracks. Yet there were no senior officers or NCOs to ensure their safety. "Shali understood the problem. He convinced the engineers to create a separate entrance, showers, and the like for women. This was at a time when the army wasn't ready for this problem, wasn't thinking about it."

When Shalikashvili commanded the 9th Infantry Division, one of his battalions was to be deployed for six months to the Sinai as part of a peacekeeping operation. Shalikashvili was concerned about the burden of deployment for both the soldiers and their families. Because service members move so often, they rarely have the diverse local networks that typically help civilians problem solve. He thus tasked the brigade commander and the deploying battalion command with creating a booklet, one "that would be a kind of bible to the company commanders, and then once they deployed, to the wives," Shalikashvili explained. It listed out what military families should do, the places to go, and the division and even base phone numbers to call if they had any problems. No such standard manual existed at the time. Recognizing such a booklet could help soldiers and their families army-wide, Shalikashvili requested that the army's deputy chief of staff for personnel turn their model into a generic manual.

Nowhere was Shalikashvili's concern for soldiers and their families more evident than in his role as a community commander, the de facto mayor for overseas military communities.

His first stint came as assistant commander of the 1st Armored Division in Germany in the early 1980s. As the community commander of Nuremberg, Shalikashvili oversaw four sub-communities and five major installations, totaling over twenty-seven thousand soldiers, family members, and civilians. "Because we generally live in our own communities," Shalikashvili explained, "we make sure [they] are wholesome, safe, and filled with opportunities for our service members and their families."

Major Allen Ohlstein, the division's provost marshal for the duration of Shalikashvili's command, was responsible for the community's security. This gave him opportunity to observe firsthand how the general dealt with challenging disciplinary issues. "Sometimes hard decisions have to be made in order to fulfill our oath of office," Shalikashvili impressed upon him, "but we should still do it with humanity."

For example, there was a major problem with drugs at Nuremberg High School. "Shali cleaned up the schools and made them safe," Ohlstein recalled. "Anyone caught dealing with drugs was sent home." He also lowered the DWI rate. Before Shalikashvili took over, the military police would wait outside the bars and arrest tipsy soldiers as soon as they put the key in the ignition. "Under Shali the MPs began helping out by ensuring drunk soldiers got safely home without putting themselves or others in danger."

"He had a unique ability to size people up," Ohlstein added. "If you were doing your best and being honest—honesty was a big thing for Shali—he would support you even if you'd somehow managed to get yourself into trouble." This mirrored the judgment of Warrant Officer Ed Ney: "If the kid was a good kid and the incident not that big, Shali and I would do what we could to not end his career."

Overall, "Shali could get impatient," admitted Ohlstein, "if he was getting a bureaucratic response to why something couldn't be done to help the soldiers," which happened particularly often on the issue of family housing. "Basically Shali tried to get all organizations looking for ways to say yes. If he couldn't bring about the desired change, he'd still report back to those he was trying to help and explain why he failed."

Shalikashvili's boss back at Nuremberg was none other than Butch Saint. A demanding leader not shy of offering forceful criticism, Saint labeled his 1st Armored Division deputy "the best community commander I have known"—"and that includes my own performance as commander of two different communities in USAREUR." "German-American relations could not be better, citizen spirit is sky-high, quality of life programs are copied by virtually every other community in USA-

REUR, and standards of discipline are of the highest order; all of that is due to his leadership—it did not exist at the time he came." Shalikashvili "has installed happiness as an ingredient in Nuremberg—a difficult and large community in Europe."

And now, over a decade later, Shalikashvili was once again serving as Saint's deputy at USAREUR. The community Shalikashvili now oversaw was Heidelberg.

"Serving as community commander was one of Shalikashvili's lesser commands—he had many responsibilities," Colonel Gerald Thompson, Shalikashvili's deputy community commander, later recalled. "But Shali was not some three-star that people only saw periodically. Shali *loved* community."

Heidelberg's needs were great, but the money was often lacking. "One problem is that a community commander has only limited influence over the entities he is responsible for—the schools, for instance, were funded by DoD," noted Major Ruth Collins, who served as X.O. to Saint's chief of staff. "It was also hard to effect change because the community was in a foreign land. Shali thus did two things. He sought to improve the community's ability to handle its own needs. And he also fought for increased resources."

He'd achieve both goals through one campaign: the Army Communities of Excellence program. Each year the army gave out six awards—of a whopping $1 million each—to the best small, medium, and large communities both overseas and stateside.

Shortly after arriving Shalikashvili announced his intention to win the award for their class. "It's a program designed to capitalize on pride," he explained to Heidelberg. "Pride in the service that the communities provide to the soldiers and family members, and pride that we feel in the appearance of the facilities in which we live, work, and play." But then came his critical message: "It's not so much the money we put into a building, as it is the effort we put into providing service with a smile."

The first step was engagement. At the time there were few institutionalized mechanisms for exchanging information between community leaders and the community itself. "Rumors could easily spread," explained Collins.

So they set up a 24/7 hotline for the community to offer ideas on how to improve Heidelberg's services, facilities, and procedures, with the best suggestions being recognized by a significant monetary award. To further increase two-way communication, they held town hall meetings to bring together soldiers, their families, the community staff, and the heads of the various services. They also set up a volunteer mayor and a family support center in each housing area to provide leadership and assistance for families.

They also created support groups. "At that time the military didn't take care of families well," recalled Mehar, "so under Shalikashvili's leadership we began trying ideas out." "We all but invented family support groups," holding meetings every week or two. "We'd even do such things as bring family cars in for tune-ups. Perhaps we overdid it in the beginning, doing too much rather than teaching how to do it."

The next two years were a full-court press. They started a Drug Abuse Resistance Education (DARE) program in schools, instituted a quality of life survey, established the Community Family Force Forum, and created the "Working Friendly" campaign to recognize people for enthusiastic and hospitable service to the community. To increase volunteerism, there was the Adopt-a-Facility campaign. They set up a Self-Help U-Fix-It facility, a summer hire program run by the students themselves, mechanisms to allow service members to share annual leave with ill fellow workers, and the Families Learn About Germany (FLAG) program.

These programs proved invaluable—particularly when the VII Corps was unexpectedly sent to the Persian Gulf for Desert Storm. "When a soldier deploys from the States," Shalikashvili explained, "if his family did not feel very comfortable, they could get on a plane or in a car and go home to mother." But military families couldn't do that from Europe. "And the last thing you wanted was young families trying to leave and go back to the States, [to] god knows where." It's a financial strain as well, because the family foots the bill for both transportation costs and living expenses. Thus the multiple community support efforts that Shalikashvili, Thompson, and his team created in Heidelberg helped reduce the burden on military families. And that, Shalikashvili explained, in turn helps "the fighting men and women of the Armed Forces to focus on their job wherever and whenever duty called without worrying about the welfare of their loved ones."

This message—that big improvements in the quality of life of soldiers and their families can be achieved if people were willing to go the extra mile—was summed up in one of Shalikashvili's favorite phrases: "It only takes a nickel more to go first class."

And by investing that nickel, Shalikashvili knew, a huge rate of return could be won. That's because he'd done it before. Back when he oversaw Nuremberg, he'd successfully led the community to win a similar army-wide community competition—and used the substantial award money to build a new commissary and PX.

And now here in Heidelberg Shalikashvili would pull it off once again. In 1991 they'd be awarded the Community Excellence Prize for best large overseas community. And the $1 million in award money? Heidelberg spent it improving childcare and youth services.

Why did Shalikashvili exhibit such care for both people and community?

When later asked that question, Ohlstein immediately recalled Shalikashvili's arrival in Nuremberg. The new boss called the senior NCOs and commissioned officers together. The meeting began with an inspirational film and ended with a talk from the general. One sentence floored the major: "If you don't love soldiers," Shalikashvili challenged, "then you have no business being a leader."

Ohlstein was shocked because he'd never heard a senior officer use the word "love" before. Looking back from the vantage point of retirement, he judged that Shalikashvili's articulation of the need to love soldiers hadn't been "general speak." Rather, "it was a man conveying his convictions to us."

Why did Shalikashvili hold such convictions? "Was it possible," mused Ohlstein, "that Shali's lack of community as a lad—or perhaps better said, his fragile community—created a void in his life?"

Ohlstein hadn't known about the loss of Shalikashvili's first wife and newborn daughter. Was it possible, then, that these two voids—the lack of stable community given his wartime upbringing and the tragic loss of his young family—explained why love of soldiers and their families became so central to him?

It might, particularly if viewed in the light of that curious thing Shalikashvili did—zealously throwing himself into the simple task of decorating brigade headquarters—when his pregnant wife was dying.

Perhaps it had been an effort guided by memories from his childhood in Europe. The hallways of the New Schloss had been lined with the portraits of the Pappenheim ancestors, as had the walls of the schloss's beautiful twin spiral staircases. As a child, he'd walked by them many times. Maybe he'd stared up at them purposefully. Or perhaps they'd meant nothing in particular, yet some part of his young brain had internalized their significance.

Tasked to decorate brigade headquarters, Shalikashvili, a man struggling with the crippling specter of the loss of his new family, had similarly filled the walls with photographs of air defense weapons, past and present, with unit histories, and with replicas of the organizational insignias of all of the units ever assigned to the command. The display was perhaps a way of capturing the continuity and strength of the US Army. Perhaps it also meant that he now viewed the military as a family—something John Shalikashvili could devote himself to without fear that it would ever abandon him.

His boss's review at the time supports this: "He is the upper limit of the professional soldier; completely dedicated to the military service and the purpose for which it exists and magnanimously equipped and eternally willing to perform any task or duty, at any time any place. . . . I would fight to have this officer in any capacity and if the situation ever was presented, I would gladly work for him."

After the death of Gunhild and Christina, moreover, there'd be no more reports of colleagues noticing him privately showing arrogance, boasting about his career goals, or harshly criticizing things he disliked or found wanting.

Interestingly, in letters home from Alaska he never mentioned his mentor Sergeant Grice by name, let alone the lessons he was imparting. But after the death of his young family, as he threw himself totally into serving the military family, that's when Shalikashvili began to talk openly about what he'd learned from Grice. And later, when imminent retirement was motivating him to articulate the insights about leadership he wanted to pass on, that's when he would crystalize the lessons from Grice into what he termed the Three Pillars of Leadership.

Two of the pillars—*professional competence* and *character*—came directly from Grice's teaching. The third pillar, though, took to a higher level one of Grice's main lessons: "Those you lead will want to know that you sincerely care about them and will sacrifice for them, that you simply enjoy being with them." For Shalikashvili it meant more: "Words—even actions—weren't enough. If you don't feel it in your heart, if you don't love your soldiers in your heart, they will know it."

John Shalikashvili's third pillar of leadership, then, was *love of soldiers*.

It's probably no coincidence that when choosing a second wife Shalikashvili found someone who would share his commitment to service members and their families.

He met Joan Zimpelman in an officers' club in Germany in the mid-1960s, not long after Gunhild and Christina had passed. Joan was a schoolteacher from Oregon on vacation.

"Joannie has Pacific Northwest sensibilities," judged Dr. Steve Livingston, a former officer who knew her well. "She's straight talking, independent, believes in fairness and not getting too big for your britches."

In November 1966, fifteen months after Gunhild's passing, Shalikashvili proposed. The next month they were married in Kaiserslautern, Germany. Since brother Joe was unable to attend, Shalikashvili asked Richard Graham, a colleague who did not feel particularly close to the groom, to serve as best man.

As there were no curtains for the soldiers' barracks, Shalikashvili got hold of some passable yellow cloth and his bride made curtains for the troops. It was the first step on the couple's long road of supporting service members and their families.

In Nuremberg, "Shali wouldn't have been successful without her," judged Ohlstein. She'd do small things—like prepare snacks for the provost marshal's Saturday meeting with the boss. She'd do big things—like being there when Ohlstein's wife was giving birth. She'd regularly accompany her husband to check in with sub-community groups, families, hospitals. "What can we do to help?" they'd ask.

Shalikashvili's wife would also make rounds on her own. "If I heard something was going wrong, like with housing or problems facing young wives," Joan later recalled, "I'd go tell him. And I knew he would listen, and that he had the authority to fix things."

"She's the finest example of what it takes to be a commanding general's wife," recalled Colonel Bob Jones, who worked for Shalikashvili at the 9th Infantry Division in the late 1980s. "She leads all the volunteers *by example*. Under her the Wives Club is not a social club but rather a volunteer support group for the troops."

"The army talks of a 'command team,' half of which gets paid," noted Heidelberg's Thompson. "Well, Joan was a good companion. She had the same love for soldiers and knew how to make the system work." After attending community meetings, she'd say, "John, we really should do such and such." "She was a difference maker, a big player in family issues and taking care of soldiers."

The Shalikashvilis departed Heidelberg in August 1991. Right before leaving Thompson said to Joan: "Your husband really cares about people." Her reply? "I told you that." "But you might have just been saying that," countered the colonel. "But I wasn't," she shot back.

* * *

The commander of Operation Provide Comfort stood drinking in his last glimpse of Isikveren. The only way to end this refugee crisis was to move them. But before Shalikashvili could concentrate on the intense logistical preparations necessary to make that move a reality, one critical task awaited.

He turned to make his way to the Black Hawk standing by to whisk him over the mountains. Next up was a meeting on the Iraqi side of the border. There the general was going to sit down with the Iraqi military and deliver some assuredly unwelcome news.

He boarded the helicopter, and a whir of blades lifted him skyward. As the aircraft rose over Isikveren, Shalikashvili was leaving with one impression burned particularly deep into his memory.

It was the sight of young Kurdish refugee children, muddy, dirty, and near death.

15

Warning the Iraqis

Friday, April 19, 1991
—Harbur Border Crossing, Northwestern Iraq

The Harbur border crossing area, an outpost on Iraq's expansive northwestern border, was a ghost town. Twin bridges that connected the outpost to its Turkish counterpart across the Harbur River stood crippled and impassable. Unexploded ordnance dotted the landscape. Neighboring villages lay in ruins, and the hollowed out city of Zakho, the closest urban area, held just three hundred of its original fifty thousand Kurdish denizens.

Today, however, the outpost's customs house was surprisingly abuzz with commotion. Atop the building a fresh Iraqi flag radiated sovereignty. Around the perimeter, a newly posted Iraqi border guard detachment maintained vigilance. And outside the main entrance a clutter of international media had gathered, drawn by the biggest story since this crisis began: the first face-to-face meeting between the Provide Comfort task force and the Iraqi military.

Why the meeting? Because President Bush's orders to relocate the refugees had come with an almost perverse twist: the Kurds were coming back to Iraq.

Shalikashvili and his deputy commander, Jim Jamerson, had almost laughed at the irony: "We have to go back into a country we just fought a war with and tell them we want them to back off as we bring these Kurds back in?!"

But there was no alternative. "The nearest valleys that had the road network that would support such a massive relief effort," Shalikashvili would later explain, were "in northern Iraq." And time was short: the Kurds needed to leave the mountains by mid-June, when searing 100-degree heat would dry up all natural water sources.

"Our challenge," Jamerson later explained, "was to create a security zone so the Kurds would be willing to go back home, but to do so in a way that didn't restart the war."

190

The potential for conflict loomed large. Even before the Kurdish uprising, Baghdad had two corps stationed in northern Iraq. Currently two infantry divisions and several independent tank units were in the vicinity of the planned zone, including three brigades within Zakho itself. Not only did Iraqi artillery outnumber and outrange American guns, but Iraqi antiaircraft artillery and surface-to-air missiles remained in the nearby hills and the supply route from the Turkish border to Zakho was guarded by four Iraqi forts.

This was all cause for concern. Bush's announcement had been clear: this was a humanitarian mission only, not the continuation of the Gulf War under false pretenses. Warned to "protect the president" two days ago, Shalikashvili couldn't embarrass Bush by allowing armed conflict to break out during the resettlement.

Yet the diplomatic front was offering little cause for optimism. Yesterday Bagdad had agreed only to refugee centers staffed by United Nations civilian personnel. When questioned about the planned US security zone, Deputy Prime Minister Tariq Aziz was adamant: "We refuse this. They have no right to send troops to our territory. This is interference in our internal affairs."

"We see the U.S. and UN efforts as complementary," a State Department spokesman publicly glossed over the difference. "We are pleased that the Iraqis have formally agreed to the UN's plans to provide for humanitarian relief for Iraqi refugees."

So now the task force had to accomplish what the diplomats could not. Shalikashvili's goal for today's tête-à-tête was to establish ground rules to prevent clashes between the task force and Iraqi troops.

Originally scheduled for noon, the Iraqis had pushed the meeting back to the evening; given the no-fly zone imposed in northern Iraq by the cease-fire agreement, the task force would just have to wait for Saddam's delegation to make the seven-hour-plus drive from Baghdad.

The Iraqis arrived first, their white Mercedes sedan coated in dust. The car doors swung open, and two generals emerged, accompanied by guards sporting pistols. They stood outside the building, waiting in silence.

Shalikashvili too could use his arrival as a means to communicate. Arriving amid a thunder of Black Hawk helicopters, his retinue then made its way to the building accompanied by four marine guards toting M16 assault rifles. Across the river, sixty more marines kept watchful eye, while two US A-10 Thunderbolt II ground attack aircraft patrolled the otherwise empty skies above. The message was clear without being aggressive: Shalikashvili was here in a position of strength.

Shalikashvili meeting with Iraq's Brigadier General Nashwan Thanoon at the Harbur border crossing area in northwestern Iraq on April 19, 1991, to discuss Combined Task Force Operation Provide Comfort's imminent plans to move the Kurdish refugees back into Iraq. The outcome of this meeting was reportedly disastrous for Thanoon. (DoD photograph, courtesy of the NBR Gen. John Shalikashvili Archives.)

Shalikashvili's contingent stopped to shake hands with the Iraqi officers. Then, without speaking, the two sides entered the building.

On the grounds of the customs house, Shalikashvili and Iraq's Brigadier General Nashwan Thanoon sat side by side on an ornate rattan couch. The remaining delegation members occupied chairs around an extended coffee table in the center. The armed guards from both sides formed a larger perimeter.

Shalikashvili spoke first. He informed the Iraqis that as early as noon tomorrow coalition forces would cross the border and enter Zakho to begin constructing a security zone for the Kurds. He required two things. First, before then all Iraqi troops had to move south of the security zone by at least nineteen miles, the approximate range of Iraq's medium artillery. Second, their military needed to refrain from interfering in general with the rescue effort. Shalikashvili then suggested setting up a military coordination council so the two sides could communicate.

Then Nashwan spoke. Though acknowledging Shalikashvili's démarche, he passionately reiterated his government's protest of coalition forces on Iraqi soil. He never directly agreed to withdraw his troops, but his follow-up points—including Iraq's desire to maintain a police force in Zakho and to keep Harbur open "for commercial purposes"—signaled that the Iraqis would comply. Nashwan agreed, moreover, to establishing the council.

Shalikashvili then closed by asking for maps of Iraqi minefields in the mountains and promising to look into the points raised by the Iraqis. Finally, he emphasized that the mission was humanitarian in nature and that the task force was ready to cooperate with the Iraqis, but that they'd protect themselves with force if necessary.

It was done. But would the Iraqis actually follow through? In the days ahead how hard would they test his resolve?

Yet this was just the start of Shalikashvili's challenges. As CTF commander he sat at the center of an extensive web of actors, each bringing to the table not just resources but demands and opinions. Prospects for conflict —over what should be done when, how, and by whom—were enormous.

For starters, Shalikashvili was still a lower link in a chain of command that ran from the president to the secretary of defense, in consultation with the chairman of the Joint Chiefs, to the EUCOM commander.

"You work directly for me," Galvin had made clear before Shalikashvili departed. Galvin actually held two major positions concurrently, and thus could exercise two types of control. As EUCOM commander, he could affect the organization of the operation itself by drawing on all US military resources in Europe. As SACEUR, the military head of NATO, he could work the political relationships with many of the countries involved. Unsurprisingly, the major players in the task force were mostly NATO members.

Little wonder Colonel Steve Gulyas, Shalikashvili's X.O. both at Heidelberg and during Provide Comfort, would later judge that the operation went so smoothly and efficiently "because there was a synchronicity, these existing linkages between people, that expedited decision-making."

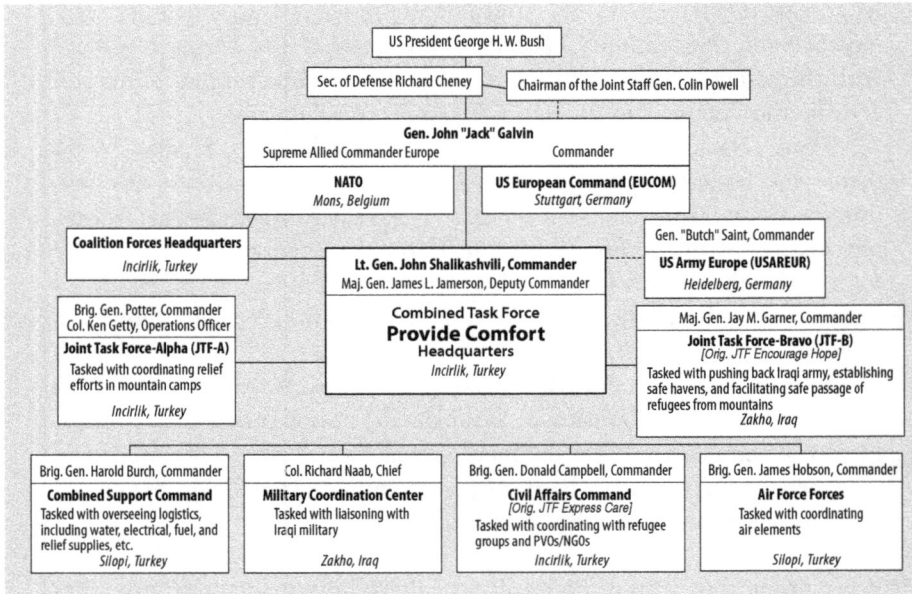

Operation Provide Comfort Organizational Structure

But these linkages came with strings. "EUCOM's mission concept has been accepted," Galvin instructed, "so get started quickly. Be very open to cooperation from the French, British, Canadians, and others. Put them on the CTF staff. You focus on securing the zone. Let your deputy manage the camps."

Galvin's orders would often come through EUCOM deputy commander General J. McCarthy. Tonight Shalikashvili would phone McCarthy. Proceed at noon tomorrow as planned, the deputy would order, and tell the Iraqis the CTF will assume temporary responsibility for law and order in Zakho. "Do military correct things," but also "do not create any incidents—make sure the marines do not look for trouble."

Jamerson later explained McCarthy's concern: "Our forces needed to be muscular enough so we wouldn't get into a fight with the Iraqis, but there were some who felt they'd missed their own chance in 'the big war'"—the Gulf War. "They had the bit in their teeth and wanted to get into things."

Some felt this way about Garner, commander Task Force-Bravo (JTF-B), the sub-task force charged with establishing the security zone. "He was kind of a cowboy," recalled JTF-A's operations officer, Ken

Getty. "Garner was gung ho," concurred Brian Holt, a British colonel who served as the CTFs operation's officer. "His career was in jeopardy of ending, and the main war had passed him by."

Garner had gone into northwestern Iraq yesterday, without Shalikashvili's knowledge, to scout suitable locations for the security zone. Later that evening he'd briefed Shalikashvili, identifying the city of Zakho—with its level land, good water supply, and proximity to the Iraqi-Turkish border—as the best location. "I am glad you did that," Shalikashvili responded, "but I don't want you doing anything like that on your own again."

As head of EUCOM, Galvin oversaw all support for the operation, including by tapping Butch Saint, Shalikashvili's immediate boss, to assist. As pointed out by Gulyas, "Saint was very instrumental in providing logistics because he was in the theater and had the assets." "My organization knows how to feed people and move things," the USAREUR commander himself would later say, adding: "Our job was to make a hero out of him. . . . All Shalikashvili had to do was ask for support. Even if he didn't ask, I'd give it to him. Galvin eventually complained to me that I was providing too much."

Yet that support too came with strings. "I understand that you work for someone else now," Saint had told Shalikashvili, "but I'm your daddy. This is not a test to see if you fail. If you do fail and don't tell me why, I'll have your ass. I'm going to make you succeed if you help me out." Before Shalikashvili left for Turkey, Saint had briefed him on how to approach the mission, while also providing a list of people, including Garner, to bring with him to Turkey.

Saint also offered warnings: the civilian organizations were not always doing their job, not always cooperating. "But," he reminded Shalikashvili, "you can't give orders to either volunteers or allies."

Saint's admonition was spot on. Provide Comfort was atypical because countries were sending their elite forces into the crisis zone without the formal agreements that typically structure such multinational operations. The only way to achieve cohesion would be through cooperation and persuasion.

"We want the British and French to provide the security forces, not the United States," McCarthy would instruct during the evening phone call. Yet soon after a British air vice-marshal would warn Shalikashvili: "We are fully content to contribute to security but it is unacceptable to be seen doing it alone. We need to be seen as a part of a total humanitarian effort." The Brits, in effect, were unwilling to play bad cop to the good cops handing out food. Nor did they want their service members split up: "We are prepared to put our troops under U.S. tactical control," the vice-marshal continued, "but we want to be part of a geographic or functional responsibility."

And the British were just one of the twelve military coalition partners Shalikashvili would have to juggle. One big sticking point would be the different "rules of engagement" that dictated what each national component could do. For instance, French rules prohibited their infantry platoons from aiding other coalition platoons under attack. ("The French didn't want to be part of *any* structure," Getty later grumbled.) British rules, despite the pressing need, didn't allow their artillery battalions to be deployed to support either coalition forces or even their own troops. And some troops, like the Spanish, were plain inexperienced: "We haven't been deployed out of Spain since the Spanish-American War in 1898," Jamerson later paraphrased their plea. "We aren't sure what to do. Please put us somewhere safe."

Potter, the JTF-A commander, later identified one key strategy used to head off conflict: "Shali was absolutely astute in realizing that because there was no U.S. embassy, he was the senior US official in Iraq. So he effectively defined his role as *both* the senior political leader and the task force commander," giving him great room for initiative. Gulyas offered a second strategy: "Shali set up the task force so that the senior military rep from each country plugged in under him. So it was really a joint rather than combined in terms of operations. This helped to avoid the problem of different protocols. Despite being under operational control of Task Force-Bravo, the individual forces were controlled by their own respective generals"—a great compromise.

Integrating the nonmilitary organizations would actually prove the greater challenge. "This was all new territory for us," Shalikashvili's deputy later recalled. "We didn't know what UNHCR was. We all went in with a totally blank slate on everything: NGOs, the UN, PVOs." When the US ambassador to Turkey, Morton Abramowitz, first mentioned DART—the Disaster Assistance Response Team at the United States Agency for International Development, which would play a critical role in this operation—"I had no idea what that was," Jamerson admitted. "My mind first leapt to the game of darts, but of course I knew that wasn't it."

The feeling was mutual. "We've landed on Mars," Susan Carroll, the UNHCR protection officer responsible for the Kurds in Turkey, communicated back to headquarters soon after arrival in Incirlik. "How weird that so many militaries are here, especially the United States. We should be in charge!" And figuring out who was who, what ranks meant, was overwhelming for her. "And they were equally perplexed by who I was." So her organization purposefully displayed its independence. "It was a conscious decision by the UN," Carroll later explained, "to have women and not men on the ground to distinguish us from the military operation." At one point she'd even fly back to Geneva to bring back dresses and skirts in order to make the point even clearer.

Furthermore, many NGOs and PVOs lacked a strong command and control network to support their own operations. Some couldn't even maintain agents both in the field and back in Incirlik, let alone coordinate efforts with others. Some were completely green: "Many church groups would show up with a half dozen nurses and doctors," recalled Potter, "and say, 'Okay, what do we do?'"

Many didn't get along with each other. Very few had trust in the military, and some had outright distrust. Oftentimes they'd want to do their own thing or wouldn't go where most needed. At first Doctors Without Borders didn't even want to be associated with the military, recalled Getty, though they "came around once they saw what military doctors could do."

The civilian relief organizations would have conflicting views on many issues. In setting up the refugee camps, for instance, there'd be heated discussions over the planning, design, and placement of latrines, burn pits, water storage tanks, and drainage facilities. Just as there'd be frank exchanges over how to move the refugees down from the mountains.

They were tricky subjects. The refugee centers in Iraq, for instance, needed to be attractive enough to lure the Kurds out of the mountains but not sturdy or comfortable enough so they'd stay. Orders from Washington, Shalikashvili later explained, were "to return as many as we possibly could back to their own homes and into their own villages and towns where the existing infrastructure could take care of them and they wouldn't be dependent on this artificial camp structure that we see all over the world."

Washington was also pushing Shalikashvili to turn the refugee centers over to UN control as quickly as possible. Not only was the UN "initially very skeptical about dealing with the military," noted Jamerson, "but their standards for the camps and support infrastructure were high." Locating acceptable tents, for instance, would prove a major challenge.

"The UN human rights commissioner himself came," Getty later recalled, "and said he wanted the Kurds registered before being moved back to Iraq, something the Kurds were obviously opposed to [for fear Saddam would get hold of the list] and we realized was ridiculous."

Shalikashvili explained yet another challenge: "If our transportation system depended on military trucks [or] helicopters to bring things in," it would be "extraordinarily difficult to turn over [to the] UNHCR or any other private organization. We had to build a transportation system that depended on commercial trucking, which then in a form of a contract could be turned over. And that was true of communications and the whole system."

But setting up such infrastructure wouldn't be easy. For one, quickly pumping too much money into the system could wreak havoc with the local economy. The task force also needed to insulate itself from the appearance of allowing corruption. "You could almost see some Turks drooling over the potential for making money or for pilfering," recalled Ronsick, the CTF's liaison to the super governor. Press reports of aid supplies being diverted to military channels would at one point prompt Shalikashvili himself to meet with the highest levels of the Turkish Armed Forces.

Then there were the Kurds themselves. "Our goal was to convince them to move back to Iraq, but for us not to get sucked up into their internal politics," recalled Jamerson. "Many of them viewed this humanitarian intervention as a chance to gain freedom." White House orders, passed on by McCarthy, were thus to "never raise the word 'sovereignty' in any discussions." Above all avoid "the K word"—some variation of Kurdistan, Kurdish Autonomous Region, or Kurdish independence.

"But that was all the Kurds talked about!" Potter later groused. Shalikashvili's challenge, then, would be to entice the refugees back to Iraq, including securing their help in both the repatriation effort and running the refugee centers, all while deflecting their vigorous demands to widen the security zone or otherwise maximize Kurdish political autonomy.

"But the Kurds," Jamerson added, "were distrustful of both the UN and the US." Divisions within the Kurds themselves would further complicate negotiations: there were six major political parties, and the leaders of the two biggest Kurdish factions, Talabani and Barzani, quickly began fighting for credit, politicking for advantage.

There'd also be cultural challenges. Female Kurds, for instance, were reluctant to be examined by male doctors, especially for OB/GYN problems. And the issue of latrines would cause no end of headaches. The public bathrooms in camps were lined up military style, facing one direction—far different than family-style bathrooms that afforded privacy. In one location the latrines were even installed facing Mecca—a serious faux pas. Many Kurds were instead just relieving themselves on the ground.

The thorniest challenge, however, would be the Turks. "The only way to move the Kurds was with their [the Turks'] cooperation," explained Jamerson. All manpower and matériel needed to be flown into the bases and ports in Turkey, transported to Silopi, and then humped over the mountains into northwest Iraq. "The Turks could shut the whole operation down in an instant."

But the Turks were downright ornery, judged Jamerson. "They felt that the U.S. caused the problem. They didn't think we understood their political problems, that we'd be manipulated by the Kurds and the Kurdish political parties."

So the Turks were being demanding. For one, "the super governor told the task force outright that he wanted *all* Kurds back over the border," recalled Jamerson, including those who'd entered Turkey in the days before the border closed.

At the very start of Provide Comfort, the joint task force had been established before the Turks knew exactly what was happening, recalled Getty. The Turks hadn't thought the US military could move so much people and equipment so quickly—"they were so pissed they couldn't see straight!" Early on there'd been "interesting discussions" in the mountain camps between Turks, who'd been reluctant to let the task force move beyond airdrops, and US special forces, even escalating to the point that shots were fired.

With this upgraded combined task force, though, the Turks were getting smarter. For one, they were demanding close oversight of the mission. Whenever dissatisfied, they'd ratchet up customs inspections and other regulations. "The requirements for crossing the border changed daily, in some cases hourly," one after-action review would state—interference that sometimes delayed the delivery of supplies into Iraq for days.

Decades later, Getty would recall the toughest part of Provide Comfort: "Working eighteen- to twenty-hour days in the beginning, from 7 a.m. to at least 10 p.m. and sometimes to midnight and thereafter, trying to get control over the competing demands—from up above, down below, and from the sides—in order to build a coherent plan for moving forward." "It was," the JTF-A operations officer summed up colorfully, "a goat rope."

As commander of the upgraded CTF, Shalikashvili was going to be subject to an even grander array of conflicting demands from these multiple directions: orders but little guidance from top US policymakers; oversight from the military chain of command; the involvement of both a new boss, Galvin, and Shalikashvili's old boss, Saint; prickly and finicky coalition members; the large US military bureaucracy itself; competing branches of the US government; powerful international organizations (IOs); squirrelly PVOs and NGOs; a dyspeptic host nation; and the wild card of a defeated and humiliated Iraqi leader and his military.

It had the potential to be much more than a goat rope. To have any hope of successfully completing this unprecedented mission, Shalikashvili would need to prevent a full-blown three-ring circus.

* * *

Asked in retirement to name his greatest weakness, Shalikashvili gave a curious reply: "I don't like confrontation."

And he didn't. Upon assuming battalion command, Shalikashvili told Billy Brooks, his new X.O., he wanted to use a "good cop, bad cop" approach to run the unit. "Sir, which one do you prefer?" asked the X.O. "Good cop," replied the boss, leaving the bad cop role for Brooks—a man so gracious and kind by nature that he'd later be entrusted to handle the delicate task of roasting hot-tempered Norman Schwarzkopf at the general's retirement event.

Not liking confrontation was an eye-raising admission for a man with Shalikashvili's career success. Being conflict-averse is often viewed as a weakness; the macho Pattonesque persona, a strength.

But in the US Army, explained Getty, "95 percent of army officers feel the same way Shali did: If things get confrontational, it means you have failed." Jack Walker, once the youngest army brigadier general, agreed: "You can't be a designer of confrontation within the U.S. military—it just won't work." Lieutenant General Tom Jaco noted that Shalikashvili seldom got into a situation where there was confrontation. And General John Abizaid, who first worked under Shalikashvili during this Kurdish operation and would later become his executive assistant, saw firsthand how "instead of avoiding confrontation, Shali positively sought consensus!"

It started with the introduction.

"Look at the name on this guy! How am going to pronounce that?"

Major General J. B. Taylor, the 9th Infantry Division deputy commander, later recalled thinking when he first met his new boss. "But when you first meet him . . . he says: 'Hi, I'm John Shali.' It's a much less formal approach than you'd expect. He disarms everyone this way."

Stewart Wright had taken pains to learn his new battalion commander's name. But on the day they met, Shalikashvili merely smiled and said, "Just call me Shali. I've found that's easiest." Why divide the unit into those who could and couldn't pronounce it?

Putting others at ease—it was a key lubricant in Shalikashvili's interactions with others. In part it was a talent. "He could talk to the president or talk to a private. If he was on an elevator, he's the kind of guy that can get off and talk to people on each floor," recalled Lieutenant Colonel Roger Cirillo, Saint's subordinate. It was also a deliberate strategy. That's surely partly why Shalikashvili used special "tick cards" to track whether he was indeed having at least one personal interaction each week with a set list of personnel—from top brass down to administrative assistants.

"And not just quick platitudes but sincere, full attention," added Major General John Herrling, a subordinate during the late 1970s. Many noted what Cirillo did: that during meetings Shalikashvili did not keep looking at his watch or glancing over at the work on his desk. Regardless of who you are, "he has this way of listening to you," explained Allied Forces Southern Europe commander Admiral Mike Boorda, "and while you are talking he makes you feel you are the only person in the world."

"And he meant what he said," continued Herrling. That was another characteristic people noticed—Shalikashvili's ability to make others feel he was trustworthy. An officer can judge character in how the boss runs meetings, asks questions, things they say they want done, explained Heidelberg's Ruth Collins. There are many gray areas, and that is where you can evaluate how he responds—in his actions, voice, and words. "With some bosses, many actually, one can quickly tell if they are just concerned with looking good as quickly as possible. Shali never did."

He was known for giving the limelight to others, while, as noted by Butch Saint, "also personally accepting the responsibility for any less successful outcomes." But when privately evaluating subordinates, explained navy captain Sharon Shelton, a subordinate from Shalikashvili's final career assignment, "he gives immediate feedback if good, but no false pat on the back if otherwise. And if something goes wrong, he doesn't sugarcoat."

Many appreciated the trust he automatically extended. When taking a new assignment, for example, he didn't bring in handpicked staff. "Shali assumed that if someone in the office had gotten that far to start with, they must be competent," explained Cirillo, "until you proved otherwise." Many subordinates would be surprised that Shalikashvili wouldn't ask them to leave the room when an important phone call interrupted.

One major benefit of Shalikashvili's method of interacting with others was that he could move people in the right direction without having to push. "He always had integrity and high standards," continued Ruth Collins, adding, "he taught by example . . . I felt Shali would never want me to do anything untoward." Noting Shalikashvili was very loyal to both superiors and supporting staff, Heidelberg's Mike Molino explained: "I knew not to be disloyal to Shali and he wouldn't do it to me."

Shalikashvili also trusted people with 100 percent ownership of their job—a wise approach, noted Colonel Mike Kendall, who'd worked under Shalikashvili multiple times, because even if subordinates don't produce something great, a commander can always make adjustments later. "Shali had unique faith in his staff," agreed Nuremberg's Ohlstein, "but he still himself knew when to be at the right place at the right time."

But this checking up was done gently. Normally one can fear the visit by a division commander, explained John Lee, a 9th Infantry Division command sergeant major. "But when Shali would come by, which he did relatively often, people were not fearful. It was done in a low-key way. He did not jump in and start making loud and public corrections. He never yelled, degraded, or belittled. . . . He'd ask provoking, open-ended questions and he was okay with silences, wouldn't jump in to provide the answer." "If Shali did get very involved in the details," added Kendall, "he'd explain why."

His style also allowed people to gracefully shift direction. "Jesus, that's a nice report," he'd say before going on to ask a detailed linkage question in order to suggest a change. Or "do what you want," he'd sometimes advise, "but if you give it a month the other way, maybe you'll see it might be okay." And when he did take a different approach, he would explain why. Once he even said to Ohlstein: "Just this once will you trust me? Because I know things you don't."

As noted by Colonel Frank Adams, Shalikashvili's brigade commander at the 9th Infantry Division, Shalikashvili's personable, calm, nonthreatening approach was very good in making even prominent people not feel like they've come out of a discussion having lost, even if their ideas were not adopted. "That's a great way," explained X.O. Gulyas, "to get people to buy into decisions and thus execute them with dedication and not just pay lip service."

These bonds Shalikashvili quickly formed with others did not, however, breed a familiarity that weakened his ability to lead. That's because the closeness, explained Major General Jim Kessler, Shalikashvili's aide in the mid-1990s, doesn't come from him opening up or allowing things to get terribly personal. "It was *not* 'open kimono.'"

Take Bruno Schact, Shalikashvili's command sergeant major in the mid-1970s. Though both were German immigrants, the boss never spoke to him in German, never used their shared cultural background to connect. "Shali had a way of making me feel like a trusted advisor, but he also clearly kept the commander-subordinate relationship intact."

For he was no pushover. "Humility doesn't equal weakness and quiet doesn't equal meek," explained Brigadier General David Armstrong, who worked for Shalikashvili at the height of his power. "He's polite, listens, works mostly through suggestion, and cares about people," agreed General Montgomery Meigs, who'd worked under Shalikashvili at the 1st Armored Division, "but Shali is a hard guy. His standards are high. He's not passive, he's just quiet and subtle," an approach helped along by "his polite Old World manner." "If you wanted to go bare knuckles," Meigs added, "Shali could do that, but he'd prefer not to." Brigadier General Stan Kwieciak from the 5th Infantry Division concurred: "He's *not* a cupcake. He can be a hard ass, though a reasonable hard ass. He might listen to many opinions, but once he made up his mind. . . . Maybe he didn't yell or scream, but he could be cutting when he needed to be."

The crux, then, of what defined Shalikashvili as a consensus-building military leader was perhaps best articulated by Walker: "Shali wouldn't get too strong, which is a standard military technique, until it was really necessary."

And with Shalikashvili, it often wasn't.

"Sure, Shali was very confident in himself and what he could get people to do," explained Cirillo, "but very soon you get to competency. And Shali was competent." Part of his competency came from one of his greatest intellectual abilities: the ability to empathize with different perspectives but not get paralyzed by the complexity.

Much credit goes to the US military, which offers officers almost unparalleled opportunity to develop a "holistic" outlook: an understanding how the parts relate to the whole in a complex system.

A unit commander, for instance, learns the interlocking holistic skills of how to resource, equip, and train service members in preparation for combat. Every officer starts out small, commanding a platoon of about 40 soldiers. Then comes company, called a battery in the artillery branch, comprised of four or more platoons, totaling 62–190 troops. The units keep combining, and the number of troops keeps growing. There's battalion command (4–6 companies; 300–1,000 troops) and brigade command, known as DIVARTY in the artillery branch (2–5 battalions; 3,000–5,000 troops). At general officer level, the responsibilities are enormous. Division commanders, for instance, oversee three or more brigades for a total of 10,000–15,000 troops. That's a lot of parts coming together to comprise one whole.

Shalikashvili held all these commands, and gained similar holistic experience in a number of jobs directly supporting a commander—like serving as X.O. at junior officer level and deputy commander at the more senior levels.

Shalikashvili was deputy commander now at USAREUR. He would have preferred to instead be leading a corps (3 or more divisions; 30,000–80,000 troops), but at least Butch Saint had given him oversight of various units lacking an overall commander that together equaled a corps. And serving as de facto mayor of Heidelberg gave Shalikashvili additional oversight responsibilities for a community of twenty-five thousand soldiers and their family members, including their housing, school system, hospital, and security and police force, and an annual budget of $100 million. (A decade earlier, his Nuremberg community had twenty-seven thousand soldiers and a budget of over $65 million.)

Yet another type of holistic training is "jointness," or how different service branches cooperate in battle. Consider that artillery training, in addition to teaching logistics and the importance of precision, also provides holistic skills: "Infantrymen look ten meters ahead and one hundred meters to the sides," explained OCS graduate Colonel Robert Lindsay, but "artillerymen fight battles down-range up to fifteen thousand yards away." That's because in order to properly support a maneuver force, the artillery commander must fully understand how infantry and armor units operate. At Shalikashvili's very first posting as a forward observer for the mortar battery in Alaska, for example, he accompanied an infantry company on maneuvers and directed supporting mortar fire. This required understanding the larger flow of the infantry battle in order to determine target locations and assist with fire support plans. Reconnaissance for future positions is also critical, and must be done in conjunction with the plans of other supported maneuver or even artillery units.

Early on Shalikashvili also benefited from a year's study at the Naval War College. There he studied naval warfare, including modeling submarine warfare in computer simulations. He also enjoyed studying the complex field of mine warfare. Listening to his classmates' questions and concerns regarding his class presentation on the Mark 23 torpedo, the major had an epiphany: "I realized that depending on how you grew up in what service, you had a totally different perspective on what our business is all about." "Most people in those days understood jointness to be managing the seams between services," like how the air force provides close air support to ground troops. In the years that followed the Army War College, Shalikashvili would be part of the military's growing awareness that jointness could and should mean something much more: the services joining together as a cohesive and exponentially more effective fighting force.

A year after the Naval War College, he was at UN headquarters in Korea. "It was essentially run by the air force," Shalikashvili later recalled. "I was the exercise officer in J-3 so these big exercises like Ulchi Focus Lens were my responsibility." "Somebody invades Korea and we defend. Specifically, my work involved running the army desk in the command center, . . . keeping the [air force] staff and general informed on what the army was doing and relaying to the army what the general wanted them to do." "I learned what it was like not only to manage joint forces but also combined forces. There was a big South Korean flavor to all of that, and that came in very handy years later."

This Korea assignment was his third in what would become a string of postings in operations—known as J-3 for operations in a joint command, G-3 for the staff of a general officer, and S-3 for a brigade or lower. Operations would provide Shalikashvili significant exposure to the complexity of maintaining and utilizing a fighting force—including setting objectives, gathering intelligence, planning missions, and the administration of mobilizing, equipping, training, and staging of forces.

A three-year stint at the army's Military Personnel Center offered Major Shalikashvili yet another flavor of how the parts relate to the whole. There he guided the careers of almost 14,500 field artillery majors and lieutenant colonels by trying to match their career development needs and the needs of the larger army when making position assignments. A second holistic responsibility was helping set up US Army standards for promotion to these ranks. His superiors noted that Shalikashvili demonstrated "the rare combination of confidence and humility, ambition and selflessness, which enable him to be sensitive to the problems of an individual or drive an Army-wide requirement."

From 1981 to 1989 he would have a series of Pentagon assignments—all high-level staff positions in the army's Office of the Deputy Chief of Staff for Operations and Plans—that afforded him an increasingly important role in determining how the army as a whole both thinks and acts across a wide range of geographical areas and security issues.

As chief of the Politico-Military Division he advised the chief of staff of the army on any foreign policy region or topic that could affect the army. According to his performance reviews, it was "probably the most demanding Division Chief task on the entire Army staff."

Next, as senior army planner for joint affairs, he threw himself into the then-voluntary intensive six-week CAPSTONE course, designed to make officers "more effective in planning and employing U.S. forces in joint and combined operations." This took him to key US military commands within the continental United States and on trips to Europe, the Pacific, and the Western Hemisphere to interact with combatant commanders of US unified commands, American ambassadors, embassy staffs, and senior political and military leaders of foreign governments.

He performed so well that when the director of the Strategy, Plans, and Policy Directorate was reassigned and the deputy director retired, Shalikashvili "was thrust into a turbulent situation as an acting director" and then moved to the deputy slot when the new director was appointed.

The deputy slot, one of the most responsible positions for a one star on the DA staff, meant dealing with the most important national security issues addressed at the highest levels of government. Shalikashvili not only helped direct multiple divisions—Politico-Military, Strategic Plans and Policy, War Plans, Security Assistance, Long-Range Planning, Central American Task Force, and Interim Permanent Secretariat of the Conference of American Armies—but also integrated their individual concerns into overall army planning. The deputy also served on the Inter-American Defense Board and the Joint Mexican-United States Defense Commission, as well as being the army representative on a variety of general officer steering groups: NATO Policy, Strategy for Southwest Asia and Central America, Issues in the Pacific, Master Restationing Plan, and Light Infantry Division. Finally, in the director's absence he also vetted Joint papers and provided coordinated army positions on all issues addressed at Joint Chiefs of Staff meetings.

None of these positions, including the Pentagon assignments, earmarked Shalikashvili as being on a fast track to the top. But they did allow him ample opportunity to practice, over and over again and in myriad different scenarios, how to wrap his mind around complexity and then determine the best course of action, often in real time and on pressure-filled issues. While on the Joint Staff in the early 1990s, subordinate Kori Schake would notice: "Shali thirsted for the ability to separate the wheat from the chaff. This was especially true when things were moving so fast. And he wanted to meet people who could do the same, and to learn from them."

And clearly he had talent. Even at the beginning of his career, his second battery commander in Alaska had noted: "His mind is exceptionally quick and he has the capability of getting to the root of a problem and solving it expeditiously." And per his current boss, Butch Saint: "He is as agile-minded and flexible in changing situations as any officer I have known."

This type of intellect, though, was a potential danger within the military. Montgomery Meigs draws a distinction between "E"s and "I"s. The former is emotional intelligence, which is very powerful—it is going to the gut, instinctive, and great for combat. The latter, intellectual intelligence, is a bit slower; it's trying to look at the big picture and beyond the horizon and it's about trying to solve problems a bit more creatively than by just going by the standard operating procedure. "Shali is both," judged Meigs. "But in an 'E' environment like the U.S. Army, the 'E's will get annoyed, thinking the 'I's are disloyal to the rule set."

Kori Schake was more blunt: "The army is somewhat anti-intellectual, especially compared to the Marine Corps. The army cares about doctrine: bringing everyone up to a minimal level by setting standards. Stupid people can become generals."

So Shalikashvili was careful. "He's very smart, but hides it very well. It took me a long time to figure out he was really a smart guy," noted David Armstrong. Brian Haig agreed: "Too many smart people are enamored with themselves and want to show it," which is a sure way to create ill-will and inhibit consensus building. What's more, added Schake, "Shali could persuade people based upon the means *you* care about, not the ones he cares about," yet another way a highly intelligent officer can lead without flaunting his or her intellect.

Shalikashvili's intelligence was also made exponentially more effective because "he has both incredible intellect *and* common sense," noted Jaco, adding, "that's a very rare combination." Put differently, there was no "analysis to paralysis" that, in Meigs' typology, often sharply limited an 'I's effectiveness and annoyed the 'E's.

Shalikashvili himself agreed: "If I have a strength, it is hopefully that I have a great deal of common sense. I might not do the most brilliant thing, but hopefully I won't do the dumb thing. And hopefully I have the good sense to surround myself with the right people who can help me do the more brilliant stuff, and I can keep them from going over the edge with my common sense."

Furthermore, his analysis of the situation did not get clouded under stress or pressure. Jon Schreyach, Shalikashvili's S-3 at the DIVARTY, recalled what happened when the head of the Nuclear Surety Program informed the boss they weren't ready for inspection: "A vein on the right side of his head pulsed. That's how we all knew when he was stressed. But I never saw Shali lose his temper." "Shali doesn't get distracted by frustration or emotion. He takes things in a calm way," added Walker. "Nor does he seem to get biased by those around him."

Instead he remained low key and let logic do the talking. Jaco recalled his first impression of Shalikashvili at the Naval War College seminar meetings: "He'd come in, sit down, wave, and then say very little. He had the ability to listen—which carried the day. He would never try to impress you. He'd just ask the right question or ask no question; when he did open his mouth he said what was important."

At the Pentagon Shalikashvili used this same approach during many pitched defense budget battles or while helping determine the army position on the reduction of medium-range nuclear missiles in Europe in the in the 1980s. General Robert W. Riscassi, his boss at the time, recalled the moderating influence Shalikashvili had on nuclear missile reduction: "There were camps that said we can't give up one iota of anything, and those who said maybe there are some things we can give up." "Shalikashvili just brought logic to the table. He's relaxed, nonintrusive. His forte is knowledge." Dr. Perry M. Smith, the air force planner when Shalikashvili was the deputy army planner, agreed: "We negotiated on a number of interservice issues. I remember him as a quiet-spoken man who was well prepared, was scrupulously honest, tried to find the best solution for the nation rather than just for the army and who was not afraid to admit he didn't know something."

While speaking to Joint Staff interns toward the end of his career, Shalikashvili would admit: "This is my fifth tour in the Pentagon. I must tell you I hated four of them. . . . But each one of them was absolutely essential, I think, to build on, and to understand my business better, the business of the military."

Shalikashvili surely detested the inherent conflict in those first four Pentagon assignments. But he got through them—and excelled—in no small part due to an approach to human interaction based on both style and substance that together worked to minimize conflict and maximize productive consensus.

The effectiveness of this approach was reflected in Shalikashvili's demeanor. One subordinate from the general's very last career assignment summed it up this way: "Shali had this air of 'I know who I am, and I don't need to tell you who I am. You will get to know me, and when you do you will like me.'"

The task force commander was under intense media scrutiny during the Kurdish rescue operation. (DoD photograph, courtesy of the NBR Gen. John Shalikashvili Archives.)

<u>16</u>

A World Figure?

Friday, April 19, 1991
—Harbur Border Crossing, Northwestern Iraq

After fifty minutes, the two sides emerged from the customs house and shook hands in front of the media. The Iraqi delegation then departed without a word. Shalikashvili would never see Nashwan again—rumor would later have it Hussein executed him for accepting Shalikashvili's demand for a pullback beyond artillery range.

The CTF commander, however, did stop to chat with reporters.

"This operation," Galvin had warned two days earlier, "will be as much a public relations effort as a humanitarian one." With some 350 news media already in the crisis zone and the Defense Department considering sending a national news media pool, Washington wanted the task force to offer a daily news briefing. And with hordes of VIPs—including governmental dignitaries, military leaders, and representatives of major international agencies—flying in to inspect the operation or hold meetings with the task force, including five US congressmen visiting Incirlik just today, Shalikashvili had been told to quickly establish a visitor bureau.

"You are now a world figure," Butch Saint drove home. "People will want to talk directly with you, will want to plumb your thoughts."

* * *

A world figure?

Shalikashvili did not have a reputation as a climber. "He's not a 'star gazer,'" offered Caroll Dickson, a colleague from the mid-1970s who later became Shalikashvili's subordinate. Thomas Kelly, a Pentagon colleague in the 1980s, concurred: "Some officers only look upward because they want to get ahead. He looks downward because that's where the work gets done." Ohlstein from the 1st Armored Division agreed. "If promotion was in the back of Shali's mind, none of us ever knew it. His focus was always on what was needed now—not politicking for future career."

211

"I don't think at any time did I really have any great aspirations or any dreams beyond the next grade," Shalikashvili himself would later say. "When I made first lieutenant I was hoping that by hook and crook I would make captain. By the time you're a major, you hope that you'll be lucky enough to make lieutenant colonel. And if you're really lucky, someone will give you a battalion to command. That's the sort of thing that excited me. That's what moved me along."

During two decades of service, Shalikashvili was one of about 75 percent of captains who make major, 60 percent of majors who make lieutenant colonel, and 50 percent of lieutenant colonels who make colonel.

As a junior officer, he twice made decisions that could have limited his prospects. His marriage to Gunhild, the East German, in 1963 was one. "I was afraid that John would lose his security clearance," recalled brother Joe, "which would have ended his career."

The second came when the Air Defense Artillery branch split in 1968. Shalikashvili went to his commander's office to sign his preference for artillery. But the boss pushed back. Couldn't he see that air defense was the better career choice? Given his past seven years away from artillery, wasn't he worried about catching up to his peers? But staffing some concrete missile silo far removed from battle held no appeal; Shalikashvili hungered to "move, shoot, and communicate." After he left the room, the boss reportedly prophesied: "That guy has no future."

The Army War College, occurring at twenty years of service for most, marks the transition to senior leadership. Attendees are usually colonels, on the cusp of flag grade. Upon graduation, responsibilities dramatically intensify, as does competition for fewer available assignments. It's a time when officers, particularly those unsure about their future as a general officer, consider switching careers.

Only 4 percent of colonels get selected for the war college; the odds of a lieutenant colonel making the cut, even slighter. When chosen in 1977, Shalikashvili was a young lieutenant colonel—he'd been one of the fewer than 10 percent of majors who'd been selected "below the zone" for early promotion in 1973.

Yet after hearing he'd been admitted, Shalikashvili hesitated. "I might not go," he told his X.O. Instead, he just might pursue a dream of his.

Shalikashvili often did home improvement. In the early 1970s he stripped wax off the floors of his government-provided housing. In South Korea he crafted a cradle and changing table for his newborn son, Brant. Returning stateside for a new Pentagon job in the mid-1970s, the Shalikashvilis bought a home in Virginia where he fixed plumbing, wired lights, installed a garage door opener, and even laid a substantial brick patio and retaining wall.

So, when faced with the Army War College invite in 1977, what Shalikashvili told his X.O. was he was considering opening a hardware store. "Hardware stores have always fascinated me ever since the first time I walked into one of these old-fashioned musty [shops] where you can rummage and find old bolts and nails. It's a dream," he later explained. "The idea of being able to have something that you do and still have plenty of time to sit in the sun and read a book and contemplate life. . . ."

Yet, perhaps pointedly, Shalikashvili did attend the Army War College, graduating as "one of the most outstanding students in the class." And his next posting—as assistant chief of staff for operations, G-3, for the US Army Southern European Task Force (SETAF) in Vicenza, Italy—gave the lieutenant colonel a chance to prove himself in a position of senior responsibility doing high-level Cold War work at a bi-national NATO-oriented headquarters.

Here at this two-star command, he served as the principal advisor for all matters related to airborne operations, training, and conduct of contingency missions. His responsibilities included exercising control over extremely sensitive conventional and nuclear artillery units in Italy, Greece, and Turkey, and helping counter the Soviet threat on the inner-Germany boundary—high-level stuff for sure.

The position allowed many of his particular skills to come into play, noted John Herrling, a subordinate. Shalikashvili worked with not only US Air Force and Army units in Europe but also a variety of allies, including many flag-grade officers. "Few army officers brought in any language training at all. But Shali did well with all host nations—the Germans, Italians, and the Greeks. The Europeans knew his background, they knew Shali understood them." Additionally, "Shali could see what needed to be done at every level: USAREUR, SETAF, Shali's level, the levels below him. And, unlike many, he could take everything and put it together in a logical way; and when he told you about it, he put it in a language that everyone could understand."

And he did it all under one of his most challenging bosses he'd ever have. "My boss, a two star, had just fired his operations officer," Shalikashvili recalled. "When I reported in that first day, he said to me: 'I have been an S-3 in battalion. I've been a G-3 in a division, and I've been a corps G-3. Now what is it that you think can you do for me?' I went home and told my wife: 'We are in for a very tough time here.'"

Yet his boss would later evaluate: "When accepting Shalikashvili as the G-3, I knew that he would serve in that capacity for only one year. At that time the G-3 section was in shambles." But in the end "I was amazed at the results which he achieved and the short time in which he accomplished the task . . . I would be delighted to have him serve in my command as a Brigadier General *now*. Potential for greater responsibility is unlimited."

"During his time in Vicenza," explained 9th Infantry Division deputy commander J. B. Taylor, "Shali realized that he could make an impact on the international stage, and this was a big turning point for him." The assignment stimulated Shalikashvili in a way unfelt since his military career began in Alaska—making SETAF John Shalikashvili's second "aha" moment.

Within six months he was promoted to full colonel. Six more months and he held DIVARTY command—a "must have" position to reach flag grade. So, did the newly energized artillery officer appear to finally start star gazing then?

Many felt no. One subordinate later recalled how one of Shalikashvili's brigade commanders, Nick Andrachio, worried the boss was keeping himself from advancing "because he wouldn't toot his own horn." Only 5 percent of colonels make brigadier general. "I'll never make flag officer," Colonel Shalikashvili was known to say, even wagering $5 with a fellow officer's wife in Italy that he'd never be given even one star. Yet he made the cut at the Pentagon in 1983. "I can't believe they gave me that!" he exclaimed.

Upon reaching brigadier, many flag-grade officers don't survive long. That's because the US Congress limits the total number of general officers serving on active duty in the army to only 230 (unless posted to a "joint" billet, such as the Joint Staff). "When I was a one star, I was very hopeful that I would have the chance to serve as an assistant division commander," Shalikashvili continued. "For a young brigadier, that's sort of a culmination of many dreams and hopes. And if I'm lucky enough, I might make two star. And then if I'm really lucky, someone might give me a command of a division. But that's as far as you think."

Shalikashvili got off to a good start, serving as an assistant division commander to Saint in the early 1980s. Yet despite the support of two key board members, he failed to be promoted to major general the first time around. "I said to myself, 'If I have the board president on my side and my division commander on my side and I didn't make it, I will never make it." The next time, however, while working at the Pentagon in 1986, he became one of the 50 percent of brigadiers that typically make major general. "Nothing changed between my record that year and the next year," he recalled, so "I became convinced that much of it was luck."

Command of a division was now in Shalikashvili's sights. But there were only ten army divisions at the time. At his promotion ceremony, someone asked when he'd get a division. "I'm not going to," he replied. "I'm an artilleryman."

Shalikashvili returned to the Pentagon in 1986, taking with him his mantra that each new assignment would be his last. His tune did not change, even when ultimately picked to command the 9th Infantry Division at Fort Lewis. "This is it!" Shalikashvili said before leaving D.C. in 1987. The opportunity to end his career as a division commander was better than he could've hoped.

But was John Shalikashvili being truthful? Did he actually have career goals that extended beyond just the next grade or assignment? It's certainly possible—and, following his eye-opening tour in Italy, probably likely. But such an intensely private man with a reputation for humility could easily have kept such ambitions well hidden.

Clearly nobody enters the war college as a below-the-zone lieutenant colonel or rises to division command without substantial ambition. That's especially true for officers like Shalikashvili, who hadn't taken any shortcuts: not only did he lack significant combat experience, a critical skill for senior command, but he also never had a patron, a senior officer who fast-tracked his career.

"Certainly military officers have to have some ambition," agreed brother Joe, "and John certainly has had ambition all his life." This wasn't easy to pick up on, however: "Shali was really good at covering his competitive spirit," noted Tom Jaco.

Yet some did sense a certain vibe. A French army officer who played alongside Shalikashvili on a Fort Bliss soccer team in the early 1960s later remarked: "I was aware that you would achieve something great. You were already very impressive and, although extremely kind, somehow intimidating."

Part of his intensity was his work ethic. He was known for bringing home stacks of paperwork, sometimes even falling asleep while reading. As an X.O. to a battalion commander, his boss praised: "I have purposely overloaded Maj. Shalikashvili to determine at what point his efficiency would drop. To date it has not." Butch Saint recognized this: "If you gave him responsibility, he took it. You could heap things on him and he wouldn't flinch. Unless there was a rational reason he couldn't accept it, and then he'd tell you."

This intensity served him well. All his strengths—logistical prowess, diplomatic acumen, and the abilities to separate the wheat from the chaff, set and enforce clear standards, and work with a diverse group of people and forge productive consensus—would have been much weaker without repeated chances to develop them.

Yet it was exactly because he'd honed these skills, explained J. B. Taylor, that Shalikashvili hadn't needed to politic in order to rise in rank: "As a professional, smart, and dedicated officer, he was able to stand out and advance without pushing. People would say, 'Hey, let's get Shali for this.'"

Such distinction would carry him far. That's because in the "closed loop" of the US military—a system in which all leaders are chosen from within the organization—reputation is critical.

But what do you do when your tried-and-true approach to achieving success suddenly might not be enough?

The 9th Infantry Division would prove to be Shalikashvili's toughest assignment yet. If there ever was a time for an officer to start tooting his horn, to perhaps start letting the ends justify the means, to become more aggressive in order to further his career, this new position was it.

"The 9th Infantry Division was one of the largest, if not the largest, division in the army at the time," recalled Lieutenant General William Harrison, Shalikashvili's corps commander. "Many people didn't like that."

The division was also doing unusual things. In the late 1970s many felt that the army's focus on heavy tanks had left it without adequate maneuverability and that it was too slow in developing new equipment and tactics. In the early 1980s the division was thus given the go-ahead to turn itself into a division that was light in terms of deployability but, through an infusion of high technology, fielded significant armor-killing firepower.

The 9th Infantry Division sought to develop an "experimental mechanized/motorized" brigade of lighter, faster vehicles. "Instead of a tank with a gun, how about a truck with a big gun?" explained Frank Adams, the test brigade commander. "We had this new thing called a Humvee as well as dune buggies. We added weapons and radios and we drove them places people said they couldn't go. We tested everything: mobility, communication, command and control, weapons. We sought to create the capability to stay incredibly dispersed, rapidly mass at last minute, and integrate all the combined arms—heavy, motorized, and light—using high technology."

Yet "the 9th Infantry Division had been trying to make this motorized concept work for a number of years before Shali," recalled Deputy Commander Taylor. "There was doubt about its potential."

The biggest problem was that it lay outside the purview of TRADOC, the command that oversaw the US Army's training and operational doctrine. Shalikashvili was instead supposed to work directly with the chief of staff of the army—an arrangement that was sometimes problematic.

Once when Shalikashvili was visiting the general officer's mess at the Pentagon, the chief stopped by. "Is there anything I can do for you?" the general asked. "Yes, I need an assistant division commander [ADC] who is an infantryman, an experienced warfighter," replied Shalikashvili. Soon thereafter he received a call from the FORSCOM commander: "Don't you ever do that again. I decide what kind of ADCs you get. Don't talk to the chief of staff of the army about that." The head of FORSCOM at that time was none other than Colin Powell.

The 9th Infantry Division's financial resources also stirred resentment. "Our high-tech test bed had a separate budget stream," explained Stan Kwieciak, the division's DIVARTY commander. His DIVARTY once got $20 million to modify a TACFIRE 70 computer system for fire and control. But the artillery branch was heavily invested in a different system at the time. Someone from Fort Sill reached out to complain: "'God damn it, Stan Kwieciak, what are you doing up there? The program is AFATDS. Stick with it!'"

Yet the division would never be given enough money. "We just couldn't get that gun on a truck to work," recalled the division provost marshal, Larry Saunders, who later commanded the 509th Military Police Battalion. "You need a big gun to shoot tanks," explained Adams. "Yes, Humvees were quite maneuverable, but they were not good for either that size gun or for carrying troops."

And it wasn't solely about the money. Creating a new type of fighting force meant creating a battle concept, fighting doctrine, weapons systems, and training program. "A division commander," Shalikashvili later explained, "doesn't have the firepower to do that."

This was true. It would eventually take the chief of staff of the army, TRADOC, General Dynamics, and substantial sums of money to create such effective vehicles, which would become known as Strykers, and integrate them into the army.

This was the weak hand Shalikashvili knew he'd be playing when he was entrusted command of the division. And not long after arriving at Fort Lewis, he received a phone call that further dimmed his prospects to shine.

On the line was Major General Dutch Shoffner, an army staff officer in the Pentagon, with tough news: the 9th Infantry Division was being disbanded, and the downsizing would begin under Shalikashvili's watch.

Shoffner was expecting pushback. Earlier in his career Shoffner had fought back when told his own 3rd Infantry Division was being disbanded. "But Shali, unlike how many other people might react, did not piss and moan," Shoffner said. "It was an army-level decision. He knew that standing down was not something the organization does lightly. Shali trusted the decision-makers."

Shoffner was picking up on something that Joe Shalikashvili well understood: Yes, "John certainly has had ambition all his life," but "ego is something in this context where you try to bring yourself to the forefront or to make yourself the centerpiece of things. He did not have that and does not have that today."

Shalikashvili's lack of ego could in fact be viewed as the very foundation of his career success. The 1960s Fort Bliss soccer team is again illustrative. The team's coach later remembered Shalikashvili as a "tenacious, perseverant, courteous, loyal, and remarkable team-player, always showing the proper example, and exhibiting high quality of fair-play and respect to teammates and adversaries as well."

This wasn't simply a string of superlatives casually strung together. It was precisely because Shalikashvili had no ego need that he'd been able to take his traits of ambition, tenacity, and perseverance—things so often directed at self-promotion—and apply them instead to the larger group. By focusing his talents this way, it was understandable he'd gain a reputation for being courteous, loyal, a team player, a solid sportsman.

"Because Shali is a 'we' person and not an 'I' person," one close subordinate would later judge, echoing a common refrain, "he has the ability to generate innovative ideas and solutions from groups of people, solutions that might not have been generated from just one person."

This dynamic was evident in Shalikashvili's command of the 9th Infantry Division.

As a team player, he knew his role. Command Sergeant Major John Lee noted that, unlike many generals he'd worked under, "Shalikashvili did not major in minor affairs. He focused on the higher-order role of a division commander: how to resource, equip, train a many-thousand man division." He didn't micromanage. "He was very good at holding the leadership levels accountable for what was under their particular purview, and used the chain of command effectively."

Shalikashvili also stressed both teamwork and fair play throughout the division. "It was a test bed," explained Butch Saint, "and there were a lot of prima donnas." Frank Adams concurred: "Brigade commanders are colonels and, because they do much of the heavy lifting in the army, they can sometimes be full of themselves." Adams noted that "Shali, who had a say in determining who gets promoted to general some day, wouldn't let us colonels jockey for his favor. He wouldn't let us get into a pissing contest. 'Let's knock it off,' he'd say. Or 'you need to work a bit harder on getting along with your fellow brigade commanders.'"

Once, while visiting Fort Lewis, brother Joe, then a retired colonel, asked what division command was like. "I'll give an example," the younger Shalikashvili replied. "We had a new brigade commander and shortly after he arrived we were going to have to send him to Yellowstone to fight the forest fires that were engulfing the park. Two of my brigade commanders sat up all night to help that guy get prepared. We don't have one guy pitted against the other. I give these guys a job to do and they do it. They aren't looking for the glory."

Neither was he.

Take deactivation. "Think about what it would take to lead the shutdown of the 9th Infantry Division?!" Stan Kwieciak later asked rhetorically. He labeled it a "gut-wrenching" and "unglamorous" job, one requiring the division to turn in thousands of items of equipment, transfer thousands of soldiers, stand down flags, yet still keep the division a combat-ready organization.

But Fort Lewis commander Bill Harrison had this to say: "Faced with the Army decision to deactivate a brigade-sized element, [Shalikashvili] has maintained the morale, esprit, and warfighting confidence of his officers, noncommissioned officers, and soldiers," all while leading them in a "textbooks case" of how deactivation should be done. "In a situation in which it would have been very easy to limit one's expectations and allow a slackening of pace and a lowering of standards, he has ensured continued top performance by all, by setting a personal example."

Then there was his leadership on the division's experimental efforts. Though almost assuredly doomed to fail, he still applied enthusiasm and creativity. For one, "there was *no* doctrine for a motorized vision. John had to make one," recalled brother Joe. "Most would assume it would be based on infantry, given the division was an infantry division. But John to his credit thought cavalry/army."

According to subordinates, in trying to make the motorized brigade work, Shalikashvili was able to "operate in chaos without operating chaotically." Many found his appetite for creative solutions to both logistical problems and operational challenges infectious. "Yes, you can do it!" Shalikashvili would urge his team. "Don't give me five to six A-level ideas, instead give me twenty or thirty B-level ideas. We can improve later. Let's just keep the pace going."

Harrison recognized this: "He has an innovative, creative, and conceptual mind, and is constantly seeking ways to improve his division, the training for his soldiers, and the overall betterment of the U.S. Army."

The team, in other words, came first. "I never saw him exhibit career concern," recalled Rick Sinnreich, another DIVARTY commander. Asked if Shalikashvili was ambitious, Sinnreich responded: "Yes he was. He was ambitious for the division." Shalikashvili actually volunteered to take this experimental division to the National Training Center for the army's very first war game simulation for a division commander. "You had to be pretty sure of yourself to do that," Joe Shalikashvili later explained. And the division did not embarrass itself. Joseph Palastra, the FORSCOM commander at the time, recognized the division for its high level of unit tactical competence.

Before leaving the division, Shalikashvili tasked his staff with compiling a thick report for the chief of staff of the army detailing what the division had learned in the course of ten years of experimenting. "Shalikashvili wouldn't sugarcoat," recalled Mike Kendall, the division's chief of staff. "He told us to get the true story, warts and all." The army needed to know what worked and what didn't.

So what would be Shalikashvili's next job assignment? "Maj. Gen. John Shalikashvili," judged Harrison, "would be a superb corps commander, DCSOPS of the Army, and an eventual four-star general officer."

But the jump just from two to three stars is steep: only about 10 percent of major generals are selected annually for lieutenant general. Just prior to moving to Fort Lewis, Shalikashvili had sold his Virginia house.

This would be his last assignment, he'd said, and he'd be retiring in the Pacific Northwest, where his wife was from.

He kept an open mind however. They sold their house knowing that, because he was in the military, "we will have six years (at least) to buy a new one before we have to pay taxes on the money we make on this house." That gave him ample time to see if the army had further plans for him.

During his command of the 9th Infantry Division Shalikashvili was in fact selected for a third star, with FORSCOM commander Colin Powell rating him "one of the best division commanders in the entire Forces Command."

Like most senior generals, Shalikashvili aspired to command a corps. Yet his next assignment would be neither as a corps commander nor in a coveted Pentagon staff position. The slot offered to him—"DCINC" or deputy commander in chief, US Army Europe—was viewed by many as a terminal assignment. In the history of the US Army no DCINC, USAREUR, had gone on to a next posting. As USAREUR commander Butch Saint himself said: "The DCINC position *was* a dead-end job."

"Are you trying to send me a message?" Shalikashvili responded when the offer came. "Shut up and go," was the answer. That's all the army had available for him at this time.

Why did the army want him for the job?

One reason was the USAREUR commander himself wanted Shalikashvili. "I handpicked all people who worked for me," explained Saint in retirement. When commanding the 1st Armored Division in the mid-1980s, "I made some calls about Shalikashvili." Feedback was that he's "smart, a hard worker, honest, and that he got the job done and quietly"—all qualities critical to serving as Saint's deputy.

Saint's standards were high. He appreciated that Shalikashvili, unlike many of his other commanders, didn't need to go into the field as often in order to maintain gunnery standards to Saint's satisfaction. Hating bureaucratic paperwork and long studies, Saint wanted to get to the heart of the matter quickly, to implement a decision rapidly and effectively. "With Saint," judged Montgomery Meigs, "you had to listen to him very carefully to see if you could look over the horizon and give him only what he wants . . . and Shali was an expert at reading the Butch Saint tea leaves."

Saint also found Shalikashvili a reliable sounding board, someone who was on time, thorough, thoughtful, and if asked would offer candid thoughts. "He frequently surprised me with his insights." He also "wasn't afraid to tell me when it wasn't doing well or what needed to be done." "He's not a wilting wallflower."

Yet Shalikashvili knew his role. Saint, by his own admission, had to be top dog. "Even if my deputies made promises to other big players, I wouldn't recognize them. *I* make the decisions." But "Shali was not looking for the limelight," recalled Saint. "He never wanted my job." As noted by Saint's X.O., Tom Molino, Shalikashvili was loyal—he never complained about Saint. "Many others would have."

Additionally, commanders often pick deputies who complement them. And quite a few who knew Saint judged him not a strict rule-follower. According to Dave Mehar, who ran the Staff Action Division under Saint before going to work for Shalikashvili on the community side, "while at Fort Hood, Saint had respect for law but not necessarily for process. He had go-go dancers in the officers club. He kicked people out of the army for drugs, with no due process." Here in Germany, "he once changed orders from the chief of staff of the army in order to appoint the colonels he wanted." "He even once moved some helicopters without getting permission, because he knew it wouldn't be allowed. This pissed off both the US and the Germans. He almost got fired for that one."

Gay Van Brero of USAREUR's Housing Management Program, who knew both Shalikashvili and Saint, had privately nicknamed the former "the Gentleman Soldier" and the latter "the Rebel." Others felt similarly. "Saint would gleefully crash through obstacles that Shali would go around," noted Deputy Community Commander Thompson. Mike Molino agreed: "Shali had a remarkable way of avoiding confrontation, but Saint was a bully. He was totally confrontational," and "it was easy to piss Saint off." "Saint also had a long memory," added Mehar, "he'd get back at people who crossed him." Saint himself would say that "at the Pentagon, when I was walking down the hall, people would jump out of the way like fish from the path of a motorboat."

As "opposite ends of the spectrum," judged Mehar, "Shali and Saint needed each other. Saint knew Shali could get stuff done that he could not. If Butch Saint had been put in charge of Operation Steel Box, the Dutch—who weren't keen on the Gulf War to start with—probably would've left NATO." Thompson in turn felt "Shali would smooth out Saint." So much so, added an amazed Mehar, "he could turn Saint 178 degrees without ever actually disagreeing with him."

Saint himself recognized this: "Shali was both my student but also sometimes my teacher." Usually any differences between them, judged Saint, arose because his deputy "wanted to be nicer, to do things nicer. . . . Shali would work around it, not run over it."

What did Shalikashvili get out the relationship?

In retirement, he'd be asked if he'd had a mentor. "I really didn't. But if I had one that I learned more from than anybody else it was probably Butch Saint. He was an absolutely superb trainer. When he gave you a task he held you accountable for whatever you did." "When I came to Fort Lewis and took command of the division I had watched how the master commanded a division and how he dealt with his brigade commanders."

But there was more to it than that. "Saint was a community focused guy!" stressed Thompson. Shalikashvili had warned Thompson early on: "Saint has more spies than you, and will know more about your community than you do. But don't let it bother you." Almost every week Thompson would get notes from Saint with ideas on how to improve the community. He'd even get called to the carpet over little things, like when Saint learned that other communities had decorative flowers but Heidelberg did not. It had been Saint's idea to set up a volunteer mayor in each housing area within the community to provide leadership and assistance for families.

Like Shalikashvili, Saint understood that proper care of soldiers was critical for fighting effectiveness. Take Saint's focus on troop welfare in "Reforger," a NATO exercise to ensure troops from the United States and other NATO countries could quickly deploy to West Germany in the event of a conflict with the Warsaw Pact. The four star was deeply conversant in the details of moving and caring for the exercise's ten thousand participants: "How many commodes do you have? Do you have running water? How about duckboards for when things got muddy? This type of thing is *very* important, for troop morale and the ability to concentrate on fighting," Saint would explain.

"It was Shali and Saint's combined command environment that let me do the things necessary to get the community of excellence award," Thompson later recalled. "But the four star after Saint cared almost nothing about community. It is much easier to get things done as a community commander when you have the support of your boss."

Thus a second reason Shalikashvili agreed to once again become

Saint's deputy was assuredly that the job would allow him to make a positive difference in the lives of thousands of soldiers and their families.

"The only problem with him," Shalikashvili noted of Saint, "was if you screwed up you could never recover. So there were a number of officers that he fired needlessly and ended their careers." Thompson agreed: "You either did very well or you were gone. He'd wield a hatchet in a heartbeat." Like what happened to Shalikashvili's predecessor at the 1st Armored Division: "He didn't make brigadier general," crowed Saint. "I saw to that."

And that was a worry for European Commander Jack Galvin.

"Saint didn't always listen to EUCOM, didn't always go through McCarthy, my deputy in Stuggart, as he should," Galvin recalled in retirement. "I knew Shali would be a good buffer for Saint."

Additionally, while "Saint was good for war," Galvin added, "Shali was good for peace." EUCOM was now wrestling with the peace dividend. Home to almost 150,000 US soldiers before the Berlin Wall fell, Europe held "most of the U.S. Army." Now it had been ordered to reduce its troop strength by a whopping 50 percent. "This was a complex task," recalled Galvin. "There were rotations to consider—personnel were rotated every three years. And the families of some of soldiers sent to Gulf had decided to stay in Germany, and thus needed to be looked after." Galvin needed an expert manager to handle this, and Shalikashvili's 9th Infantry Division experience reducing troop strength while maintaining both morale and fighting trim was a huge draw.

For Galvin, then, Shali's rapport with the USAREUR commander was important—Saint's hatchet would not likely come out if his old deputy commander was once again given to him. In fact, Saint himself had an eye out for Shalikashvili. Fort Lewis commander Bill Harrison later recalled Saint asking: "So what are we going to do when Shalikashvili leaves the division?"

Unsurprisingly, the first name the chief of staff of the army offered Saint as his deputy was Lieutenant General John Shalikashvili.

Shalikashvili surely had a third calculus for accepting the job.

When his cohort of newly minted one stars was going through B. G. Charm School, the chief of staff of the army made clear: "Congratulations on your selection to become a brigadier general. You are now part of Army management. Your days of career development are over. So don't come to me to ask me for an assignment because it will be good for you. I am not interested in that. You will go on the assignment that I want you to do because it is good for the Army."

So, as a solid team player, Shalikashvili was predisposed toward accepting the USAREUR deputy job. But not without first discussing it at home. "If you don't want to leave, I don't have to do this," he told his son, who was starting his senior year of high school and had a girlfriend. "We can retire now." No, Brant replied, the family should go. "And I knew without a doubt that my dad would not have taken the position if either I or my mom had asked to stay."

Many lieutenant generals have only one posting. Moving on requires another three-star or a four-star assignment to open up. And given mandatory retirement laws, Shalikashvili needed to be promoted to a waivered position before September 1, 1991, or he'd be forced to retire.

The Gulf War had been an unexpected flash of opportunity. It gave many officers, including the irrepressible "Stormin' Norman" Schwarzkopf, the chance to distinguish themselves in combat. But not Shalikashvili. By assisting in the move of the VII Corps, he'd been only a logistical cog, albeit an important one, in the overall war machinery.

With only two or three lieutenant generals usually selected annually for full general, little wonder that, not long after Kuwait had been liberated in February 1991, Shalikashvili told his deputy community commander: "I'm at the end of my road."

But Shalikashvili's road had not ended. Luck intervened—perversely, in the form of a command error by Schwarzkopf himself.

On March 3rd the international coalition had met with the defeated Iraqi military to set the terms of the cease-fire agreement, which included establishing no-fly zones in northern and southern Iraq. A distracted Schwarzkopf agreed to Iraq's last-minute request to allow helicopters in the restricted zones "for administrative purposes." But later, following the Kurdish uprising in the north, the Iraqis then turned these helicopters into gunships—which turned the tide of the fighting and ultimately led to the massive exodus of refugees.

So Shalikashvili had been in the right place at the right time. For one, because the operation was based in Turkey, a NATO member, Provide Comfort fell under EUCOM's purview. And if the refugees had been fewer in number, the operation wouldn't have been upgraded from a joint to a combined task force. Or if Turkey had accepted the refugees, there wouldn't have been a pressing need to move them. And while no lieutenant general in the US military is expendable, Shalikashvili, as Butch Saint's deputy commander, could be freed from his position more easily than other senior generals. Finally, Shalikashvili's good relationship with his boss was critical. "Saint could have kept the DCINC from getting promoted," said Roger Cirillo, Saint's speechwriter, "including stopping Shali from commanding Provide Comfort."

* * *

So Seneca's quote—that luck is when preparation meets opportunity— had continued to hold for Shalikashvili. That's why he was here, standing in front of a customs house in Iraq, finishing up media interviews about how the international coalition was going to ameliorate this unprecedented humanitarian crisis.

But could Shalikashvili pull it off? It would be a "bear" of a problem, he told the assembled press, to move those Kurds out of the mountains. His next step would be to return to operational headquarters in Incirlik to begin working out a detailed plan.

So once again the task force commander climbed aboard the Black Hawk. And once again the whirl of helicopter blades lifted him into the air. As the aircraft banked toward Turkish territory, the two bridges of the border crossing area came into view. One span was destroyed, the other partially damaged. Tomorrow JTF-B would survey the bridges in preparation for making repairs—a critical first step because trucks, not helicopters, would be the most effective way to pull together the planned refugee camps in the security zone.

It wouldn't be the first time that the dismantling and rebuilding of a bridge marked a key turning point in John Shalikashvili's life.

17

Briefing Congress

John Shalikashvili was once again assigned to the Pentagon, only this time it was a plum assignment: serving as assistant to the chairman of the Joint Chiefs of Staff. "I saw Gen. Shali as a commander of troops work a miracle in northern Iraq," Colin Powell later explained. So "I knew that this was somebody that, even though I had known about, I had to get to know better."

Now Congress too was itching to meet the miracle worker. The former task force commander was here today at the Rayburn Office Building, ready to give testimony before a House Armed Services Committee defense policy panel.

Panel chairman Representative Les Aspin called the hearing to order. "President Bush has said he won't stand by this winter while starvation strikes the Soviet Union—or what was the Soviet Union. I believe he's right to make this pledge. I've suggested to my colleagues that some of the funds from the defense budget might be made available for aid to help prevent the chaos this winter in a nation with nearly thirty thousand nuclear weapons. It's defense by a different means, but it is defense nonetheless. Better to forestall chaos now than to deal with its impact on national security at greater cost later." Maybe "Provide Comfort can offer some kind of a model to tell us about the role the U.S. military could play in delivering aid to the Soviet Union."

Congress's curiosity made sense. As noted in a Provide Comfort after-action report, there were "no doctrine and training publications/programs for refugee/displaced civilians operations. The UNHCR has it only. Few military or civil agencies know of it."

"I am very pleased to discuss some key aspects of Operation Provide Comfort," Shalikashvili began, "in which I of course had the privilege to participate." Eschewing prepared remarks, the general instead requested permission to walk the panel through a forty-five-minute slideshow describing the Kurdish rescue operation.

First he overviewed the operation. It had been an unprecedented gathering of manpower: over 30,000 service members from thirteen countries, including 21,700 soldiers, sailors, marines, and airmen directly assigned to the combined task force as well as 10,000 additional supporting personnel in the area of operations. Deployed by air and sea from locations all over Europe, the United States, the Persian Gulf, and as far away as Australia, they ran the gamut of specialties—special forces, engineers, signal, medical, civil affairs, pilots, riggers.

There were also untold numbers of staff sent by some fifty international and nongovernmental organizations. "I'm sure there are many more in the world, but I'm hard-pressed to think of any names that don't appear here," Shalikashvili chuckled in seeming disbelief as he offered up a multislide list of the operation's civilian partners.

Then there was the Herculean effort of gathering and distributing matériel. "We had to develop a distribution system in an area where there was absolutely none." From the seaports and airports of debarkation in Turkey continuing on 350 miles overland via just one road into the mountainous border, across bitter, dangerous peaks, and then down into the Iraq lowlands, Provide Comfort's area of operations covered eighty-three thousand square miles, over half the size of the state of California.

The task force had to bring in the equipment and supplies to build a distribution system, including forward logistics bases, that would deliver a whopping 17,000 tons of relief supplies. About 6,200 tons was distributed each by airdrop and helicopter, with the rest by surface transport. The airlift component alone—from the first delivery of 27 tons on April 7 to a high of 969 tons on April 23—was the largest in human history, larger even than the famed Berlin airlift.

How does one visualize such numbers? If packed into standard forty-foot shipping containers maxed out on carrying capacity and then hitched up to tractor trailers arranged bumper to bumper, such a convoy would extend 6 miles, circling the Pentagon—the world's largest office building—an astounding 6.9 times.

After stabilizing the mountain camps, the rescuers then repatriated the Kurds. How many refugees did they move in all? Shalikashvili pegged the number at about 500,000, though others held higher estimates. To move such a mass of humanity under normal circumstance would have required a fleet of 5,556 of the largest school buses, each 45 feet long and seating 90 passengers. Lined up bumper to bumper, that caravan would have stretched 47.4 miles. With one bus embarking every sixty seconds, it

Kurdish refugees travel by truck between their mountain campsites and tent cities established back in the Iraqi lowlands by US military personnel. (DoD photo, DN-ST-91-03171.)

would've taken 92.6 hours—almost four full days—to launch the Kurds on their way home.

"It's no easy task to take half a million people from the mountains, who by now have been greatly weakened by this ordeal they'd gone through, and move them down very treacherous mountain passes into the valleys of Iraq," Shalikashvili continued. "From the security standpoint, Mr. Chairman, the thing that gave us the biggest fits . . . were the absolutely untold number of mines and booby-traps that we ran into in this area. . . . I've never seen an area mined so heavily. Mines of every description, every make."

Yet despite all these obstacles the task force pulled it off—and in only six weeks. "On June 6 we transferred operation of all our temporary camps and food distribution and medical support . . . to the UNHCR," with the last coalition soldiers departing northern Iraq on July 15.

Amazingly, no serious armed clashes had broken out with the Iraqi military. Sure, there'd been plenty of resolve testing. The task force had monitored the Iraqis almost nonstop—including undertaking a prodigious fifty-two ground reconnaissance missions. But their efforts paid off, because the very few task force casualties, Shalikashvili told the panel bittersweetly, had come from land mines.

And there was a happy ending even beyond the happy ending. Shalikashvili's great fear—that IOs and PVOs would be stuck indefinitely maintaining the "temporary" refugee centers in northwestern Iraq—never materialized. "There was never more than 60,000 in these centers at one time," the general explained, with most Kurds returning to their homes. "As of two days ago, only 1,300 were in any kind of temporary camp. Not in my wildest dreams would I have imagined that would have been possible."

How had such a miracle come about?

Shalikashvili first credited the US military itself: "We bring some very unique capabilities that we can project very quickly." This included engineering units to widen roads and repair bombed out airfields; long-haul communications systems, including tactical, theater, and especially strategic airlift; and the security forces to create the umbrella under which this all operated. The greatest of these assets was strategic airlift: "When you consider that we had to project ourselves 10,000 miles it is no small feat. Others perhaps have [a similar range of capabilities] but it takes them longer to project."

He listed out and offered praise to not just the coalition partners but all countries who sent relief and other logistics supplies. None was too small to escape his appreciation, including Romania, which donated blankets. "Badly needed," the general impressed on the panel.

What else made the operation successful? It was the people. And here is where Shalikashvili liberally used superlatives. Like how Deputy Commander Jim Jamerson was an "absolute professional." Or that JTF-A's Dick Potter was a "super soldier," and his 10th Special Forces Group performed an "absolutely magnificent effort through and through." And "by every measure" JTF-B's Jay Garner also "did an equally outstanding job."

There was high praise too for Colonel Richard Naab and the Military Coordination Center. "When they saw something that the Iraqis were doing that was interfering with the operation, Naab was on them in a flash and was . . . absolutely key in an operation such as this."

He praised Brigadier General Harold Burch, who "had the thankless task of building that logistics infrastructure . . . that turned out to be our greatest challenge and also to be our greatest savior." "I don't know of a single incident worth mentioning here where we weren't able to do what we set out to do because we could not get the supplies forward."

Then there were the voluntary organizations. "Without their help and guidance to me personally and to every one throughout the organization we would have been extraordinarily hard pressed to complete the effort in the way we did. It absolutely has to be said that they are [an] indispensable piece of the kind of operation we were asked to run in northern Iraq." Working hand-in-hand with them was Donald Campbell and his "magnificent" reserve soldiers from Civil Affairs. Without them "we could not have achieved our timelines."

Finally, he mentioned the temporary way stations the task force constructed in the mountains to aid the repatriation effort: "Each one had medical facility, food distribution facility, temporary housing for those that needed it. We had a number of people who fled in their cars and abandoned them in mountain passes when they couldn't travel further. We sent mechanics out to fix cars, brought new batteries in, and had gas stations at these way stations. A very elaborate effort, but [it] paid great dividends because I don't think that you back here read any sort of headlines about mishaps as we brought nearly half a million people out of these mountains." "I truly don't know of a mishap, because of folks like Potter, Garner, and all the other folks who did such a masterful job."

One major aspect of the operation mostly absent from Shalikashvili's testimony was the sizing of the security zone. "We'd put a lot of thought into the refugee centers we built around Zakho," Deputy Task Force Commander Jamerson later explained, "but we were surprised to find that people didn't want to stay. Many wanted to continue on southward, toward home in Mosul, Erbil, and even Kirkuk."

On May 12—with many refugees still remaining in the mountains—fifteen hundred Kurds actually held a demonstration in Zakho demanding the allies not only expand the zone to include the city of Duhok, just south of Zakho, but also work out a political settlement on an autonomous Kurdistan that would protect them from Saddam Hussein. The Iraqis, clearly wanting the international coalition to leave, agreed to meet with Kurdish elders on the 13th to discuss Duhok's inclusion in the zone. Potter recalled accompanying Shalikashvili to meet the Kurdish faction leader Jalal Talibani. "A big topic of discussion was how the US was going to guarantee Kurdish autonomy." "It was clear that the Kurds, without mentioning it by name, really wanted the Mosul oil fields" to be included in the security zone.

But that was dangerous. There was huge pressure coming from Washington not to expand the zone beyond the area of Zakho—this was a humanitarian mission, not US involvement in local politics.

Whatever decision he made, Shalikashvili faced substantial risks. "You know, we could get fired," he actually told his deputy. At one point the commander confided in the task force's operations officer that he was thinking of retiring. "I've been dragging my wife and family around the world. I really enjoyed my posting at Fort Lewis, and when I retire I might go and organize the base history museum archives."

Shalikashvili ended up choosing a middle path. "He made the decision not to go past Duhok," recalled Jamerson, which lay midway between Zakho and Mosul. Yet toward the end of the operation, a visiting US government official told Jamerson: "We almost fired Shalikashvili for that." "That was indicative of how the United States operates in a crisis," the deputy commander reflected. Washington had instructed them to get the Kurds home, without offering any guidelines or talking points. "Yet they can punish you after," the air force general noted, "for doing it the wrong way."

But in the end Shalikashvili hadn't been fired. Instead he was a welcome guest here before the House Armed Services Committee.

"It was an eye opener to me," the general admitted as he wrapped up his testimony, "how much can be done by men and women who see an awesome task ahead of them and come to the task with enthusiasm and not to fight over turf, wire diagrams, and who works for whom or what. . . . I don't recall one meeting where someone started pointing at someone else and saying that is your job, why don't you start doing this. It was just great."

At the end of Shalikashvili's remarks, Representative Norman Sisiki, who'd traveled to the region to see the operation firsthand, looked pointedly at Shalikashvili from the dais. "General, you talked about all your commanders," he said, "but I can tell you that it was your enthusiasm over there that really did the job. And you really are to be commended."

Was this enthusiasm motivated by more than just professionalism? In the midst of the operation, one reporter asked Shalikashvili: "I understand you were a refugee yourself, fleeing Poland. Does that give you some empathy with what's going on here?"

"I suppose so," Shalikashvili replied. And in fact once, during one visit to Duhok to oversee the expansion of the security zone, a particular memory had flooded back. While opening a can of fruit salad, he remarked that he couldn't eat such fruit—a luxury his family never could have secured in wartime Europe—without thinking of the trip to he took to the New World on the SS *America*. But his refugee experience, he

A beaming Shalikashvili visiting with Kurdish refugee children during Operation Provide Comfort. Throughout his career he'd be well known for caring
about and enjoying spending time with kids. (DoD photograph, courtesy of the
NBR Gen. John Shalikashvili Archives.)

explained to that reporter, "was a very long time ago. I think any one of
us, regardless of our background, who sees the suffering in those mountain passes would be moved to tears."

In a later interview Shalikashvili would reflect on Provide Comfort:
"All you had to do was look at the soldiers, marines, holding children.
You could tell in their eyes, after having been trained to fight wars and
kill, what excitement it was for them to be saving lives on such a vast
scale. I think all of us at one time or another were Boy Scouts or Girl
Scouts or something. We all learned to do good and to take our coat off
and put it over the water puddle so the old lady can cross the street safely.
But very few of us ever have the opportunity to help others on such a vast
scale as these operations."

Interestingly, very few people knew that Provide Comfort was actually not the first time Shalikashvili had helped the US military provide
substantial humanitarian relief to needy war refugees.

* * *

John Shalikashvili did not have a typical Vietnam War experience.
Because of the relatively limited positions for artillery and armor,

Major Shalikashvili served his one-year tour as a senior district advisor with the Military Assistance Command, Vietnam (MACV).

Arriving in June 1968, he was assigned to the Trieu Phong district, located north of the city of Quang Tri, not far from the demilitarized zone. His district stretched from the Gulf of Tonkin to the border in the west and from about five miles south of the DMZ to just above Quang Tri.

Being a senior district advisor meant assisting the district in both counterinsurgency and pacification efforts. "It was a position," explained Shalikashvili's boss, Provincial Senior Advisor Harvey Mooney, "that gave both joint and combined experience." Joint because the senior advisor worked with the marines, air force, and even the CIA. Combined in part because the MACV teams themselves were multinational: there were Australian advisors, many who served as warrant officers, as well as Filipinos, on the pacification side, in charge of boosting rice production. It was also combined in that a district advisor served the district chief, a major in the Vietnamese army, who was both a government administrator and local military commissar. As such Shalikashvili dealt with Vietnam's local and regional forces on a daily basis, and occasionally with the regimental commander of the main force Vietnamese army. "We were combined before the term became popular!" Mooney enthused.

Shalikashvili lived alongside 150 Vietnamese and ten to fifteen other nationalities in a triangular French-built fort. "My team," he wrote to his parents, "consists of a captain as my assistant, a lieutenant, an Australian warrant officer, and three sergeants." The team had their own separate living quarters and prepared their own food. They relied on generators for electricity, well water for washing, and canned water to drink. There was a medic on site, and a nearby hospital was just a two- or three-minute helicopter ride away. They had radios to listen to and, unless floods came, received mail daily. He'd regularly receive packages of magazines and even canned fudge from his wife; he'd string up the empty cans to use as perimeter lights. "So life is quite comfortable," he assured his parents, "and we don't lack anything in particular."

Yet "it was *very* hard to be a major and only have four or five men to lead," explained Peter Luitwieler, an intelligence officer who served under Shalikashvili. "But Shali had a good way of pulling the team together. He wasn't an egotist. He didn't raise his voice but led by example, led with a smart mind. And he was good at delegating, which is a must if you are going to be a MACV."

But he could be firm when needed. David Millie, an Australian who served as a senior advisor in a nearby district, recalled: "There were six different Australian warrant officers under Shali. He kept dismissing them because they would violate his no-alcohol policy."

Shalikashvili needed his men to stay sharp, of course, for this was wartime. And combat, a main metric for judging an officer's abilities, was a critical assignment.

To assist his district chief in counterinsurgency, he helped train the local militia and, as Shalikashvili later recalled, helped "to patrol [up to] the demilitarized zone and to keep track of how many North Vietnamese units were coming across."

Shalikashvili's experience was again atypical in that he was paired with a capable and professional counterpart, Major Nim of the Vietnamese army. "Nim was so respected in the District that we gave him the money we'd collected to buy tractors and plows and put him on a plane to Saigon to make the purchases himself," recalled Mooney. Like Shalikashvili, Nim too was an outsider. "He really was a North Vietnamese who had come over to the South," Shalikashvili later recalled, "but he was a very well respected leader and very competent. By the time we got through we were quite a team."

Another uniqueness of Shalikashvili's tour of duty was that because he arrived after the Tet Offensive, he was spared that violence and the subsequent blow to morale. Yet he did experience his share of local firefights, particularly at the outset. "You ask what we do when we go searching for [Vietcong]," he wrote his parents. "Well, usually we fly by helicopter to an area where we think the VC are hiding, surround it and then start a detailed search. Depending on how many VC we think are in the area, that's how many troops we take. This can vary from 10 to 20 people [even up] to 600. So far we have been extremely fortunate and have captured or eliminated quite a number of VC."

Shalikashvili would earn a Bronze Star for leading an assault on a North Vietnamese command post that had been turned into islands due to heavy flooding. "We had a fairly good-size firefight. And what I remember of it is—no particular heroic action on my part. Except that we were all in boats and they were on land. And we were trying to make it to that land so we could overwhelm them. And take them prisoners." "In the end, we succeeded."

"He turned the most populated District of the Province from a heavily infested VC dominated area to the most pacified District," his superiors noted. They credited this and many other advances made in the district to "the unique rapport between Maj. Shalikashvili and his Viet-

Major John Shalikashvili served as a senior district advisor in Trieu Phong, Vietnam, near the demilitarized zone, from June 1968 to June 1969. For his counterinsurgency efforts, he was awarded a Bronze Star with a "V" for heroism. His work on "pacification," or economic development, provided his first glimpse into the military's effectiveness in providing humanitarian relief. (Courtesy of the NBR Gen. John Shalikashvili Archives.)

namese counterpart." They noted that enhanced security of the district allowed Shalikashvili to prompt the district chief into programs to stabilize and develop the area—like helping organize local elections, building wells, and working with officials on rice production.

"I gather that the press and TV are reporting all kinds of horrible things in our area here," Shalikashvili wrote in another letter, "but I hate to say it, we haven't had a good fight in almost two months and no matter how hard we look, we just can't find any VC in our area . . . so the majority of time continues to be taken up with feeding people, building houses, etc."

"Right now I'm engaged in building a road from district headquarters up north to a place called Cua Viet," went yet another letter. "Since we never had a road to that part of the district, it should do a lot to improve the economy of this area. Right now I have about five bulldozers and countless trucks working on this road and I hope that before I leave on R&R I will be able to take the first drive on my new road." And in yet another: "Today I spent half the day at a dedication of a new children's hospital that the 3rd Marine Division is building for the Vietnamese children from this area. It's really a beautiful big hospital and I'm sure will be much appreciated." "However," he added, "as good as the idea of a children's hospital is, the ceremony was very boring and I got tired of all the speeches."

Then a rare opportunity came his way—to serve as senior advisor for Operation Fisher, a refugee relocation project in Gia Dang, out on the east coast. "What we are doing is relocating all the people who now live on the coast into a central camp where we can provide security for them. It involves some 12,000 people and so I have my hands full. In order to oversee this operation I moved my headquarters out here to the coast." The resettlement, including constructing a road linking the camp to Quang Tri, would take about a month.

"Nobody is really sure why the enemy is so quiet," Shalikashvili wrote after moving back to his district headquarters after Operation Fisher ended, so "we do most of our work in civic action"—"that is helping the people get on their feet." "Let's hope it stays this way."

On one occasion he'd return to the resettlement area to open a new school. "If you would see those little guys going to school for the first time," he wrote, "you would know that we not only should be here, but will understand when I say that I sincerely hope we will not desert Viet Nam. . . . Had you heard the people—10,000 of them—telling me that this was the first Tet in many, many years that they were able to spend without having to worry about war and shooting and bombing you would understand that what we did there was good and worthwhile."

"I really believe that we can help these people," he later wrote. "For the almost nine months that I have been here, in our district alone, we were able to bring about 45,000 people under government control. That means giving them schools, dispensaries, a place to grow their rice, relative security from VC terror."

"In other words, what I'm saying is that I really believe in what I'm doing here. So don't worry too much—your son is very happy because he is doing what he likes to do."

<u>Part V</u>

To Confirm a Chairman

Defense Secretary Les Aspin worked hard to ensure President Clinton "hit a home run" with his choice of nominee for chairman of the Joint Chiefs of Staff. (DoD photo, DN-SC-93-0169.)

18

Getting to Yes

August 11, 1993—Washington, D.C.

It was Wednesday midafternoon, and Secretary of Defense Les Aspin, working from a borrowed office at the White House, was teeter-tottering between anxious and apoplectic. The president had said that given the outsized figure of Colin Powell, he wanted to "hit a home run" with his choice for the next chairman of the Joint Chiefs. So Aspin had labored his damnedest to make it happen. But complication after complication had arisen. And now here on the phone was White House counselor David Gergen threatening to postpone the decision until the end of the month. "The only way on God's green earth we get out of this thing," Aspin barked back, "is to do it *now*."

That made it the bottom of the ninth. Today they'd taken a second swing at their best candidate, but to Aspin's mortification the ball once again seemed headed straight toward the foul pole.

Was it going to bounce the wrong way this time too?

* * *

It wasn't supposed to be this way. On July 22 Aspin sent the president a memo that stressed: "It is very important that there be sufficient time for the confirmation process and an orderly transition," because "by law, the new chairman must be sworn in by October 1st."

The president needed to appear decisive in naming his new chairman, if only to dispel the residual stink from the administration's "Ground Hog Day"–style mishandling of the recent Supreme Court nomination: candidate after candidate had been summoned to the White House, each then left dangling offstage as Clinton ogled the next.

Keeping with strong tradition, the administration limited consideration to the fifteen top officers: the five on the Joint Staff (the vice chairman and the army, navy, air force, and marines service chiefs) and the ten combatant commanders or CINCs With all of them assembling in D.C.

in mid-August for the annual "Chiefs and CINCs" conference, Aspin had timed the selection process well.

He also prepared meticulously. In early August he provided Clinton not only a checklist of a dozen qualifications required for the chairmanship and the names of the eight strongest candidates but even a video screening highlighting their qualifications.

Two names topped the list: John Shalikashvili, serving now as SACEUR/EUCOM commander, and marine general Joseph P. Hoar, leader of Central Command. The army general was the front-runner—not just for Aspin and Powell but for most White House notables who'd helped determine the selection criteria.

There was just one problem: Shalikashvili's enthusiasm for the job hovered below lackluster.

On Sunday, August 8, Shalikashvili flew in from Belgium for a meeting on Sarajevo with Aspin. He'd already told Powell he wasn't interested in the post, but Aspin wanted to hear it from Shalikashvili himself.

Powell had requested the general first stop by Quarters 6, the chairman's residence at Fort Myer, before heading to the Pentagon. "I am honored to be considered," Shalikashvili told his boss shortly after arriving. But then he drummed out a three-beat response he'd offer Aspin later that day: "But I would prefer to remain as SACEUR because I can serve the country best in that capacity," "I don't wish to follow in the footsteps of Colin Powell," and finally, ever dutiful, "but if asked I would salute and do my best."

The nation's top military man wasn't necessarily put off by Shalikashvili's reticence, however. Not a year after taking him on as assistant to the chairman, Powell had nominated Shalikashvili to replace four-star general Butch Saint, Shalikashvili's former boss, who was retiring as head of USAREUR. "You shouldn't do that," Shalikashvili protested, "I am a three star. . . . There are a lot more senior three stars with more experience and also four stars." But Powell persisted, and Bush signed off on the job promotion.

As Shalikashvili was preparing to leave for Heidelberg, fate intervened. George Joulwan's nomination to replace Jack Galvin, who was retiring from his SACEUR post, was derailed by National Security Advisor Brent Scowcroft, who hadn't gotten along with Joulwan back in the Nixon administration.

"Listen, Shali. George is just too much high maintenance. I am not going to send him to replace Jack Galvin as SACEUR," Shalikashvili later recalled Powell telling him. "I am going to send you."

"Shali, I think, was a little shocked when I said, 'Shali, you are the man,'" Powell himself later remembered. This premier job traditionally went to a senior four star and even once to a four star *after* he'd served as chairman of the Joint Chiefs. "He kind of braced back," Powell continued, "and I said, 'John, you are the man, and I have no doubt about your ability to do it.'"

"You can't do that for the same reason that I wasn't quite the right guy for USAREUR," Shalikashvili again objected. "There are lots of very senior European four stars that will be working for me. They are not as cavalier about this rank issue as we are." "I will take care of that, don't worry," the chairman countered. So once again Powell submitted Shalikashvili's name to the president, this time also recommending him for a fourth star.

That's when Shalikashvili actually urged then-President Bush not to consider him. "I thought it was bad precedent," the general explained. "Never in our history [had] a three-star general been promoted to a four-star general and his first job be Supreme Allied Commander of NATO. After all, this is the job Eisenhower had."

But with Galvin himself backing Shalikashvili as his replacement, the president accepted Powell's recommendation. On June 24, 1992, the chairman pinned a fourth star on Shalikashvili's uniform and leapfrogged him over dozens of more senior officers to make him the top US military man in Europe.

It was an improbable achievement. In the entire history of the US Army, hundreds of thousands of officers had watched their careers end well before this point. By adding that fourth and final star, Shalikashvili had come to fill one of the only seven slots, plus a handful of exceptions, that Congress allows for four-star generals in the army at one time. He was only the 148th full general to serve in the US Army.

Then, just one year into Shalikashvili's five-year tenure as SACEUR, "it was time for me to step down," Powell recalled, "and we were looking for the best person to replace me." "We looked over all the admirals and generals who were available, and I said to [Aspin], 'Once again, it is Shali.'"

And, lo and behold, Shalikashvili was again demurring.

One of his reasons—"I didn't wish to be reading in the papers for four years 'He's OK, but he's no Colin Powell'"—was almost ironic. The administration wanted Shalikashvili precisely because, although possessing many of Powell's positive attributes, he differed from the current chairman in critical ways.

Take the president's first requirement—what Aspin's memo described as "somebody who can run military operations." Shalikashvili had held operational command at every level from platoon to division, and now led the US military's most important warfighting command. Powell in contrast never led a division and spent far more time than Shalikashvili in staff jobs and in Washington policy posts.

Therein lay a huge part of the problem. Extremely politically savvy and enjoying sky-high popular support following the stunning Gulf War victory, Powell could frustrate policies he disagreed with—especially those that disrupted the military as an organization. "You've got to see our force as a human living organism and treat it as such," he once warned.

Little wonder Clinton's bold campaign promise to end the ban on gays in the military became the administration's first big controversy. The armed forces had pushed back forcefully, leading openly gay Representative Barney Frank to charge Powell with "trying to submarine the President politically."

"Homo[sexuality] is a problem for us," the chairman told Aspin early on, listing out the reasons: there was a ban on sodomy under military law, an "absolute right to privacy simply does not exist" in the close quarters of military life, AIDS was a concern, and deciding if straight soldiers would then be forced to live with gay soldiers was a thorny issue that would be of grave concern to parents of young soldiers.

Not wanting his military to be sucker punched, Powell offered a possible compromise: "We stop asking." As part testimony to Powell's political virtuosity, "Don't Ask, Don't Tell" would become a Defense Department directive by the end of 1993—and stay in place for over seventeen years.

Selecting a new chairman was thus the administration's opportunity to tilt agenda-setting power back toward the civilian leadership. And nowhere was the need greater than on the two interrelated issues of the use of force and defense cuts.

In terms of the former, Powell had helped shape the Bush administration's policy of remaining hands-off in Eastern Europe despite the expanding conflicts in Bosnia, Slovenia, Macedonia, and Croatia.

The roots of Powell's outlook lay in his two years of duty in Vietnam, first as a rifle company commander advising South Vietnamese units and then as infantry battalion X.O. During his first tour, he was surprised that the small outpost he'd been assigned to was built in a highly vulnerable location. The camp was located there, explained his Vietnamese counterpart, to protect the accompanying airfield. And why the airfield? To supply the outpost, of course. In the subsequent decades Powell spent trying to wrap his head around US involvement in that country, "Vietnam rarely made much more sense than Captain Hieu's circular reasoning on that January day in 1963."

"We kept adding troops, we kept adding bombers, we kept adding fighter planes," Powell critiqued. "There were 3,000 advisers when I got there, and my contingent brought it up to 11,000. But it wasn't enough. We kept adding, adding, adding, and we deceived ourselves into thinking we were making more progress than we actually were."

The lessons he learned in the Vietnam quagmire solidified into what would become known as the Powell Doctrine: no force should be used unless it is overwhelming; has clear, achievable, and finite goals; and is broadly supported by the American people.

This doctrine meant that, despite the ethnic cleansing being carried out by the Serbs, Powell was firmly against setting up an air-exclusion zone over Bosnia, just as he rejected the stance by Prime Minister Margaret Thatcher and others that the West should undertake limited air strikes to deter the Serbs from shelling Sarajevo. "As soon as they tell me it is limited, it means they do not care whether you achieve a result or not," Powell warned. "As soon as they tell me 'surgical,' I head for the bunker." So cautious was the military that when administration officials prepared a diplomatic protest to warn Serbian combat planes to stop shadowing international relief flights, the Pentagon scrubbed the document of any implicit threat of military action.

Many in the new administration, however, were unwilling to accept the notion that military force couldn't be used prudently short of all-out war. The defense secretary was one of them. "If we say it is all or nothing and then walk away from the use of force in the Balkans," Aspin warned, "we are sending a signal to other places that there is no downside to ethnic cleansing. We are not deterring anybody."

Yet another was the US ambassador to the United Nations. Madeleine Albright later recalled that whenever policymakers discussed taking action in the Balkans, Powell "replied consistent with his commitment to the doctrine of overwhelming force, saying it would take tens of thousands of troops, cost billions of dollars, probably result in numerous casualties, and require a long and open-ended commitment of US forces. Time and again he led us up the hill of possibilities and dropped us off on the other side with the practical equivalent of 'No can do.'" At one National Security Council meeting, she even challenged the chairman: "What's the point of having this superb military you're always talking about if we can't use it?"

The doctrine of overwhelming force didn't just mean "a skewed set of intervention choices that seem driven more by favorable force ratios, as in Somalia, than by national interest," a *New York Times* editorial critiqued, but had also "become the rationale for larger-than-necessary military budgets." That's because maintaining a decisive force to win any major war was an expensive proposition—one that seemed increasingly less necessary with the demise of the Cold War.

So, in February 1993 Aspin ordered the Pentagon to cut $14 billion from the next year's budget, a first step toward trimming two hundred thousand troops beyond what Powell had publicly argued was prudent. A whopping $60 billion was to be cut by 1997.

In staunch disagreement with such steep downsizing, the chairman in turn introduced measures to reduce overlapping roles and missions in the military that fell far short of the administration's expectations.

He also took the unusual political step of responding to critics by publishing a subsequent *New York Times* opinion piece entitled "Why Generals Get Nervous." After offering recent examples when US troops had indeed put themselves in harm's way, Powell then spelled out his case for why the complexity of the Bosnian crisis called for a political rather than a military solution.

With this seemingly unbridgeable gulf separating the chairman from the administration, Powell wanted out. Just as he'd done even earlier with Defense Secretary Dick Cheney, Powell had unsuccessfully petitioned Aspin to let him step down months before his term expired on September 30, explaining that he wanted to give his successor more influence this summer in shaping the Pentagon's long-term budget.

With Powell's exit by October a given, the Clinton administration wanted a chairman who'd be as much a flexible visionary as Powell was viewed conservative and unimaginative. But—as warned by former chairman Admiral William Crowe, a key Clinton advisor—the hard part would be finding a military man with an open mind. A lifetime of manuals, checklists, and standard operating procedures almost precluded it.

So who should replace Powell? The loose tradition was to rotate the position among the services. Next up should be the air force. But airmen and seamen, long sparring partners, were now at each other's throats over recent defense cuts. With deeper reductions looming, appointing another army man seemed a sensible compromise.

One army general known for his flexible mind was Shalikashvili. In no small part because of Operation Provide Comfort, Chief of Staff of the Army General Gordon Sullivan would liken Shalikashvili to the great jazz improvisational artist Dave Brubeck: "highly trained in the classical approach but able to operate successfully, almost magically so, in new conceptual territory."

In terms of budget cuts, Shalikashvili had repeatedly found creative ways to maintain an effective fighting force in the face of deep downsizing. He did so as a two star when beginning the deactivation of the 9th Infantry Division. As a three star he'd helped manage the steep drawdown of army forces in Europe. And now as a four star, the SACEUR was overseeing the continuing drawdown of all US troops in Europe.

Shalikashvili was more accepting of budget cuts in part because he believed that a key part of readiness was the quality of life of service members, and not just expensive machinery and weapons systems. Shalikashvili also believed that, given years of defense budget wrangling, what the US military and America's allies now needed was for the Pentagon to settle on a final reduced force structure, whatever that was, and stick with it. The uncertainty itself was doing harm to US military readiness and reputation.

He also held more flexible views on the use of force. If Powell's hypercautious approach was forged in Vietnam, Shalikashvili's outlook was similarly rooted in his own experience there. He later recalled that when leaving Vietnam, "I was convinced we were winning because [in] that sector where I was we were doing very well. The VC were not controlling anything. The North Vietnamese weren't either." "I thought that we were very successful in bringing peace and stability to that small world where I lived." That's why "I didn't have the feeling of trauma. I didn't have the feeling of the emotional pull and tug that the nation experienced back here."

Recent media reports were thus describing Shalikashvili as an adherent to the "Vietnam-plus" school of military power. While agreeing to the importance of having clear objectives, using decisive force, and working with allies, this group still believed force could be a usable and versatile instrument of statecraft. "They didn't make the lesson of Vietnam a constraining dogmatism."

Following his tour in Indochina, Shalikashvili continued to be part of missions involving the flexible use of military force. While working at the Pentagon in the early 1980s, for instance, he was awarded the Legion of Merit for participating in the policy planning phase for the Multinational Force and Observers in the Sinai and for providing support to the US members of the UN Truce Supervisory Organization in the Middle East.

Then, of course, there was Provide Comfort. "We always think of military forces as going to war, and that's our primary mission," Shalikashvili later said, "but [Provide Comfort] was the first time that I saw firsthand what an enormous capacity the armed forces have for doing good."

In many ways that operation marked a turning point in modern military warfare. During the Cold War military conflicts tended to be proxy wars; other armed conflicts across and even within borders tended to be kept in check by the superpowers. But following the fall of the Berlin Wall, new conflicts were becoming the rule, particularly ones spurred on by nationalism. And to ameliorate both the violence and the subsequent humanitarian crises they often created, elements of both peacemaking and peacekeeping would be needed.

Because of this shift, it was getting harder for proponents of the Powell Doctrine to hold sway. Indeed, upon assuming the mantle of SACEUR, Shalikashvili privately expressed intense frustration that NATO was doing nothing in the face of the continent's worst bloodshed since World War II. Only months later he was making unusually frank public statements for a serving officer, including critiquing that the West had overestimated the Serbians' fighting prowess and that the United States especially had displayed a lack of leadership at the start of the Bosnian crisis in 1991.

Like Powell, Shalikashvili knew that only massive numbers of ground troops could stop the slaughter in Serbia, a step he too believed "unrealistic." But while Powell preferred the rare use of the big stick, Shalikashvili was more comfortable with a mix of carrots and sticks of different sizes.

Thus the new SACEUR threw himself into directing a thorough planning process designed to give the US president the means to intervene in the Balkans. Given the notorious contention and quarreling among NATO's sixteen political leaders, "it wasn't easy," Shalikashvili later recalled, to turn NATO from being solely a collective defense against the Soviet Union.

But he did it. He got the organization to agree to peacekeeping missions both in words and in actions: NATO was now considering airstrikes to supplement diplomatic efforts, a change that earned Shalikashvili the respect of Secretary of State Warren Christopher, and by October 2, NATO's new Allied Rapid Reaction Corps would stand ready to take military action for peacemaking both within and beyond NATO territory.

The Serbian conflict, in fact, was why Shalikashvili had met with Aspin at the Pentagon on Sunday. He then returned to Mons that same evening because on Monday the 9th NATO was meeting to officially approve his concept to allow air strikes in Bosnia. This was a historic step—never before had the alliance positioned itself to take military action not in defense of its members.

On Tuesday, August 10, Shalikashvili was back stateside for the start of the Chiefs and CINCs conference that morning. But first he had a more pressing engagement: the commander in chief wanted to see him.

The first-ever meeting between the two men occurred in the president's upstairs office in the West Wing. Freshly showered after his morning jog, Clinton was dressed casually. After enthusiastically explaining the historic documents and pictures on the wall, the president then engaged the general on a wide range of issues, from Bosnia to women in the military, to the need for the chairman to proactively interface with Congress.

After about an hour, Clinton asked if Shalikashvili had anything to add. At first the general said no. Then yes. "I prefer to remain in NATO. I'm making a real difference there and there isn't anyone as qualified as me for this position." Second, "I don't cherish following Powell's footsteps." The third beat, however, was slightly different: "I'm not sure I'm the best guy to convince Congress."

After thanking Shalikashvili for the discussion, the president asked advice on a good candidate. "I told him Larsen, Hoar, and Butler. He asked who would have highest credibility with the military. I felt Joe Hoar. He thanked me and walked me out of the office." Interestingly, "I don't remember him ever asking me if I wanted the job."

Clinton had good reason to ask whose credibility in the military was highest. The president's vocal campaign pledge to reverse the ban on gay service members had worsened his already poor reputation in the armed forces. Having avoided the draft during Vietnam, he was the first chief executive since Franklin D. Roosevelt without military experience. He'd smoked pot. He'd womanized. Reports that a young woman at the White House told visiting general Barry McCaffrey "I don't talk to soldiers" perfectly captured how elongated the hyphen in "civil-military" had become.

To overcome these barriers, Clinton needed a chairman who the entire military could get behind. Someone who'd perform well in what one reporter called the "bear pit" of the Joint Chiefs of Staff. Someone who could "get the bears who head the Army, Navy, Air Force, and Marines Corps to work together rather than chew each other up."

Credibility was important for broader reasons. Clinton needed a chairman who could work effectively with all the key stakeholders—the military, defense officials, Congress, and allies and enemies alike.

Shalikashvili had a proven ability to forge consensus on policy implementation across a range of tough issues. There were his recent accomplishments as SACEUR, of course. And as assistant to the chairman he'd served as Powell's liaison to the secretary of state, a job requiring close coordination with the secretary of defense. In that post he'd played a critical role particularly in reducing nuclear proliferation and securing loose nukes in the former Soviet Union.

His breadth of knowledge and command of the facts were key parts of all these successes. This was yet another reason why Shalikashvili was a natural to succeed Powell: the Goldwater-Nichols Act of 1986 had made both the chairmanship and the Joint Staff much more about being expert in all areas of advice to the secretary of defense and the president.

Furthermore, "Shali wasn't like the stereotypical soldier," explained one subordinate. "He didn't see things in black and white or hold rigid morals, and the civilians thus found it easier to relate to him."

And so, assuredly, would the president. "Clinton will probably have more room to maneuver with Shalikashvili than he did with Powell," opined one news report, noting for example that Shalikashvili likely would not have openly criticized Clinton on the gay policy as Powell had done.

As Richard Holbrooke summed up: Powell "regarded the new team as children. And the new team in turn regarded him with awe." "Part of the problem," Madeleine Albright later explained, "was that we were all new and Powell seemed like the grown-up. And this may sound crazy . . . but somebody walks in with a uniform and has a chest full of medals and is the hero of the Western world . . . there is a certain something about a winning military commander." General Merrill McPeak would later describe how Powell's eminence allowed him to overstep: "It was appropriate for a chairman to advise the president: 'This is a bad idea, but if you have to do it, here's four options that range from bad to worse. Pick one and sign me up for it. And remember, I said this is a bad idea.' But

Powell was more of a 'This is a bad idea, and the hell with you I'm not going to do it' kind of a guy."

Powell was indeed "grouchy with Clinton," added Kori Schake, who'd worked on the Joint Staff when Shalikashvili was Powell's assistant and whose husband was working for the Chiefs of Staff at Clinton's White House at the time. "He knew Clinton needed a person Clinton wouldn't bridle at—either at the person or the message."

Enter John Shalikashvili. He was "a consummate staff man who has never tailored a public or political image, and whose authority is built on consensus," summed up one recent media report. Two men who knew Shalikashvili well agreed. He "is not a Washington animal," noted one. But he is still "politically savvy," clarified another.

A document "for the president's eyes" circulating at the Pentagon and White House opined: "Gen. Shali would most likely lead the Joint Staff to operate more collegially . . . than we have consistently seen in recent years." John Shalikashvili was being seen as a candidate who'd likely help Clinton shorten the wide gulf now separating the West Wing pinstripes from the Pentagon's boots and brass. One who would also work well with Congress and allies. One who could help forge consensus on how best to tackle the many new problems of this new post–Cold War era.

On Tuesday evening John and Joan Shalikashvili accompanied the other CINCs, chiefs, and spouses to a dinner reception at the White House.

It was a chance for Clinton to review the candidates as a group, many of whom were all-but-openly running for the position. According to media reports, General George "Lee" Butler, head of the Strategic Air Command, and Paul David Miller, commander of US forces in the Atlantic, had already been dropped from consideration precisely for campaigning too openly for the post.

Shalikashvili, however, wasn't feeling the pressure. "I thought I was finished," he later recalled. So he enjoyed himself. During the tour the president gave of the White House that night, Shalikashvili was impressed by Clinton's knowledge. "He told me he has been interested in the White House and presidency for many years."

The president was also downright fascinated by American success stories. He'd reportedly "swooned" over the biographies of such nominees as Attorney General Janet Reno, who'd spent years chasing drug dealers in Miami and whose mother had wrestled alligators, and Supreme

Court Justice Ruth Bader Ginsburg, a shining gender-equality role model. And according to recent media reports, Clinton was just as taken by Shalikashvili's "compelling personal story."

The general's image was further boosted that night when David Gergen overheard Shalikashvili whisper to Vice Chairman Admiral David Jeremiah: "I hope I never get to the point where I become so jaded that I consider a personal tour of the White House living quarters to be a routine event."

But there were two front-runners to consider. So, after the music stopped and the guests departed, the president met for a private one-hour discussion with the man Shalikashvili himself was recommending: General Joseph Hoar of the US Marine Corps.

Hoar had at least one thing the army general lacked: an immediately obvious command presence. Tall and articulate, he was "an Irish Gary Cooper" according to a biography prepared by Aspin's office. Yet the two generals shared much in common. Based on his experience in Iraq and Somalia, currently the only two hotspots where US forces were fighting, Hoar also believed in the flexible use of force. Like Shalikashvili, he had a reputation as a straight shooter.

And for being humble. "What would you say if I offered you the job?" Clinton asked. Hoar's reply—that for long his goal had been battalion command and that he continued to marvel at how far he'd come—meant he was leaving the decision up to the commander in chief.

But Hoar had one significant downside: he ardently opposed lifting the ban on homosexuals. The next day, in fact, the Human Rights Campaign Fund would picket the White House, alleging the marine general had conducted witch hunts after gays at Parris Island.

When the sun dawned on Wednesday, August 11, Colin Powell and John Shalikashvili would meet yet again. Pulling Shalikashvili aside before the conference started, the chairman chided: "You've caused some concern with your answers to the president."

Earlier Powell had been briefed by Aspin. The secretary relayed that Clinton, though still favoring Shalikashvili, was nervous. In the president's experience, a person did a better job when he really wanted it. This was surely a reference to Vince Foster, a prominent Arkansas lawyer Clinton convinced to serve as deputy White House counsel; suffering from depression that was surely magnified under the pressure-cooker life of D.C., he'd committed suicide in July. Thus the defense secretary and the chairman needed to find out what was really up with the front-runner. Was it real ambivalence or just modesty behind his tepid response? Powell suggested that Shalikashvili would be more candid without Aspin in the room.

So Powell was now meeting one-on-one with Shalikashvili. "This job is too important for you to be keelhauled into it, pissing and moaning," Powell harangued. "Go talk to yourself, go talk to Joannie, because it's coming your way and the only way you can stop it is if you really, really don't want it."

So the immigrant general first talked to his wife. She in turn talked to their son. And then the family made the decision: "I would stick to my line, but assure Colin that if the president picked me—there would be no doubt about the energy and enthusiasm I would have for the job."

After Shalikashvili relayed the family's decision to the chairman, "Powell observed that I still didn't show much enthusiasm. I told him I can't fake it."

> * *

That's why Aspin, working from a borrowed White House office, was in a tizzy that Wednesday afternoon as he awaited Shalikashvili's arrival for a second meeting with the president.

"Would you accept if asked?" the defense secretary pounced when the general walked in. It was the sixth time in just a few short days this question had come Shalikashvili's way. This time, however, the general offered only one beat: "If the president wants me, I would accept and give him my best."

Soon National Security Advisor Sandy Berger appeared and immediately started asking the same question. Aspin, who'd already put out word to the media that a decision was imminent, cut him off; that question had been asked and answered, he snapped.

Someone then showed Shalikashvili a statement they'd be recommending the president make to the media. "Told them less on me—more on job," the general later recalled, but "didn't do any good." Aspin then suggested the general collect his thoughts. So Shalikashvili asked for paper, and someone in the outer office typed his statement on 5x8 index cards.

Aspin should have known better, however. There was no guarantee the president was ready to make a choice. The ball could indeed bounce foul yet once again.

This time the meeting was held in the Oval office. The two men sat alone, taking chairs near the fireplace. On the opposite end of the room, separated from them by two long couches, was the Resolute desk. Gifted to President Rutherford B. Hayes by Queen Victoria, it had been placed in the Oval Office during the administration of John F. Kennedy, Clinton's boyhood hero.

This was the place where decisions were made.

The president began by listing about a dozen points he was looking for in a chairman. They struck Shalikashvili as well thought out. The ones that stuck in his mind were about being the best: Being the best at organizing and directing war efforts. At providing honest advice. And at representing the chiefs and the armed forces to the civilian leadership, representing soldiers and their families' welfare, and working with Congress. The president also wanted someone who could gain and retain the respect of the chiefs and CINCs, someone who both the people and the president will trust is providing the unvarnished truth.

"I'm convinced you best meet the requirements," Clinton said.

But then came hesitation. Once before he'd offered the job to someone who didn't want it. And that, the president explained, had turned out a disaster.

"So that's why I need to look you in the eye and ask: 'Do you want the job? Are you willing to do it?'"

"I believe I'm better suited for SHAPE," the general responded, referring to Supreme Headquarters Allied Powers Europe, or NATO operational headquarters. "You have a number of top-notch guys to be chairman—but you don't have anyone as qualified as I am for SHAPE. So I would rather stay where I am."

But then came a change in tone. "But if you want me to be chairman . . . I am deeply honored, I would accept it, and I would give it my best shot. Actually I would approach it with the same drive and enthusiasm as I approached the job as SACEUR."

It was his seventh and final time answering the question.

A smile broke across Bill Clinton's face. The president got up from his chair, shook hands with a rising Shalikashvili, and said: "Okay, let's tell them."

19

The Ghost of Dimitri

September 22, 1993—Washington, D.C.

It was the day of the Senate confirmation hearing—the day John Shalikashvili was to fully achieve the American dream.

He'd seemed a shoo-in for the chairmanship when Clinton nominated him over a month earlier. But then, two weeks later, controversy broke with a *Defense Daily* headline that trumpeted: "Documents Appear to Link JSC Nominee's Father to Nazi Forces."

It was oddities in Clinton's nomination speech that had jumpstarted the news story. In the Rose Garden that day, the president had related how in 1944, when the "Warsaw-born Shalikashvili" was eight years old, "his family fled in a cattle car westward to Germany in front of the Soviet advance."

What? A Pole escaping to *Germany*? This "wrong-way bolt for asylum" raised the eyebrows of, among others, syndicated columnist Jacob Weisberg. That Clinton referred to the nominee's father only as a Georgian army officer prompted Weisberg to write: "The drama of the Georgian patriot caught between Hitlerism and Stalinism . . . smacked of exculpatory mythology, the sort of thing kids are told about their grandparents to gloss over darker realities." "The widely repeated details of the general's immigrant saga inspire similar doubts," he continued. "Does anybody really believe, for instance, that Shali learned English by watching John Wayne movies in Peoria?" Columnist Richard Cohen agreed: "The fable radiates idealization. The Statue of Liberty herself must have shed a tear."

Similarly suspicious, the *Defense Daily* enlisted the Simon Wiesenthal Center, a Los Angeles-based organization that hunts down Nazi war criminals. The center soon unearthed writings by Dimitri archived at Stanford University. Foremost was his unpublished memoirs chronicling his childhood in Georgia up to the Shalikashvilis' departure from Germany in 1954. Penned in Russian and translated into English by his wife and a hired translator, both versions, along with other documents, had been donated to the Hoover Institution by Missy Shalikashvili beginning in 1980, two years after Dimitri's passing.

On August 27 the *Defense Daily* went to press. It reported that according to Dimitri's own memoirs not only had Clinton's nominee "received his early education in Nazi Germany during Hitler's Third Reich," but his father had actually joined the "regime" in 1941. Then came the explosive main reveal: Dimitri Shalikashvili had "ultimately served as a major in the Waffen SS," which was "among history's most notorious militias" and "a fighting secret police that was a vicious enforcer of Hitler's ideas about race and ethnicity."

This revelation, avowed the Wiesenthal Center in a concurrent press release, was "not an attack on the nomination of John Shalikashvili as the next Chairman," and nor should the general "be judged on the basis of what the father did." Yet "the public trust is best served," the center argued, "by a full disclosure of how it was possible for an officer who openly collaborated with the Nazis and at one point earned the rank of Major in the Waffen SS, to have been permitted into the U.S. after World War II."

Perhaps the current administration had been negligent, suggested the *Defense Daily*: "Clinton has been scored repeatedly for failing to investigate thoroughly backgrounds of some appointees." Or maybe the powers-that-be had purposefully swept embarrassing details under the rug: "The father's ties to Hitler's Germany raise questions about whether the Clinton administration knew the family history when the president picked the general to replace Powell and whatever DoD officials were aware of the matter in the course of Shalikashvili's 35-year U.S. military career." "If the press reports are right," posited Cohen, "then the Clinton administration or the Pentagon—or both—have combined the smug arrogance of the ignorant with an attempt to repackage a Nazi into a political refugee."

The Pentagon, for its part, soon acknowledged it had been aware of Dimitri's service in the German army, though not his ties to the Waffen-SS. A senior official stated that the Defense Department had relayed everything it knew to White House aides, and that the president's moving description on August 11 of his nominee's family origins had been carefully phrased to skirt the issue of the father's service in the German army.

How was this controversy likely to play out? When complications had arisen during several recent nominations, including the administration's backing of Judge Kimba M. Wood for attorney general, Clinton had cut the candidate loose. Shalikashvili's fate, then, might well depend on Dimitri's past. The more in bed the father had been with the Nazi

Dimitri Shalikashvili and "close family friend" Walter Schellenberg, Hitler's chief of German military intelligence during World War II.

regime and especially the infamous SS, the greater either the administration's negligence or its cover-up—and, by extension, the greater the chance that the son's confirmation could be derailed.

In the days that followed, the media detailed the concerns of both the *Defense Daily* and Wiesenthal Center founder Rabbi Marvin Hier. This included how Dimitri "wrote of briefly being taken prisoner by the Germans and then released after being treated with kindness." That Walter Schellenberg—Hitler's chief of German military intelligence during the war—had been "a close family friend." That the nominee's father "might have begun cooperating as early as 1939 after his release from POW camp" when he remained in Warsaw with his wife, "who came from a wealthy German family," and when he "appears to have enjoyed a comfortable lifestyle, including vacationing in a fancy villa, in the midst of the war—a fact, that, along with other descriptions in the [memoirs], indicates he was collaborating with the Nazi occupiers of Poland."

Though not mentioned by either Hier or the *Defense Daily,* Dimitri's memoirs had indeed made clear he'd done an end run around US regulations. He hadn't followed the example of many Georgian friends in Pappenheim of applying for a visa through the International Refugee Organization; that, he wrote, "was a difficult and lengthy procedure, which required the presenting of . . . evidence that the person was never involved in any collaboration with the Nazi regime. Such documents had to be certified by a notary, and in many cases witnesses were required to testify for the individual who had not sufficient evidence to prove his case."

Instead, Dimitri waited. In letters home from boarding school, son John repeatedly asked about progress in the family's plans to move to America. Or to Spain, which along with Italy were two major "ratlines," or escape routes, for Nazis looking to flee Germany after the war.

Eventually the US government reinstituted regular visa applications. Dimitri's memoirs listed their less-stringent requirements: certificates proving the Shalikashvilis were in good health, an affidavit from a relative in the United States stating the applicants had no political ties with the Nazi regime, and an institutional sponsor to act as guarantor the applicants wouldn't become a burden on the government once they reached the New World.

Alice Tym, reacting to the controversy stirred by the *Defense Daily,* told the press: "It was my Aunt Win [Luthy] who brought his family over, with some helpful persuasion [put on US authorities] from the Episcopal church in Peoria." The Luthy family, of course, could also be persuasive. Not only was George Luthy, Tym's uncle, a prominent Illinoisan, but Ferdinand Luthy, her father, had served on the War Production Board, which rationed raw materials among allies during World War II. Illinois senator Everett Dirksen, Joe Shalikashvili would later recall, had been enlisted to help bring the family to the United States, while John himself once commented that Adlai Stevenson II, the state's governor, had been involved.

Why the need for such power brokers? What exact sins did Dimitri need papered over? The foreign units under Nazi command, Hier told the media, committed several terrible atrocities during the course of the war. Ukrainian, Latvian, and Lithuanian units had helped round up, and in some cases kill, Jews and other prisoners. Though admitting there was no evidence of any Georgian Legion culpability, the rabbi charged that overall there were certainly enough red flags to warrant a closer look at Dimitri Shalikashvili.

Making headlines was one thing. Making a case, however, was quite another. And, indeed, the portrait the Wiesenthal Center and the *Defense Daily* were attempting to paint of Dimitri possibly being a favored pro-Nazi collaborator was quickly challenged.

"Nonsense" was how Marek Jan Chodakiewicz, a Polish-American historian with expertise in occupational politics in Poland, responded to Hier's claim that the Shalikashvilis' comfortable lifestyle meant they'd collaborated with the Nazis. "The Nazis," he wrote in the *New York Times,* "unlike the Communists, did not expropriate all members of the upper classes in Poland."

In fact, Dimitri's memoirs clearly described how, after defending Poland against Hitler's invading force, he was rescued from a German prisoner camp by the combined help of a Jewish Pole who had set up a fake POW hospital and then the financial resources of his wife's family. The autobiography further explained how the Shalikashvilis lived in his mother-in-law's apartment and relied on her income—and not any Nazi largesse—to survive German-occupied Warsaw. "We were from Georgia. Georgia was not fighting against Germany," Joe Shalikashvili would later add. "We weren't Poles. We weren't subject to the restrictions they were."

The memoirs also made clear that during the Warsaw Uprising the Shalikashvilis endured weeks of living underground. Chodakiewicz's characterization—that the family had been "reduced to eating grass"— was only a slight dramatization over what they'd been forced to eat: corn husks. The family, Chodakiewicz continued, had not simply moved to Germany "once the war ended." No, they'd fled in fear: given the Russian forces gathering outside of Warsaw, "to stay would have meant death." This too was chronicled in Dimitri's memoirs.

Nazi Germany, moreover, was no glorified sanctuary. Contrary to the original *Defense Daily* story, John Shalikashvili had not "spent the war's final two years in the Nazi capital of Berlin attending schools run by the Third Reich." As outlined in the memoirs, the newly reunited family splurged for a few days in Berlin by visiting the zoo and dining at a fancy restaurant, but then Dimitri shuttled his wife and kids off to pastoral Pappenheim, far from the Nazi capital, to live off the charity of Missy's relatives.

Although many of the suspicions raised by Hier and the *Defense Daily* were quickly refuted, some legitimate concerns remained: Why had the nominee's father joined the German military in the first place? How had his eventual service to the SS come about? Most importantly, what atrocities might Dimitri have committed as a uniformed soldier of the Third Reich?

A firestorm of activity ensued. Joe Shalikashvili hunted down old documents to send to his brother. Angry calls came in to Hoover demanding copies of the English-language version of the memoirs, with some fact-finders journeying to Stanford to read the original Russian version. Faxes and phone calls volleyed between SHAPE, Shalikashvili's current office in Belgium, and Stanford University, the Pentagon, the US embassy office in Berlin, and the chief of staff of the German armed forces. The media and even Shalikashvili himself would reach out to European history experts.

With so many individuals and institutions in pursuit, how could the truth about the nominee's father's service in the Georgian Legion not eventually come out?

* * *

On January 3, 1943, Dimitri Shalikashvili took leave of his family and boarded a train heading south out of Warsaw. His destination was the Polish village of Krushina, an enlistment station for the German army's newly formed Georgian Legion. The former foreign contract officer for the Polish cavalry was joining the Nazi war effort.

As detailed in his memoirs, Dimitri held mixed feelings about both Germany and its war machine. Germany had lent troops to Georgia back in 1918 when the country regained independence following the Russian Revolution. This, Dimitri appreciated, allowed his homeland to "start organizing her internal affairs without having to worry about defending her borders." Berlin of course had self-interest in "maintaining a strong Georgia as a key to the Caucuses," Dimitri recognized, but the German presence was an assurance against Turkish aggression as well as a stabilizing factor in Georgia's relationship with the governments of the Northern Caucasus. "The Georgian nation," he wrote, "is well aware of the help she received from Germany and will record this in her history."

He also admired how the German military had comported itself professionally in Georgia—unlike the Brits, who took over his country after the Germans left: "Noticeable during the British occupation was the arrogance of the British soldiers toward the civilian population." He judged these soldiers often "aggressive, rude, and tactless. They bothered women and often beat up their male companions."

Dimitri's greatest adulation, though, was reserved for the Poles. A natural affinity, he believed, existed between Georgia and Poland, two smaller countries locked in a perpetual cycle of independence from and subservience to the Russian monolith. The Poles were "the best patriots in the entire world"—"not just in words or fancy parades and military display of troops but when it comes to real sacrifices for their beloved land." In the Polish-Russian war of 1919–21, "the deeply rooted hatred towards the Russians was so great that women were joining the partisans and even children served as messengers in the underground organizations." They often "accepted torture and died silently, never answering the questions put to them under torture by the Russians."

Dimitri had proudly served Poland as a contract officer, and was even more honored to have defended the country during the Nazi invasion. At the campaign's end, he'd surrendered to German troops only to escape the fate of being killed by the Soviets. During the entire German occupation of Poland, moreover, he "never accepted any job connected with the German administration, and never worked for the Germans." After his release from the German POW camp, for example, a connection of Aunt Julie's offered Dimitri work in the German archives office in Danzig, which needed someone with Russian and Polish language skills. "Fearing that this might involve some work directed against Poland, I politely refused the job." Missy's first cousin, George Manteuffel, later offered Dimitri a job supervising Polish laborers in Germany. "This proposition I certainly categorically denied." The job he eventually took, president of the Georgian Colony, was "strictly administrative," he stressed, requiring "no contact with the German Authorities."

On June 22, 1941, Germany finally declared war on Russia. "The first weeks of war, German troops kept advancing in the enemy's territory," Dimitri later recorded. Entire divisions, even armies, including soldiers from both the USSR and from the countries annexed by Russia after 1939, were surrendering and even enthusiastically offering to help Germany defeat Russia. Thus Dimitri judged there "seemed sufficient proof that the respective nations of the Soviet Union do not support the government and [that] this regime that has been coerced upon the people [would] soon collapse." For Dimitri and his fellow members of Warsaw's Georgian Colony, these "first victories on the Eastern front gave us new hope to see the Day of [Georgian] Liberation come true!" "All we could think of was to get the chance to fight for Georgia!"

While Hitler was opposed to Soviet citizens participating in the war against Russia, his commanders on the Eastern Front felt differently. In autumn 1941, against the Supreme Command's clear orders, they created the *Hilfswillige,* volunteers who served as sentries, drivers, depot workers, and the like. Then came the *Osttruppen,* uniformed volunteers who guarded communication lines, fought Soviet partisans, and held less important sectors on the front. By the time existence of these Eastern volunteers came to light, the Reich's hopeless military situation in the east forced Hitler to accept broader recruiting efforts.

One institution he allowed to form was the Eastern Legions, or the *Ostlegionen,* which Hitler limited to non-Russian volunteers living far from the frontiers of the "Great Reich." So on December 30, 1941, the Supreme Command provided the legal authority for the Wehrmacht, or the German armed forces, to create four such groups: the Georgian, Armenian, Turkestani, and Caucasian-Mohammedan Legions.

Dimitri later recalled how, in the lead-up to this decision, the Warsaw Georgian Colony was "frequently visited by German officers who wanted to find out how we looked at the idea of organizing fighting units of Georgian prisoners of war," and if "Georgian civilians, as well as former officers of the Polish Army, would consider joining."

"We knew they would not refuse our help to fight in their ranks against Russia." But "we did not trust the Germans," he added. "We knew they were determined to be the only ones who would shape the future of Georgia, as well as other nations of the Soviet Union."

It was worth a gamble, though, because circumstances might change. Dimitri knew that many Germans "did not approve [of] the official [policies] and did not sympathize with the Hitler regime." Georgians also "had quite sincere friends among the Germans that wished us well and expressed their hopes that Georgia would become an independent nation." This, Dimitri later recounted, included Walter Schellenberg, Hitler's chief of German military intelligence and a close friend of Dimitri's brother David.

In December 1942, Dimitri and two other compatriots were chosen to join the Georgian Legion. Their group, just like a similar group of Georgians summoned from Warsaw earlier that year, were ecstatic "at the thought of soon again becoming active in the military service."

"We were harshly criticized by the majority of the Polish people," Dimitri later wrote, but "what really counts is we did not hesitate to volunteer to serve our country and to risk our lives for her freedom. In their blind hatred towards the Germans, the Poles, once again, displayed a complete lack of objective reasoning." "Had the Polish people been in our position, they would have done the same." That's because the "Poles never stop before obstacles nor do they fear any danger when it comes to fighting for their country."

When Dimitri finally arrived at the enlistment station in Krushina, he met with Colonel von Hildendorf, commander of the Eastern Formations. Upon submitting his application, Dimitri was taken aback when the colonel returned the paperwork. "Do not sign your name 'Prince Dimitri

Shalikashvili,'" von Hildendorf warned. It could stir up ethnic tensions: "All the Legionnaires—Russian, Ukrainian, and the like—come from the Soviet Union, and your title might prove an obstacle to being admitted. In fact, never use the title of prince again if you wish to serve in the Georgian Legion."

What choice did he have? In hopes of freeing Georgia and in order to continue his military career, Dimitri swallowed his pride and simplified his signature. Only then did he get his badge, whose number signified he was the 7,019th man to join the Georgian Legion.

More harsh lessons awaited. The Germans had given assurances that all former Polish contract officers joining the Legion would retain their rank. An empty promise, it turned out. Most were appointed only second lieutenant or lieutenant. Dimitri, despite being told he was part of a smaller group that would be accepted as captains, a one-rank demotion for him, was also demoted to second lieutenant. Adding insult to injury, the legionnaires were given uniforms with strange looking emblems that, Dimitri disdained, didn't signify they were officers at all.

Aware of the motivations of the legionnaires, the German military refused to send them near their respective homelands. Dimitri was instead assigned with the Georgian 2nd Battalion in France, first in Bricquebec and then La Haye-du-Puits, where he "barely felt the presence of war." Next was with Georgian Infantry Battalion 797 in Castres. One of his first tasks there was to translate during executions of Georgians caught listening to radio broadcasts.

He treasured his few furloughs home. Yet so much did Dimitri detest that bastardization of a uniform the Germans provided that he'd immediately change to civilian clothes upon arrival. During one visit, his son Othar noted "there was a German NCO with him—his task was clearly to keep an eye on my dad. The Germans weren't trusting Georgians at this point." Many officers of the Georgian Legion were in fact maintaining contact with their Polish colleagues in the anti-Nazi underground Home Army, undoubtedly supplying intelligence to the Poles.

By the summer of 1944, the German war effort was weakening in France and the Wehrmacht was in full retreat in Russia. Germany was now concentrating its forces, including the national units, in the west.

This made Dimitri livid. "Only the unforgivable, truly insane mistakes of the Germans, their short-sighted politics in the East, [and] their stupid criminal behavior towards the native population of Russia have led to a defeat that not only had a devastating effect on the end of the war, but also destroyed the hopes and expectations of the countries that fought on the German side to liberate themselves from Russia."

On July 20 there was a failed assassination attempt on the fuhrer. At the time, Dimitri, after having been wounded in battle, was serving as a military affairs specialist in the Liaison Office for Georgian Affairs in Paris. Hitler's close call, and Germany's ever-weakening military position, resulted in changes for both Dimitri and the legions. Dimitri was elevated to captain on October 1 and, as the German military began evacuating from Paris, returned to Germany to serve as advisor in military affairs at the headquarters of the Georgian Liaison Office in Berlin.

The Liaison Office, according to Dimitri, was focused on "saving Georgians." The Allies and the Russians had reached agreement that after their anticipated victory all Russian citizens who had been transported to work camps in Germany, as well as all POWs who served in the national formations, had to return to Russia. Dimitri's office, with the help of the German authorities, thus began providing many Georgian POWs with proper identification papers so that they could instead dissolve into German society after being released.

To further protect their countrymen, his office worked with both German and Italian authorities to construct an agreement allowing Georgian organizations, including family members, to move to northern Italy. A Georgian delegation was also soon sent to Turkey to try to contact the Americans in order to "work out an agreement to protect our units, to make absolutely sure they would not be delivered to the Russians" after the eventual Allied victory.

The failed attempt on Hitler's life resulted in a second significant change: "All new National Units were to be under the direct command of the SS," the *Schutzstaffel*, the paramilitary organization of the Nazi Party. More specifically, they'd be under the "Waffen" or "Armed" SS subgroup, which were combat units within the military. Dimitri judged the Waffen-SS troops excellent, efficient, and liberal—even unorthodox—in outlook, a fighting force that retained high morale and their combat readiness to the very end of the war, even when the regular army started to falter.

Yet they "should not," Dimitri wrote in his memoirs, "be mistaken for [the Allgemeine or General SS, responsible for enforcing the Nazi government's racial policy], that left a most unpleasant memory."

On December 11, 1944, the first new national unit, the Caucasian Cavalry Division, was created. This included the regiment *SS Waffengruppe Georgien,* under the leadership of Colonel Michail Fridon Tsulukidze. The entire division was assigned by the German Command to northern Italy. The Georgian Regiment would operate from a small town called Comeglians.

To aid in the new unit's formation, the Waffen-SS asked the Georgian Legion to lend them an expert cavalry officer. "It was me who was chosen," Dimitri later recalled. "However, my assignment was to be a temporary one and I was to stay on as an officer of the regular army." With this posting also came a promotion in rank to major.

With intense air-raids occurring over Berlin and the latest news from the front all bad, the decision was then made to transfer all Georgian fighters—even the original units fighting under the Wehrmacht—to northern Italy. The Italians agreed.

So, in mid-February 1945 Dimitri went to Salzburg to register Georgian families eligible to go to Italy, escorting over seventy of them on his first trip. He returned to Berlin by end of April.

Catching wind that these Georgian families might be transferred to yet another location, Givi Gabliani, Dimitri's boss at the Liaison Office, convinced the commander of the Eastern Formations to send Dimitri back to Italy, but not before giving Dimitri a document appointing him the Georgian Liaison Office's representative in Italy. "In that capacity," Dimitri explained, "I would be authorized to assist the Georgians in Italy in any way I could."

So Dimitri returned to Italy, now second in command of the Georgian Cavalry Regiment. "We wore our [Waffen-SS] uniforms with the respective colors of our National Formations. All officers and sergeants in our Regiment were Georgians. The only German was the treasurer." Their main task? "There were many Italian partisans actively harassing the Germans; the national units were Germany's plan to help fight the partisans."

But soon "there was a noticeable gloom and spirits were low" in their unit. The Georgians knew the war had been lost and a tragic fate awaited them if they fell into the hands of the Russians. Soldiers began abandoning their posts. One night an entire squadron deserted. The next night it happened again.

One day when Tsulukidze was away, Dimitri was given temporary command over the regiment. Dimitri seized the opportunity to meet with the chief of the North Italian partisans who were fighting the communists. Looking to secure his regiment's postwar security, Dimitri agreed that his unit would join their cause—under the condition they wouldn't fight Germans. "From that moment, our position changed significantly. We received secret orders from the national Partisans of Northern Italy that we were accepted as members of the Partisan Division whose task is to liberate the region."

What if they had instead joined the German army in retreating from Italy? "We all would have been delivered to the Russians by the British," Dimitri knew. "They did that to other National Units who bravely fought against the communists, they would have done the same to us." The British had cold-bloodedly delivered hundreds of north Caucasians and Cossacks to the Russians in the small town of Lientz, in the Alps. "The Russians tortured them by hanging, not by the neck, but by driving hooks through their ribs." "By signing the agreement with the North Italian partisans, we saved hundreds of lives."

Instead, the war ended quite differently for the remainder of Dimitri's unit. The Georgians soon left Comeglians and settled in another small town. Preparing for the imminent end of hostilities, Tsulukidze decided to promote his officers. "However ridiculous as it may seem, this was not a completely illegal act," Dimitri later recalled. "So I was promoted to [lieutenant] colonel . . . but nobody took it seriously!"

A few days later the British army arrived. Tsulukidze invited their senior officers to dinner to enjoy food, wine, and Georgian music and hospitality. "The British Commander could not understand what actually is going on! Here they found a regiment that belonged to the German Army and wore uniforms of the [Waffen-SS]. But at the same time these men were north Italian partisans of the region Comeglians and they wore the insignia of Italian National Partisans on their German uniforms!" "And it became even more confusing when we explained . . . that the majority of the Georgians were citizens of the Soviet Union . . . a country fighting on the British side. But here we had to add that the same men were fighting against the communists. At that point the British officers simply refused to understand!"

Soon thereafter the Georgians were taken away by military truck, eventually reaching Udine, the local point of assembly for prisoners of war. Because they'd given assistance to the Italian Partisans and because of the favorable words from the first British commander who'd broken bread with them, Dimitri and his fellow Georgian Legionnaires were not sent back to Russia to face either hard labor or death.

"Providence," Dimitri judged, had "saved us all from a most tragic end!"

* * *

Based on her review of Dimitri's memoirs, Olga Dunlop, an archivist at Stanford's Hoover Institute, told the press that the nominee's father "was an ardent Georgian nationalist, but he doesn't seem to have been a Nazi by conviction." Charles Palm, deputy director of the Hoover Institute, agreed, saying the picture painted in the memoirs was of a Georgian patriot who sided with the Nazis as an anti-Communist crusade to liberate his native land.

This was backed up in pages pulled from the unpublished memoir of Gabliani, Dimitri's boss at the Georgian Liaison Office, that Joe Shalikashvili had passed on to his brother. Gabliani, who'd worked to create the new Georgian cavalry unit, had written that Colonel Tsulukidze, chosen by Germany to command the unit, lacked critical skills. Because many Georgians, both civilian and legionnaires, would soon be in Italy, as would be other Eastern Formations, Italy was going to be an important base for the Georgian Legion, particularly after the likely Allied victory. Gabliani thus needed representatives in the unit who'd be "astute negotiators with the Western Allies, Italians, and the 'Eastern peoples.'"

So a safety measure was built in: "I knew that Tsulukidze was in dire need of well-trained and experienced cavalry officers while putting his unit together. My military advisor, Dimitri Shalikashvili, surpassed such qualifications. In fact he was more qualified than anyone in Tsulukidze's formation so far, including the colonel himself. Even more importantly Dimitri was a true gentleman, level-headed, cautious, a born diplomat and in spite of all of this (or maybe because of it) he kept a low profile. He also spoke several foreign languages. I remembered how in Paris, M. Kedia and I half-jokingly told Dimitri that he would be our Ambassador with the Western Allies."

Gabliani didn't immediately discuss these details with Dimitri, who would just help put together and train the unit. Given that Tsulukidze's officers had already asked Gabliani for help, "for my part I just had to arrange Dimitri's temporary transfer from the Georgian Liaison Staff to Tsulukidze's unit. I did so and as a result I worried much less about the safety of the Georgians in that unit, knowing that my friend would be there and exercise good influence on the colonel's temperament and judgment."

That Dimitri had been temporarily lent out, or "seconded," to the SS was backed up by multiple sources. One was his paybook, which bore no Nazi stamps and listed all his ranks and titles as army. All promotions were signed by army officers, all wages recorded as paid by the army paymaster. Critically, at the point Dimitri transferred to the *SS Waffengruppe Georgien,* the paybook clearly showed continuing assignment to the Georgian Liaison staff of the Wehrmacht, without change of status to SS officer.

There was more corroboration. The Berlin Document Center of the US embassy office in Berlin uncovered no record of a Dimitri Shalikashvili having been a member of the Waffen-SS. Germany's ministry of defense, responding to a request from the military attaché to the German embassy in the United States, searched the archives at the Freiburg Military Records Center as well as the Federal Archives in Aachen-Kornelimunster. They found no record of any such affiliation.

So where did the Clinton administration come down on all this? Defense Secretary Les Aspin, for one, stated that the father "was not a member of the SS. He was a member of the Georgian Legion. His unit was administratively assigned to the SS. But he did not individually join the Waffen SS."

Furthermore, the distinction Dimitri's memoirs drew between the Waffen-SS and the Allgemeine-SS, which the media didn't seem to even pick up on despite the *Defense Daily's* original mischaracterization of the Waffen-SS's role, was borne out. It was affirmed, for instance, in first-hand information John Shalikashvili received from a former US Army Counter Intelligence Corps officer in the occupational forces in Germany. Charged with arresting war criminals, he explained that in the immediate postwar period many elements of Himmler's national security establishment, including the Allgemeine-SS, were placed on the automatic arrest list, to be held and investigated. "Former Waffen-SS members were not in the same category," however. Because the Waffen-SS, which basically consisted of military combat units, were not the secret police, "they were arrested only when evidence of specific war crimes was already at hand."

But was that a distinction without a difference? It was certainly possible Dimitri could have committed atrocities while serving with the Waffen-SS, regardless of his official capacity. As correctly noted by Hier, Dimitri's memoirs did not describe much of the *SS Waffengruppe Georgien's* activities in northern Italy.

In the weeks since the *Defense Daily* story broke, however, nobody had uncovered any damning records implicating Dimitri or his unit in atrocities in Italy. There was only conjecture, including by John Shalikashvili himself: "I think what happened was that my father never thought of [his service with the Waffen-SS] as something horrible. If he had, why would he have written about it? Why would he have taken his papers and given them to Stanford University?"

Hier was not swayed by such logic. The SS major's uniform "wasn't a tuxedo you rent for 24 hours," he challenged. Dimitri "wore it from late 1944 to the end of the war." Because the nominee's father lived in Warsaw when the Germans invaded, he "had a firsthand view of what the Nazis were up to and how they were treating the Poles and the Jews." "What kind of moral argument is that," the rabbi added, that "I should be excused on the grounds that I was really fighting to liberate Georgia?"

The larger question of morality aside, however, the danger to Shalikashvili's nomination seemed almost over. Given that no further incriminating information had come out, Shalikashvili's defenders needed only parrot just one line the Wiesenthal Center itself had offered at the controversy's outset.

So that's what they did. "Any allegations about his family members are not relevant to General Shalikashvili's impressive career serving his country," a Pentagon spokeswoman stated on day one of the controversy. Aspin too praised the nominee's "superb record of achievement," adding that "allegations about his father's history are not relevant to Gen. Shalikashvili's nomination." A White House spokeswoman concurred: "Gen. John Shalikashvili's record of achievement stands on its own and his father's history is irrelevant."

When the reports of Dimitri's Nazi connection first surfaced, the Armed Services Committee reviewed the archival materials and held individual meetings with the general. The result? "What is relevant is that Gen. Shalikashvili has done a great job at NATO and that he'll make a magnificent chairman of the Joint Chiefs of Staff," stated Senator Carl Levin, a Democratic lawmaker noted for his efforts to promote awareness of the Holocaust and someone who, as a member of the Armed Services Committee, would be voting at Shalikashvili's confirmation hearing. "I think he's extremely highly regarded," said Senator John McCain, a Republican committee member, and "I don't see any repercussions about his father." From Democratic senator Jeff Bingaman: "I don't know of any opposition. I certainly support him."

One thing, however, could still trip up the nomination. If Shalikashvili knew of his father's service, noted then-Republican senator Arlen Specter, the fact that he didn't reveal this association would be grounds for disqualification. Back in January another Clinton nominee had paid the price for knowingly trying to cover up illegal activity. Zoe Baird, who'd employed illegal immigrants as household help and also failed to pay social security taxes for the workers until just before the story broke, had been forced to withdraw her nomination.

John Shalikashvili's nomination was not necessarily out of danger yet.

* * *

In the cavernous wood-paneled hearing room of the Hart Senate Office Building, Senate Armed Services Committee Chair Sam Nunn called the meeting to order. But if the ghost of Dimitri Shalikashvili was haunting this room today, it was not immediately apparent.

In his opening remarks, the Democratic senator from Georgia overviewed the nominee's recent responsibilities as both assistant to the chairman and SACEUR, highlighted the importance of the chairman position in this new era of Goldwater-Nichols, and laid out the challenges Shalikashvili would soon face. Then ranking minority member Senator Strom Thurmond, a Republican from South Carolina, spoke briefly, affirming the chairman's evaluation that Shalikashvili was highly qualified to serve as the next chairman of the Joint Chiefs of Staff.

In these back-to-back remarks, not one word about the controversy over the nominee's father had been spoken.

Then came Shalikashvili's opening statement. Reading from prepared remarks, the general focused mainly on overviewing the professional challenge of assuming the torch from Colin Powell's capable hands.

But then the nominee spoke to the personal.

"Before concluding, allow me to comment briefly on the recent deeply disturbing reports that my father had been a member of the dreaded Waffen-SS, and that I perhaps withheld this information. I did *not* withhold this information, for I never had the slightest hint that my father was associated with the Waffen-SS."

The general, from time to time looking up from his prepared statement to make eye contact with the committee, continued: "While my father's official German record shows uninterrupted service in the Georgian legion under the German army of Wehrmacht, it is most troublesome to me that according to his own writings apparently in the last months of the war my father was associated with some Georgian unit that was under the control of the Waffen-SS."

"I am deeply saddened that my father had this tragic association. To me, and I believe to all those who knew him, that is so absolutely out of character. To me he was a kind and gentle man, and I loved him very much. He was a man who perhaps loved his native Georgia too much, certainly a man caught up in the awful tragedy of World War II."

Then for the next three hours Shalikashvili and the committee proceeded to discuss the security issues facing the nation. During the marathon hearing, what minimal commentary senators made about the controversy all reflected well on Shalikashvili.

"I would like to say that I was deeply touched by your continuing and everlasting reverence for a father who allegedly made a mistake," said Senator John Warner, "but the son still stands by with affection for his father. In this time of troubled parenthood, I think I find that very reassuring and a sign of the strength of your personal character."

Or these words by Senator Joseph Lieberman: "Obviously the revelation of contact with the Waffen-SS touched the nerves of a lot of people around this country, and yet I'm convinced, having heard you this morning and spoken to you previously about this, that there's no one who's suffered more pain from this revelation than yourself. I'm also convinced that it would be grossly unfair, and I'm sure everyone on this committee feels that way, to judge you based on anything your father had done. It would be unfair, and it would be un-American . . . this country has built itself on the premise of opportunity for every succeeding generation and, indeed, opportunities within a single generation to remake themselves."

Before ending the hearing, the chair reiterated a point he'd made in his opening remarks: "General, I see clear sailing. I do think we're going to have to talk to the executive branch about when to confirm you, not because there is any doubt about your confirmation or your qualifications." "But," continued Nunn, "the question is can we afford to lose you with the hat you have on right now at this particular juncture?" With so much going on in Europe—including the political crisis unfolding in Russia, potential for NATO involvement in Bosnia, and events in Yugoslavia—the senator was concerned that the committee had not yet received a nomination of an officer to replace Shalikashvili as head of EUCOM and SACEUR. "I hope we get [a nominee] soon, and then we can move very rapidly. If you could take that message back I'd appreciate it."

"I will do that sir," responded Shalikashvili, thereby bringing to an end the last real hurdle to the president's nominee becoming the next chairman of the US Joint Chiefs of Staff.

20

Blondi and the Boy on the Bridge

February 22, 1995—Fallbrook, California

Donna Kurtz was at home, babysitting her young grandson. They'd just settled in for the evening, ready to watch John Shalikashvili on television.

The first time she'd heard his name on the news was during that 1991 humanitarian operation in Iraq. John had pulled it off—feeding, clothing, and ultimately saving those at-risk Kurds. Whether ironic or just amusing, she wasn't sure, but hadn't he done similarly for her back in Peoria—by providing her lunch, smuggling out his mother's clothes for her to wear, and boosting her fragile ego? "He was a wing-mender, even then," Donna reflected.

John was chairman now. The Senate had unanimously confirmed him on October 6, 1993, just two days after General Joulwan was appointed to Shalikashvili's SACEUR job in Belgium.

Once he became chairman, *Parade, Reader's Digest,* CBS, and other media had clamored for interviews. "But Shali had no interest," recalled Public Affairs Officer Larry Icenogle. "Sir, I'm trying to take the long view, I'm your legacy guy," Icenogle pressed. "I appreciate that Larry," Shalikashvili replied, "but to the extent that I've done anything good in this life, the people who need to know that already do. For me, that's enough." Yet eventually "I wore him down," Icenogle recounted with a grin. "He gave an interview to *Parade.*"

Shalikashvili did have a reputation for being allergic to the spotlight. But was his media shyness as chairman motivated by more than humility? When the controversy over Dimitri's SS service broke in August 1993, "that was the angriest I've ever seen my dad," recalled Brant Shalikashvili. "Phenomenally angry." "Angry at the malice toward his father's memory." After receiving a congratulatory note lauding his cleverness in being Clinton's choice for the job, the general had written back with sarcasm: "I'm not capable of 'incredibly clever decisions' or I would not have agreed to this nomination. But then I would have denied the media

272

this latest attack." At Shalikashvili's request, his October 25 swearing-in ceremony was private, with no media in attendance.

But now—after sixteen months on the job—the chairman had finally agreed to his first major television appearance. He was at CNN's studio office in Washington, D.C., seated across the table from perhaps the most recognizable interviewer in America. Over the next hour the public would finally get its first in-depth look at the man who—as Larry King had just introduced in the opening credits—"has the president's ear when it comes to protecting the United States and its citizens."

"General John Shalikashvili's life reads like the American Dream," Donna heard King begin. Since his nomination, she'd come across much romanticization of John's life. What annoyed her was the oft-repeated anecdote that he'd learned English by watching John Wayne movies. It had been her constant coaching, for Christ's sake, that had done it. Of course, she realized, "he couldn't very well say 'my girlfriend slapped me around until I got it right!'"

Before interviewer and interviewee could charm the nation with the general's immigrant success story, something needed to be settled. "You like to be called Shali?" the host asked. "Please, yes," the guest replied. He's a "regular guy," King would subsequently proclaim to the cameras.

Then they began jawing. They covered the chairman's unusual background, including how he and both parents had been stateless. They spoke of Shalikashvili's life in Peoria, his "dropping out" of ROTC and obtaining his first and only citizenship, and then getting drafted shortly after graduating from college. The general told of how he'd supposedly been talked into going to OCS, and how Alaska made him fall in love with military life. They touched upon the role of luck, his humble ambition just to make the next grade, and how his wife and son had been very supportive of his career.

Right before cutting to one commercial, King said: "We'll be right back with . . . it's hard to call him Shali when you're sitting with four stars and all those ribbons, but we'll try. We'll be right back with Shali."

That's when the realization came to Donna. "His mom's dreams," she almost purred at the thought, "they *did* come true."

And, unknown to anyone else, the chairman's high school girlfriend had actually played a key role in his improbable success.

* * *

Back in Peoria, as his senior year of high school was winding down, John kept bringing Donna applications to Bradley. "Who's going to pay?" she challenged. "Don't worry about it," he countered. Terrified he'd somehow come up with the money, she'd told him a lie—she was planning on going to art school.

"And then I disappeared."

Why did she do it? The secret would burden her for decades: "It was my fault I got pregnant, being carried away in the moment. The passion of it all drove me a little mad."

What was Donna to do? All options seemed devastating.

"I loved the baby already and could never think of aborting such a darling child." "But my mother would have made me . . . that's for damned sure." That's because she'd tried "every way on earth to abort me," just as during junior year after the gang rape her mother had paid off a friend to shove her down the stairs in that failed attempt to induce a miscarriage.

Donna was still haunted by what had happened thereafter at that doctor's office. There was the sound of screaming—these operating rooms didn't use anesthesia. And the smell of astringent, and the feeling of her hair, ringing wet, sticking to her head when it was over. Then in the morning, when they took the packing off, "I prayed to die in those moments . . . but I promised I would not let myself scream." The biggest torture, however, came at the end. They made her look at the fetus—to shock her into being "a good girl thereafter."

There was no way in hell Donna would go through that again.

Should she tell John about the pregnancy? He'd certainly once again stand up to her mother, ready to fight for their future together and the future of their child.

But Donna couldn't let that happen. She knew in her heart that John, "who was so precious to his family, whose mother adored him, whose father adored him, whose teachers and buddies, the entire junior and senior class all admired him . . . would go on in life to be someone." But "I was a throwaway kid," a product of "a truly fucked up family." Worried almost from the beginning that she'd "truly wreck his life," Donna had promised herself she'd never drag him down.

"I thought his family would be furious with him, risking his future, straddled with a baby at a time when he should be bearing down studying. I never considered for one moment that they would all love his child."

So "I had to take myself out of the way." And despite the pain it

Donna Bechtold in nursing school in Texas, circa late 1959, around the time John Shalikashvili called from Alaska to propose marriage. (Courtesy of Blaine Blystone.)

would cause them both, she couldn't breathe a word to John about either the whys or wheres. Because he'd surely chase after her—and by doing so jeopardize his promising future.

So, by leaving without a word Donna had changed his life. "If he'd had a child," she'd often wondered, "would John have gone to college?" Either way, when his Selective Service number was chosen in July 1958 "it would have been likely John would have been deferred and never served."

Donna was probably right. Although Eisenhower's executive order of July 11, 1953, ended the paternity deferment for married men, those whose induction would cause extreme hardship to dependents could qualify for a Class 3-A deferment—very likely the case if John had had a young family. Not wanting to join the military in the first place, he'd likely have jumped at deferment. Or perhaps he'd never have been drafted in the first place: the executive order of February 15, 1956, gave men who became fathers after August 25, 1953, a lower priority of call behind those without children.

So Donna could take solace in at least one truth: by running away with their unborn child, she'd kept the door on a military life from closing on him prematurely.

She was grateful for the time they'd spent together—"He changed my life forever. I would never have gone to nursing school without a restored ego." Yet Donna still had one regret, one that returned full force when John's career successes had finally thrust him into the national spotlight.

It was the "idiotic decision" she'd made during that marathon phone call he'd placed to her while she was at nursing school in Texas. At one point he brought up graduation night. John told her he'd been sure that night that they'd always be together. Hearing the hurt in his voice carry across the phone line, Donna had an urge to blurt out why she'd left Peoria: "I wanted to say, 'I left for you. So as not to besmirch your name, your family.'" But she couldn't. "I didn't want him to feel guilty or sad, so I left it alone." She said nothing—either about the pregnancy or the heartrending miscarriage, likely helped along by the stress of running away, that she'd suffered weeks after leaving Peoria.

Given all the pain she'd caused him, John should have given up that day. But no. Even learning she'd had a son who'd been kidnapped by her crazy ex-husband hadn't shaken his determination.

Why then hadn't Donna just said yes to his marriage proposal?

At the time John reconnected, Donna's sole focus was getting her baby back from Cuba, where he was being abused by his mentally ill father. "The kidnapping had me so tormented that I could barely keep up with my studies."

But "John had very small hands for a man—small and soft. My father, uncles, and grandfather all were auto mechanics and their hands of course were large and rough." "I thought to myself over and over during John's proposal, which was elegant and tearful, that he had these tiny little hands, and what in the hell could a man like that do to get my baby back, to even find my baby?"

"It was a heart-wrenching decision for me and I bawled all night and for weeks to come, but I needed an attorney husband and I was good looking enough to get anyone I wanted." "Those little soft hands—what in the living hell was I thinking?" *Of course* "this darling man could have located my child, prevented his abuse, changed all of our lives."

* * *

The televised discussion between suspenders and stars continued, with the more sober issues of national security dominating the remainder of the show.

It was perhaps a testament to King's softball style of interviewing that the only possible elephant in the room—his father's wearing of a German uniform during World War II—wasn't raised until the final minutes of the broadcast.

"Everyone hates 'sins of the fathers,'" King began. "Would you clear up . . . there was a story about your father when you first got appointed. I never got the end of it."

"Well," the chairman began, demeanor calm and collected, a smile appearing as the question was being asked.

As was well known by his staff, the chairman favored a particular analogy. In all things, imitate the duck: no matter how furious the paddling underneath the water may be, the surface should appear placid. And when responding publicly to these accusations about his father back during his nomination, Shalikashvili had indeed kept his cool.

Tonight, however, Larry King's inquiry seemed to be flapping the normally unflappable general. "Well, the story was that my father during World War II served in a German . . . ," Shalikashvili began, but then stopped mid-sentence, umming and ahhing before continuing, ". . . in a Waffen-SS unit, which I guess he technically did not, but in fact was associated with one." But the real question, Shalikashvili explained, "was whether I ever knew that. And I never knew that."

"Well . . . he wasn't a Nazi?" King blurted out almost before his guest had finished answering.

Upon hearing that follow-up question, Donna felt her body go rigid. The French doors of her bedroom were open, and her brain absently registered a mild breeze blowing across the room. She sat there without breathing, praying that he'd get through this awful moment.

"*Did he know his dad was a Nazi?* Were they all kidding?!" Her grandson, craning up to look at her, asked why she was crying and pinching his hand. Only then did Donna lie back, allowing her body to loosen up, her blonde hair spilling over the pillows.

"Oh God, John," she thought to herself, "get out of this one!"

"Well . . . he wasn't a Nazi?" Larry King's question hung in the air.

Yet in his rush to ask, the host had glossed over what his guest had barely finished explaining: that the real controversy had been whether the general had been aware of his father's service in the SS, as well as his follow-up affirmation: "I never knew that."

Oh, but John Shalikashvili had known.

He'd shared an awful secret with Donna, one that seemed painfully evident to her in how John, sitting there face-to-face with Larry King, was continuing to answer that question the host had just blurted out: "Well . . . he wasn't a Nazi?"

"I don' . . . I never . . . I . . ." Shali fumbled. Then he found the right tack: "The only thing I can tell you is that I loved him dearly. He was the kindest, gentlest man and I always thought of him as such. Um . . . and it was a great shock when such a story broke."

Having been glued to the media following his nomination, Donna knew John had given that same evasive answer when asked then about his father's SS service. On one National Public Radio (NPR) segment, Shalikashvili had gone even further: "Everything that I am is because, to some respect, because of my parents."

John was reacting to these charges about his father, Donna knew, by both lying and being truthful. And she was perhaps the only one watching tonight's broadcast who understood the deep, bittersweet motivations behind this paradoxical response.

* * *

Back in Peoria she too had credited his parents—for the good genes they'd assuredly passed on and the high standards of behavior she guessed they'd taught him.

Though initially reluctant to discuss them, "he mentioned his mother first and talked about how he loved her, and I admired that. She sounded like a dream come true." The things he'd said, particularly of her spirit in guiding the family through wartime Poland, reflected qualities Donna saw in the son. This woman would never admit to suffering, being weak, or having suffered a loss in status. "Chin up, elegant pose" was the main mental image she'd formed of the mother. "If she didn't know something, she'd fake it," John had said. It echoed the description later offered by Joe Shalikashvili. When asked about what John had inherited from their mother, the first two traits he ticked off were goal orientation and perseverance—"she found ways to overcome obstacles."

But the amazing thing, Donna intuited, was that although Missy was *not* a shrinking violet, she was still tender and kind. "When things went wrong, Mom had her arms around us," John had told her. Again, Joe later concurred, saying John had also inherited her "good manners," fierce "loyalty," and just plain "concern for others." Examples of Missy's character abounded. Like how she'd brought the Shalikashvili's nanny from the family's bombed out home in Warsaw back to her mother's house in the suburbs, how she'd volunteered with the Red Cross and tended to wounded Polish soldiers and Georgian POWs, or how she twice braved dangers in seeking to rescue her husband from being a prisoner of war.

And what had John inherited from his father? In that 1993 NPR interview he also professed: "I love my dad just completely and he is the one person in this world that I look up to more than anybody."

It made sense, actually, because father and son were in fact almost the same person. Anyone familiar with one who then perused the officer efficiency reports of the other could be forgiven for doing a double take. The similarities are jaw-dropping.

Take Dimitri's evaluations as a Polish cavalry officer: "A quiet man, self-controlled in words and gestures. A man of great moral values. He fully represents the concept of an English Gentleman, maintaining the highest standards of behavior, appearance, and self-control. He is ever-professional, ever-capable, and behaves as a person of culture and honor."

Or consider what prompted the head of the Georgian Liaison Office in Berlin to lend him out to the SS-affiliated Georgian cavalry unit in the first place: "Dimitri was a true gentleman, level-headed, cautious, a born diplomat and in spite of all of this (or maybe because of it) he kept a low profile."

This concept of being a "gentleman" was reflected in John's evaluations too: "He is respected by all, not only for his professionalism, but also for his tact, sensitivity to the problems of others, gentlemanliness, and quiet dignity." Or he's "outstanding in every way. Intelligent, perceptive, decisive, imaginative, responsible, efficient and above all a gentleman."

When asked what qualities Dimitri had passed on to brother John, Joe replied: "Temperament." "Good—no—excellent manners." "I never saw him raise his voice, be harsh, speak harshly of anyone." John also shared Dimitri's "tremendous appreciation for what is right or wrong." "In bringing us up," Joe summed up, "father would always come back to the need to be a 'gentleman,' a gentleman of the 'old school.'"

In another interview Joe brought up that critical force behind Shalikashvili's improbable American success—that he had no ego despite being fiercely competitive. "Where does that come from? I'm not sure," offered Joe. "But I put much credit on my parents. We were raised, and

John especially because of his personality, to put the mission first instead of putting himself first."

It was more than just putting mission first, of course. That's why, after telling NPR "everything that I am is because, to some respect, because of my parents," John Shalikashvili added, "and a big thing with them is being honest and being kind to others; being concerned with others' feelings and others' needs and wants rather than solely my own."

But for a man with deep appreciation for the two people who created him, John did a strange thing when he first arrived in the United States.

Many high school and college classmates would later recall he was closemouthed about both his family and European background. "John was indicating for us not to pry," said one. Another classmate wasn't even sure if his parents had actually come to the United States: "I could never figure that part out." Yet another recalled that John actually portrayed the Luthys as his own parents, "though people suspected."

Of course people suspected. Not only did the Shalikashvilis live near the Bradley campus but their house was a few doors down from John's fraternity. How could friends miss Dimitri, clad in lederhosen, sitting on the porch or going for walks? John couldn't have hidden behind a curtain of total denial forever. There was "a rumor that his father was a Nazi," recalled Steve Harrison, who later regretted that, because he was Jewish, he thus didn't befriend John.

When John did eventually mention his father, he described him as a professional soldier, explaining the family had moved around because of his dad's career. Bill Rapp, a PHS classmate and mechanical engineering student at Bradley, could tell John was proud his dad was a professional soldier and wanted to be like him. Yet Rapp also couldn't recall John ever mentioning any other family members and never knew if John had any siblings. Another friend recalled John saying Dimitri had been a colonel in the White Army, one who lost everything during the Bolshevik revolution. It was a partial description, one that promoted a sympathetic image.

Yet with Y. King Liu, an ethnic-Chinese student from East Bangladesh studying on scholarship at Bradley, John could be more open. "Having gone through war myself, I know all things can happen," explained Liu. His own father had been high up in the Kuomintang and, in order to get his family out of Chiang Kai-shek's China during the closing days of the war, had commandeered a postal truck at gunpoint and syphoned off needed gas.

With a fellow war refugee, John could be more honest. My dad, John admitted to Liu, served with the Georgian Legion, which "had essentially been under the control of the Nazis." But John still offered a lie: "He was told at gunpoint either join or we will shoot you."

To perhaps his closest high school friend, Jim Suffield, John told an even more dramatic story—that the whole Shalikashvili family would be dealt with if Dimitri did not join the German war effort.

What did John say to Donna about his Old World upbringing?

She too was misled about his parents at first. "I live with my aunt and uncle," he said, which Donna soon surmised meant George Luthy and his wife, "the bankers." Eventually, though, he began sharing details about his father. "He described his dad as being gone a lot, a military serviceman. And I got the feeling that the father was both strict and gentle, not a tyrant."

But then came the painful reveal—"he spoke of his dad's military career ripping up the family."

* * *

On that day in January 1943 when Dimitri Shalikashvili took a train bound for Krushina to enlist in the German army's newly formed Georgian Legion, it wasn't just Polish friends who were upset at his decision.

His wife Missy was, in fact, livid. She was "violently opposed" to the idea of her husband fighting for the Nazis, her elder son later recalled. She of course understood Dimitri's motivation: he wanted the Soviets out of Georgia, and Germany's war against Russia might make that happen. Missy too was sympathetic to the plight of Georgians. That's why she'd braved many dangers working for the Red Cross helping care for Georgian soldiers in German POW camps around Warsaw. But to her way of thinking, Dimitri's joining the Georgian Legion was quite different, the equivalent of making a deal with the devil.

One day she was sitting with her children in a Warsaw park and the subject of the Jews came up. "May the dear lord forgive the Germans for what they are doing," she said. "What for?" asked Othar. "For what they are doing to the Jews and the Poles," she sighed.

She'd looked on helplessly as the walls of the Warsaw Ghetto were constructed in the fall of 1940—the route from their apartment to the cemetery where Missy's father was buried passed by forced laborers erecting part of the barriers.

One summer, when the family was vacationing with Georgian friends in a suburb outside Warsaw, they came across a starving Jewish man.

Missy did what she felt she had to do—she fed him. Her elder son understood the significance: "It was an insanely brave or stupid thing to do.
She would have been killed if word of this had gotten out."

Dimitri felt differently. He believed his wife too often let her emotions
and caring cloud her judgment. This kept her from seeing the larger picture, and often put others—including their own family—in danger.

It wasn't just feeding the Jews. In Warsaw she naively went back to
plead for mercy on the robber who'd invaded their home. She also turned
back from the train station because she couldn't bear to leave her mother
behind, a decision that put the lives of her and their children at risk.

About one year after Dimitri's admission to the Legion, Missy jour-
neyed to his post in Salzburg to float the idea that the family accompany
him on his imminent transfer to Italy. Though knowing it was too dangerous, Dimitri left the decision up to her. He was proud when she decided
she and the children should remain in Pappenheim. "This time," Dimitri
praised, "Missy did not allow her feelings to prevail over reason."

Reason must dominate over emotion. That's exactly what led him to
join the German military. He and his wife had both experienced Stalin's
atrocities firsthand, and Dimitri firmly believed that even if Hitler was
a devil, he was a lesser one than Stalin. Decades later he'd explain his
decision to wear a German uniform: "Those were hard times and they
called for hard decisions. I am deeply convinced that those of us who
volunteered to serve in the ranks of the Georgian Legion made the right
decision."

He'd also recall parting with his wife that day at the station: "Missy
was very sad about my leaving her. However, I knew her well enough to
be confident that she understands the reasons that motivated me to take
such an important step as joining the Legion. Missy was not that kind
of woman who would ever put herself, or even our children, before the
highest priorities that are so dear to me. Those priorities are to sacrifice
everything for Georgia and the Georgian people."

And he was right. When she first laid eyes on Dimitri that day in
1931 she knew she would marry him. And with marriage came loyalty.
Missy Shalikashvili would always stand by her husband.

*　*　*

It had taken Donna all of senior year to understand how deeply the
father's service in the German military had affected John.

It was clear right off, however, that John struggled with the question of his German background. He told her emphatically he was never German. He hated the German language; it sounded so "gruff." And German art, that was "crap—dreary and morose, like most things of that culture."

But he also oft expressed how beautiful he found her German features. How attracted he was by her body type, skin, hair color, and facial features. His first year at PHS, before he'd even met Donna, he'd in fact dated a German exchange student.

Donna's overall impression was that John disliked girls with dark hair or girls that looked Jewish, period. He once called a Jewish girl, one who'd been Donna's friend since grade school, "a pig." "I asked him why he didn't like her but he wouldn't tell me. I asked him just half-joking if it was because she was Jewish. He just stared at me. Holding his stare, I said, 'John?' but he refused to discuss it." Another time, when John once said he thought his mother would love her, Donna asked if it was because she looked so German. He replied "It would be difficult if you were a Jew."

This troubled Donna greatly. Most of her friends were Jewish, and she was also close with some of their parents, cultured people who were highly encouraging of her creative talents. What about John's past would ever make him say such horrible things?

There were a number of possibilities. It might've been just a mix-up or a few thoughtless comments that held no larger significance. Or maybe dating a Jewish girl wasn't "difficult" for him but rather for someone at home, perhaps his father? (The image Donna held in her head of Missy would be antithetical to his mother being anti-Semitic.) Well, for whatever reasons, maybe this recent immigrant to the States just couldn't completely and immediately shut out either the old values of hatred he'd been exposed too in Europe and especially in Germany, particularly against the Jews, or the narrow-mindedness "that he could only love a German girl."

Yet Donna never challenged him. "I didn't want to know." Because if he confirmed it, it would surely "split us to pieces."

John eventually offered one story from his childhood that suggested that an inner struggle of good versus evil was indeed roiling within the newly arrived immigrant.

It was about a friend he'd made, a scrawny kid about his age. The two would meet up on this bridge, where they'd while away the time spitting into the water below or just chatting.

Often each boy would bring food to share: potatoes, carrots, and—

once in a blue moon—sweets. That John tended to bring more and better offerings suggested that his friend was from a poor family.

Once the kid commented that many he knew were being arrested, which made John surmise he was Jewish. The boy seemed unaware, though, of why this was happening. "I pretended that I didn't know much about the fate of the Jews," John admitted to Donna, "when I really knew about all there was to know"—including about the camps, he told her. Understanding the danger his Jewish friend was in, John urged him to flee with his family.

One day John arrived at the bridge at the appointed time. The boy was nowhere to be seen. John waited. And waited. Glancing around in boredom, he spied an odd clump of leaves by the railing. Taking a closer look, he noted the stems were meticulously intertwined, with the leaves forming a tight package.

Peeling it open, John discovered there were cookies inside. "He knew I had a sweet tooth," John told Donna, so "I knew it was the kid who left them there."

He went by the bridge many times thereafter, but eventually gave up hope. John would never see the boy on the bridge again.

"Of course I knew what had happened to him," he told Donna, "and eventually I stopped putting my mind to which camp he'd been sent to, how far away, and what the records would show if I ever got to see them." "The Germans," he explained, "kept immaculate records."

It was a poignant memory. But it was a second wartime recollection John shared that just about floored her.

His father and mother had been arguing fiercely. Dimitri was in uniform and Missy had on a nice dress. They were going to an event, he was told, and he was coming along. Realizing his mother was almost in tears, John in his naivete wondered if she feared she wasn't attired nicely enough. But later he'd realize it was somehow a big event in his parents' life, a nerve-racking experience, and they were anxiously debating what was to be said, and not said, and how his mother was to act.

He remembered a fancy car, one with a driver in military uniform. "No talking," his parents warned before the ride began. Each time he spoke up during the drive, his mother would shake her head sternly and put her fingers to her lips.

After a long journey through the woods they finally arrived. They were escorted to a huge patio overlooking the forest. He remembered it being a beautiful day. There were throngs of people, including general officers. The hors d'oeuvres were fancy—fish, eel, octopus, and other delicacies that belied the wartime restrictions in place. The vibe, John remembered, was "tense, political, a who-knows-who" gathering with groups of people standing together like cliques, each seemingly suspicious of the other.

As the reception dragged on, whenever anyone came to talk to John, Missy would grab for his hand. Whenever he spoke up, her grip tightened.

As John was describing the event, Donna noticed he was actually sweating with nervousness. "He had my rapt attention," she later recalled.

Feeling stifled by his mother's attention, John eventually noticed a welcome distraction—a beautiful German shepherd lying on the veranda. He went over to the dog, knelt down, and began stroking its fur.

A thin man with a thin mustache appeared.

"His name is Blondi," came the explanation in German. And that's when Adolf Hitler, extending a hand downward, patted blue-eyed John Shalikashvili on the crown of his golden head.

"When he said 'Hitler'" Donna later recalled, "I knew instantly that he was telling me the truth."

But was he? Perhaps yes and perhaps no. Donna would never know about the embellishments John would later make in his letters to woo back Anita Ziegler. Neither would she hear that Joan, his eventual wife, would later chide her husband for aggrandizing stories. It's quite possible John Shalikashvili was being similarly dramatic in his telling of the Blondi story to Donna.

Regardless, the record still shows that Shalikashvili knew of his father's association with the SS. Fast-forward to 1993. A few weeks before Shalikashvili was nominated for the chairmanship, Hoover Institute senior fellow Colonel Richard Staar, a Polish-born international security expert, sent a letter to Shalikashvili's office in Mons, providing him a list of all of Dimitri's materials held at the Hoover archives. The timing of this apparently unsolicited note suggests a subtle heads-up.

But Shalikashvili needed no hints. He was in fact intimately familiar with the memoirs. As a student at the Naval War College in the early 1970s, Shalikashvili, on behalf of his parents, asked Stephen Ambrose, his thesis advisor and a famed historian who'd edited the Eisenhower

Papers, for advice on getting Dimitri's manuscript published. John also dutifully told his parents he'd be happy to do a rewrite once they produced a basic translation.

Almost a decade later, his mother began sending drafts. The son's letters back were full of encouragement. "Your translation of father's life in the Legion arrived and I cannot tell you how interesting it was for me to read." "This and all the previous writings that you sent will be read and reread." He expressed happiness that she was continuing with her translation of Dimitri's time in the Legion because it was "a priceless account with special meaning."

And then the last installment of his father's time in the Georgian Legion arrived—the one recounting Dimitri's service with the Waffen-SS unit. "I found it extremely interesting, not only from a personal view, but also from a historical perspective. I am sure few people had the insight as to the position of the Legion during the last few months of the war, particularly its relationship with certain Italian elements."

Thus, irrespective of whether John Shalikashvili had actually met Hitler, he still clearly knew about his father's association with the Nazi regime in general—and the SS connection in particular—well before his confirmation hearing.

Back in Peoria, though, it was clear to Donna that John was struggling with Dimitri's service to the Nazi regime. And she believed she understood why.

Through both genes and upbringing, John had inherited such wonderful qualities from his parents—like being empathetic, kind, and treating others with respect and trust. From his mom, particularly, John had gained deep empathy for people. But his early childhood had likely bombarded him with Nazi propaganda, including hatred for the Jews.

Those two childhood stories reflected the deep conflict she guessed was going on in his young mind: On one side, his childhood friend, the boy on the bridge, probably killed by the Germans because of his ethnicity. On the other, his father, working for the very man who created the campaign to wipe out the Jews.

That young, mixed-up boy from the Old World had then stepped off the SS *America* into the fresh environment of the New World. Peoria in the 1950s, Donna later recalled, was a time "when World War II, Hitler, the Nazis, etc. were fresh on everyone's minds."

No wonder John was tight-lipped about both his family and European upbringing. And no wonder John would get so enraged when friends called her Blondie. It likely touched the rawest of nerves within him—his discovery of his father's betrayal of the very qualities his family held so dear.

This interpretation allowed Donna to find new meaning in the words of comfort John had offered her that day with the watermelon: "These aren't your real parents. Your genes are from past generations. . . . Genes skip generations sometimes." Could John have encouraged himself with those exact words—that perhaps he himself didn't have the seeds of his father's weakness growing inside him?

By the same token, however, John's very genes and upbringing had surely compelled him not to be disloyal to his father. John, like both parents, was faithful to a fault. That time he came to her house and did battle, her mother made so many references to Hitler that Donna half-worried John would believe she'd shared his secret. "Of course I hadn't. And he knew I'd never do that. Even at that age, he had great trust in the people he loved."

"Whenever he mentioned his dad," Donna noted, "he was more pensive and more insistent about his own love." She'd first guessed it was because his father didn't love him back. But now, knowing these twin stories of the Jewish boy on the bridge and Blondi, she believed John's insistence about his love for his father likely reflected his compulsion to loyalty despite the damage Dimitri had done to the family.

And perhaps this cognitive dissonance—simultaneously hating and loving his father—could well explain why a young John Shalikashvili had equivocated so long about joining the military and why he later obfuscated his reason for wanting to become an officer in the first place.

Fortunately, Peoria had been a period of at least partial healing.

During that long phone call from Alaska, John admitted he hadn't wanted to remember those childhood years in Europe. But he was thankful she'd pulled it out of him: "Talking it out with you was a wonderful and therapeutic thing," for it allowed him to find a way back to his old self, to finally think of his past as something he didn't have to conceal or fear. Just as it then likely allowed him to put wartime hatreds behind. "And because I came through it as cleanly as I had without cracking up, for that you deserve the love I still feel in my heart for you."

Decades had since passed since that phone call. But John had likely remained deeply thankful. A couple of years into retirement, he would sit for a Q&A session with the *Peoria Journal Star*. The resulting two-page spread—published on June 27, 1999, his sixty-third birthday in fact—would include three photographs "courtesy of John Shalikashvili." One photo included the two of them at their senior prom, with Donna wearing that longest, most beautiful corsage he'd given her.

By reputation Shalikashvili was "not a shoot-from-the-hip kinda guy." He would roundly criticize the expression, "Lieutenant, do something!" that he'd learned early in his career; it inhibited thinking, he said. His choice of photograph and both publishing venue and date thus speaks volumes. Perhaps he was reaching out to Donna across the many miles and decades that separated them. Perhaps he wanted to say: "Thank you, because without your help back then, I never would have realized my American success."

Part VI

The Twilight of an American Dream

21

Retirement Day

September 30, 1997—Fort Myer, Virginia

Summerall Parade Field at Fort Myer, Virginia, was packed with VIPs. Topping the list was the rare joint appearance of President Clinton and Vice President Gore, along with the First Lady and Mrs. Gore. Many high-ranking defense officials also crowded in, including the current and past secretaries of defense, William Cohen and William Perry; Undersecretary John Hamre; former deputy secretary John White; and the current secretaries of both the army and navy. There were many administration heavyweights, including Secretary of State Madeleine Albright, National Security Adviser Sandy Berger, and CIA Director George Tenet. Also rubbing shoulders were members of Congress as well as a multitude of boots and brass, such as the next chairman of the Joint Staff, General Hugh Shelton; at least two former chairmen; current service chiefs and combatant commanders; such retired four stars as former SOUTHCOM commander General Barry McCaffrey; and even the chairman of NATO's Military Committee, General Klaus Nauman.

This unusually large "who's who" turnout was testimony to the reputation of one man: General John Malchase David Shalikashvili. After being on active duty for thirty-nine years, three months, and one day, he was finally retiring from the US military.

Shalikashvili had been an "effective chairman," Representative Robert Michel told the media, someone "not given to personal grandstanding or self-promotion," someone "able to keep all the branches of the military happy." "I never heard any behind-the-scenes quibbling about him," he added, "and that kind of stuff is pretty common in Washington."

Cohen's aides had even broached the idea that Shalikashvili stay on for a third two-year term. The chairman—who had noted the previous year, "I am the most senior and oldest general on active duty. Lately, when I go jogging at night I feel like the oldest"—offered a polite but firm no thank you. His wife's response was reportedly less diplomatic.

With Shalikashvili set to hang up his uniform for good, it was time

292 BOY ON THE BRIDGE

for affectionate gift giving. Noting the general's long-held dream, Susan Berger, wife of the national security adviser, crafted the Grand Order of Nuts and Bolts—an array of ribbons and miniature hardware tools. "You may not think I will really open a hardware store," the general had told reporters at the National Press Club in his final public speech as chairman, "but you are wrong and you will all get a ten percent discount!"

The ceremony opened with the march-on, with Clinton, Gore, Cohen, and Shalikashvili taking their place on the red-brick reviewing platform as their names were announced.

As the cannoneers kicked off a nineteen-round salute in his honor, Shalikashvili stood his usual ramrod straight, right hand raised in crisp salute. As explosion after explosion reverberated across the parade field, his mind began to drift.

He recalled another memorable salvo, that one he'd witnessed some thirty-eight years earlier in Alaska. Firing off one too many rounds for the visiting secretary of the army, the artillery battery X.O. had earned himself a demotion. "That afternoon, the X.O. was transferred to the position of motor officer," the memory flooded back, "and I became the new X.O."

Luck. Without it, this stateless war refugee would not have come to realize this momentous day.

First and foremost, he and his family had been fortunate to survive the violence and bloodshed of World War II. How doubly fortunate that, after they'd lost everything, wealthy relatives in Bavaria had taken them in. "Europe was devastated, an ugly scar was forming between the East and West . . . a sign of the beginning of the Cold War," Shalikashvili later recounted of this pivotal time, and for "a kid from Poland and Germany without the knowledge of a single word of German, the world didn't look full of promise and opportunity, I can assure you." But next, in an improbable hat trick of luck, Winifred Luthy, an empathetic and generous stranger, offered passage to the New World.

The start of his military career too had been shaped by circumstance. Donna's decision to flee Peoria without a word once becoming pregnant, for instance, had probably kept him from seeking deferment from the draft. Or the problem with his eyes. If he'd actually realized his dream of becoming an air force pilot, his career might have been much less stellar. His natural affinities—for logistics, simplifying complexity, setting and communicating standards, empathizing with and motivating the common man—were less needed in the smaller, more elitist, and more technology-centered air force. A slower rise, in turn, would have dampened the development of his greatest skills: diplomacy, holistic thinking, and productive consensus building.

Or what about the small mound of snow that had kept the Morris Minor from spiraling off that towering cliff back in Alaska? The careers of many promising officers have been unexpectedly cut short—by accidental death or injury, an affair, a blowout with a vindictive superior officer, or just once getting caught tipsy behind the wheel.

Sometimes the mistakes of others prove a windfall. If Schwarzkopf hadn't allowed Iraqi helicopters in the post–Gulf War "no fly zone" in northern Iraq, there'd have been no gunships raining fire down on the Kurds and thus likely far fewer refugees fleeing into the mountains. Operation Provide Comfort, in turn, would have remained a JTF under General Jim Jamerson of the US Air Force.

But the golden opportunity of Provide Comfort had meant that his stint as Saint's deputy in Heidelberg hadn't been his swan song. "Because the operation was a good human interest sort of story," Shalikashvili recognized, "it caught the imagination of the press, and so my name came to the forefront."

That then led to the platinum opportunity to serve as Colin Powell's main liaison to key policymakers on international relations and politico-military concerns. "So I got to know the decision-makers in Washington, in and out of the Pentagon," Shalikashvili continued, which meant his skills were similarly fresh in people's minds when Joulwan's nomination to SACEUR was derailed, in turn helping him land the job.

That was a critical change of fate.

For one, "as soon as I arrived in Europe," Shalikashvili noted, "Bosnia became a hot issue. Consequently, my name was attached to many of the actions being worked in Washington and when . . . it came time to replace General Powell my name once again made it on the list."

Not only that, but if the SACEUR job hadn't unexpectedly opened up, Shalikashvili would have instead replaced Butch Saint as head of USAREUR—a position outside of the fifteen-candidate pool the Clinton administration had considered for Powell's replacement. Shalikashvili likely would have retired in that post, not as he was today as chairman of the Joint Chiefs.

As the last salvo rang out across Summerall Parade Field, Shalikashvili

General John Shalikashvili's September 30, 1997, retirement ceremony at Fort Myer, Virginia. (DoD photograph by R. D. Ward, courtesy of the NBR Gen. John Shalikashvili Archives.)

felt pleased. "Today everything went perfect. A nineteen-gun salute it was supposed to be, and nineteen guns it was."

Soon thereafter, once the drum and bugle corps in their red revolutionary war uniforms had finished trooping the line, it was time to inspect the formation. It would be Shalikashvili's final time leading this military tradition that dated back to the Revolutionary War.

Shoulder-to-shoulder, Shalikashvili, Clinton, Cohen, and the Commander of the Guard strode down the line of troops from each service—army, navy, air force, marines, and coast guard. As they marched along, Shalikashvili's mind once again began to wander. This time he recalled an even earlier memory: the night World War II ended for Pappenheim.

He remembered how, in the very early morning hours, the village's old people and children were ordered to take down the bridge over the Altmühl River to buy time for the German soldiers escaping south into the Alps. By first light, however, that wooden span still hadn't been completely disassembled.

As the inspecting party marched passed the American flag, Shalikashvili threw up a salute. That's when an image jumped vividly to mind: those GIs on the other side of the river, rifles at the ready, preparing to cross the Altmühl. "These," he reminded himself, "were my first Americans."

"How strange life can be," he mused. "Now, fifty-two years later, one of these small boys they saw on the other side of the half disassembled bridge was inspecting the United States Honor Guard, accompanied by the president of the United States."

"Never in my wildest dreams," Shalikashvili awed, "did I think such a thing could happen."

A retirement ceremony is an occasion to reflect on a person's accomplishments. And after the inspecting party returned to the reviewing stand and once the colors were brought forward, it was time for words to be spoken about John Shalikashvili.

First came the presentation of awards. As the words accompanying each was read aloud, Cohen bestowed the general with his fourth Defense Distinguished Service Medal, the highest military peacetime award, and the president draped about his neck the Medal of Freedom, the highest civilian award. Then the defense secretary and the president took turns at the podium.

Cohen opened by quoting Justice Oliver Wendell Holmes: "Alas, gentleman, that is life. We cannot live our dreams. We're lucky enough if we can give a sample of our best." "Well," the defense secretary said, "today we express our gratitude to a man who has given more than a sample of his best, he's also lived his dreams."

Cohen listed some of the best qualities the general had offered to the country: "firmness, not harshness; understanding, not weakness; humaneness, not intolerance; generosity, not selfishness; pride, not egotism." Clinton, during his turn at the microphone, praised "the humility, the honesty, the graciousness, the respect he always shows to others; and the wonderful way he listens, even to bearers of bad news." Even when "I could see the pain in his eyes that he couldn't tell me what I wanted to hear . . . with a clear and firm voice and a direct, piercing gaze, he always told me exactly what he thought the truth was. No president could ever ask for more."

And by giving more than a sample of his best, Shalikashvili had made substantial contributions over the last four years. The words accompanying the Distinguished Service Medal captured three of them—how he confronted historic change, responded to nontraditional military missions, and prepared America's armed forces for the challenges of the twenty-first century.

For one, historic change had indeed defined his tenure. At the general's confirmation hearing in 1993, Senator Nunn had noted that Shalikashvili was the first chairman to be nominated and confirmed in the post–Cold War era.

"When I became chairman in 1993," the general would reflect in retirement, "it was the collapse of the orderly life after the end of the Cold War." In World War II, he contrasted, everyone knew the fighting would draw to a close and that the world would look very different afterward. But "there wasn't anyone who seriously asked, 'how do we work with a Europe that is no longer confronted by Communism?' Nobody was prepared for it to end."

One huge question was what to do about NATO, an alliance against an enemy now fractured into its constituent pieces. So Shalikashvili proposed a plan, which President Clinton approved. "Shali's idea," Madeleine Albright, his colleague and good friend, later explained, "was to invite the emerging democracies of Europe and the former Soviet Union to enlist in a new entity, the Partnership for Peace, whose members would participate in military training exercises with NATO countries. This meant that former enemies of the Alliance would learn how to operate with it, while old rivals such as Romania and Hungary would now work together. The countries that did the most to upgrade their militaries, develop peaceful relations with their neighbors, and solidify their democratic institutions would become eligible for full Alliance membership"—what became known as NATO expansion.

This new European security structure, Albright praised, "would preserve and strengthen NATO, while creating a meaningful role for all, including Russia and Ukraine." To gain support among skeptical countries, particularly Poland, Clinton sent Albright and Shalikashvili to Central and Eastern Europe immediately prior to the January 1994 NATO summit.

When the times called for a leader with "the touch and toughness of a warrior-diplomat," Cohen told the crowd at Summerall Field, "General Shali was there, reshaping the alliance to meet the demands of a new era." And Clinton would tell the audience that "standing with Shali in Warsaw as we celebrated NATO's enlargement and welcomed the people of his original homeland back home to the family of freedom" was "one of the proudest moments of my presidency."

Herein was the last major injection of luck into his career. During the 1990s, managing the chaos and uncertainty of the end of the Cold War, particularly in Europe, was the main preoccupation of national security policy. At a different time in history, John Shalikashvili's Old World roots and Europe-focused military career might not have made him the most attractive candidate for chairman.

His second contribution as chairman was increasing nontraditional military missions. At his last National Press Club speech, the general had articulated how the end of the Cold War had unleashed nontraditional security threats. "During the Cold War, when and how to use military force was relatively simple. Locked into the bipolar confrontation, both sides were forced to husband their military strength for that one massive confrontation. . . . Neither side dared employ force on a grand scale unless the survival of the nation or some other vital interest was at stake."

The demise of the Cold War, however, unleashed the instability that the East-West rivalry had been keeping in check. We "found ourselves with failing states, humanitarian tragedies, ethnic conflicts, and regional bullies." "We've kind of taken the lid off a lot of these things," he'd state in another interview, "and until they run their course we have to be prepared to ensure that we don't allow any of this to get out of hand. One of the tools that ought to be available is the military."

The chairman's willingness to use US military might short of war, for peacekeeping and low-intensity conflict, was a radical departure from Powell's fixation on preparing for big, conventional wars: "U.S. forces just can't post a sign that says we only do the big ones," was Shalikashvili's signature refrain. His thinking would prove prescient: for the foreseeable future the Gulf War would remain the US military's last corps-level engagement.

His new policy for the Balkans, for example, proved a force for good. In sharp contrast to the ineffective UN Protective Force, Shalikashvili helped end the savage war by structuring air operations and creating a seventeen thousand-strong Implementation Force based on "close coordination between the diplomat and the soldier," a clear and concise mission statement, and a "straightforward chain of command." Notably, the force included a Russian brigade, a landmark exercise in great power cooperation.

But there were noticeable failures to take action. Wesley Clark, when heading the Joint Staff's Strategic Plans and Policy Directorate as a three star, prepared a response plan to support any UN effort to stop the large-scale massacres in Rwanda. "Wes, do you seriously believe anyone in Congress will support such a plan now, in Africa, eight months after Mogadishu?" Shalikashvili asked, referring to the specter of the "Black Hawk Down" incident.

Overall, serving as chairman at this critical historical juncture, Shalikashvili would later summarize, was "like sitting on a powder keg." "There was no day during my four years that we were not involved in active operations overseas. In fact, there were never less than ten operations on any given day. Some of these were small and you didn't read about them. But others like Bosnia and a couple of dust-offs with Saddam Hussein were much larger and were in the public eye." And "I can't tell you how many times we had to make emergency evacuations of Americans from places in Africa that were collapsing."

Old problems also continued to need attention. Like responding to China's intimidation of Taiwan, this time via missile tests during Taiwan's democratization in 1995–96. And in 1994, when it was clear Pyongyang was making nuclear missiles, "we were very close to the brink. One of the things we were considering was a blockade of North Korea, which the North Koreans informed us would be considered an act of war." According to one estimate Shalikashvili saw, armed conflict would have cost 52,000 US military casualties, killed or wounded, and 490,000 South Korean military casualties in just the first ninety days. Fortunately, the problem was resolved diplomatically.

Whether because of the increasing chaotic world, Shalikashvili's greater willingness to use force, or both, his tenure as chairman was marked by more than forty separate military operations. Powell, in contrast, oversaw about thirty.

Shalikashvili's third contribution, as noted by Clinton, was "managing the downsizing of our forces while upgrading their capability and readiness," or what Cohen praised as "building a military force that was both smaller and better."

It was definitely smaller. Since the Berlin Wall fell, the United States had reduced its active force by seven hundred thousand—about a third of its manpower, the largest drawdown since the Vietnam War. The services, Shalikashvili would point out, had lost more personnel than the total current British, German, Dutch, and Danish armed forces combined. And with the significant 40 percent reduction in its defense budget, the United States was now spending less of a percentage of national wealth on defense than at any time since before World War II.

Yet despite these steep cuts Shalikashvili had still made the military better. He'd done it, Clinton noted from the podium, by "dramatically improving joint doctrine and training, and taking joint planning far into the future for the very first time." Shalikashvili set the tone by enhancing collegiality of the service chiefs—including letting them, contrary to the news rules of Goldwater-Nichols, express opinions directly to the president. He also sought to solidify jointness beyond his chairmanship through *Joint Vision 2010,* the first in a planned series of conceptual templates to provide "a common direction for our services in developing their unique capabilities within a joint framework of doctrine and programs as they prepare to meet an uncertain and challenging future."

All these steps, Cohen offered up to the crowd, meant that the US military "would remain the best-trained, the best-led, the best-equipped force in the world."

Implicit in this retirement celebration, though, was a fourth major contribution. "If one lesson is to be learned from European history," Shalikashvili believed, "it's that the military shouldn't control the government." As chairman, he'd thus sought to rebalance the civil-military relationship.

He began straight out of the gate. A reporter at the Rose Garden nomination ceremony had asked if Shalikashvili would try to enlist the member states of the now-dissolved Warsaw Pact into NATO. "I have just been nominated for the position of chairman, not president of the United States," Shalikashvili responded, eliciting laughter.

A year into the general's chairmanship, Senator Jesse Helms created an uproar by telling the media that Clinton wasn't "up to the job" of commander in chief and that many military officials shared this view. The president was so unpopular on military bases, Helms warned, that Clinton "better have a bodyguard" if he visited the senator's home state of North Carolina. Shalikashvili immediately took action. Not only did his office release an official statement, he personally reached out to many journalists to affirm the president has, and will continue to have, the loyalty and full support of the Joint Staff.

The first big military confrontation of Clinton's presidency was over Haiti. Clinton wanted to use the US armed forces to ensure that the generals who ousted Jean-Bertrand Aristide would step aside and reinstate the Haitian president. The operation would be led by Special Forces Commander Hugh Shelton. "Shali, the military thinks I'm crazy, don't they?" "Yes," was the reply, "but that is what we have a constitution for. You get to decide." Clinton pressed: "Shelton doesn't agree with me, does he?" "I don't think so," the chairman confirmed, "but it doesn't matter. You get to decide. And he'll do a fine job." And after Aristide was successfully reinstated, Shalikashvili told the president that even if Clinton's decision had proven disastrous, the military wouldn't have regretted it because "the founders decided that it would be better to let the political leaders make the mistake than the military leaders."

Shalikashvili further rebalanced the relationship by improving interagency cooperation. He not only personally worked smoothly and effectively with two defense secretaries, one from each of the major political parties, but was also an early advocate of "whole government" solutions to problems of complex contingencies.

This included working closely with fellow Slav Madeleine Albright, who'd served as US ambassador to the UN and was currently secretary of state. Secretary of Defense Perry, who judged Albright the best UN ambassador he'd known, felt "the great support she got from Shali was an important part of her success."

One shining example of the interagency cooperation Shalikashvili made happen was his assignment of General Wes Clark to work with diplomat Richard Holbrooke in the negotiations that led to the historic Dayton Accords, which finally brought an end to war in the Balkans. Wanting to institutionalize such cooperation, Shalikashvili then set up a more inclusive interagency process and a better national security-making process.

Yet there were those, especially in the military, who weren't always comfortable with the closer civil-military relationship under Clinton. "Shali had to defend a lot of unpopular policies," explained Mike Gallagher, the chairman's public affairs officer, "like going to Vietnam for the normalization ceremony. Many in the military were against it." Brian Haig, the chairman's speechwriter, agreed: "Many wanted Shali to stand up to Clinton," but "if Shali didn't agree with Clinton, only a very small core of people knew Shali's real thoughts."

Was it this kind of criticism of his tenure as chairman, then, that would prompt Shalikashvili to say in retirement that his greatest weakness was not liking confrontation?

Out on the Fort Myer parade field, it was now the chairman's turn to speak.

"It is a great day to be a soldier," Shalikashvili began from the podium, setting the tone of his remarks. Today he'd only touch on his European roots, immigrant experience, and key people and places from his career. His emphasis in these very public remarks would center on the "magnificent soldiers, sailors, airmen, Marines, and Coastguardsmen" of the US military.

While taking his usual morning run today, the chairman had passed by Arlington Cemetery. "I've always liked this place," he'd thought as he took in the rows and rows of silent white crosses that were "representative of the military I'd served so long: from lowest private to the most senior generals; black, white, red; all religions; male and female; and those whose forefathers came over on the Mayflower and those whose accent was as thick as mine remains to this day." "That's the military I love," he reflected, "the army that has been my home for nearly forty years."

During this goodbye speech he'd thus credit his fellow service members for the achievements made during his tenure as chairman. "Each time the call came, America's forces were ready, and each time they performed magnificently." "Others might envy us our high technology equipment, but they stand in awe of our young men and women in uniform and the sergeants and petty officers who lead them."

"People aren't in the armed forces: people are the armed forces," he continued, paraphrasing Vietnam War commander General Creighton Abrams. "Not personnel, but living breathing people, tough people, ethical people, trained people, people working together to get the job done, worldwide, year after year."

And Shalikashvili had taken care of his people. "There isn't a single soldier in our military today who has not benefited from the concern Gen. Shali has consistently displayed for his or her well-being," Senator Tom Daschle recently told the press. "His commitment to improving the quality of life for those serving in the Armed Forces has been second to none."

Speaking at an in-house retirement event, Joint Staff director Vice Admiral Dennis Blair noted how Shalikashvili "worried about every one of the 110,000 some-odd service people who are away from their home ports and bases every night." Blair recalled having once been involved in the deployment of two army sergeants to a dangerous area of the world. "General Shali forced, by conservative count, eight iterations of the deployment order authorizing the deployment of those two soldiers, personally reviewing every detail to ensure that they were not committed to a mission which their skill, training, and instructions could not handle."

Why such dedication? Because "I think we're a family that takes care of one another," Shalikashvili noted in a recent media interview. "We're a family that is committed to ensuring that everyone would have a fair

The Shalikashvilis in a private moment at his public retirement ceremony. Like her husband, Joan was "a difference maker, a big player in family issues and taking care of soldiers." (DoD photograph, courtesy of the NBR Gen. John Shalikashvili Archives.)

chance to rise to the full measure of their abilities. We're also a family that when they see something wrong try to come to grips with it quickly and fix it and get on with our business."

As head of this military family, Shalikashvili had overseen a symbolic project. In April 1996 the chairman wrote to the widow of Omar Bradley, the first chairman of the Joint Staff, to explain that for the first time ever, oil paintings of all the chairmen were being commissioned for display at the Pentagon. Shalikashvili's portrait had been completed in time for his retirement ceremony.

It was a project that seemed to channel two earlier occasions in his life: first, walking the halls of the New Schloss as a child staring up at those portraits of Pappenheim ancestors, and second, as a newly widowed captain in Germany, decorating headquarters with pictures depicting the military family that had historically made up his unit. Seen in this light, the creation of a chairman portrait gallery had particular meaning for Shalikashvili. It would be his way of honoring the family he felt so deeply attached to, the family that he'd forever be a part of: the US armed forces.

Perhaps that is why he chose to end his retirement speech this way: "Now let me close with a word to the soldiers with whom I shared this 39-year journey," Shalikashvili said. "Many years ago, when he was asked what his last wish would be, Black Jack Pershing said: 'that when the last bugle is sounded, I want to stand with my soldiers.' And so when in years hence the last bugle sounds, I hope to stand with you, as ramrod straight and as proud as you stand before us here today. In the years to come, no matter what I do, no matter where I go, no matter what I will become, in my heart I pray I will always remain one of you—a soldier."

A soldier in a family of soldiers.

22

The Final Inheritance

August 7, 2004—Steilacoom, Washington

Though based in the sleepy town of Steilacoom, Washington, John Shalikashvili kept an energetic pace in retirement. Ultimately deciding against that hardware store, he instead stuck to his clear strengths—helping maintain military readiness, caring for service members and their families, and improving international security policy.

He served on the boards of many organizations, like Boeing and L-3 Communications; the Tragedy Assistance Program for Survivors and the Fisher House Foundation, a housing provider for military families wishing to be near a hospitalized love one; and the National Bureau of Asian Research. He was also both a visiting professor at Stanford University's Institute for International Studies, working alongside friend and mentor William Perry, as well as a senior advisor to the Preventive Defense Project, which Perry ran from Stanford and Harvard Universities.

He joined three other chairmen—David Jones, William Crowe, and Colin Powell—in endorsing the ratification of the Comprehensive Test Ban Treaty, with Shalikashvili himself serving as President Clinton's special advisor on a CTBT feasibility report. He and Hugh Shelton, his successor, led a campaign to combat childhood obesity, which is an increasing barrier to recruiting new troops and just plain bad for America. He also undertook his own concerted and ultimately successful campaign to persuade the government to repeal Don't Ask, Don't Tell.

Yet despite four years as the country's top military advisor and these additional efforts in retirement, his name still hadn't risen much in prominence since causing head scratching in the Rose Garden back in 1993. He'd recently been the victim of identity theft, the guilty party not recognizing the unique name attached to the social security number he'd stolen. While on an unofficial reacquaintance tour of Fort Lewis, Shalikashvili and his former brigade commander had accidently stumbled into a Stryker exercise, their car being quickly surrounded by nineteen-

John Shalikashvili on a visit to Georgia, the birthplace of his father, Dimitri Shalikash-vili. (DoD photograph, courtesy of the NBR Gen. John Shalikashvili Archives.)

ton war machines. In the process of clearing up the confusion, the soldiers hadn't even recognized the former chairman.

Sure, his penchant for avoiding the spotlight explained part of it. Yet, disappointingly, his legacy as chairman also was waning. For example, the Joint Vision documentation he started, and which Shelton continued, would fizzle out, in part for "failing to emphasize the salience of international terrorism in general, and the growth of al-Qaida in particular."

"Well, nobody remembers the name of the chairman who came before Powell either," some would argue, defending Shalikashvili's obscurity. Following in the footsteps of Powell had indeed been tough. When Shalikashvili was chairman, people would walk by his office and say: "That's where Powell used to be."

Yet opportunity wasn't finished with Shalikashvili. In 2004 he was invited to deliver a speech at the Democratic National Convention in Boston to support Senator John Kerry's bid for the presidency—exposure that could well jumpstart the general's full-time return to national policymaking.

A few days before flying out, he was driving home from a haircut when a numbness spread across his face. He'd felt it twice before, but this time it continued on to his left hand, prompting him to fearfully change course for Madigan Army Medical Center. There he was diagnosed with a transient ischemic attack, a temporary blockage in the brain that sometimes precedes a stroke. Luckily no damage was done. Kept on for observation, Shalikashvili drafted his convention speech from a borrowed hospital desk.

After Boston, two more spells followed. But he'd been busy, the effects had been minor, so he simply pressed on.

On the evening of August 7, 2004, the hammer finally fell. He was at home brushing his teeth when the numbness again stretched across his face. But with each passing second it kept spreading, first along his arm and then inexorably down his leg. He stumbled toward the bedroom. Within seconds his wife was dialing 911. Over the next terrifying minutes his speech would slur and the left side of his body would fall completely limp.

The diagnosis this time was massive hemorrhaging. A vessel in his brain had ruptured, flooding his right front temporal lobe with blood. The medical team had to drill through his skull to stop the bleeding, relieve the pressure on his brain, and remove the damaged tissue.

For three weeks the sixty-eight-year-old remained in intensive care. Fatigued from the violence to his body, he mostly slept. Then, after medicines were adjusted, he found his way back to consciousness.

John Shalikashvili had, in fact, been expecting it.

"Most of my adult life I have suspected that I was a candidate for a stroke since both my parents had them." His mother's stroke came with no bleeding. His father first suffered a stroke, and thereafter, to help prevent a second, underwent surgery to clean out the arteries in the back of his neck. He was later felled by a heart attack. Dimitri's brother David was returning home from a café one afternoon when he collapsed from a heart attack, dying before the doctor arrived. "Everyone on both sides of the family as far back as we can trace died of either heart attacks or strokes," relayed John's sister, who herself died of heart failure in 2016.

A family history of heart disease—defined as a father or a brother diagnosed before age fifty-five or a mother or sister before age sixty-five—doubles one's risk. Dimitri's heart problems began in his early forties. John's too; he was taking pills for the condition as early as battalion command in the mid-1970s. Though he strove to keep the career-jeopardizing condition to himself, once while out riding in a jeep he suddenly slumped forward. Luckily his driver, who'd been taking EMT classes, knew to push the commander's head back to open his air passages. After coming to, Shalikashvili had simply said: "Nobody else needs to know about this."

Toward the end of his career, the specter of this particular family legacy loomed increasingly large. On one flight back to D.C., while sketching out the retirement home he'd build in Steilacoom, the chairman included double-doored entrances to accommodate the wheelchair he might someday need. He upped his tempo of medical checkups. On one trip to Walter Reed, he posed an unsettling question to his driver: "Rich, do you know one of the last things a person often sees before dying?" Though thinking the question odd, the driver dutifully replied: "No sir. What?" From the back seat came the answer: "A hospital."

So Shalikashvili was careful in retirement. "My blood pressure was under control, as was my cholesterol, I didn't smoke or drink alcohol excessively . . . I went to the gym every other day and I took long walks into Steilacoom on those days I didn't work out in the gym. So when the stroke came, I was in good physical shape."

But when it came, it was still devastating.

His lack of ability to walk unassisted or drive a car was frustrating. "I have discovered just how much every-day tasks call for two good arms and hands," he vented. Privacy was also stripped from him, as thus was his ability to control his image and the respectful distance he could keep between others and himself. "Whenever you have to have help in going to the bathroom and every day a different person comes to help, you cannot retain any sense of modesty."

Also taken away "was my ability to think through complex problems or tasks." "If ever I had a need to make myself lists of what needs to be done and prioritize them . . . that time is now." But writing or even reading was difficult. He suffered from "left side neglect": absent considerable concentration, his eyes kept focusing center-right on the page. He'd also lost natural cease-and-desist functions: once he put pen to paper, only intense focus could bring his hand to a stop as the right side of the page drew near. When he failed, he felt miserable. He'd recall how, following his mother's stroke, she had used sheer force of will to train herself to write with her off-hand.

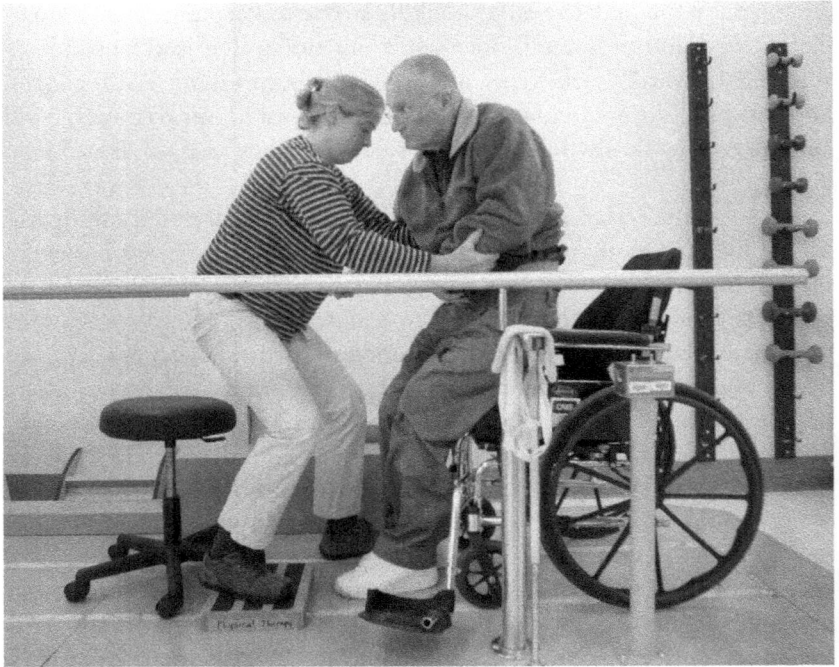

John Shalikashvili undergoing physical therapy following his first major stroke in 2004. (Dan DeLong/SeattlePI.)

There was good news, though. "Fortunately, my speech was not affected like was my father's." Nor had the general's hearing been impaired. Dimitri had already lost some of his by the time he reached Peoria.

Most transforming though was the loss of his iron-clad grip on his emotions.

Rich Hill served behind the wheel during Shalikashvili's stints as both SACEUR and chairman, the general's highest-pressure assignments. "Drivers have a unique vantage point," Hill explained. "We see the boss a lot—at work, at home, right after getting out of tense meetings, and during important discussions held in the car." "I saw Shali get agitated, sure, but he never cussed or threw things. This is *not* typical," stressed Hill. "Many high-ranking officers will swear after they hang up after a tough phone call," but "as the heat rose, Shali got even more calm. It was strange!" Ron Parent, who served many four stars—William Westmoreland, Al Haig, Johnny Dee Wilson, and Hugh Shelton—as well as US

Coast Guard commander Admiral James Loy and Secretary of Defense Caspar Weinberger, agreed: "Shali was the kindest, most soft-spoken, gentle, self-confident general that I ever worked for."

When asked how his father handled the intense stress of his career, Brant Shalikashvili posed: "I think he internalized a lot. That man has probably one of the most tremendous wills of anyone I know. And part of that was the will to keep stress inside, rather than subject those around him to it."

This iron control over his emotions was a critical enabler of Shalikashvili's career success. It allowed him to maintain what Brant termed his "polite and caring unruffled persona," which enabled him to excel at the punishing task of finding common, productive ground with diverse groups of people across a variety of issues.

"I think it would have done him some good if he'd yelled a little bit more, screamed a bit more. Not necessarily at people, just in general," said Brant. And "there is a part of me that thinks the person who he's been since the stroke is simply him without the filter. Without the thing that says 'internalize the stress.'"

Others agreed. According to Mike Clark, senior enlisted aide during the general's years as both SACEUR and chairman: "After the stroke, officers didn't want to escort him because he'd say what was on his mind." Rachel McLain, Shalikashvili's executive assistant in retirement, noted that whenever the general went to board meetings, they never knew how he'd be. "This place is boring," he suddenly exclaimed at a celebratory event at one such organization, following up with a crude expression about wanting to leave. McLain convinced him to stay—until he slammed his fist on the table, insulted a key board member, and then demanded to go. He'd strike out verbally at caregiver staff at home, and once threatened to hurl weights at physical therapy staff. And though his control over his emotions was gone, his ability to read people wasn't. "The general would lash out based on people's unique weak points," McLain observed.

"I never knew I had so little patience," a frustrated Shalikashvili admitted less than a year after his stroke.

Over the years his body and mind continued to diminish. At one point he was hit by a seizure so severe it fractured his pelvis; he returned to a wheelchair and never walked again. As the years continued, dementia began to grab hold of his mind. On July 15, 2011, a second stroke hit.

It was a most unwelcome family legacy. It stripped away almost everything that made Shalikashvili who he was. Dimitri, toward the end of his life, once mused that when horses are hurt we shoot them out of kindness. "Too bad it's not the same for people" was the implication John's sister Gale drew.

Did John Shalikashvili have regrets? "Prior to the stroke I have had a very full and successful career. So I don't have to think of this stroke as preventing me from having a purpose in life. I have had that."

On the morning of July 23, 2011, John Shalikashvili passed away at Madigan Army Medical Center, Joint Base Lewis-McChord, Washington. The cause of death was complications from the second stroke. He was seventy-five years old. He is buried in Arlington National Cemetery.

Gravesite of John Shalikashvili, Section 30, Grave 832-2, Arlington National Cemetery. The wreath was laid by the prime minister of Georgia. (US Army photo by Rachel Larue/Arlington National Cemetery/released.)

Epilogue
The Meaning of a Life

So how *did* John Shalikashvili do it? How did the penniless, stateless refugee boy who stood out on that bridge watching GIs stream into Pappenheim at World War II's end go on to become the thirteenth chairman of the US Joint Chiefs of Staff?

Based on my many years of research into the man, I believe that—putting aside luck, or circumstances beyond his control that serendipitously fell his way—Shalikashvili realized the American dream because of his skill in carrying out a certain philosophy.

Consider this curious anecdote. Joe Shalikashvili was once asked which career achievement made his brother, now retired, the most proud. "It was his decision [as a three star]," Joe replied, "to name the parking lot sections at Heidelberg's new PX after animals—hippos, giraffes, and the like—so that kids could help their moms find the car."

Why such immense pride in what many might view a minor improvement in people's welfare? I believe it stems from Shalikashvili's de facto life philosophy, which he articulated, poignantly enough, in a letter sent out the very day of his retirement ceremony. Responding to a college professor's request for advice for his students, the outgoing chairman exhorted: "Every person has a responsibility to see the world as it really is, imagine it as it should be, and then work to make it better."

Shalikashvili developed and excelled at realizing this tripartite philosophy because of the very combination of things, both good and bad, benevolent and malevolent, that this biography has striven to show made him such an unusual senior US military officer: his wartime upbringing, aristocratic background, parental influence, betrayals by loved ones, and immigrant experience. Together these experiences allowed him to understand and appreciate many often-conflicting ideals, but without being ardently predisposed to any one. They made him sensitive to the needs of others yet allowed him to remain levelheaded.

It began with his wartime past. "Seeing people killed had been part of

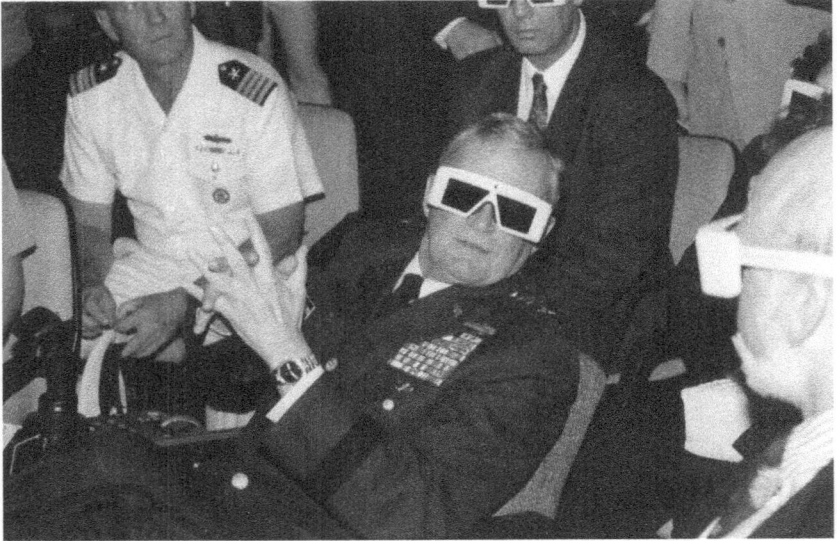

"Every person has a responsibility to see the world as it really is, imagine it as it should be, and then work to make it better."—John Shalikashvili, shown here wearing 3D glasses. (DoD photograph, courtesy of the NBR Gen. John Shalikashvili Archives.)

my growing up," he once reflected. Having spent half his childhood in the most bombed city of World War II, he knew firsthand the devastation conflict could unleash and how even an entire race could be targeted for annihilation. While living underground, his family had been forced to pay others to carry his grandmother's stretcher, a lesson in the selfishness of people during trying times. "You deal with it," he explained, "by trying not to let it demolish you."

Many seek self-preservation by expecting the worst from the world. Shalikashvili once served as an X.O. for a battalion commander who told him: "I believe people are no damn good, so when they screw up it is no big deal for me because I expect them to do so." But Shalikashvili deemed that outlook unhealthy: "I think people want to do good; you just have to make sure that they know what the goal line is and help them get there."

He likely felt so because during World War II and its aftermath he'd also seen the better side of humanity. He'd witnessed, for example, the compassion of escaping Polish partisans who, rather than leaving their war dead behind, carried them through the sewers in order to give them a proper burial. Even total strangers extended life-saving kindness—such as Winifred Luthy, who first sent badly needed care packages and then enlisted her brother to make the Shalikashvilis' dream of US immigration possible. "He didn't know us from beans," Shalikashvili later voiced his appreciation. Winifred's niece, Alice Tym, recalled the Shalikashvilis' arrival in Peoria: "They looked pitiful, all thin and with threadbare clothes—like the pictures you see of huddled masses at Ellis Island." The Luthys arranged housing, furniture, and clothing for them, even securing jobs for Dimitri and Missy. "We were so kindly received," Joe later appreciated.

Seeing the extremes of human behavior as a child thus gave John Shalikashvili early exposure to "seeing the world the way it is," not just how he might otherwise have thought or wished it to be. It provided wisdom that, in looking ahead, one should neither downplay the risks of bad things occurring nor prematurely dismiss possibilities for a better world.

And certain aspects of his aristocratic upbringing motivated him to make the world a better place. This biography has demonstrated how the ideal of noblesse oblige—the responsibility of the privileged to give back to the world—motivated especially Missy, Oma, and Aunt Julie to help others in need.

But aristocracy also teaches prudence. That's why the Pappenheims gave the Shalikashvilis free rent but not free electricity and offered them jobs rather than financial support. Interestingly, being a *fallen* aristocrat also taught prudence. Like how poverty encouraged John Shalikashvili to differentiate needs from desires—recall his letters home from boarding school in which he returned money and other items he thought unnecessary. Thriftiness would continue throughout his life.

Both noblesse oblige and poverty, then, would have primed Shalikashvili for the deliberate but judicious use of US power and resources to make the world a better place. One example is Operation Provide Comfort's approach to caring for the Kurds. "The more comfort you provide, the more it costs," Aspin noted at that congressional briefing, so "how do you decide in an operation like this the level of comfort you are going to provide?" The task force decided not to impose US or British standards for medical support, dietary needs, shelter, or clothing, replied Shalikashvili. "We did very much try to go by the standards that [the Kurds] were used to before they fled."

Another key aristocratic ideal is graciousness. Many aristocrats in his life—his parents, grandmother, Aunt Julie, and Julie's son Ludwig and even granddaughter Ursula—habitually interacted with others in a kindly manner. Though atypical for aristocracy, many of them were also down-to-earth. With such role models, it's no surprise John Shalikashvili rose through the ranks in part because of his gracious and low-key way of working with others.

Aristocrats also understand the value of appearances. I've presented numerous examples of how Shalikashvili purposefully cultivated images that strengthened his leadership. His "international mystique" was one. "Leadership by example" was yet another. Recall the remark that battalion commander Shalikashvili's volunteering for the unappealing job of "walking the rails" while his crew unloaded the howitzer in the rainy Pacific Northwest was "the kind of thing that gets around the grapevine in a hurry!" And by cultivating a reputation of purposefully not politicking for assignments, he thus encouraged the "let's get Shalikashvili for this" dynamic that helped bring him new leadership opportunities anyway. Finally, he promoted his office, not himself. Before moving into the chairman's quarters just vacated by Powell, Shalikashvili had extensive renovations done to the downstairs. That's where the new chairman would host an unusually large number of social gatherings, events that allowed his people skills full effect. The upstairs where the family slept, though, was left as is.

A third and related dimension was certain key orientations/values, whether inherited from his parents or instilled by them during his upbringing—like honesty, perseverance, loyalty, bravery, professionalism, and gentlemanly ways. *Boy on the Bridge: The Story of John Shalikashvili's American Success* has detailed how this inheritance enhanced Shalikashvili's ability to see the world as it was, imagine how it could be, and work to make a difference.

As readers too have learned, his father's ultimate betrayal of these family values perversely ended up being a major catalyst for his son's life philosophy, as Dimitri's participation in the Nazi war effort motivated John to never repeat his father's great weakness of putting his own narrow desires or self-interest first. Little wonder that Shalikashvili advised Hugh Shelton, his successor as chairman: "This is a tough town . . . avoid at all costs trying to do other than what you know is the right thing, to say other than what you know is the right thing."

Missy Shalikashvili's actions also served as warning. Like his mother, John too was empathetic. Recall how he'd told Donna that her trials in life "would help her better understand the lives of others who suffer." It had done so for him. As chairman, for example, he was once leading a meeting of the Joint Staff department heads. At the time waves of Haitian refugees were fleeing the country, often in unsafe boats, and the US Navy had been picking them up and depositing them on Guantanamo Bay Naval Base. The head of the Manpower and Personnel Directorate informed the chairman she was having trouble getting the mail system for the camps up and running, and then continued with her briefing. Shalikashvili—whose own mother had suffered the excruciating wait for news of her missing husband—stopped her and said: "There is nothing more important you can do for these people than this." As one attendee recalled: "It's so nice when the senior guy has his head on straight."

But empathy can be dangerous. Missy's urge to protect the individual—whether feeding a starving Jew or remaining in Warsaw because she couldn't bear to leave her mother behind—often put a greater number of lives at risk, as Dimitri had noted.

It's perhaps unsurprising that John Shalikashvili, when later asked about his experience growing up in wartime, answered: "You disciplined yourself not to become so emotionally involved that it robbed you of your perspective."

One needed a clear head to weigh costs and benefits. In 1995 Shalikashvili and National Security Advisor Anthony Lake together toured Gettysburg, where three days of fighting had produced at least forty-five thousand casualties. While in the battlefield bookstore, they reflected on how the recent Somali mission had been judged a disaster because the "Black Hawk Down" incident claimed the lives of eighteen soldiers. "Something has broken down in the debate about the use of force," Shalikashvili critiqued. "Eighteen people died so thousands and thousands could live. To me, that's glory."

Here it is worth revisiting Shalikashvili's childhood experiences. Growing up in wartime Europe also taught him the world is rarely a simple struggle between black and white. Many shades of gray exist.

The story of his father's unit surrendering at the end of World War II epitomizes the complicated politics of nationalism and war. Recall Dimitri's bemusement at the British finding a German army regiment, clad in Waffen-SS uniforms, most of whom were Georgians and thus citizens of the Soviet Union, a country fighting on the British side, but also now officially serving as north Italian partisans fighting the communists. Just imagine how few aspiring officers at OCS had family experiences marked by such complexity!

Family dynamics also taught him people can be just as complex. Take the fluid views Missy and Oma had of their nationality, which rotated between being Georgian, Russian, German, or Polish. Shalikashvili himself would see himself at turns as American, Polish, German, and—as he told not only Donna but decades later also Madeleine Albright—Georgian.

With an appreciation for life's complexities and the resulting conflicts they can create, it is little wonder Shalikashvili attacked problems by plunging into the details, by appreciating nuance. This mentality, backed by his engineer's mind, helped him excel in all those "holistic" postings that required fathoming how the parts relate to the whole. By more clearly seeing the world the way it actually was, he could better understand how to make it better. By seeing the complexities, Shalikashvili could also keep from being overly optimistic about possible solutions.

Counterbalancing that caution, however, was his imaginative mind-set. Yes, "John was a creative, outgoing, and naughty boy who could always cute-talk his way out of trouble," and he'd retained that spirit into adulthood, even if it lay below the surface.

Unless, of course, he was around children. Once, at a wedding, Shalikashvili noticed a little girl off by herself. "Come here, I'm going to teach you something your dad will *love*," he said with a conspiratorial wink, and then demonstrated how to whistle with an acorn top. "Dad isn't a disciplinarian with kids," Brant Shalikashvili explained, "because he believes this devilishness allows people to see things differently."

During my interview with William Perry, who'd worked closely with Shalikashvili on the thorniest US security policy issues, the former secretary of defense began by showing me framed photos of key historical peacemaking moments the two men helped bring about. Looking at one I remarked: "There's that devilish grin." Perry, clearly mourning the recent death of the general, looked at me in alarm. But later he paused our discussion to admit: "Yes. He did have a devilish grin."

And he took devilish actions. In retirement Shalikashvili would talk of his efforts to combine the services in new ways to increase capability. When dealing with the Haiti crisis as chairman, for instance, "I took an aircraft carrier and took all the aircraft off it and put army helicopters on. And the navy and the army almost fainted." He'd tried something similar during Provide Comfort when he insisted all army helicopters be put on an air force tasking order. "Folks at Leavenworth thought I was a heretic."

Perhaps the strongest motivator for John Shalikashvili's life philosophy, however, was his immigrant experience. Tellingly, being nominated chairman was "the second greatest honor of my life." The first? "The day back in 1958 when I became an American citizen."

He was proud of what the United States stood for: "While I know the dark side of war, I also know first-hand about the bright side of America. The America that from its earliest days has been a land of boundless opportunity and a beacon of hope and of liberty around the world."

And by settling in Peoria he'd steeped himself in that bright side of America right from the start. "Because it was the Middle West," Shalikashvili appreciated, "it has its rock-iron value system, this clear sense of right and wrong." It was a place that offered "important lessons about hard work, helping others." "And people are not flashy . . . I feel very comfortable with that."

Similarly, upon joining the US military Shalikashvili felt fortunate "to belong to an outfit where everyone expected a young officer's values and character to be his credentials." "I don't want to sound corny, but it was a life that had some kind of meaning. It wasn't just making a buck. You were doing something for your country. For me, that meant twice as much as most, because I feel I owe this country so much."

As this biography has shown, Shalikashvili's dedication to the military was enhanced by the painful experiences of being betrayed or hurt by loved ones—whether Donna's leaving Peoria without a word or the premature deaths of Gunhild and Christina. These blows gave him the incentive, at a critical early stage in his career, to emphasize caring for his military family rather than just his own career.

John Shalikashvili's allegiance to his new home was akin to Countess Julie Pappenheim's devotion to the Pappenheim family after the untimely death of her husband, which she symbolized by remaining forever attired in black. "Dad was a great patriot toward Georgia," Joe Shalikashvili explained, "John is like that to the United States." In Germany in the mid-1960s, P. J. Volk witnessed how patriotism once prompted Shalikashvili into a rare public outburst. "I was standing in line at the PX to pick up laundry. Shali was ahead of me. The German girls behind the counter were saying critical things about the American soldiers, that they were stupid or something, and Shali said to them, 'I speak perfect German. These soldiers are here keeping your country safe. If you say anything bad about Americans again, I will have you fired!'"

Yet unlike the father, the son strove not to let patriotism blind him from seeing the way things actually were. Consider his takeaways from Vietnam. "We think of ourselves as correct and morally proper force, and in Vietnam time and again American troops participated in absolute atrocities or mistreatment of prisoners," Shalikashvili once pointed out, "so I came out of that convinced that we cannot just live on the assumption that we are Americans and we don't do those things. We are just as human, just as prone to fall into that trap. Particularly when it seems like we have encouragement to do that from our senior leaders."

A good way to prevent moral failures, he believed, was to uphold the high standards the US publicly espouses. Such as openness. In Vietnam, "another thing that I learned is that we became paranoid about the press." But "the press is invaluable [for] telling that part of the military operation that the government does not want to be known or to dwell on." As chairman, whether in the Balkans or in Haiti, "I always insisted that we make sure that we are as open as we should be with the press."

"The best spokesmen for the military that we have are our soldiers, our young leaders, sergeants," he added. But in terms of being open with the press, "all I ever asked them was to 'stay in your lane.' If you are a platoon leader, talk about the life of the platoon. Don't talk about what the president should be doing or not doing. Just stay in your lane and you will never go wrong."

Lastly, being *both* a war refugee and a senior American military officer was a force multiplier. Because of his wartime upbringing, "I gained a first-hand appreciation for what Americans fight for and how very important it is that when we do fight, we win." And this dual identity also meant he'd be a leader who'd look beyond just the interests of the United States.

Examples abound. When Shalikashvili was assistant to the chairman, he took trips to the former Soviet Union with Deputy Undersecretary of Defense for Policy "Scooter" Libby. "We had long talks," Libby later recalled, ". . . in which he would talk very proudly about his family history, of a sense of being rooted in tradition, in understanding the perils of people who live outside the glow of democracy and what it means to be dedicating your life to bringing freedom to those areas."

Or just ask William Perry: "All, and I mean all, of the European leaders, civilian and military, had enormous respect for Shali. They knew he always represented his own country very well. But they also knew he cared deeply about their countries. They also knew he'd be totally honest with them. As a result he was more effective than any other SACEUR I know of."

That Shalikashvili played such an unusual and critical role in NATO—the centerpiece of global stability in the turmoil of the immediate post–Cold War era—perhaps explains his most serious violation of his own values: the lie he told Congress during his confirmation hearing.

When the controversy broke, the "right thing" for Shalikashvili would have been to tell the truth—that he knew of his father's SS affiliation. Nobody was looking to punish him for the sins of his father. To be confirmed, as noted by Senator Specter, he'd just need to say he himself did not hold any pro-Nazi views.

And he didn't. Except for Donna's recollections of him as a newly arrived refugee, in all my years of research and in hundreds of interviews I've uncovered no further evidence of any such outlook, no further hint of any anti-Semitic views, in this US Army officer. As a battalion commander in the mid-1970s, Shalikashvili once kicked a soldier out of the army for being a neo-Nazi. "Shali got so angry during the meeting with him," one subordinate later recalled; it was the only time he'd ever witnessed the boss lose composure.

Here is where the paradox is deepest: by lying, John Shalikashvili went against the very principle that had fueled his rise to the top. Why then did he lie?

I asked Joe Shalikashvili this question. When presented with evidence that his brother had indeed known, Joe replied: "John was under immense pressure. He was very worried about how it would affect his ability to interact with allies." Whether he became chairman or returned to his SACEUR post, the general would be working closely with many of the same military leaders. That's why, after being confirmed, John told his brother: "I've passed the nomination, but it didn't do anything to enhance my position."

It's hard to independently judge how much admitting the truth would have undermined Shalikashvili's credibility with other European leaders, and thus his ability to work with them to make the world a better place. But for a man known for "priding himself that he always told the truth, even if people didn't like what he had to tell them," it's an awkward explanation at best. My guess is his complicated feelings about his father played an important role.

But one thing is certain: by accepting Clinton's nomination to the post, a strategic thinker like Shalikashvili would have understood the substantial risk that his father's transgression would come to light during the confirmation process. Was that the real reason he'd equivocated so long before mustering up a decent yes to the president's offer?

* * *

"To see the world as it really is, imagine it as it should be, and then work to make it better."

John Shalikashvili took his first steps toward this philosophy at the small world of Officer Candidate School. Thereafter, the higher he got promoted, the larger this "world" became. Each step upward provided opportunity to apply his approach on a wider scale—whether commanding units from platoon to division, guiding the careers of army majors and lieutenant colonels as a major, helping steer army policymaking across a range of issues at the Pentagon as a colonel on up, or being responsible for the transatlantic alliance as the military head of NATO or for the entire globe as chairman.

It wasn't just that his skills reduced conflict. It was that by reducing conflict Shalikashvili so often helped both save lives already in danger and prevent further conflict down the road. Consider that under his leadership Operation Provide Comfort both prevented renewed fighting with the Iraqi military from breaking out and removed a half-million Kurdish refugees from harm's way. His later efforts to secure loose nuclear weapons in the former Soviet Union similarly also made the world a much more peaceful place. Just as, while SACEUR and chairman, he helped guide the transatlantic alliance and beyond through the chaos of a post–Cold War world.

It's sad to think of the last time I saw the general, that spring day in 2011 when his stroke-affected mind, agonizing over the potential consequences for the relatively few lives taken under his watch, had conjured up those frightful images. So many famous military leaders are known for their prowess in commanding troops in battle. But the proof of Shalikashvili's genius lies elsewhere: in the many lives he helped keep from harm. It's the case of the dog that didn't bark—because John Shalikashvili so often kept it quiet. Little wonder that in retirement he chose to join William Perry's Preventive Defense Project, where he continued his efforts to avert conflict. To me, that's glory.

Unfortunately, compared to leading troops in battle, defusing current and future conflicts is a contribution that is much harder to quantify, and thus less likely to be celebrated. Furthermore, because Shalikashvili worked via a low-key style of treating others with respect, rather than a more dramatic confrontational or self-promotional approach, he garnered even less of the spotlight.

It was precisely to make explicit Shalikashvili's overlooked contributions to peace and leadership, then, that I've written this very unusual biography.

It's an unusual biography for an unusual success story, and John Shalikashvili held deep appreciation for the country that made it all possible. "Where else," he posed, "could my story have happened?" "Where else but in this land of boundless opportunity could a kid born on the wrong side of the Iron Curtain who came here as a 16-year old not knowing more than two words of English, one who started out as a private in the Army, in time rise to become the most senior general? Where else but here, here in America? There just isn't a place like it."

Shalikashvili's assertion rings true. Consider that he and his father shared almost the exact same skill set. Dimitri, however, never had the fortune to serve in the US military. He fought for the Russian tsar, Free Georgia, Poland, and Germany—and was on the losing side every time, twice becoming a POW to boot. He retired as only a major. By the time he arrived in the United States, Dimitri looked like a broken man, recalled Alice Tym: "His shoulders were stooped. It must have been so difficult to go from being a somebody to being threadbare and getting assistance from someone he didn't even know." After arriving in Peoria, this Georgian prince who'd been too proud to do menial work in Pappenheim took an auditor job at Central Illinois Light Company to support his family. But Shalikashvili's parents knew that making the sacrifice to come to the United States was the right move: "We did it for the children."

And Shalikashvili held such deep gratitude for his adopted country well before he reached the top. Back when he was a colonel serving as DIVARTY commander in Germany, a command post exercise required Shalikashvili to fly to a tactical operations center deployed in a sleepy town near the Czech border.

As his chopper touched down in the town square, Major Grover

Ford, Shalikashvili's operations officer, was waiting for him a bit at a remove. The sound of the helicopter blades had long since reverberated across the town, and the town center was now filled with curious children. Upon disembarking Shalikashvili went to greet them. By the time Ford made his way over, Shalikashvili was down on one knee, chatting.

"It was obvious the kids were flabbergasted," Ford recalled. "How could a German-speaker fly in an American helicopter? How could this man be a high-ranking officer in the U.S. Army?!"

After five minutes Shalikashvili turned to Ford and said: "I'm going to talk to these kids a bit more."

About twenty minutes later, the commander was finally done.

"You probably won't believe this," Shalikashvili said on the drive to the tactical operations center, "but this is the most important thing I will do today." The commander then began sharing with Ford the questions the kids were asking.

After he finished, Shalikashvili felt compelled to add something: "I needed to tell them about the melting pot, about how in the United States you can be anything you set out to be."

Acknowledgments

First and foremost, without the unflagging enthusiasm and multifaceted support of my trophy wife, Dr. Rachel Marcus, and the flexibility and fun of my stepchildren, two-legged Abe, Saul, and Rose and four-legged Lily, bringing *Boy on the Bridge: The Story of John Shalikashvili's American Success* to life would have been neither possible nor bearable.

Additionally, John, Joan, and Brant Shalikashvili shared their time, candid reflections, photographs, letters, and combined Rolodex; provided a signed letter of support; and authorized access to restricted materials—all while placing zero restrictions on how I answered my research question. I deeply appreciate their generosity.

Colonel Othar Joseph Shalikashvili and Gale Sever just as graciously offered their recollections, shedding invaluable light on their brother's upbringing and character.

Then there's Donna Bechtold Kurtz—without her unexpected openness and insights this would have been a radically different biography indeed. Special thanks also to Donna's grandson, Blaine Blystone, and friend Merilee Hudson for their assistance, as well as to Anita (Ziegler) Hollweck and granddaughter Anna Handrischik for reaching out to share old letters and memories.

I'm also grateful to the George C. Marshall Foundation for financial support via its Baruch Fellowship Award; Susan Lemke at the Special Collections, Archives, and History Section of the National Defense University Library and Frank Shirer at the Center of Military History, both at Fort McNair; "Mike" Perry at the Army Heritage and Education Center of the Military History Institute, Carlisle Barracks; Carol Leadenham at the Hoover Institution Archives, Stanford University; Dorothy Hart at Peoria High School, Charles Frey of the Special Collections Center, Bradley University Library, and especially Bradley's ever-genuine former registrar Kathie Beaty. A hearty "*ganxie*" also to both Lieutenant Colonel Roy Kamphausen for wide-ranging support and the National Bureau of Asian Research for foresight in creating its Gen. John Shalikashvili Archives.

In addition to my better half, many others generously read and improved various drafts/proposals or offered financial, research, translation, legal, and even living arrangement assistance.

Above all, without the yare and flair of Dr. Ellen Frost's logistical support services, this book would have long-since stalled out. I owe an ineffable debt too to Sandra Ward, who earnestly gave much, and in many ways, to the project. A hearty shout out as well to the rock stars Cary Grief, Claire Topal, and Dr. Yuan-kang Wang for going above and beyond the duties of friendship.

Other kind souls include General Wesley Clark, Lieutenant General Daniel Christman, Major General James Kessler, and Lieutenant General Gary Speer, as well as Colonel Frank Adams, Colonel Billy Brooks, Dr. Joseph Collins, Claudia Dreifus, Dr. Evelyn Farkas, Dr. Rachel Leow, Dr. Bettina Matthias, Colonel Robert Ross, and particularly "Opinions Unlimited" Colonel Jon Schreyach. Special thanks also to UPK's Melissa Hammer, Ila McEntire, Natalie O'Neal, Derik Shelor, and Stephanie Williams; Umair Kazi and Michael Gross of the Authors Guild; Ellis Levine, Andrea Pedolsky, and Susan Rabiner; and, of course, Rachel McClain.

Equally warm appreciation goes to Dr. John Atwood, Elizabeth and Jack Beardsley, Debra Birt, Dr. Michael Birt, Erica Cavanagh, Kim and Chip Collins, Kailani Cordell, Ann Coulston, Dr. Simone Derix, Karen DeYoung, Dr. Maurice East, Arthur Eldar, Dr. Gayle Feldman, Hilde Goetz, Chris and Amy Faldt, Georg Frank, Dr. Carla Freeman, Sourabh Gupta, Aurie Hall, Erna Handke, Karin Hanta, Jonathan Harr, Leslie Harris, Karolos Karnikis, William Krolicki, Nicholas Lanciani, James Lanham, Deirdre Launt, Debra Layers, Dr. Steven Livingston, Dr. Tabitha Mallory, Paul Marble, Sharyn Marble, Adam Marcus, Dr. Robert Marcus, Dr. Peter Mattis, Dina Melnichuk, Bonnie Miller, Irakli Nadareishvili, David Nedde, Deborah Nedde, Bill and Caryl O'Keefe, Jay O'Keefe, Ronit Piper, Dr. Charles Robertson, Dr. Sandra Sardjono, Dr. Andrew Scobell, Dr. Yvonne Sim, Cathy Topal, Dr. Samuel Topal, Marlene Welsh, Quincy Whitney, Sonja Williams, Dr. Gaby Weissman, Sandra Yin, and—last but never least—Dr. Joshua Ziemkowski.

Illuminating John Shalikashvili's character required channeling hundreds of human "points of light" spread across the firmament of his life (listed alphabetically):

Old World: Jonas Anderson, Kyra Cheremeteff, Zurab Kobiashvili, Friedrich Paulsen, Countess Ursula Pappenheim, and Pappenheim historians Hans Navratil, Renate Prusekow, and Thomas Karl.

Peoria: Bruce Bagge, Gary Bragg, Caroll Connor, Lou Deardorff,

Gayle Deynzer, Dorothy Gregoire, Steve Harrison, John Hoehne, Merilee Hudson, Anita Johnson, Peter Knost, Y. King Liu, Charles Luthy, Paul Matlock, William McCarty, Joyce Murphy, Jon Nelson, Bill Rapp, Gary Rice, Roger Roszell, Brigadier General Horace Russell, Valerie Markman Schwartz, Richard and Barbra Sterling, Ron Streibich, Jim Suffield, Lawrence Tadie, Alice Tym, Richard Verkler, Ray Voigt, Max Wessler, and Audrey Whitney.

OCS: Randy and Penny Dunham, as well Colonel "Bill" Austin, Lieutenant Colonel Jim Barber, Wilson Blake, William Cheal, Robert Coggsdale, Colonel Byron Crawford, Laurence Crawford, Colonel Russell Davis, Colonel James Doukas, Bob Errico, Melvin Eubanks, Captain Larry Frye, Major Daniel Furman, Lieutenant Colonel Bobby Godwin, Bob Hartley, Lieutenant Colonel Robert Jenks, Andrew Kner, George Krumbhaar, Colonel Gerald Lauzon, Gerald Leungen, Colonel Robert Lindsay, Colonel Karl Lorenz, Lieutenant Colonel John Marti, Captain James McGary, Richard McKay, Mike McMahon, Roger O'Dwyer, Anthony Ostrom, Ole Face, John Ruoff, Lieutenant Colonel Robert Sandla, Dwight Schumann, Richard Seignious, Albert Shook, Coy Short, Colonel James Slagle, Colonel Wilbert Sorenson, SP4 Hubert Stang, Major James Stotler, James Swann, Raymond Tetreault, "Colby" Thresher, Donald Toney, and "Jerry" Ward.

Alaska: Paul and Helen Buckley, First Lieutenant Dale Cunningham, Colonel Roger Donlon, Samuel Foster, Colonel Charles Glenn, Sergeant First Class William Grice, John Haynes, Colonel William Howerton, Tedd Hummel, SP4 Henry Phillips, Charles Skillman, and Gail Vodopich.

Field Artillery/Missile Defense. Dr. Boyd Dastrup, Lieutenant Colonel John Hamilton, Colonel Jon Schreyach, Lieutenant General "Dutch" Shoffner, and Colonel Frank Siltman.

Fort Bliss: Carl Burgdorf, Mark Garcia, and William Grubbs.

32nd AADCOM: Lieutenant Colonel Richard Graham, William Hoover, Master Warrant Officer Edward Ney, Colonel Peter Poessiger, Colonel Al Roller, and Lieutenant Colonel P. J. Volk.

Vietnam: Frank Gramer, Melissa Hart, Colonel John B. Haseman, First Lieutenant Peter Luitwieler, Lieutenant Colonel David Millie, Brigadier General Harley Mooney, Lieutenant Colonel "Karl" Schelhammer, First Lieutenant James Smith Jr., and Mrs. Robert Weary.

Military Personnel Center: Colonel Bob Becker, Colonel Roy Herron, and General Binford Peay.

Battalion Command: Sergeant First Class Paul Bates, Colonel Billy Brooks, Major General Jimmy Collins, Tony Forsyth, Lieutenant Colonel

Kevin Gregory, Dr. Richard Holyoke, Lieutenant Colonel Bob Kukich, Dr. Steven Livingston, Dan Nelson, Colonel Thomas Ross, Command Sergeant Major Bruno Schact, Lieutenant General Howard Stone, Major General Jack Walker, Stephen Witt, and Sergeant Stewart Wright.

SETAF: Major General John Herrling and Mrs. Russell Merical.

DIVARTY Command: Colonel Roger Bernardi, Dr. Frederick Bussey, Command Sergeant Major Roger Casinger, Colonel Grover Ford, Brigadier General Stan Kwieciak, Sergeant Don Sparks, and Brigadier General Rex Weaver.

Pentagon in the 1980s: Major General George Bombel, Colonel Bruce Clarke, Colonel Ralph Hallenbeck, Lieutenant General Tom Jaco, Colonel Mike Kendall, and General Robert Riscassi.

DCINC, 1st Armored Division: Colonel Caroll Dickson, Colonel Bob Jones, General Montgomery Meigs, Chaplain Joseph Miller, Colonel Mike Molino, Lieutenant Colonel Allen Ohlstein, and General Crosbie "Butch" Saint.

9th Infantry Division: Sergeant First Class Brett Chamberlain, Mrs. Jack Costello, Lieutenant General William Harrison, Sergeant Major John Lee, Colonel Robert Ross, Colonel Larry Saunders, Colonel Richard Sinnreich, Major General J. B. Taylor, and Marilyn and Chuck Wender.

DCINC, USAREUR: Lieutenant Colonel Martin Anderson, Susan Caroll, Lieutenant Colonel Roger Cirillo, Colonel Ruth Collins, Ambassador David Fisher, General John "Jack" Galvin, Colonel Stephen Gulyas, Lieutenant Colonel David Merhar, Colonel Tom Molino, Admiral "Snuffy" Smith, Colonel Gerald Thompson, and Gay Van Brero.

Operation Provide Comfort: General James Jamerson, Brigadier General Richard Potter, and Colonel Ken Getty, who provided multiple interviews, key insights, and supporting material; and General John Abizaid, Ambassador Morton Abramowitz, Brigadier General Brian Holt, Colonel Eugene Ronsick, and Kurdish Representative Qubad Talabani.

Assistant to the Chairman through Chairman: Madame Madeleine Albright, Frank Angelo, Brigadier General David Armstrong, Lieutenant General Daniel Christman, Command Sergeant Major Mike Clark, General Wesley Clark, President William J. Clinton, Dr. Joseph Collins, Deputy Secretary of Defense Rudy de Leon, Colonel Scott Deibler, Claudia Dreifus, Dr. Sidney Drell, Admiral Thomas Fargo, Dr. David Finkelstein, Colonel Mike Gallagher, National Security Advisor Stephen Hadley, Lieutenant Colonel Brian Haig, Rich Hill, Nancy Hughes, Lieutenant General Patrick Hughes, CW3 Jack Hurley, Colonel Larry Icenogle, Major General James Kessler, General Nicholas Krawciw, John Lancaster, Lieutenant General Ed Leland, Rear Admiral Mike McDevitt, Elizabeth Zaldastani Napier, Ron Parent, Secretary of Defense Dr. William Perry, Robert Peurifoy, General Colin Powell, Edgar Puryear, Dr. Kori Schake, Captain Sharon Shelton, General Gordon Sullivan, General Henk van den Breemen, Damon Wilson, and Ambassador Temuri Yakobashvili.

Retirement: CW3 Steven Abernathy, Dr. Brian Beldowicz, Kathleen Blanchet, Major Adam Cecil, Major General Anthony Cucolo, Lieutenant General James Dubik, Karolos Karnikis, Rachel McLain, Marcus Dee McRee, Dr. Melinda Moir, and Debra Preston.

Please note that ranks are listed as per interview date and some interviewees knew Shalikashvili during multiple assignments. My apologies to those inadvertently left out and for misspelled names or missing or incorrect ranks.

Appendix A
Timeline: Old World

From Russian Empire to Soviet Union (1721–1922)

Nov. 21, 1864	Marie Rudiger born, Lublin, Poland (under Russian rule).
Feb. 16, 1896	Dimitri Shalikashvili born, Gurjaani, Georgia.
?	Marie Rudiger marries Alexandre Bielaieff.
Apr. 8, 1906	Maria "Missy" Rudiger born, St. Petersburg, Russia.
1914	Dimitri Shalikashvili graduates high school, Tbilisi, Georgia.
Jun. 28, 1914	World War I begins.
Jun. 1915	German army advances on Warsaw, Rudiger-Bielaieff family flees Lublin back to St. Petersburg.
Jun. 7, 1916	Dimitri Shalikashvili pauses study at Russian Lyceum in St. Petersburg to volunteer with the Russian Empire's Regiment of the Horse Guards.
Nov. 1916	Dimitri Shalikashvili commands platoon in fight against Turks.
Dec. 1916	Alexandre Bielaieff assigned to Supreme Headquarters.
Oct. 1917	Bolshevik Revolution cancels Dimitri Shalikashvili's officer exams in St. Petersburg.
Feb. 1918	Dimitri Shalikashvili returns to Georgia.
May 26, 1918	Democratic Republic of Georgia declares independence.
Jun. 1918	Dimitri joins newly forming Georgian national military.
Nov. 11, 1918	World War I ends.
Oct. 1920	Bielaieff family flees Russia.
Dec. 1920	Dimitri leaves for Georgian diplomatic mission to Turkey.

Feb. 15, 1921	Communist Russia invades Georgia.
Dec. 28, 1922	Soviet Union founded.

Poland (1922–1944)

1918	Poland regains independence.
Nov. 12, 1922	Dimitri Shalikashvili leaves Turkey for Poland to become foreign contract officer.
1923	Dimitri Shalikashvili graduates from eight-month course on Poland's language, politics, and military, in Bydgoszcz.
1924	Dimitri Shalikashvili graduates from Polish Central Cavalry School, Grudziontz.
1924	Rudiger-Bielaieff family returns to Poland.
Mar. 1925	Dimitri Shalikashvili graduates with honors from Polish General Staff Academy, War College, and is formally admitted to Polish army as foreign contract officer.
Jun. 1931	Dimitri meets Missy Rudiger.
1932	Dimitri and Missy marry, Warsaw.
Jun. 27, 1936	John Shalikashvili born, Warsaw.
Aug. 23, 1939	Russo-German Nonaggression Pact.
Sep. 1, 1939	Germans invade Poland, launching World War II; Shalikashvilis home moved to Skolimow; Dimitri Shalikashvili taken POW by Germans.
Dec. 28, 1939	Missy Shalikashvili frees husband from German POW hospital; Alexandre Bielaieff dies.
Oct. 1940	Shalikashvilis move back to Warsaw.
1941	Dimitri Shalikashvili begins Georgian Colony job.
Jun. 21, 1941	Surprise German invasion of Soviet Union.
Dec. 30, 1941	Germany legalizes creation of German military's Eastern Legions.
Jan. 3, 1943	Dimitri Shalikashvili joins the Georgian Legion.
Fall 1943	Dimitri Shalikashvili posted to France.
Aug. 1, 1943	Warsaw Uprising begins.
Late 1943	Dimitri Shalikashvili posted to Georgian Liaison Office, Berlin.
Oct. 1, 1944	Missy Shalikashvili, her children, and mother flee Warsaw.

Germany (1944–1952)

October 1944	Shalikashvili family arrives in Pappenheim, Germany.
Dec. 11, 1944	Germany forms SS Waffengruppe Georgien.
Feb. 1945	Dimitri Shalikashvili makes first trip to Italy.
Apr. 24, 1945	US soldiers arrive in Pappenheim.
Spring 1945	Dimitri Shalikashvili seconded as deputy commander to Georgian Cavalry Regiment, Italy.
May 1945	Dimitri Shalikashvili surrenders to British military; thereafter Missy Shalikashvili makes unsuccessful trip to Italy to free him.
Summer 1946	Dimitri Shalikashvili released from British POW camp.
Dec. 1946	Dimitri Shalikashvili returns to Pappenheim.
Jan. 17, 1950	Julie Pappenheim dies.
Nov. 22, 1952	Shalikashvili family departs Pappenheim.
Nov. 24, 1952	Shalikashvili family boards SS *America*.
Dec. 1, 1952	Shalikashvili family lands in USA; Marie Rudiger-Bielaieff passes away.

Appendix B

Timeline: New World

Peoria, Illinois (1952–1958)

1952–1954	Peoria High School.
Summer 1954	Donna flees Peoria.
1954–1958	Bradley University.

Private (1958–1959)

Jul. 30, 1958–Oct. 9, 1958	Basic Training, Fort Leonard Wood, Michigan.
Oct. 24, 1958–Jan. 22, 1959	Advanced Individual Training, Fort Chaffee, Arkansas.
Jan. 24, 1959–Jul. 6, 1959	Field Artillery Officer Candidate School, Fort Sill, Oklahoma.

Second Lieutenant (1959–1961)

Jul. 7, 1959–May 13, 1960	1st Battle Group/Brigade, 9th Infantry Division, Eielson AFB, Fairbanks, Alaska.
Jul. 7, 1959–Nov. 17, 1959	Forward Observer, Mortar Battery.
Nov. 18, 1959–May 13, 1960	Platoon Commander, Mortar Battery.
May 14, 1960–Feb. 27, 1961	Battery B, 2nd Howitzer Battalion, 15th Artillery, US Army, Ladd AFB/ Fort Wainwright, Fairbanks, Alaska.
May 14, 1960–Aug. 2, 1960	Aide-de-camp for General Wheeler.
Aug. 3, 1960–Oct. 31, 1960	Forward Observer, Battery B; then Assistant S-3, Howitzer Battalion.
Nov. 1, 1960–Feb. 27, 1961	Assistant X.O., then X.O., Battery B.
Dec. 14, 1960	Becomes Regular Army officer.

First Lieutenant (1961–1963)

Feb. 28, 1961–Apr. 9, 1963	Instructor, US Army Air Defense School, Fort Bliss, El Paso, Texas.
Apr. 18, 1963	Marries Gunhild Bartsch.
May 2, 1963–Dec. 13, 1963	Student, Artillery Officer Advanced Course, USAADS, Fort Bliss, El Paso Texas.

Captain (1963–1967)

Dec. 14, 1963–Feb. 9, 1964	French Language Class, Presidio of Monterey, California.
Feb. 10, 1964–Dec. 1964	Staff Officer, Plans and Operations Division, G-3, USAADS, Fort Bliss, El Paso Texas.
Feb. 5, 1965–May 17, 1965	Assistant Information Officer, 32nd Artillery Brigade, USAREUR, Kapaun Barracks, Kaiserslautern, Germany.
May 18, 1965–Jan. 1968	Operations Officer, Detachment Commander, and Operations Officer, 32nd Army Air Defense Command, USAREUR, Kapaun Barracks, Kaiserslautern, Germany.
May 20, 1965	Christina Shalikashvili born.
May 22, 1965	Christina Shalikashvili dies.
Aug. 9, 1965	Gunhild Shalikashvili dies.
Dec. 27, 1966	Marries Joan E. Zimpelman.

Major (1967–1974)

Jan. 24, 1968–Jun. 20, 1968	Language training, Fort Bragg, North Carolina, and Biggs Air Force Base, Texas.
Jun. 21, 1968–Jun. 4, 1969	Senior District Adviser, Advisory Team 19, US MACV, Trieu Phong, Vietnam.
Aug. 15, 1969–Jun. 22, 1970	Student, US Naval War College, Newport, Rhode Island; M.A. in International Affairs, George Washington University, Washington, D.C.

Jun. 22, 1970–Aug. 13, 1970	2nd Battalion, 18th Field Artillery, 212th Field Artillery Group, 9th Infantry Division, Fort Lewis, Washington.
Jun. 22, 1970–Jun. 7, 1971	Executive Officer, 2nd Battalion, 18th Field Artillery, 212th Field Artillery Group, 9th Infantry Division, Fort Lewis, Washington.
Jun. 15, 1971–Aug. 12, 1971	Acting Commanding Officer, 2nd Battalion, 18th Field Artillery, 212th Field Artillery Group, 9th Infantry Division, Fort Lewis, Washington.
Sep. 11, 1971–Sep. 17, 1972	Operations Officer, Current Operations, Office of the Assistant Chief of Staff, J-3, UN Command/US Forces Korea, Eighth Army HQ, Seoul, South Korea.
Mar. 6, 1972	Brant Shalikashvili born.
Oct. 31, 1972–Jul. 3, 1975	Assignment Officer/Personnel Management Officer, Field Artillery Branch, and Chief, Assignment Branch, Lieutenant Colonels Division, Officer Personnel Management Directorate, US Army Military Personnel Center, Alexandria, Virginia.

Lieutenant Colonel (1974–1978)

Jul. 30, 1975–Dec. 9, 1975	Assistant Fire Support Coordinator, Division Artillery, 9th Infantry Division, Fort Lewis, Washington.
Oct. 12, 1975–Jun. 22, 1977	Commander, 1st Battalion, 84th Field Artillery, 9th Infantry Division, Fort Lewis, Washington.
Aug. 8, 1977–Jun. 12, 1978	Student, US Army War College, Carlisle, Pennsylvania.
Mar. 8, 1978	Dimitri Shalikashvili dies.
Jun. 13, 1978–Jun. 12, 1979	Assistant Chief of Staff, G-3, SETAF, Vicenza, Italy.

Colonel (1979–1983)

Jun. 13, 1979–Aug. 1981	Commander, Division Artillery, 1st Armored Division, USAEUR and Seventh Army, Zirndorf, Germany.
Sep. 14, 1981–Jan. 20, 1983	Chief, Politico-Military Division, Office of the Deputy Chief of Staff for Operations and Plans (ODCSOPS), US Army, Pentagon.
Jan. 21, 1983–Jul. 22, 1983	Senior Army Planner for Joint Affairs, US Army, ODCSOPS, Pentagon.

Brigadier General (1983–1986)

Jul. 23, 1983–Jul. 27, 1984	Acting Director, then Deputy Director, Strategy, Plans, and Policy Directorate, HQ, US Army, Pentagon.
Aug. 21, 1984–Jun. 12, 1986	Assistant Division Commander, 1st Armored Division, USAEUR, and Commander, Nurenburg Military Community, Ansbach, Germany.

Major General (1986–1989)

Jun. 15, 1986–May 30, 1987	Assistant Deputy, then Deputy, Chief of Staff for Operations and Plans (Joint Affairs)/Director of Strategy, Plans, and Policy, ODCSOPS, US Army, Pentagon.
Jun. 1987–Aug. 1989	Commander, 9th Infantry Division, Fort Lewis, Washington.

Lieutenant General (1989–1992)

Sep. 1989–Aug. 1991	DCINC, Seventh Army/USAREUR, Heidelberg, Germany.
Apr. 1991–Jun. 1991	Commander, Operation Provide Comfort, Turkey/Iraq.
Aug. 1991–Jun. 1992	Assistant to the Chairman, Joint Chiefs of Staff, Pentagon.

General (1992–1997)

Jun. 23, 1992–Aug. 21, 1993	SACEUR, SHAPE, Mons, Belgium, and CINC, EUCOM, Stuttgart, Germany.
Apr. 1993	Missy Shalikashvili dies.
Aug. 25, 1993–Oct. 1, 1997	Chairman, Joint Chiefs of Staff, Pentagon.
Sep. 30, 1997	Retirement Ceremony, Fort Myer, Virginia
July 23, 2011	John Shalikashvili dies, Madigan Army Medical Center, Joint Base Lewis-McChord, Washington.

Notes

Abbreviations

CJCS	Chairman of the Joint Chiefs of Staff
DBK	Donna (née Bechtold) Kurtz
DS	Dimitri Shalikashvili
GS	Nina-Alexandra Shalikashvili (Gale Sever)
JMDS	John Malchase David Shalikashvili
JSA-NBR	Gen. John Shalikashvili Archives, National Bureau of Asian Research, Seattle Washington
JZS	Joan (née Zimpelman) Shalikashvili
MS	Missy Shalikashvili
NYT	*New York Times*
OCS	Officer Candidate School
OJS	Othar Joseph Shalikashvili
OPC	Operation Provide Comfort
SC-NDUL	Special Collections, National Defense University Library, Washington, D.C.
JSFA	John Shalikashvili Family Archives
WaPo	*Washington Post*

Note on Sources

201 File: JMDS's official 200+ page military record, including performance reviews and other evaluations from his thirty-nine-year career. JSA-NBR.

4SPC-V: Video of JMDS four-star promotion ceremony, 6/19/92, JSA-NBR.

CJCS-C: 15,000+ sets of JMDS correspondence, both as CJCS and from his nomination period while SACEUR, Special Collections, Archives, and History Section, National Defense University Library, Fort McNair, Washington, D.C.

CJCS-SS: *CJCS-SS, Testimony and Interviews by General John M. Shalikashvili, Chairman of the Joint Chiefs of Staff: October 1993–September 1997* (US Joint Chiefs of Staff, 1997).

DSM: Dimitri Shalikashvili memoirs, English-language version. Hoover Institution Archives, Stanford University, Stanford, California.

-*WWI*: "Beginning of World War One."
-*RHG*: "Regiment of the Horse Guards."
-*BDI*: "Bright Days of Our Independence."
-*GMA*: "Georgian Mission in Angora, 1920–21."
-*C*: "Constantinople."
-*P1*: "Poland, Part I."
-*P2*: "Poland, Part II."
-*P3*: "Poland, Part III."
-*WWII*: "World War Two: Polish Campaign of Sept. 1939."
-*WP*: "Warsaw, Poland (Sept. 1939 to Jan. 1943)."
-*GL1*: "World War II: The Georgian Legion, Part I."
-*GL2*: "Georgian Legion, Part II."
-*GL3*: "Georgian Legion, Part III."
-*G*: "The Year I spent in Germany After World War II."

DBK interviews: From 11/2011 to 10/2012 the author conducted almost one hundred phone and email interviews with DBK. Many stories were confirmed by DBK friend Merilee Hudson.

Letters to AZ: Seventeen letters by JMDS to Anita (Hollweck) Ziegler, mostly from 1951 at boarding school in Dinkelsbuhl to his first years in America. Courtesy Anita Ziegler.

Letters home: Over 150 missives JMDS wrote to his parents, 1950–1991, SFA.

JMDS-NB: 97 volumes of JMDS personal notebook, 7/18/86–9/30/97, JSA-NBR.

JMDS-OH: Frank Siltman and John Dabrowski, *An Oral History of Gen. John Shalikashvili* (Carlisle Barracks, Pa.: US Army Military History Institute, 2008).

NBR-SC-PV: Promotional video for launch of the National Bureau of Asian Research's John M. Shalikashvili Chair in National Security Studies, 4/5/2006.

OPC-AAR: Operation Provide Comfort After Action Report, US European Command Headquarters, 1/29/1992.

OPC Briefing: "U.S. Aid to Kurds as Model for U.S. Aid to the Soviet Union," Defense Policy Panel, US House of Representatives Armed Services Committee, 2110 Rayburn Office Building, 9/4/1991, https://www.c-span.org/video/?21027-1/operation-provide-comfort-aid-kurds.

Preface

"He's a quiet, decent man": "Shalikashvili: A Peorian in the Pentagon," *Peoria Journal Star* online Legacy Project, 6/27/1999. **"No ego need"**: John Lancaster, "Shalikashvili: A Military Man from the Start," *WaPo*, 9/21/1993.

Consistent positive reputation: "When we were equal, I always felt we were equal. When he was my superior, I never felt threatened by him," Caroll Dickson interview. Lieutenant General Tom Jaco, once a fellow major, recalled in author interview: "About every time I thought Shali was so high I couldn't pick up the phone and talk to him, he'd do something that, rather than bringing himself down to my level, instead pulled me up to his level."

Prologue

Village history, trades, and architectural landmarks: http://www.pappenheim. info and *DSM-G.*

Burg: "Geschichte de Burg" [History of the Castle], Pappenheim County website, http://grafschaft-pappenheim.de/burg/geschichte/.

Pappenheim ancestry: "House of Pappenheim," Online Royal Genealogical Reference Handbook, http://www.almanachdegotha.org/id91.html; and "House of Pappenheim," http://www.almanachdegotha.org/id91.html. **Imperial Marshal:** "Reichserbmarshall," https://de.wikipedia.org/wiki/ Reichserbmarschall. **Ulrich:** Philip Schaff, *History of the Christian Church* (New York: Charles Scribner and Sons, 1910), 145. **Carl:** Jeroen Duindam, "The Habsburg Court in Vienna: Kaiserhof or Reichshof?" in *The Holy Roman Empire, 1495–1806. A European Perspective,* ed. R. J. W. Evans and Peter H. Wilson (Leiden: Brill, 2012), 104.

Burg destroyed in war: "Pappenheim im Dreißigjährigen Krieg" [Pappenheim during the Thirty Years' War], http://www.pappenheim.de/en/tourism/living-history/town-history/the-30-years-war/. Blown up by ancestors: *DMS-G,* 5.

Altmühlbrücke: http://www.pappenheim.info/Altmuehlbruecke.2804.0.html.

Ending of war for Pappenheim: "Kriegsende in Pappenheim" [War in Pappenheim], http://www.pappenheim.info/Kriegsende.264+M54a708de802.0.h tml; and Hans Navratil and Tom Karl interviews.

Burn pit: OJS interview. **Tin soldiers:** Zurab Kobiashvili interview. **Painted backdrop:** Ursula Pappenheim interview.

Boredom and shattering glass: OJS interview.

Volkssturm: H. W. Koch, *The Hitler Youth: Origins and Development 1922–1945* (New York: Cooper Square Press, 1975), 247–48.

Bridge deconstruction: JMDS and OJS interviews.

"These were my first Americans": JMDS-NB, 9/30/1997.

1. Only in America

Nomination ceremony: C-Span video, http://www.c-spanvideo.org/ program/48461-1.

Size of military: "Active Duty Military Personnel, 1940–2011," Infoplease Database, http://www.infoplease.com/ipa/A0004598.html.

Name pronunciation: "'Shally' as in Alley: Clinton Selection of Shalikashvili Tangles Tongues," *Baltimore Sun,* 8/14/1993; and "General's Name Proves to Be a Real Tongue Twister," *San Antonio Express News,* 9/13/1993.

Height: He'd shrunk an inch since 1958. JMDS naturalization certificate, JSA-NBR.

"Physically unimposing": James Pinkerton, "Yuppie Military: No More Powells, Shalikashvilis?" *Long Island Newsday,* 9/19/1993. "Like a businessman": "General John Shali," *Times of London,* 7/26/2011. "Doesn't ooze
charisma": Peter Grier, "Joint Chiefs Nominee: Low Key, High Experience,"
Christian Science Monitor, 9/13/1993.

JMDS as top choice: Brian Duffy, "The Rules of the Game," *U.S. News and
World Report,* 8/15/1993; Fred Barnes, "Aspin 'Filmed' Strategy in Guiding Clinton to General," *New Republic,* reprinted in *Salt Lake Tribune,*
9/1/1993; Michael Gordon, "NATO Commander Is Picked to Lead the Joint
Chiefs," *NYT,* 8/12/1993; and Art Pine and John Broder, "Polish-Born General Picked to Head Joint Chiefs," *Los Angeles Times,* 8/12/1993; and William Perry interview.

"Dark horse candidate": David Evans and Terry Atlas, "New Military Chief
Picked: 'Gen. Shali' to Replace Colin Powell," *Chicago Tribune,* 8/12/1993;
and Tim Weiner, "Man in the News: Four-Star Military Mind," *NYT,*
8/12/1993.

"GI's general": *The Chairmanship of the Joint Chiefs of Staff* (Washington, D.C.:
Joint History Office, Office of the CJCS, 1995), 44.

NATO strength: "Globo-Cops: Deciding How and When to Use the U.S. Military
Is the Challenge for America's New Top Soldier, John Shalikashvili," *Newsweek,* 8/23/1993, 16. Most critical command: Barton Gellman, "Army General to Lead Joint Chiefs; Polish-Born Shalikashvili to Succeed Powell as Top
Military Officer," *WaPo,* 8/12/1993.

SS *America* trip: JMDS and GS interviews.

Three milestones: John O'Connell, "A Conversation with General John Shalikashvili," *Peoria Journal Star,* 6/27/1999. "First piece of mail": Helen
Buckley interview.

Defense spending: For 1992–93 fiscal year, *The Military Balance 1993–94* (London: International Institute for Strategic Studies, 1994).

Malchase: The Georgian version, Malkhas, was Anglicized to Malchase when he
became a US citizen. See 3/25/1994 letter to Rene Noorbergen, *CJCS-C.* Storied ancestry: see chapters 4, 6, and 9.

"Straightforward," "low-key," "self-effacing," and "informal": Lancaster, "Sha-
likashvili: A Military Man from the Start." "Understands teamwork,"
"adjusts to realities," "firmness," and "compassion": Melissa Healy, "Quiet
Ascent: Joint Chiefs Chairman-Designate 'Shali' is Soft-Spoken but Steely,"
Los Angeles Times, 8/12/1993. "Extraordinarily sensitive": Sean Naylor,
"'Shali' Born in Poland, Fled to Germany, Came to U.S. at 16," *Air Force
Times,* 8/23/1993, 6. "Bone deep": "Joint Chiefs Nominee John Shalikashvili Profiled," NPR's *All Things Considered,* 9/21/1993. "Seldom raised,
always heard": "Colin Powell's Replacement Knows Human Side of Com-
bat," *Seattle Times,* 8/12/1993. "Enormously loved and respected": Pine and
Broder, "Polish-Born General Picked."

Clinton-Powell tensions: Eric Schmitt, "The Top Soldier Is Torn Between 2 Loyalties," *NYT*, 2/6/1993, and "Joint Chiefs' Head Is Said to Request Early Retirement," *NYT*, 2/10/1993.

2. How Many Shalikashvilis Can There Be in the World?!

All references in this book to DBK, including her discussions with JMDS, are from DBK interviews. DBK and JMDS's romantic relationship was confirmed by classmate Jim Suffield, JMDS's closest high school friend, DBK classmate and friend Valerie Markman Schwartz, and classmate Joyce Murphy.

3. Will It Play in Peoria?

"Will it play in Peoria?": Amy Groh, "The Phrase that Put Peoria on the Map," *Peoriamagazines*, 6/2009, www.peoriamagazines.com/ibi/2009/jun/phrase-put-peoria-map.

PHS: "A Look Back at Peoria High's History," http://www.psd150.org/Page/1298. **Graduation:** Speeches by John Voelpel and Anita Tosetti. See Art Andrews, "Peoria High Commencement: Honor Students Stress 4 Freedoms' Importance," *Peoria Star*, 6/3/1952.

Accent: JMDS's ratcheting up his Germanic accent to impress women was noted in Lou Deardorff interview.

Maturity: Another classmate judged him "mature beyond his years." Bill Rapp interview.

Clothes smuggling: In author interviews, OJS and GS affirmed Donna's identification of key pieces of Missy's clothes and jewelry; and DBK said of the shoes belonging to Gale: "They were four inches too small for me!"

4. Missy and Wartime Warsaw

Fleeing Warsaw to Poznań: *DSM-GL2*, 10; and OJS interview, which contain occasional discrepancies. For example, DS lists the final camp as being in Lodz, not Poznań; DS identifies freight cars, while OJS says cattle cars.

Alexandre Bielaieff: See chapter 6.

Mikhael Bielaieff: Virginia Rounding, *Alix and Nicky: The Passion of the Last Tsar and Tsarina* (London: St. Martin's Press 2012), 267.

Most bombed city: O'Connell, "A Conversation."

Births of children: *DSM-P3*, 8–9; and *DSM-WP*, 6–7. Ivan is Russian for John.

Contract officers and Polish citizenship: Leszek Molendowski, "*Marriage of Convenience: Georgians on the Side of Hitler,*" 5/12/2009, unpublished essay translated from Polish by Arthur Eldar, including a section on "Georgian Officers in the Polish Army 1921–1939."

Stateless: In 1958, DS and MS became US citizens "after being stateless for 37 years." Helen Colvin, "Retiree Dimitri Finds U.S. Land of Opportunity," *CILCO News*, 2/3/1961.

MS in Skolimow: *DSM-WWII*, 1; *DSM-WP*, 2–5; and OJS interview. **First-aid courses:** *DSM-P1*, 17.

Julie letter: *DSM-WWII*, 24.

MS to Warsaw and DS rescue: *DSM-WWII*, 24, 26–29; and *DSM-WP*, 1, 5. Hasso von Manteuffel: "Globo-Cops," 16.

Death of MS's father: *DSM-WP*, 1.

German-occupied Warsaw: *DSM-WP*, 6–18.

Katyn argument: *DSM-WWII*, 18, 22. **Massacre in Katyn:** Czeslaw Zak, "Szkoda, ze Jest Oficerem Kontraktowym" [Pity That He Is a Contract Officer], *Polska Zbrojna* [*Armed Poland*], no. 187 (9/24–26/1993).

Georgian Colony job: *DSM-WP*, 7.

MS and Georgian POWs: *DSM-WP*, 12–17.

Care packages from DS: *DSM-GL1*, 11, 14.

Grenade blast: GS interview. **Robbery:** *DSM-GL2*, 2–4; and OJS interview.

Aborted flight from Warsaw: *DMS-P3*, 8. **"If we'd been caught":** OJS interview.

Spy accusation: *DMS-GL2*, 14–15. **"Our backs were against the wall":** Jim Suffield interview; *DMS-GL2* states that Missy was under threat of execution.

Polish partisans' arrival: OJS interview.

Forced underground: JMDS and OJS interviews; Lancaster, "Shalikashvili: A Military Man from the Start"; and "Shalikashvili: A Peorian in the Pentagon." **"Through the sewer lines" and "piece of bread":** "A Peorian in the Pentagon." **Pay for help and Geneva Convention:** OJS interview.

DS journal: *DSM-P1*, 39; and *DSM-GL2*, 17.

Godmother: GS interview.

5. Countess Julie Pappenheim

Julie in black: *DSM-G*, 3.

Postwar Pappenheim: *DSM-G*, 5–7, 9; and Ursula Pappenheim interview.

Pappenheim privileges: *DSM-G*, 2. **"That's how I know my Pappenheimer":** "Pappenheimer," http://vanderkrogt.net/statues/object.php?. **Count Joachim:** *DSM-WP*, 13.

Population increase: *DSM-G*, 1, 5; and Hans Navratil interview.

Pappenheim family deeds/reputation: *DSM-G*, 2–3.

Shalikashvili apartment: *DSM-G*, 6; and GS interview.

Pappenheims' view of Shalikashvilis: Ursula Pappenheim interview.

Shalikashvilis' introduction to Pappenheim: *DSM-GL2*, 11; *DSM-G*, 6–8; and OJS and GS interviews. **Lack of electricity:** GS interview.

MS's attitude about assimilation: GS interview. **OJS/GOS adjusting:** OJS and GS interviews.

"Sink or swim": "CJCS remarks delivered at the American Academy of Achievement, Las Vegas, Nevada 6/18/1994," in *CJCS-SS*. **Poor grades:** JMDS and JZS interview; undated postcard and undated letter home; and 10/11/1951 letter to AZ. Grades for final year in Germany recorded on his PHS transcript.

Feistiness in class: Many stories mentioned in Von Horst Wolf, "The Most Powerful General in the World—He Was My Classmate," *BILD*, 8/14/1993, translated from German in 2/16/1994 letter from Gerd Konarsky, *CJCS-C*.

Fascination with Wild West: 8/19/1992 letter to Mr. Marek Stanczuk and 5/18/1995 letter to John Adams, *CJCS-C*.

Shalikashvili spelling: The Georgian spelling is "Schalikachvili"; the Polish, "Szalikaszwili"; and the Russian, "Shalikov." The family changed from the German "Schalikaschwili" to the English spelling of "Shalikashvili" when naturalized. See 3/25/94 letter to Rene Noorbergen, *CJCS-C*.

"Creative, outgoing, and naughty": Kyra Cheremeteff interview.

Artistic talents: JMDS's childhood sketches, SFA. **Teacher note home:** GS interview.

"John was well-liked": "Joint Chiefs Nominee Profiled." **"I envied him":** Lancaster, "Shalikashvili: A Military Man from the Start." JMDS's ease in making friends and connecting with people confirmed in GS, OJS, and Ursula Pappenheim interviews. **"Easy flow":** GS interview. **"Chased me with an axe":** JMDS interview.

DS introducing vices: JMDS and JZS interviews.

Chocolate: GS interview. **Cigarettes:** Carol Smith, "New Orders: John Shalikashvili, Once the Nation's Top General, Works to Regain Command of His Life After a Stroke," *Seattle Post-Intelligencer*, 7/7/2005. **Syphoning gas:** Gerald Thompson interview. **Fisticuffs:** JMDS interview. **"Back in business":** Smith, "New Orders."

Convivial: Letters home, 1951–52. **Sister's caretaker:** GS interview. **"Hero was mother"** and **"good at connecting/relationships with girls":** OJS interview.

MS's absences from Pappenheim: *DSM-GL3*, 17, 19–20; and GS interviews. **DS letter:** *DSM-GL3*, 15.

DS's return to Pappenheim: *DSM-G*, 6–9.

DS's personality: JMDS, OJS, GS, and Ursula Pappenheim interviews; and *DSM*, passim. **Love of horses:** *DSM-WWII*, 20–21. **Appreciation for steeds:** *DSM-RHG*, 3. **Bedtime stories:** GS interview. **No household chores:** Jim Suffield interview.

Local economy and DS's employment: *DSM-G*, 5, 7.

MS and *Hofgarten*: *DSM-G*, 7; and GS interview. **MS hawking items:** Hans Navratil interview.

"Hard, calculating people": *DSM-G*, 6.

Consider alternative cities: *DSM-G*, 7.

6. Oma and the Passing of the Old World

Hospital visit: *DSM-G*, 11.

Rudiger sisters' deaths: Author's visit to gravesites.

Oma: In interviews, OJS and GS recalled that Oma was also committed to giving them a fulfilling life and never letting them feel like displaced persons. They also recalled visits by Tante Julie and Tante Sophie. **One cookie each:** Zurab Kobiashvili interview.

Landing in New World: "Ship Sightings in the Port of New York," World Ship Society, http://worldshipny.com/pony1952.shtml.

Lublin, birthplace, and nationality: *DSM-P3,* 8.

Johann Friedrich Rudiger: *Men of the Time: Biographical Sketches of Eminent Living Characters* (London: G. Barclay Press, 1856), 679–80; and OJS interview. Rudiger served Grand Duke Vladmir Alexandrovich and then, on his death, his youngest son, the Grand Duke Andrei Vladimirovich.

Krusenstern's Swedish roots: Family genealogy table provided by OJS.

Admiral Krusenstern: trip recounted in Ivan Fedorovich Kruzenshtern and Richard Belgrave Hoppner, *Voyage Round the World, in the Years 1803, 1804, 1805, & 1806: by order of His Imperial Majesty Alexander the First, on Board the Ships Nadeshda and Neva, Under the command of Captain A.J. von Krusenstern* (Printed by C. Roworth for J. Murray, 1813).

Baron Krusensztern, Dojlidy estate, and tsar's visit: Jolanta Szczygiel-Rogowska, "Historia Palacu Lubomirskich" [History of Lubomirskich Palace], *Kurier Poranny* [*Poranny Courier*], 7/14/2009.

Ladies-in-waiting: "Globo-Cops," 16; and GS and OJS interviews.

Alexandre Bielaieff: *DSM-P3,* 6; OJS interview; and http://www.geni.com/people/ Alexander-Alexeevich-Beliayev/6000000018502270138.

MS's early life: From birth to mid-1920s Poland, *DSM-P3,* 6–8. **Court life:** GS and JMDS interviews; and Claudia Dreifus, *Interview* (New York: Seven Stories Press, 1997), 160. **Godmother:** GS interview.

From arrest to Pappenheim: *DSM-P3,* 8–9.

Reclaiming Polish property: *DSM-P3,* 9; OJS interview; and Szczygiel-Rogowska, "Historia Palacu Lubomirskich."

SS *America:* "SS America," http://www.ssmaritime.com/SS-America.htm. Earlier that year a larger vessel, her sister ship the SS *United States,* was launched.

Matchabelli: *DSM-BDI,* 46; and Winifred niece Alice Tym interviews.

Dmitry Starosselsky: *DSM-WWI,* 7.

Winifred Luthy and Luthy family role in emigration: Winifred nephew Charles Luthy, Alice Tym, OJS, and GS interviews; "Memories of the Shalikashvilis Coming to Peoria, Illinois as Told by Mrs. Alice Luthy," 3/9/1996 oral history recording by Barbara Evans of the Rotary Club of Peoria, SC-NDUL; Brown, "The General and the Grandmother"; 5/24/1994 letter from Alice Tym, *CJCS-C;* and *DSM-G,* 6, 10–11.

JMDS letters: Letters home, 1951–52.

Looking to emigrate: *DSM-G,* 6, 9–12; JMDS, OJS, and GS interviews.

Displaced Persons Program: 5/18/1994 letter from former Church World Service employee, Joseph B. Mow, *CJCS-C.*

Missy deferring to husband: GS and Jim Suffield interviews.

"I am German": OJS interview.

7. Betrayal

"Ramrod straight": Walter Winget in *PHS Lion's Alumni Newsletter*, winter 1994. **Military bearing:** Tad Szulc, "What We Need to Do," *Parade Magazine*, May 1, 1994. **"Absolutely gorgeous"**: Audrey Whitney interview. **"Very Germanic!"**: John O'Connell, "Above All Else a Real Gentleman," *Peoria Journal Star*, 6/27/1999.

Athleticism: In Germany, 9/21/1951 letter home; at PHS, JMDS high school transcript. **Soccer:** Peter Knost interview. **Runner:** "I ran track both in high school and at Bradley. I was a miler," JMDS-OH, 5. **State-ranked:** Gerald Thompson interview.

Bashful smile: 7/19/1994 letter from Barbara Anderson Guthrie, *CJCS-C*. **"Eager to learn/steady"**: Ray Voigt interview. **Personality:** Multiple author interviews; and 10/13/1993 letter from Anita Johnson, *CJCS-C*, particularly "very bright, very kind, very unassuming, and calm and measured in any situation." **"Honorable"**: Ron Streibich interview. **"Straight shooter/trustworthy"**: Bill Rapp interview.

"First foreigner": Classmate Joyce Oberlander, in John O'Connell, "Above All Else"; and John Hoehne and Gary Rice interviews. **"A deserving guy"**: Richard Verkler interview.

JMDS critique: Of PHS teaching, DEK interview; of language instruction, Peter Knost interview.

Classmates' kindness: Szulc, "What We Need to Do."

Initial English ability: JMDS in O'Connell, "A Conversation."

Class ranking: PHS transcript. **"'A-plus' for initiative"**: Lancaster, "Shalikashvili: A Military Man from the Start."

JMDS recollections of PHS: John O'Connell, "A Conversation."

"Clicked their heels": "Peorian in the Pentagon." **Swagger stick and gloves:** Alice Tym interview.

More than meets the eye: In author interviews, Peter Knost recalled how JMDS easily fit in with others, that "he'd watch and wait before making his move, before opening his mouth when in a group that includes people he didn't know." Ray Voigt noted he wasn't particular close to the partiers. Bill Rapp judged him as having "maturity beyond his years," noting he wasn't part of the "elite" or "high-society" clique.

8. To Become an Officer?

Sneaking out: William J. Clinton, "Remarks by the President and General John Shalikashvili in Farewell Ceremony," Office of the Press Secretary, White House, 9/30/1997.

Robinson Barracks: Talbott Barnard, "OCS Today: US Army Artillery and Missile OCS," *Artillery Trends* (2/1960), 62.

Officers/enlisted men ratio: Figure 4.4—Enlisted-to-Officer Ratio, 1801–1994, in Shelia Nataraj Kirby and Harry J. Thie, *Enlisted Personnel Management: A Historical Perspective* (Santa Monica, Calif.: National Defense Research Institute, RAND, 1996), 33.

SOP: "The Challenge," US Army Artillery and Missile OCS, Fort Sill, Oklahoma (1957), 18.

First day: JMDS, James McGary, and Bobby Coggsdale interviews. **Long, punishing run:** Larry Frye, "What OCS Means to Me," in "The OCS Experience: Memories of Robinson Barracks—Artillery OCS, Fort Sill, Oklahoma, 1941–1973," compiled by Randy and Penny Dunham for the OCS Alumni Chapter, 3/26/2013, 152.

"Outstanding!": Larry Frye interview. **"Took up whole uniform!":** Mark Garcia interview. **"Lieutenant Alphabet":** Undated correspondence from Marty Blackmore, CJCS-C.

"I'll call you Shali": Larry Frye interview. **OCS nametag:** Bob Errico interview.

"He fudges rarely": Claudia Dreifus, "Who's the Enemy Now?" *NYT Magazine,* 5/21/1995, https://www.nytimes.com/1995/05/21/magazine/who-s-the-enemy-now.html.

Bradley scholarships: JMDS and OJS interviews; and Andrews, "Peoria High Commencement."

Model airplanes: PHS Class of 1954 yearbook; Dorothy Gregoire interview. **Aptitude test:** Jennifer Chambers, "Time in Peoria Provided Foundation for NATO Commander," *Peoria Journal Star,* 8/23/1992. **Aerospace engineer:** 5/12/1953 letter to AZ. **Not ruling out a military career:** DBK interview.

"Without change": OJS interview. **O'tar Shalikashvili:** *DSM-P3,* 8; and Jacques Ferrand, *Familles Princières de Géorgie: essai de reconstitution généalogique (1880–1983) de 21 familles reconnues princières par l'Empire de Russie* (Montreuil, Paris, France, 1983). **Jean "The Brave":** *DSM-BDI,* 26–27. **Golden saber:** OJS interview.

OJS's early military career: OJS and GS interviews. **OJS's setback:** Y. King Liu interview.

AFROTC: Official AFROTC website, https://www.afrotc.com/about/history. **Bradley's program:** "Air Force Reserve Officers Training Corps," *Bradley University Bulletin,* 5/1950, 58–59; and "Bradley AFROTC Draws Praise," *Hilltopics* (BU Alumni Publication), 3/1958.

Clicking heels/marching: Lou Deardorff interview. **"Like a Prussian drill sergeant!":** Gary Bragg interview and quoted in Sally McKee, "Commander of relief effort is ex-Peorian," *Peoria Journal Star,* 4/30/1991. **Kickstep:** Jon Nelson interview. **Pledge marshal:** Roger Roszell interview.

"Enrolled in Air Force ROTC": Dreifus, *Interview,* 161. **"If I can't fly":** Peoria TV news report aired on 5/12–13/1994, with reporter Fraser Engerman, videotape, JSA-NBR; and "Memorandum for the Chairman: WEEK-TV Peoria's NBC Affiliate Interview," 5/4/1994, CJCS-C. **Dropped out:** JMDS 2/22/1995 interview on CNN's *Larry King Live.*

Advanced ROTC requirements: "Enrollees must be physically qualified citizens of the United States between the ages of 14 and 27 and must be regularly enrolled students in the University," noted in "Air Force ROTC." OJS recalls JMDS explaining that the citizenship requirement barred him from continuing.

Sabres: "AFROTC Form Sabre Air Command Squad," *Bradley Scout*, 3/21/1957. President of: *Bradley University Class of '54 Yearbook*; and Horace Russell interview.

Citizenship: Because he'd immigrated earlier, OJS had already been naturalized. Greatest honor: "'Veterans of Foreign Wars,' Washington, D.C., 2/28/1994," *CJCS-SS*. "All in the same boat": "Constitution Day-Citizenship Day Speech," 9/17/1996, *CJCS-SS*.

Peacetime draft: "Background of Selective Service," https://www.sss.gov/About/History-And-Records/Background-Of-Selective-Service; David Wilma, "First Peacetime Draft in U.S. History," 10/16/2003, http://www.historylink.org/File/5572; "Statement by the President upon Signing the *Reserve Forces Act of 1955*," August 9, 1955, Eisenhower, *Public Papers, 1955*, 775–76; and "A Presidential Classroom for Young Americans, 1995," *CJCS-SS*.

Selective Service Registration: JMDS Selective Service System Registration Card, JSA-NBR. Worry about draft: 6/30/1955 letter to AZ. ROTC exemption: Selective Service Act of 1948, noted in "Air Force ROTC."

Reserve Forces Act of 1955: Public Law 305, 84th Congress (69 Stat. 598). Hershey: House Committee on Appropriations Hearing, 1958.

"Who'd draft an immigrant college graduate?": Mike Molino interview; and *Larry King Live*. Difficult to find employment: Lou Deardorff interview.

Hyster: Teresa Brown, "The General and the Grandmother," *[Peoria] Observer*, 3/20/1996; and interview with Charles Luthy.

Draft notice: "Talk before the Lancers Boys Club, The Cross Country Elementary School," Baltimore, Maryland, 4/7/1995, *CJCS-SS*; and Dreifus, "Who's the Enemy Now?"

Induction day: "Acknowledgement of Service Obligation," "Record of Induction," and "Report of Medical Examination," 7/30/1958, 201 File; and Smith, "New Orders." "I must admit" and "very proud to serve": "CJCS Remarks to American Academy of Achievement." "Felt an obligation": "Talk before the Lancers Club."

OCS application: Paraphrased from JMDS-OH, 7, and JMDS and JZS interviews. Date: "Application for Appointment: OCS," 8/28/1958, 201 File. Process: Bob Errico, Bobby Coggsdale, and Dan Furman interviews.

Basic training performance: *2nd Battalion-3rd Regiment Classbook* (Fort Leonard Wood: US Army Training Center Engineer, Oct. 1958).

Letters from OCS: 11/4/1958, 11/27/1958, and undated letters home.

"I would not want to be his superior": 5/1953 letter to AZ. Family favorite for general: GS interview.

Suppressing claustrophobia: OJS interview.
Not compete against brother: Richard Potter and JMDS interviews.

9. Dimitri, Prisoner of War

Except where noted, this chapter is based on DSM. *Official documents from DS service to Polish and German militaries provided by OJS.*

Beach swim: *DSM-GL3,* 23.
Final rank: He formally retired as a lieutenant colonel, a promotion he did not take seriously. See chapter 19.
Start of DS military career: *DSM-RHG,* 1.
DS appearance: From dated photos, SFA.
Rank at retirement: *DSM-GL3* 7. Promoted on 4/25/1945: DS's German military passbook.
"Who loved his native land": *DSM-BDI,* 23.
Early life in Georgia: *DSM-WWI,* 1; and DS, "Vospominaniaa," 1956, quoted in Bruce Grant, *The Captive and the Gift: Cultural Histories of Sovereignty in Russia and the Caucuses* (Ithaca, N.Y.: Cornell Univ. Press, 2009), 135–37. "More of a habit": *DSM-BDI,* 3.
Lyceum: *DSM-WWI,* 3–5. "Acknowledged as gentlemen": *DSM-GL1,* 7.
Princely Shalikashvili line: "Schalikachvili (Schalikoff)," 137–40, in Ferrand, *Familles Princières de Géorgie,* 109–10; and undated letter and Shalikashvili family tree outline from JMDS distant relative Mrs. Elizaveta Abramian to Margarita Choquette, Reference Consultant at the Family History Library, Church of Jesus Christ of Latter-Day Saints, forwarded to JMDS on 3/14/1994 via correspondence transmitted by Senator Orrin G. Hatch, CJCS-C.
Shalikashvili crest: SFA and OJS. The two versions sport a different fourth symbol.
Without change: OJS interview.
Siblings in WWI: *DSM-WWI,* 5–9. Starosselsky to Cossack Brigade: Cecil John Edmonds, *East and West of Zagros: Travel, War, and Politics in Persia and Iraq 1913–1921* (Leiden: Koninklijke Brill NV, 2010), 362. Tamara's Cross of Saint George: Ferrand, *Familles Princières de Géorgie,* 139.
DS in WWI: *DSM-RHG.* "Cherished tradition": *DSM-RHG,* 3. Campaign vs. Turks: Dimitri Shalikashvili conscription card, 11th Lancer Regiment, Polish Cavalry. Mission to St. Petersburg: *DSM-RHG,* 4, 6–7. "Loved and respected": *DSM-RHG,* 3.
Independent Georgia: *DSM-BDI.* Pass exams to 3rd Cavalry: 6–7. "The more work I was given": 9. Liaison Office: 28–33. Chosen for Angora: 34–35. Passport spelling: 36.
David's career: *DSM-P1,* 14; *DSM-P3,* 1–4; and "Some Blue Bloods in the Legion," Strategy Page (Issue CIC 222), http://www.strategypage.com/cic/docs/cic222b.asp.
Georgian Colonies: *DSM-P1,* 1–2.

DS in Constantinople: *DSM-C*, 41–43.

Angora mission journal: *DSM-P1*, 39. The journal is the basis of *DSM-GMA*.

Contract officer rights and responsibilities: 6/1996 letter from Jan W. Kancz, *CJCS-C*. Kancz's father, the late Brigadier General Jan Kancz, commanded the Polish 1st Light Horse Regiment, 1928–1931.

DS to Poland: *DSM-C*, 40–43; and *DSM-P1*, 3. Happiest time in life: *DSM-P1*, 2.

DS as foreign contract officer: Czeslaw Zak, "Szkoda, ze Jest Oficerem Kontraktowym" [Pity That He Is a Contract Officer], *Polska Zbrojna* [*Armed Poland*], no. 187 (9/24–26/1993)

Central Cavalry School: *DSM-P1*, 10–14. Accolades: DS Qualifications Report [Wyciag Kwalifikacyjny], Class of 1923/24, Central Cavalry School, Poland; and *DSM-P1*, 13.

War College: *DSM-P2*, 1–9. "Did not stop studying": *DSM-P2*, 2. Accolades: *DSM-P2*, 8–9; and DS War College [Ecole Superieure de Guerre] certificate, Class of 1926–28.

Enter Polish army: Zak, "Szkoda, ze jest." Unhappy with return to regiment: *DSM-P2*, 8. "Not proceeding the right way" and DS on adversity: *DSM-P2*, 9.

1st Regiment and "an honor in itself": *DSM-P2*, 9.

DS progress reports: Courtesy of OJS. Zak, "Szoda, ze jest," contains select quotes from these documents.

"English Gentleman": DS Annual Progress Report [Roczne: Listy Kwalifikacyjne], 1935. Interactions with others: DS Annual Supplement Progress Report [Roczne Uzupelnienie: Listy Kwalifikacyjne], 1930. "Stands high above": DS Annual Supplement Progress Report, 1932.

DS promotion to major: *DSM-P3*, 13. "His status as contract officer": DS Annual Progress Report, 1938.

Barred from regimental command: OJS interview.

DS and Missy courtship: *DSM-P3*, 4–5. "Life is full of surprises": *DSM-P3*, 5.

Georgian Legion: See chapter 19.

British POW: *DSM-GL3*, 8–24. Surrender to British: 8. "In a British POW camp": 15. Encountering Polish units: 11. Spartan: 17. Red Cross visits: 16. Georgian character: 22. British vs German treatment of POWs: 18.

Contact with Missy: *DSM-GL3*, 19–21. Heart problems: 19. Cat comic strip: GS interview.

Gold ring and bracelet: *DSM-GL3*, 21.

Aunt Ketouna: *DSM-GL3*, 24–27.

News of mother and sister: *DSM-P1*, 13–14; and *DSM-P3*, 4.

David's career: *DSM-WP*, 7; *DSM-P1*, 1, 14; and *DSM-P3*, 1–4.

Mother's death: *DSM-P3*, 4. David's death: *DSM-WP*, 7.

10. A Strategic Yes

BU size: Determined by comparing JMDS class rankings. Diverse enrollment: June Fejes, "Brother-Sister Team from Korea Are Two of Many Foreign Stu-

dents at BU," *Bradley Scout*, 10/25/1956; and Gary Bragg interview. OJS
was a member of the Nadi El Wah'da club.
Reaction to DBK disappearance: DBK.
"Won't be first to have a family": 9/1954 letter to AZ. **Brag:** 8/1954, 7/30/1955,
and 11/1955 letters to AZ. **"Escape from damn America":** 11/1955 letter to
AZ. **Anita engaged:** 6/5/1957 letter to AZ.
"Rebelling" with frat brothers: "Remarks by Gen. John M. Shalikashvili to Bradley University New York Area Alumni Chapter Winter Cocktail Buffet at Sar-
di's in New York City," 1/20/1994, *CJCS-SS*; and 1/27/1995 and 9/9/1993
correspondence from E. William McCarty, *CJCS-C*. **Highway Tap:** Bob Jas-
mon, 8/12/1993 Western Union Mailgram, *CJCS-C*. **Drank and played shuffleboard:** JMDS interview. **"Playboy of Peoria":** NBR-SC-PV. **"Rode his
coattails":** Y. King Liu interview. **"Not another one!":** GS interview.
Loss of scholarships: JMDS and Gerald Thompson interviews; JMDS-OH, 4; and
"John Shalikashvili Dinner Speech, 1997 Battle Standard Dinner, U.S. Merchant Marine Academy," 2/21/1997, *CJCS-SS*. **Theta Chi intervention:** Richard Sterling interview. **Class ranking:** JMDS Bradley University transcript.
Caterpillar failure: "2009–2010 Annual Report," the Elliot School of Interna-
tional Affairs, George Washington University, 37.
"Jail you for disobeying": Mike McMahon interview.
Being an engineer: JMDS also told a reporter, "The aptitude tests I took after
high school said I should be an engineer. My heart, regrettably, did not say
the same thing." Chambers, "Time in Peoria."
How Peoria shaped him: O'Connell, "A Conversation."
"Two people in one": 9/1954 letter to AZ.

11. The Crucible of OCS

*This chapter draws heavily from author interviews with JMDS, Roger
O'Dwyer, and forty-one others present during JMDS's OCS training (see the
acknowledgments).*

OCS history: "The Challenge," US Army Artillery and Missile OCS, Fort Sill,
Oklahoma (1957), 7–8.
Institutionalized hazing: Jim Stotler interview. **Indentured servitude:** Jim Slagle
interview. **"Heart-breaking, back-breaking":** Guy Wilhelm, "What OCS
Means to Me," in "The OCS Experience," 136.
Attrition rate: Barnard, "OCS Today." **"Machine gun fire":** Robert Lindsay
interview.
Class hierarchy and pressure: "The Challenge," 11; Barnard, "OCS Today," 62;
Wilhelm, "What OCS Means to Me," 146–47; and especially Robert Sandla,
John Marti, Dan Furman, and Jim Stotler interviews. **"Like an old Prus-
sian!":** George Krumbhaar interview.

"Dust storms," "harboring wildlife," and "dust on log": Coy Short, James McGary, and Jim Slagle interviews.

Smiley faces: George Krumbhaar and Wilbert Sorenson interviews.

Cavalcade of demerits: Wilhelm, "What OCS Means to Me," 141–42.

Jark March: "OCS Hall of Fame," *Field Artillery* (3–4/1999), 31; "Durham Hall," Brochure of the Field Artillery OCS Hall of Fame, Fort Sill, Oklahoma. Geronimo: "Geronimo," http://sill-www.army.mil/History/_bios/geronimo.htm. Witnessing march: Wilhelm, "What OCS Means to Me," 139–40. "Expert at those": 2/23/1959 letter home.

Sleep deprivation: Robert Lindsay interview and Wilhelm, "What OCS Means to Me," 140, respectively. "Half the class": Laurence Crawford interview. Sleep standing: JMDS interview.

Weight loss: Robert Lindsay and Larry Frye interviews, among others.

"Stand in shower": John Ruoff interview. "You miserable candidates": James Slagle interview.

Jark March breakdown: Bobby Coggsdale interview. PLF: Coy short interview. PLF required bending the knees, holding the feet together, tucking the chin down to the chest, and keeping neck muscles tensed.

"He was a very good soldier": 2/23/1959 letter home.

"Easy to get out of OCS": Wilhelm, "What OCS Means to Me," 144.

Big Brother: Albert Shook, John Ruoff, and Bobby Coggsdale interviews. JMDS as: Russell Davis, Roger O'Dwyer, Bob Errico, Robert Sandla, and Robert Jenks interviews.

"Wasn't a talker," "neat in appearance," and "going to do it right": Bob Errico, Bobby Coggsdale, Joseph Ward interviews.

Tarantula execution, heat stroke, and rattlesnake anecdotes: Roger O'Dwyer interview. JMDS's fuse debacle: Mike McMahon interview.

Contact lenses: Jim Stotler interview.

Top three: JMDS interview. His 6/15/1960 Regular Army Commission application lists him as "Distinguished Graduate of the USA Artillery and Missile OCS."

JMDS worries: Roger O'Dwyer interview. Reserve Officer status: Reserve status was nullified once the peacetime draft ended. Roger Donlon interview. "Discharged as regularly determined": Undated letter home, sent from AIT. Desire to use degree: Frank Angelo interview. Unsure of timing: 2/23/1959 letter home.

12. Savior of the Kurds?

Overflight: Untitled video, JSA-NBR; and Richard Potter interview.

Isikveren population: Gordon Rudd, *Humanitarian Intervention: Assisting the Iraqi Kurds in Operation Provide Comfort, 1991* (Washington, D.C.: Department of the Army, 2004), 67.

Number and groupings of refugees: OPC Briefing.

Timeline of rebellion and Iraqi response: OPC Briefing. **United States encourages uprising:** David Hoffman, "Witness to a Scene from Hell: What Baker Learned on a Ridge in Turkey," *WaPo*, 4/21/1991.

Halabja: "Thousands die in Halabja gas attack," *BBC*, 3/16/1988; John Pike, "Chemical Weapons Programs: History," Federation of American Scientists, 11/8/1998, https://fas.org/nuke/guide/iraq/cw/program.htm. **Follow-on health problems:** C. J. Chivers, "The Kurds: Still Suffering From '88 Gas Attack, a Village Distrusts Iraq's Report," *NYT*, 12/11/2001. **Post-gassing flight:** John Murray Brown, "Footsore and Weary Kurds Reach Makeshift Turkish Camp," *WaPo*, 4/6/1991.

Senate report on Anfal Campaign: Peter Galbraith and Christopher Van Hollen, *Chemical Weapons Use in Kurdistan: Iraq's Final Offensive*, Staff Report to the Committee on Foreign Relations of the US Senate (Washington, D.C.: GPO, 10/1988), noted in Michael Wine, "After the War: Years Later, No Clear Culprit in Gassing of Kurds," *NYT*, 4/28/1991. **Findings of Kurdish doctor:** Chivers, "The Kurds." **Human Rights Watch:** Kenneth Roth, "The Iraqis' Use of Poison Gas," *NYT*, 2/5/2003.

Post–Gulf War accusation: Caryle Murphy, "Iraqi Army Reported Advancing on Rebel-Held Northern Areas," *WaPo*, 3/31/1991.

April 3rd full flight: OPC Briefing. **3 million refugees:** John M. Goshko, "Rebel Urges West to Aid Iraqi Kurds," *WaPo*, 4/2/1991. **1–2 million:** U.S. News and World Report, *Triumph Without Victory: The History of the Persian Gulf War* (New York: Random House, Times Books, 1992), 403–4, noted in Rudd, *Humanitarian Intervention*, chapter 2, note 38.

Children dying on march: Jon Murray Brown, "International Relief Reaches Iraqi Refugees," *WaPo*, 4/8/2011.

UNHCR: Brown, "Footsore and Weary"; and Susan Carrol interview.

250,000 Kurds into Turkey: Brown, "Footsore and Weary." **General Gures:** "Dogan Gures: US-EU Want To Have Turkey Divided," *Milliyet*, 11/4/2007, BBC Monitoring same-day translation. **Halabja refugees in Turkey:** Brown, "Footsore and Weary."

Camp names: Rudd, *Humanitarian Intervention*, 66. **Estimating refugee number:** OPC Briefing; and Ken Getty interview.

Arrival in Alaska: Charles Glenn interview; 5/9/1994 letter from Henry Phillips, CJCS-C; and Henry Phillips interview. **Eielson/Ladd environment:** Helen Wheeler Buckley, Paul Buckley, and Charles Glenn interviews.

72-degree-below pin: Roger Donlon interview. **Jeep accident:** Charles Glenn interview.

500-mile ski patch: JMDS and Colby Thresher interviews. **Mount McKinley attempt:** Steve Livingston interview. **Ruddy cheeks:** Steve Hadley interview. **Veined hands:** Brian Holt interview. **Car accident:** Mike McMahon interview.

"Thirty of the biggest critics": Brain Haig interview.

Grice background: Rudy Grice interview.

Grice leadership lessons: "Remarks as Delivered by Gen. John M. Shalikashvili, USA, Chairman, Joint Chiefs of Staff," at the George C. Marshall ROTC Award Seminar, Virginia Military Institute, Lexington, Va., 4/12/1995, *CJCS-SS*; JMDS-OH, 13–16; Linda D. Kozaryn, "Joint Chiefs Chairman Cites Lessons Learned as New 'Louie' in U.S. Army," *Pentagram*, 5/12/1995; and "Remarks by Gen John Shalikashvili, Chairman of the Joint Chiefs of Staff," Rotary Club of Atlanta, Atlanta, Georgia, 4/17/1995, *CJCS-SS*.

JMDS leadership: William Howerton, Paul Buckley, John Haynes, Ted Hummel, and Mike McMahon interviews; and John Haynes, *Out of the Blue: The Legacy of John P. Haynes* (Phoenix, Ariz.: M&J Southwest, 2007), 78–79.

Chasing Regular Army Commission: Haynes, *Out of the Blue,* 9–10; and JMDS interview.

Wheeler: Colby Thresher, Roger Donlon, and Hellen Wheeler Buckley interviews.

"Didn't even catch a cold": 1/7/1959 letter home. **"Good with boundaries":** Rich Hill interview. **Glenn review:** 201 File.

Screwing up schedule: JMDS and JZS interviews.

"This lad shows promise": Helen Buckley interview.

Point Barrow expedition: JMDS interview; and Dreifus, "Who's the Enemy Now?" **"It became clear":** JMDS-OH, 9–10. **"It's impossible to describe":** 12/25/1960 letter home.

Wainwright designation: "Fort Wainwright History," https://www.wainwright.army.mil/history/FWA_history.pdf. Brucker's visit: JMDS-OH, 11; and JMDS and Helen Buckley interviews. **Ski parades:** Colby Thresher interview. **Twenty-gun salute:** JMDS-NB, 9/30/1997.

"Second parents": JMDS-OH, 14. **Best man:** Paul and Helen Buckley interviews.

Dating: 8/16/1993 letter from Stanley Calvert, *CJCS-C*; and JMDS, Charles Skillman, and Gail Vodopich interviews.

"Shy" and "reserved": Gail Vodopich interview. **"Slightly shy":** Paul and Helen Buckley interviews.

Howertons' dinner: William Howerton interview.

Off-hour activities: Undated letter home.

Phone call: DBK interviews.

13. Mushroom Cloud

"Mushroom cloud": Gene Ronsick interview.

UN condemnation and Bush proclamation: Ann Devroy and John E. Yang, "Bush Orders Airlift of Aid to Refugees," *WaPo*, 4/6/2011.

Operation order: Operation Provide Comfort Battle Staff Action, HQ USEUCOM Communications Center, 4/6/1991, 2043 zulu. **Flash gravitas:** Ken Getty interview.

Ten-day mission and "stop the dying": Jim Jamerson interview. **27 tons:** OPC Briefing.

Express Care: Ken Getty interview.

British and French planes: Ann Devroy, "U.S. Shifts on Refugee Enclaves," *WaPo*, 4/10/1991. **$180 million:** William Drozdiak, "U.S., Allies Want Refugee Havens Established in Iraq," *WaPo*, 4/9/1991.

Troop numbers: OPC-AAR, 1. **Coalition partners:** Rudd, *Humanitarian Intervention*, 226. **Civil organizations:** Rudd, *Humanitarian Intervention*, 60.

Second Bush announcement: "Excerpts from Bush's News Conference: Relief Camps for Kurds in Iraq," *NYT*, 4/17/1991.

JMDS made commander: JMDS and Crosbie Saint interviews; and JMDS-NB, 4/16–17/1991. **"I think I know":** Rudd, *Humanitarian Intervention*, 109. **Arrival at Incirlik:** Jim Jamerson interview.

Reflecting on being chosen: "Remarks to the National Security Industrial Association and the National Defense preparedness Association," 8/4/1994; and "Erskine Lecture Series, U.S. Marine Corps Foundation, Quantico, VA," 5/10/1994, *CJCS-SS*.

Movement of VII Corps: Peter S. Kindsvatter, "Jayhawk Goes to War: VII Corps in Operation DESERT STORM," 4/30/2016, https://armyhistory.org/jayhawk-goes-to-war-vii-corps-in-operation-desert-storm/; Stephen P. Gehring, "Deployment of VII Corps to Southwest Asia," interview with LTG John M. Shalikashvili, Deputy Commander in Chief, USAREUR, Oral History Interview, Military History Office, Office of the Secretary of the General Staff, Headquarters US Army Europe and Seventh Army, 9/14/1991; and Jack Galvin interview. **"Whatever fell off the table":** Crosbie Saint interview. **JMDS recollections:** Gehring, "Deployment of VII Corps." **"Military tour de force" and "Shali is looking good":** David Halberstam, *War in a Time of Peace: Bush, Clinton, and the Generals* (New York: Scribner, 2001), 321. **Galvin's praise:** Jack Galvin interview.

Field artillery complexity: Jon Shreyach interview. **Three field artillery positions:** 11/4/58 letter home.

Setting/communicating standards: Kori Schake and Dutch Shoffner interviews.

"Tricks of the trade": JMDS-OH, 14. **HAM performance:** 201 File. **"Top of the top":** William Grubbs interview.

"It went beyond zero tolerance": Dutch Shoffner interview. **Consequence of one screw up:** Stewart Wright interview.

32nd AADCOM performance: 201 File. **White gloves:** William Hoover interview.

"Russian prince": Carl Burgdorf interview. **"Necessary callouses":** Peter Poessinger interview. **Alaska war games:** Charles Skillman and Henry Phillips interviews. **Singing in German:** William Howerton interview.

Fort Bliss performance: 201 File. **"Just yesterday alone":** 9/16/1961 letter home.

NATO head praise: 201 File.

"Fluently? None": Helen Buckley interview; and *Larry King Live*. **"Because I hear them twice":** Mike Molino interview.

Galvin on JMDS: Jack Galvin interview.

Bavarian politics: David Fischer, "A 'Diplomat's Soldier,'" *San Francisco Chronicle*, 8/13/1993; and David Fischer interview.

Steel Box: Stephen Gehring, *From the Fulda Gap to Kuwait: U.S. Army Europe and the Gulf War* (Carlisle, Pa.: Center for Military History), chapter 2; Detlef Junker et al., *The United States and Germany in the Era of the Cold War, 1945–1990: A Handbook* (Cambridge, UK: Cambridge Univ. Press, 2004), 224; and Tom Molino and Steve Gulyas interviews.

"Shali stands out": J. B. Taylor interview.

Importance of Turkey and super governor: Eugene Ronsick, Ken Getty, and Jim Jamerson interviews.

14. Huddled Masses

Camp and refugee conditions: Rudd, *Humanitarian Intervention,* 69; Ronald Brown, *Humanitarian Operations in Northern Iraq, 1991* (Washington D.C.: US Marine Corps History and Museums Division Headquarters, 1995), 1, 6; Brown, "Footsore and Weary"; and Jack Galvin, Richard Potter, and Ken Getty interviews. **"The squalor":** OPC Briefing.

Population: The 2000 Decennial Census by the US Bureau of the Census defined urbanized areas as having a population over fifty thousand.

C-130 airdrop: Brown, *Humanitarian Operations,* 6. **Crushed to death:** John Yang, "Military Mobilized for Refugee Relief," *WaPo*, 4/13/1991. **Pallet weight:** Rudd, *Humanitarian Intervention,* 39. **"The weakest suffered":** Jim Jamerson interview.

Effects of poor sanitation: "Operation Provide Comfort: Lessons Learned," Department of Evaluations and Standardization, US Army JFK Special Warfare Center and School, Fort Bragg, North Carolina, 11/27/1991, 227.

"Extraordinarily severe weather": OPC Briefing. **"Medical apocalypse":** Brown, *Humanitarian Operations,* 1.

Two thousand per day: "Lessons Learned," 216. **One thousand per day:** "probably an accurate number," OPC Briefing. **Double or triple and "one of greatest challenges":** Yang, "Military Mobilized."

Organizing camps: Dick Potter and Ken Getty interviews; Brown, *Humanitarian Operations,* 69, 85–88. **Kurdish expertise:** "Lessons Learned," 42. **Hygiene programs:** "Lessons Learned," 53. **Diarrhea/nausea/vomiting:** "Lessons Learned," 111. **Four hundred per day:** Ken Getty interview. **"Best day since we got here":** John Galvin, *Fighting the Cold War: A Soldier's Memoir* (Lexington: Univ. Press of Kentucky, 2015), 439.

Airdrop problems: JMDS, Jim Jamerson, and Ken Getty interviews. **"Most inefficient way" and land across valley:** OPC Briefing. **Weather conditions:** Brown, *Humanitarian Operations,* 6. **One-third wasted:** "Lessons Learned," 48.

Entry point chaos: "Lessons Learned," 28. **Not on pallets:** Gene Ronsick interview. **Simply sent forward:** "Lessons Learned," 29, 44.

Kurdish food preferences: "Lessons Learned," 45, 58, 228; Ken Getty interview. Improving water supply: "Lessons Learned," 60–61.

Move from push to pull: OPC Briefing.

Typhoid: "Lessons Learned," 91. Measles: US Department of State daily briefing, 4/26/1991. Cholera: Dick Potter interview.

Security situation: JMDS, Dick Potter, and Ken Getty interviews. Direct quotes from OPC Briefing. Disgruntled Kurds: Brown, *Humanitarian Operations,* note 88.

$450 million: OPC Briefing.

Not logistics king: Jim Jamerson interview.

Child corpses: Ken Getty interview. Pregnant Kurds: Tom Clancy and Tony Zinni, *Battle Ready* (New York: Berkley Books, 2004), 58; and OPC-AAR, 14. Child mortality: R. Yip, "Acute Malnutrition and High Childhood Mortality Related to Diarrhea. Lessons from the 1991 Kurdish Refugee Crisis," *JAMA* 4, no. 270 (August 1993): 587–90. General suffering: John Galvin interview.

Babysit: Ed Ney interview. Play on floor: Marilyn Wender interview. "Walk the floor": Billy Brooks interview. "Great high school principal": Rich Hill interview. "Mother hen": Rex Weaver interview.

Loneliness of leadership: Frank Adams, Jim Jamerson, Ken Getty, Paul Bussey, and James Dubik interviews. B. G. Charm School: Ken Getty interview.

Schooling for possible civilian career: 9/16/1961 letter home.

Gunhild: OJS and GS interviews. Compassionate reassignment and deaths: 201 File. Premature: JZS interview.

BOQ curtains: P. J. Volk interview. TAPS speech: "Dinner Remarks to the Military Survivors/Tragedy Assistance Program for Survivors (TAPS)," 5/24/1997, CJCS-SS.

Performance reviews and decorate headquarters: 201 File.

"Professional *and* caring": Brian Haig interview. "Cut red tape": Larry Saunders interview.

Malloy: Comments posted to JMDS online obituary notice, "Shali: A Caring, Humane Leader," *News Tribune,* 8/7/2011.

Walk the rails: Stewart Wright interview.

Sitting on curb: Gay Van Brero interview.

Program for new arrivals: Roger Casinger interview.

Female MPs: Rex Weaver interview.

Deployment/support booklet: Gehring, "Deployment of VII Corps," 12.

Nuremberg community command: 201 File; and Allen Ohlstein and Ed Ney interviews. "Wholesome, safe": "A Presidential Classroom." "Best community commander": 201 File.

Heidelberg community command: Gerald Thompson, Ruth Collins, and Dave Mehar interviews.

COE competition: Multiple *Heidelberg Herald-Post* articles, including "Com-

munity of Excellence Campaign—Heidelberg Commits to the Effort,"
"Awards," "Army Community of Excellence Action Line Installed," and
"ACOE Action Line Calls Produce Changes," 11/16/1989; "Communication: Cornerstone of an Excellent Community," 1/10/1990; "Our Theme:
'No. 1 in 91,'" 2/14/1991; and "Heidelberg Wins $1 Million ACOE Competition as Best Large Oversea Community," 3/28/1991. **Sub-community mayor and Family Support Center:** Gehring, "Deployment of VII Corps," 12–13.
Deploying from Europe: Gehring, "Deployment of VII Corps," 12–13.
"Nickel more to go first class": Gerald Thompson interview.
Nuremberg award: Allen Ohlstein and JZS interviews. **Spending Heidelberg award money:** Gerald Thompson interview.
"If you don't love soldiers": Allen Ohlstein interview.
"Upper limit of professional soldier": 201 File.
"If you don't feel it in your heart": "George C. Marshall Remarks," *CJCS-SS*.
Joan Zimpelman: JZS, Richard Graham, Allen Ohlstein, Bob Jones, and Gerald Thompson interviews.
"Your husband really cares": JZS interview.
Image of Kurdish refugee children: Szalc, "What We Need to Do."

15. Warning the Iraqis

Unless sourced otherwise, references to John Abizaid, Frank Adams, David Armstrong, Bill Brooks, Susan Carroll, Roger Cirillo, Ruth Collins, Ken Getty, Steve Gulyas, Brian Haig, John Herrling, Brian Holt, Tom Jaco, Jim Jamerson, Jim Kessler, Stan Kwieciak, John Lee, Robert Linsay, Mike Kendall, Monty Meigs, Mike Molino, Allen Ohlstein, Richard Potter, Gene Ronsick, Crosbie Saint, Larry Saunders, Bruno Schact, Kori Schake, Jon Schreyach, J. B. Taylor, Jack Walker, and Stewart Wright are from author interviews.

Harbur area: Brown, *Humanitarian Operations*, 51.
"Nearest valleys" and summer heat: OPC Briefing.
Iraqi forces in area: Brown, *Humanitarian Operations*, 51–57; and JMDS-NB, 4/17/1991.
"Protect the president": JMDS-NB, 4/17/1991.
Baghdad on refugee centers: Blaine Harden, "U.S. Relief Chief Will Meet with Iraqi Officers," *Austin American Statesman*, 4/19/1991. **"We see efforts as complementary":** Blaine Harden, "U.S., Iraqi Officers to Meet on Aid," *WaPo*, 4/19/1991.
Meeting: Susan Warren, "Allies Seek Iraqi Assurance Troops Won't Be Assailed," *Houston Chronicle*, 4/19/1991; Jonathan Kaufman, "General Affirms US Role in Camps," *Boston Globe*, 4/20/1991; and "U.S. Tells Iraqis to Keep Distance," *Northwest Florida Daily News*, 4/20/2011. **JMDS statements:** JMDS-NB, 4/19/1991; and Rudd, *Humanitarian Intervention*, 114. **Tha-**

noon statements: JMDS-NB, 4/19/1991. Nineteen-mile rationale: Rudd, *Humanitarian Intervention,* 114.
"You work for me" and Galvin/McCarthy orders: JMDS-NB, 4/17/1991.
"I am glad you did that": Rudd, *Humanitarian Intervention,* 110–11.
Can't order volunteers/allies: JMDS-NB, 4/16/1991.
Air vice-marshal: JMDS-NB, 4/16/1991.
ROEs: Donald Goff, "Building Coalitions for Humanitarian Operations: Operation Provide Comfort," Individual Study Report (Carlisle Barracks, Pa.: US Army War College, 4/15/1992), 20.
NGO and PVO problems: "Lessons Learned," 2, 19, 73; Rudd, *Humanitarian Intervention,* 71; and Jim Jamerson and Ken Getty interviews. Conflicts over camps: "Lessons Learned," 66.
"Return as many as possible": OPC Briefing.
UN skepticism of task force: "Lessons Learned," 63.
Transportation/communication systems setup and pilfering/corruption: OPC Briefing.
Kurdish politics: Brown, *Humanitarian Operations,* 81. Cultural challenges: "Lessons Learned," 48 and 67; and Potter, Getty, and JMDS interviews.
Turks getting smarter: Ken Getty interview. Border control: "Lessons Learned," 41.
"Don't like confrontation": Smith, "New Orders." Good/bad cop: Bill Brooks interview.
Tick cards: Rachel McClain interview.
Boorda: Untitled American Forces Network news video marking JMDS's promotion to CJCS, JSA-NBR.
Saint on giving credit: 201 File.
Phone call: Mike Kendall and Jim Kessler interviews.
"How's about this?": John Herrling interview.
Holistic perspective: US Army War College professor Richard Meinhart praises JMDS's holistic skills in Smith, "New Orders."
DCINC/community commander responsibilities: 201 File; Crosbie Saint interview.
Naval War College studies: 201 File; and 2/24/70 letter home. Epiphany: JMDS-OH, 21.
Korea recollections/evaluation: JMDS-OH, 21–23; 201 File; and 10/18/71 letter home.
MILPERCEN and below-the-zone: 201 File.
Pentagon assignments: 201 File.
"Agile-minded and flexible": 201 File.
"If I have a strength": O'Connell, "A Conversation."
"His forte is knowledge": Lancaster, "Shalikashvili: A Military Man from the Start."
"I remember him as": 9/4/1993 correspondence from Perry M. Smith, *CJCS-C.*

"This is my fifth tour": "CJCS Remarks to Joint Staff Interns," 4/6/94, *CJCS-SS.*
"Shali had this air": Ron Parent interview.

16. A World Figure?

Unless sourced otherwise, references to Frank Adams, Caroll Dickson, Tom Jaco, Jack Galvin, William Harrison, John Herrling, Stan Kwieciak, John Lee, Montgomery Meigs, Dave Mehar, Tom Melino, Allen Ohlstein, Crosbie Saint, Larry Saunders, Brant Shalikashvili, OJS, Dutch Shoffner, Rick Sinnreich, J. B. Taylor, Gerald Thompson, and Gay Van Brero are from author interviews.

Execution: Jim Jamerson interview.
Saint and Galvin quotes and media/VIP interest: JMDS-NB, 4/17/1991; and
    OPC-AAR, 17.
"He looks downward": Healy, "Quiet Ascent."
"Beyond the next grade": *Larry King Live.*
Promotion percentages, captain–four star: Wesley Clark, *A Time to Lead: For
    Duty, Honor, and Country* (New York: Palgrave, 2007), 161–62.
Chose artillery branch: JMDS and JZS interviews. "No future": John Hamilton,
    Blazing Skies: Air Defense Artillery on Fort Bliss, Texas, 1940–2009 (Washington, D.C.: US Army, Department of Defense, 2009), 210.
War College odds: Ken Getty interview. "Might not go": Bill Brooks interview.
Home improvement: JMDS and Tom Jaco interviews; and various letters home.
    Hardware store: Dreifus, *Interview,* 168.
"One of most outstanding": 201 File.
SETAF responsibilities: 201 File. Most challenging boss: JMDS interview; JMDS-
    OH, 15. "Potential unlimited": 201 File.
Andrachio: Ralph Hallenbeck interview. "Never make flag": Caroll Dickson and
    Don Sparks interviews. Wager: Terry Mericle interview. "Can't believe!": GS
    interview.
230 army generals: 10 U.S. Code § 526. "As far as you think": *Larry King Live.*
    "Much of it was luck": JMDS-CH, 44.
"I'm an artilleryman": Allen Ohlstein interview.
"This is it!": Joe Collins interview.
"Certainly military officers have ambition": NBR-SC-PV. "Somehow intimidating": 9/21/1993 letter from J. L. Derivery, *CJCS-C.*
Stacks of paperwork: Sharon Shelton, Roger Cirillo, and Brant Shalikashvili
    interviews. "Purposely overloaded": 201 File. "Wouldn't flinch": Crosbie
    Saint interview.
Experimental brigade: Stephan Bowman, Mike Kendall, and James Saunders,
    eds., *Motorized Experience of the 9th Infantry Division, Fort Lewis, Washington 1980–1989,* 9th Infantry Division.
Assistant division commander kerfuffle and "doesn't have the fire power": JMDS-
    OH, 50–51.

"Ego is something": NBR-SC-PV. "Tenacious, perseverant, etc.": 8/12/1993 letter from John Novier, *CJCS-C*.

"'We' not an 'I' person": Steve Gulyas interview.

Harrison on JMDS command: 201 File.

"Without operating chaotically": Larry Saunders interview.

Motorized review: Bowman et al., *Motorized Experience*.

NTC test: Mike Kendall interview. Palastra evaluation: 201 File.

Harrison on JMDS future: 201 File.

Sale of house: 4/4/1987 letter home. Last assignment: Healy, "Quiet Ascent."

Powell rating: 201 File.

"Terminal assignment": "Powell's Replacement Knows."

"Shut up and go": JMDS-OH, 51.

"Not afraid to tell me" and "no wilting wallflower": "Joint Chiefs Nominee Profiled."

JMDS on Saint: JMDS-OH, 47–48.

First candidate proffered: Crosbie Saint interview.

"Congratulation on selection to BG": JMDS-OH, 42.

Few two-star advancement opportunities: Daniel Christman interview. Mandated retirement: Stew Smith, "Military Commissioned Officer Promotions," 5/1/2017, https://thebalancecareers.com/military-commissioned-officer -promotions-4055887.

Schwarzkopf error: Laurie Mylroie, "Iraq's Real Coup," *WaPo*, 6/28/92.

"Bear of a problem": Susan Warren, "U.S. May Need Force to Gain Kurd Haven," *Houston Chronicle*, 4/20/1991.

Bridge repair: JMDS-NB, 4/20/1991.

17. Briefing Congress

Unless sourced otherwise, JMDS, Les Aspin, and Norman Sisiki quotes are from OPC Briefing.

"When I saw": NBR-SC-PV. "Work a miracle": 4SPC-V.

Manpower breakdown and logistics geography: OPC-AAR, 1; and "Lessons Learned," 216.

Relief supplies tonnage: OPC Briefing; and 39th Air Base Wing History Office, "Task Force Provide Comfort Transforms into ONW," http://www.incir-lik.af.mil/News/Article-Display/Article/302584/task-force-provide-comfort-transforms-into-onw/. Larger than Berlin Airlift: "Peorian in the Pentagon."

Tonnage visualization: Such tonnage would require 581 standard 40-foot dry shipping containers, each with a payload capacity of 58,600 pounds/29.3 tons. Assuming a 15-foot day cab, the total caravan length would equal 31,955 feet. The Pentagon, with five sides of 921 feet each, has a circumference of 4,605 feet.

Total refugee population and movement timeline: OPC Briefing.
Fifty-two reconnaissance missions: Brown, *Humanitarian Operations*, 77.
Size of security zone and Duhok: Brown, *Humanitarian Operations*, 81–85; and Jim Jamerson and Dick Potter interviews.
Retirement: Brian Holt interview.
"You were a refugee yourself": *Good Morning America*. Fruit salad: Brian Holt interview. "You could tell in their eyes": Dreifus, *Interview*, 165.
Vietnam experience: JMDS-OH, 16–20. Armor/artillery opportunities: Ken Getty interview. Trieu Phong: 6/29/1968 letter home. Being district advisor: Harvey Mooney interview. Team and daily life: USAMHI, 16–17; and 6/29/1968 and 9/10/1968 letters home. Leadership: Peter Luitwieler interview. Fire Australians: David Millie interview.
Patrol DMZ: USAMHI, 17. Nim: USAMHI, 16; and JMDS and Harvey Mooney interviews. Vietcong searches: 9/20/1968 letter home. "In the end, we succeeded": Dreifus, *Interview*, 167. Evaluations: 201 File.
Pacification efforts: O'Connell, "A Conversation." "Hate to say it": 8/11/68 letter home. Building wells, laying road, and dedicating hospital: 7/26/1968, 3/10/1969, and 4/9/1969 letters home. "People's well-being": 5/1/94 correspondence from Jim Smith, CJCS-C.
Unusual opportunity: Robert Linsay interview. Operation Fisher: "Operational Report: Lessons Learned 1 August–31 October 1968," Headquarters, 1st Brigade, 1st Cavalry Division, APO San Francisco 96490, 11/10/1968, 5; 11/11/1968 and 12/3/1968 letters home. "Civic action": 1/24/1969 letter home. "Get on their feet": 3/4/1969. Opening school and "doing what he likes to do": 3/4/1969 letter home.

18. Getting to Yes

Unless otherwise noted, JMDS's itinerary and quotes are from JMDS-NB, 8/8–11/1993.

"Home run": Duffy, "Rules of the Game." "God's green earth": David Martin, "Landing the Eagle," *Vanity Fair*, 11/1993.
Memo: Fred Barnes, "Shali, Shan't He?" *New Republic*, 9/13/1993.
SCOTUS candidates: Martin, "Landing the Eagle," 150.
Candidacy: U.S. Code Title 10 for 1994, Subtitle A, Part I, Chapter 5, Section 152, Subsection (b) paragraph (1) limits candidacy to these fifteen, but paragraph (2) allows others if president deems it to be in the national interest.
Aspin's preparations: Pine and Broder, "Polish-Born General Picked"; and Fred Barnes, "Aspin 'Filmed' Strategy."
Front-runner: See chapter 1. 1st meeting with Powell/Aspin: JMDS-NB, 8/8/1993.
USAREUR/SACEUR/CJCS promotions: JMDS-OH, 48–49. "You are the man": NBR-SCP-V. Galvin backing: Gellman, "Army General to Lead."

Fourth star: 4SPC-V. Four-star slots: 10 U.S. Code § 525. 148th: https://en.wikipedia.org/wiki/List_of_United_States_Army_four-star_generals.

"Once again, it's Shali": NBR-SC-PV.

"He's no Colin Powell": "Peorian in the Pentagon."

"Living organism" and "submarine the president": Schmitt, "Top Soldier." "Homosexuality is a problem" and "we stop asking": Russell Berman, "The Awkward Clinton-Era Debate Over 'Don't Ask, Don't Tell,'" *The Atlantic*, 10/10/2014, https://www.theatlantic.com/politics/archive/2014/10/the-awkward-clinton-era-debate-over-dont-ask-dont-tell/381374/.

Hieu's circular reasoning: Colin L. Powell with Joseph E. Persico, *My American Journey* (New York: Random House, 1995), 80–82, quoted in Karen DeYoung, *Soldier: The Life of Colin Powell* (New York: Knopf, 2006), 58. "We kept adding": Chuck Springston, "Colin Powell's Vietnam and the Making of an American Statesman," *Vietnam Magazine*, 4/10/2017, https://www.historynet.com/colin-powell-vietnam-making-american-statesmen.htm. Vietnam as influence: R. Jeffrey Smith, "Following Popular Powell May Be Difficult," *WaPo*, 8/12/1993. Powell doctrine: Kenneth Campbell, "Once Burned, Twice Cautious: Explaining the Weinberger-Powell Doctrine," *Armed Forces and Society* 24, no. 3 (spring 1998): 357–74.

"I head for the bunker" and scrubbed language: Michael Gordon, "Powell Delivers a Resounding No on Using Limited Force in Bosnia," *NYT*, 9/28/1992.

"Not deterring anybody": *NYT*, 9/28/1992.

"Time and again": DeYoung, *Soldier*, 235–36. "What's the point?": Michael Dobbs, "With Albright, Clinton Accepts New U.S. Role," *WaPo*, 12/8/1996.

NYT editorial: "A Chairman for Changing Times," *NYT*, 8/14/1993.

Powell/administration tension: Eric Schmitt, "Joint Chiefs' Head Is Said to Request Early Retirement," *NYT*, 2/10/1993. Op-ed: Colin Powell, "Why Generals Get Nervous," *NYT*, 10/8/1992.

Crowe advice: Martin, "Landing the Eagle," 152.

Nomination norms: Schmitt, "Top Soldier." Break with norms: Gordon, "NATO Commander Picked." Inter-Service Rivalries and Army Man Appeal: "Hail to the Chief," *The Economist*, 8/14/1993.

Improvisational artist: Roger Spiller, "Hope Is Not a Method," *American Heritage* 44, no. 8 (December 1993).

Need final force structure: JMDS-NB, 8/10/1993.

"When I left Vietnam": JMDS-OH, 17. "Didn't have trauma": *Larry King Live*. "Vietnam-plus" school: Lancaster, "Shalikashvili: A Military Man from the Start."

Sinai/Middle East: 5/19/83 Legion of Merit award, 201 File.

"Capacity for doing good": Szulc, "What We Need to Do."

JMDS frustration on Bosnia: Lancaster, "Shalikashvili: A Military Man from the Start." Balkans use of force: Gelman, WaPo.

"Unrealistic": Lancaster, "Shalikashvili: A Military Man from the Start."

"It wasn't easy": "Peorian in the Pentagon." Earn Christopher's respect: Barnes, "Aspin 'Filmed' Strategy." Rapid Reaction Corps: "NATO's new Allied Command Europe (ACE) Rapid Reaction Corps (AARC) is inaugurated at Bielefeld," October 2, 1992. NATO website http://www.nato.int/cps/en/natolive/news_23893.htm?selectedLocale=en. Not in member defense: Gordon, "NATO Commander Picked."

Clinton/JMDS meeting: JMDS-NB, 8/10/1993. First ever: JMDS-OH, 53. "I prefer to remain": "Talk before the Lancers Boys Club," Baltimore, Maryland, 4/7/1995, CJCS-SS.

Clinton's poor reputation: Stewart Powell, "Shalikashvili Is Answer to Clinton's Call for Humanitarian Warrior," Indianapolis Star, 8/12/1993.

"Bear pit": George Wilson, "Dear General, Remember that Your Credibility Counts in the 'Bear Pit,'" Air Force Times, 9/6/1993.

"Not a stereotypical soldier": Roger Cirillo interview.

"Room to maneuver": "A Man for the Hour," Christian Science Monitor, 8/13/1993.

"Powell the grown-up": DeYoung, Soldier, 236. "The hell with you": Michael Takiff, A Complicated Man: The Life of Bill Clinton as Told by Those Who Know Him (New Haven, Conn.: Yale Univ. Press, 2010), 182. "Regarded him with awe": DeYoung, Soldier, 236. Powell "grouchy": Kori Schake interview.

"Consummate staff man": "A Man for the Hour." "No Washington animal": Roy Alcala in William Matthews, "Clinton's JCS Nominee Began as Buck Private," Air Force Times, 8/23/1993. "Politically savvy": Jack Galvin in Gellman, "Army General to Lead."

Memo to president: Martin, "Landing the Eagle," 153.

White House reception: Barnes, "Shali, Shan't He?"; and JMDS-NB, 8/10/1993.

Clinton and American successes: "Why does Clinton Fall in Love?" U.S. News and World Report, 8/23/1993. Ginsburg: Duffy, "Rules of the Game." JMDS "compelling story": Pine and Broder, "Polish-born General Picked."

"Never get so jaded": Barnes, "Shali, Shan't He?"

Clinton/Hoar meeting: Martin, "Landing the Eagle," 214. Hoar downside: Eric Schmitt and Michael Gordon, "Military's Leaders Are Jockeying in Effort to Be Powell's Successor," NYT, 8/9/1993.

Powell dialogue with Aspin/JMDS: JMDS-NB, 8/11/1993.

Aspin/Berger/JMDS dialogue: JMDS-NB, 8/11/1993.

2nd Clinton meeting: JMDS-NB, 8/11/1993.

19. The Ghost of Dimitri

Initial controversy: "Documents Appear to Link JSC Nominee's Father to Nazi Forces," Defense Daily, 8/27/1993; and "Statement on General John Shalikashvili's Nomination as Chairman of the Joint Chiefs of Staff," Simon Wiesenthal Center, 8/27/1993.

Raised eyebrows: Jacob Weisberg, "Details, Details," *New Republic,* 10/11/1993, 54–56; Richard Cohen, "Gen. Shalikashvili's Father," *WaPo,* 8/31/1993.

Dimitri's memoirs: Melissa Healy, "Shalikashvili's Father Tied to Nazi Unit," *Los Angeles Times,* 8/28/1993; and OJS interview.

Department of Defense response and Kimba Wood: Stephen Engelberg, "General's Father Fought for Nazi Unit," *NYT,* 8/28/1993.

Hier's concerns: "Documents Appear to Link," 6; Engelberg, "General's Father"; Healy, "Shalikashvili's Father"; and 8/27/1993 AP wire story.

Securing US visa: *DSM-G,* 10; five different letters home, most undated. Ratlines: https://en.wikipedia.org/wiki/Ratlines_(World_War_II_aftermath). "Aunt Wyn": Van Henderson, "Ooltewah's Alice Tym Defends Gen. Shalikashvili's Family," *Chattanooga News-Free Press,* 9/15/1993. Dirksen: OJS interview. Stevenson: Roger Bernardi interview.

Refutations: Marek Jan Chodakiewicz, "General's Father Tied to Nazis? Nonsense," *NYT,* 9/13/1993. "We were from Georgia": OJS interview. Short Berlin stay: *DSM-GL2,* 11.

Firestorm: OJS and Hoover archivist Carol Leadenham interviews; various CJCS dated faxes, letters, and notes, JSA-NBR.

Post-independence German and British assistance: *DSM-BDI,* 10–11. Polish patriotism: *DSM-P1,* 22–23. Refuse German employment: *DSM-WP,* 6–7.

Early German-USSR fighting: *DSM-WP,* 7–8. Hitler and Eastern volunteers: Wladyslaw Anders and Antonio Munoz, "Russian Volunteers in the German Wehrmacht in WWII," https://www.feldgrau.com/WW2-German-Wehrmacht-Russian-Volunteers. Ostlegioneen: George Fischer, *Soviet Opposition to Stalin: A Case Study in World War II* (Boston, Mass.: Harvard Univ. Press, 1952), 48.

Eastern legions: These "legions" were actually training centers where national units, mostly battalions, were organized and trained. Georgian Legion: *DSM-GL1–DSM-GL3,* passim. Legion formation and why DS join: *DSM-WP,* 7–9, 12, 17–18. German supporters, including Schellenburg: *DSM-WP,* 9.

Enlistment: *DSM-GL1,* 3–4, 10. Badge number: *DSM-GL1,* 13. Dimitri's entering rank: Dimitri's Germany army passbook lists him as a private on 1/1943; second lieutenant on 2/1943; and first lieutenant on 6/1993. Strange emblems: *DSM-GL1,* 3.

First assignments: *DSM-GL1,* 5–14. Furloughs home: *DSM-GL1,* 9. Helping Polish Home Army: Chodakiewicz, "General's Father."

"Unforgivable mistakes": *DSM-WP,* 8.

Transfer to Paris: *DSM-GL1,* 17–18, 22–23.

Promotion and chosen for new mission: *DSM-GL2,* 14–15.

Georgian Liaison Office and "Saving Georgians": *DSM-GL2,* 15.

New Waffen-SS oversight: *DSM-GL2,* 12–13. Caucasian Cavalry Division: Chris Bishop, *SS: Hitler's Foreign Divisions—Foreign Volunteers in the Waffen SS, 1941–45* (Staplehurst, UK: Spellmount, 2005), 74.

DS praise for Waffen-SS: *DSM-GL2,* 13.

Georgian Cavalry Regiment: *DSM-GL2,* 13, 15, 16. "In that capacity": *DSM-GL3,* 2. Events in Northern Italy: *DSM-GL3,* 2–10. Promoted to colonel: *DSM-GL3,* 7. "We saved lives": *DSM-GL3,* 6.

Dunlop: Healy, "Shalikashvili's Father." Palm: Engelberg, "General's Father."

Dimitri's lack of SS affiliation: Multiple faxes to JMDS at Supreme Headquarters Allied Powers Europe (SHAPE): 8/26/1993 fax of *DSM-GL1–DSM-GL3,* passim, from Hoover Institution; 8/27/1993 fax of Givi Gabliani memoir sample, 58–91, from OJS; 8/30/1993 fax of Dimitri's paybook from OJS via SHAPE Liaison Office; 9/1/1993 letter from US Embassy Office Berlin's Berlin Document Center faxed on 9/6/1993; and 9/9/1993 letter from German Ministry of Defense faxed via EUCOM HQ, JSA-NBR documents.

Aspin statement: Anne McIlree, "A Patriot 'On His Own Merit,'" *USA Today,* 8/30/1993.

Waffen vs. Allgemeine-SS: 3/1/1995 correspondence from Clarence W. Schmitz, *CJCS-C.* "My father never thought": Dreifus, "Who's the Enemy Now?" "Wasn't a tuxedo": Thomas W. Lippman, "Pentagon Nominee's Father Served as Nazi SS Officer," *WaPo,* 8/28/1993.

Pentagon remarks: "Documents Appear to Link," 6. Aspin remarks: Engelberg, "General's Father." White House remarks: Healy, "Shalikashvili's Father."

Initial Committee response: Donna Cassata, "Shalikashvili Says He Didn't Know of Father's Nazi Service," AP, 9/22/1993.

Specter concern: Cassata, "Shalikashvili Says He Didn't Know."

Zoe Baird: "Addressing Nannygate," *NYT,* 3/30/1994.

Confirmation hearing: https://www.c-span.org/video/?50819-1/joint-chief-staff-confirmation.

20. Blondi and the Boy on the Bridge

Unless otherwise noted, this chapter derives from author interviews with DBK, JMDS, and OJS and from the Larry King Live interview.

Confirmed: "Senate Confirms Joint Chiefs Head," *Los Angeles Times,* 10/6/1993.

Initially media shy: Larry Icenogle interview.

Allergic to spotlight: "Peorian in the Pentagon."

Angry: Brant Shalikashvili interview; Eric Sorenson, "General's Son Breaks Ranks with Tradition," *Spokesman-Review,* 5/14/1995. "Clever": 8/30/1993 letter to Jean Thompson, *CJCS-C.* Private ceremony: 11/10/1993 letter to Herbert Budnick, *CJCS-C.*

Fatherhood and the draft: Selective Service System, "Effects of Marriage and Fatherhood on Draft Eligibility," https://www.sss.gov/About/History-And-Records/Effects

Duck analogy: Jim Kessler interview.

MS qualities: Many noted by DBK and OJS confirmed in author interview with Shalikashvili family friend Kyra Cheremeteff.
NPR interview: "Joint Chiefs Nominee Profiled."
Dimitri qualities: As per chapter 9; and Givi Gabliani unpublished memoir sample, 590–91.
JMDS as gentleman: 201 File.
"Where does that come from?": NBR-SC-PV.
Close-mouthed about family/Europe: Jon Nelson interview. **"Not to pry":** Lou Deardorff interview. **"Could not figure out":** Ron Streibich interview. **"People suspected":** Lou Deardorff interview. **DS Nazi rumor:** Steve Harrison email.
Spotting DS: Peter Knost and Lou Deardorff interviews.
Proud of father: Bill Rapp interview. **"Colonel in White Army":** Peter Knost interview. **"Gun to head":** Y. King Liu interview.
MS against DS joining Legion: OJS and GS interviews. **MS and Jews:** OJS interview.
MS to Salzburg: DSM-GL2, 16. **Stalin vs. Hitler:** OJS interview. **"Those were hard times" and "Missy was sad":** DSM-WP, 17–18. **MS knew on first meeting:** DSM-P3, 5.
MS defer to DS: OJS and GS interviews.
German exchange student: Undated letter from Peter Knost, seen by JMDS on 3/16/1994, CJCS-C.
Subtle heads-up: 7/19/1993 letter from Richard F. Staar, CJCS-C.
JMDS on memoirs: 6/10/1970, 3/4/1979, 3/11/1979, and 10/14/1979 letters home.
Prom photograph: O'Connell, "A Conversation." **"Not a shoot-from-the-hip kinda guy":** J. B. Taylor interview. **Inhibits thinking:** 3/6/1997 remarks to Senate Youth Group, CJCS-CS.

21. Retirement Day

Unless otherwise noted, this chapter is drawn from "Remarks by the President and General John Shalikashvili" and https://www.c-span.org/video/?92126-1/ general-shalikashvili-farewell. JMDS's thoughts and feelings are from JMDS-NB, 9/20/1997.

Attendees: JMDS, Cohen, and Clinton speeches.
Michel's remarks: O'Connell, "Above All Else."
No third term: Eric Schmitt, "New Leader of Military Will Need Right Answer," NYT, 6/30/97. **Oldest general:** "Remarks of Gen. John Malchase Shalikashvili at the Joint Armed Forces Officers' Wives Luncheon," 11/13/96, CJCS-SS.
Nuts and Bolts: Douglas Stanglin, "Shali's Tool Chest," U.S. News and World

Report, 10/13/1997. **Ten percent discount:** "Parting Words," Pentagon's *J-Scope* 2, no. 39 (9/30/1997).

"Europe was devastated": "CJCS Remarks to American Academy of Achievement."

JMDS on luck: Edgar Puryear, *American Generalship* (Random House: 2000), 231–32.

JMDS on his chairmanship: "Peorian in the Pentagon"; and Dreifus, *Interview,* 166.

"Shali's idea": Madeleine Albright, *Madam Secretary* (New York: Miramax Books, 2003), 212.

NPC speech: "National Press Club Luncheon," Washington, D.C., 9/24/1997, *CJCS-CS.* **"Taken the lid off":** Dreifus, *Interview,* 166.

"Don't just do big ones": Dreifus, "Who's the Enemy Now?"

Balkans success: Joe Collins, "A Strategist Remembered: Shalikashvili Was Both Soldier and Statesman," *Armed Forces Journal* (9/2011), http://armedforces-journal.com/essay-a-strategist-remembered/.

Rwanda failure: Wesley Clark, *A Time to Lead: For Duty, Honor, and Country* (New York: Palgrave, 2007), 270.

"Powder keg": "Peorian in the Pentagon." **About thirty for Powell:** Noted by Nunn at JMDS confirmation hearing.

Smaller military: "National Press Club Luncheon."

Enhance service chief collegiality: William J. Clinton and Joe Collins interviews. **Joint education/training/exercises/war plans:** "National Press Club Luncheon." **Joint Vision 2010:** http://webapp1.dlib.indiana.edu/virtual_disk_library/index.cgi/4240529/FID378/pdfdocs/2010/Jv2010.pdf.

"Military shouldn't control government": Kyra Cheremeteff interview.

Helms uproar: Steven Greenhouse, "Chairman of Joint Chiefs Defends Clinton Against Attack by Helms," *NYT,* 11/20/1994; and Steven Greenhouse, "Helms Takes New Swipe at Clinton, Then Calls It Mistake," *NYT,* 11/23/1994.

Haiti conversation: William J. Clinton interview.

Improve interagency cooperation: Collins, "A Strategist Remembered"; Lyle Goldstein, "General John Shalikashvili and the Civil-Military Relations of Peacekeeping," *Armed Forces and Society* 26, no. 3 (spring 2000): 404–5.

Perry on JMDS/Albright: Bill Perry remarks at John Shalikashvili memorial service, 8/6/2011, Tacoma Convention Center, Tacoma, Washington, https://www.dvidshub.net/video/122379/army-gen-ret-john-shalikashvili-vip-memorial-part-4.

Critique of JMDS-Clinton relationship: Mike Gallagher and Brian Haig interviews.

Daschle remarks: "Senate Proceedings: Tribute to Gen. John Shalikashvili," *Congressional Quarterly's Washington Alert,* 10/3/1997.

Blaire remarks: Undated transcript of speech presented before the Joint Staff in honor of JMDS retirement, JSA-NBR.

"We're a family": Interview with American Forces Press Service, 8/11/1997, CJCS-C.

CJCS oil paintings: 4/22/1996 letter to Mrs. Omar N. Bradley, CJCS-C.

22. The Final Inheritance

Hardware store: Toward retirement, JMDS and JZS actually considered it. 8/11/1997 interview with American Forces Press Service, CJCS-C.

CTBT: JMDS, "Findings and Recommendations Concerning the Comprehensive Nuclear Test Ban Treaty," January 2001 Report to the President and Secretary of State, https://fas.org/nuke/control/ctbt/text/shalictbt.htm#report. **Obesity:** JMDS and Hugh Shelton, "The Latest National Security Threat: Obesity," WaPo, 4/30/2010. **DADT Repeal:** JMDS, "Second Thoughts on Gays in the Military," NYT, 5/7/2010; and JMDS, "Congress Should Repeal 'Don't Ask, Don't Tell' and Let the Pentagon Do the Rest," WaPo, 5/22/2010.

Identity theft: Robert Heady, "Guarding Against Identify Theft," Network Journal, 9/30/2000, 50. **Stryker exercise:** Frank Adams interview.

Joint Vision fizzle: Collins, "A Strategist Remembered," 8–10.

"Nobody remembers": Gerald Thompson interview. **"That's where Powell used to be":** Sharon Shelton interview.

DNC speech: "Gen. John Shalikashvili's Remarks to the Democratic National Convention," NYT, 7/29/2004.

JMDS's strokes: Smith, "New Orders"; Michael Gilbert, "South Sound's Own General Doing Better after Stroke," News Tribune, 9/17/2004; "General John Shalikashvili," Report to the Community, Harborview Medical Center, 2004, 23–25; and JMDS, JZS, Brant Shalikashvili, Rachel McClain, and speech therapist Kathy Blanchet interviews. Unless noted otherwise, JMDS's direct quotes are from his 4/13/2005 essay "My Thoughts about My Stroke," written as part of his rehabilitative therapy, SFA. Contrary to Smith's "New Orders," JZS recalls one transient ischemic attack, not two, following the DNC.

Family history: "My Thoughts about My Stroke"; and GS and OJS interviews. **David's death:** DSM-WP, 7. **Gale's death:** Janet Shalikashvili interview. **Double the risk:** Gina Kolata, "Seeking Clues to Heart Disease in DNA of an Unlucky Family," NYT, 5/12/2013. **DS onset:** DSM-P3, 16; DSM-WWII, 28; and Roy Herron interview. **JMDS onset:** Steve Livingston interview.

Double doors: Bill Harrison interview. **Upped tempo and "a hospital":** Rich Hill interview.

DS deaf: Alice Tym interview.

JMDS control over emotions: Kathy Blanchet, Rich Hill, Ron Parent, Brant Shalikashvili, JZS, Mike Clarke, and Rachel McClain interviews.

"So little patience": Smith, "New Orders."

Regrets?: "My Thoughts about My Stroke."
Death: Shaila Dewan, "Gen. John M. Shalikashvili, Military Chief in 1990s, Dies at 75," *NYT,* 7/23/2011. Second stroke: JZS interview.

Epilogue

PX parking lot: Martin Anderson interview.
JMDS philosophy: 9/30/97 letter to Master Sergeant Armstead Dorsey, *CJCS-C.*
"Seeing people killed" and "You deal with it": Smith, "New Orders."
"No damn good" and JMDS response: JMDS-OH, 60.
"Didn't know us from beans": Smith, "New Orders." "They looked pitiful": Alice Tym interview. "We were kindly received": OJS interview.
Chairman's quarters renovations: Fort Myer Commanding Officer Scott Deibler and Gay Van Brero interviews.
"Tough town": *PBS Newshour with Phil Ponce,* 9/25/97.
Haitian crisis: Sharon Shelton interview.
"You disciplined yourself": Smith, "New Orders."
Gettysburg visit: Jason DeParle, "The Man Inside Bill Clinton's Foreign Policy," *NYT Magazine,* 8/20/1995, https://www.nytimes.com/1995/08/20/maga-zine/the-man-inside-bill-clinton-s-foreign-policy.html.
"Georgian": DBK and Madeleine Albright interviews.
Acorn top: Zurab Kobiashvili interview.
"Almost fainted": JMDS-OH, 21.
"Second greatest honor": "Veterans of Foreign Wars."
"Beacon of hope": "Gen. John Shalikashvili's Remarks."
Peoria: Dreifus, "Who's the Enemy Now?"; Dana Brown, "Ahali and 10 Oth-ers Honored by Bradley: Distinguished Alumnus Thanks University for Its Good Lessons," *Peoria Journal Star,* 10/2/1998.
"Belong to an outfit": JMDS's 6/6/2003 remarks celebrating U.S. naturalization of Brigitte Allen-Gort, NBR, Seattle, Washington. JSA-NBR.
"Don't want to sound corny": "Peorian in the Pentagon."
DS and JMDS patriotism: OJS interview. Laundry outburst: P. J. Volk interview.
JMDS Vietnam takeaways: JMDS-OH, 16–20.
"First-hand appreciation": "Veterans of Foreign Wars."
"Long talks": Lancaster, "Shalikashvili: A Military Man from the Start."
"All, and I mean all": Perry remarks, JMDS memorial service.
Specter: Cassata, "Shalikashvili Says He Didn't Know." Kick out neo-Nazi: Steve Livingston interview.
"Under immense pressure": OJS interview.
Priding himself for honesty: Roy Herron interview.
"Where else?": "Peorian in the Pentagon." "Isn't a place like it": JMDS Remarks at Allen-Gort ceremony.
Broken man: Alice Tym interview. DS auditor job: *DSM-BDI,* 14.
"I needed to tell them": Grover Ford interview.

Select Bibliography

In addition to the mostly primary source materials listed in the "Note on Sources" section of the endnotes, key sources regarding John Shalikashvili referenced in this biography include:

"A Chairman for Changing Times." *NYT*, 8/14/1993.

Albright, Madeleine. *Madam Secretary*. New York: Miramax Books, 2003.

"A Man for the Hour." *Christian Science Monitor*, 8/13/1993.

Barnes, Fred. "Aspin 'Filmed' Strategy in Guiding Clinton to General." *New Republic*, reprinted in *Salt Lake Tribune*, 9/1/1993.

———. "Shali, Shan't He?" *New Republic*, 9/13 1993.

Brown, Teresa. "The General and the Grandmother." *[Peoria] Observer*, 3/20/1996.

Cassata, Donna. "Shalikashvili Says He Didn't Know of Father's Nazi Service." *Associated Press*, 9/22/1993.

The Chairmanship of the Joint Chiefs of Staff. Washington, D.C.: Joint History Office, Office of the CJCS, 1995.

Chambers, Jennifer. "Time in Peoria Provided Foundation for NATO Commander." *Peoria Journal Star*, 8/23/1992.

Chodakiewicz, Marek Jan. "General's Father Tied to Nazis? Nonsense." *NYT*, 9/13/1993.

Clark, Wesley. *A Time to Lead: For Duty, Honor, and Country*. New York: Palgrave, 2007.

Cohen, Richard. "Gen. Shalikashvili's Father." *Washington Post*, 8/31/1993.

"Colin Powell's Replacement Knows Human Side of Combat." *Seattle Times*, 8/12/1993.

Collins, Joe. "A Strategist Remembered: Shalikashvili Was Both Soldier and Statesman." *Armed Forces Journal* (9/2011): 8–10.

Colvin, Helen. "Retiree Dimitri Finds U.S. Land of Opportunity." *CILCO News*, 2/3/1961.

DeParle, Jason. "The Man Inside Bill Clinton's Foreign Policy." *New York Times Magazine*, 8/20/1995.

Dewan, Shaila. "Gen. John M. Shalikashvili, Military Chief in 1990s, Dies at 75." *NYT*, 7/23/2011.

DeYoung, Karen. *Soldier: The Life of Colin Powell*. New York: Knopf, 2006.

"Documents Appear to Link JSC Nominee's Father to Nazi Forces." *Defense Daily*, 8/27/1993.

Dreifus, Claudia. *Interview*. New York: Seven Stories Press, 1997.

———. "Who's the Enemy Now?" *New York Times Magazine*, 5/21/1995.

Duffy, Brian. "The Rules of the Game." *U.S. News and World Report*, 8/15/1993.

Engelberg, Stephen. "General's Father Fought for Nazi Unit," *NYT*, 8/28/1993.

Evans, David, and Terry Atlas. "New Military Chief Picked: 'Gen. Shali' to Replace Colin Powell." *Chicago Tribune*, 8/12/1993.

Fischer, David. "A 'Diplomat's Soldier.'" *San Francisco Chronicle*, 8/13/1993.

Galvin, John. *Fighting the Cold War: A Soldier's Memoir*. Lexington: Univ. Press of Kentucky, 2015.

Gehring, Stephen P. "Deployment of VII Corps to Southwest Asia." Interview with LTG John M. Shalikashvili, Deputy Commander in Chief, USAREUR, Oral History Interview, Military History Office, Office of the Secretary of the General Staff, Headquarters US Army Europe and Seventh Army, 9/14/1991.

Gellman, Barton. "Army General to Lead Joint Chiefs; Polish-Born Shalikashvili to Succeed Powell as Top Military Officer." *Washington Post*, 8/12/1993.

"General John Shali," *Times of London*, 7/26/2011.

"General John Shalikashvili." *Report to the Community*, Harborview Medical Center, 2004, 23–25.

"Gen. John Shalikashvili's Remarks to the Democratic National Convention." *NYT*, 7/29/2004.

"General's Name Proves to Be a Real Tongue Twister." *San Antonio Express News*, 9/13/1993.

"Globo-Cops: Deciding How and When to Use the U.S. Military Is the Challenge for America's New Top Soldier, John Shalikashvili." *Newsweek*, 8/23/1993.

Goldstein, Lyle. "General John Shalikashvili and the Civil-Military Relations of Peacekeeping." *Armed Forces and Society* 26, no. 3 (spring 2000): 387–411.

Gordon, Michael. "NATO Commander Is Picked to Lead the Joint Chiefs." *NYT*, 8/12/1993.

Grant, Bruce. *The Captive and the Gift: Cultural Histories of Sovereignty in Russia and the Caucuses*. Ithaca, N.Y.: Cornell Univ. Press, 2009.

Greenhouse, Steven. "Chairman of Joint Chiefs Defends Clinton Against Attack by Helms" *NYT*, 11/20/1994.

———. "Helms Takes New Swipe at Clinton, Then Calls It Mistake." *NYT*, 11/23/1994.

Grier, Peter. "Joint Chiefs Nominee: Low Key, High Experience." *Christian Science Monitor*, 9/13/1993.

Halberstam, David. *War in a Time of Peace: Bush, Clinton, and the Generals*. New York: Scribner, 2001.

Hamilton, John. *Blazing Skies: Air Defense Artillery on Fort Bliss, Texas, 1940–2009*. Washington, D.C.: US Army, Department of Defense, 2009.

Harden, Blaine. "U.S. Relief Chief Will Meet with Iraqi Officers." *Austin American Statesman*, 4/19/1991.

Haynes, John. *Out of the Blue: The Legacy of John P. Haynes.* Phoenix, Ariz.: M&J Southwest, 2007.

Heady, Robert. "Guarding Against Identify Theft." *Network Journal,* 9/30/2000, 50.

Healy, Melissa. "Quiet Ascent: Joint Chiefs Chairman-Designate 'Shali' is Soft-Spoken but Steely." *Los Angeles Times,* 8/12/1993.

———. "Shalikashvili's Father Tied to Nazi Unit." *Los Angeles Times,* 8/28/1993.

Henderson, Van. "Ooltewah's Alice Tym Defends Gen. Shalikashvili's Family." *Chattanooga News-Free Press,* 9/15/1993.

Kaufman, Jonathan. "General Affirms US Role in Camps." *Boston Globe,* 4/20/1991.

Kozaryn, Linda D. "Joint Chiefs Chairman Cites Lessons Learned as new 'Louie' in U.S. Army." *Pentagram,* 5/12/1995.

Lancaster, John. "Shalikashvili: A Military Man from the Start." *Washington Post,* 9/21/1993.

Lippman, Thomas W. "Pentagon Nominee's Father Served as Nazi SS Officer." *Washington Post,* 8/28/1993.

Martin, David. "Landing the Eagle." *Vanity Fair,* 11/1993, 150–215.

Matthews, William. "Clinton's JCS Nominee Began as Buck Private." *Air Force Times,* 8/23/1993.

McIlree, Anne. "A Patriot 'On His Own Merit.'" *USA Today,* 8/30/1993.

McKee, Sally. "Commander of Relief Effort Is ex-Peorian." *Peoria Journal Star,* 4/30/1991.

Molendowski, Leszek. "Marriage of Convenience: Georgians on the Side of Hitler," 5/12/2009, unpublished essay translated from Polish by Arthur Eldar, including section on "Georgian Officers in the Polish Army 1921–1939."

Naylor, Sean. "'Shali' Born in Poland, Fled to Germany, Came to U.S. at 16." *Air Force Times,* 8/23/1993, 6.

O'Connell, John. "Above All Else a Real Gentleman." *Peoria Journal Star,* 6/27/1999.

———. "A Conversation with General John Shalikashvili." *Peoria Journal Star,* 6/27/1999.

"Parting Words." Pentagon, *J-Scope 2,* no. 39 (9/30/1997).

Pine, Art, and John Broder. "Polish-Born General Picked to Head Joint Chiefs." *Los Angeles Times,* 8/12/1993.

Pinkerton, James. "Yuppie Military: No More Powells, Shalikashvilis?" *Long Island Newsday,* 9/19/1993.

Powell, Stewart. "Shalikashvili Is Answer to Clinton's Call for Humanitarian Warrior." *Indianapolis Star,* 8/12/1993.

Puryear, Edgar. *American Generalship.* New York: Random House: 2000.

Schmitt, Eric, and Michael Gordon, "Military's Leaders Are Jockeying in Effort to Be Powell's Successor." *NYT,* 8/9/1993.

"Senate Proceedings: Tribute to Gen. John Shalikashvili." *Congressional Quarterly's Washington Alert,* 10/3/1997.

Shalikashvili, John. "Congress Should Repeal 'Don't Ask, Don't Tell' and Let the Pentagon Do the Rest." *Washington Post,* 5/22/2010.

———. "My Thoughts About My Stroke." Undated and unpublished essay.

———. "Second Thoughts on Gays in the Military." *NYT,* 5/7/2010.

"Shalikashvili: A Peorian in the Pentagon." *Peoria Journal Star* online Legacy Project, 6/27/1999.

"'Shally' as in Alley: Clinton Selection of Shalikashvili Tangles Tongues." *Baltimore Sun,* 8/14/1993.

Smith, Carol. "New Orders: John Shalikashvili, Once the Nation's Top General, Works to Regain Command of His Life After a Stroke." *Seattle Post-Intelligencer,* 7/7/2005.

"South Sound's Own General Doing Better After Stroke." *News Tribune,* 9/17/2004.

Sorenson, Eric. "General's Son Breaks Ranks with Tradition." *Spokesman-Review,* 5/14/1995.

Spiller, Roger. "Hope Is Not a Method." *American Heritage* 44, no. 8 (December 1993).

Stanglin, Douglas. "Shali's Tool Chest." *U.S. News and World Report,* 10/13/1997.

"Statement on General John Shalikashvili's Nomination as Chairman of the Joint Chiefs of Staff." Simon Wiesenthal Center, 8/27/1993.

Szulc, Tad. "What We Need to Do." *Parade Magazine,* May 1, 1994.

Weiner, Tim. "Man in the News: Four-Star Military Mind." *NYT,* 8/12/1993.

Weisberg, Jacob. "Details, Details," *New Republic,* 10/11/1993.

Wilson, George. "Dear General, Remember that Your Credibility Counts in the 'Bear Pit.'" *Air Force Times,* 9/6/1993.

Zak, Czeslaw. "Szkoda, ze Jest Oficerem Kontraktowym" [Pity That He Is a Contract Officer]. *Polska Zbrojna* [*Armed Poland*], no. 187 (9/24–26/1993).

Index

Page numbers in italics refer to illustrations.

A-10 Thunderbolt II ground attack aircraft, 191
Abizaid, John, 200
Abramowitz, Morton, 196
Abrams, Creighton, 301
Acknowledgment of Service Obligation, 95
Adams, Frank, 202, 216–17, 219
Adopt-a-Facility campaign, 185
Advanced Individual Training (AIT), 95, 96, 130, 158
air defense, 159–62
Air Defense Artillery, 212
Air Force ROTC, 92–93, 94
AIT. *See* Advanced Individual Training
Alaska: indigenous people, 146, 147; Shalikashvili and the social and dating life in, 148–49; Shalikashvili and the physical challenges of, 140–42; Shalikashvili and the Point Barrow fire mission, 146–47; Shalikashvili's assignment to the 9th Infantry Division, 140; Shalikashvili's career advancement, 147–48, 293; Shalikashvili's development as leader and, 142–45, 146–47; Shalikashvili's phone call to Donna and proposal of marriage, 149–50, 287; Shalikashvili's pursuit of Regular Army Commission, 145–46; Shalikashvili's worldly mystique, 162

Albright, Madeleine, 245–46, 250, 291, 296, 300
alcohol, 183, 235
Alexander II, 90, 101
Alexander III, 66
Alix of Hesse, 66
Allgemeine-SS, 264, 268
Allied Rapid Reaction Corps, 249
Altmühlbrücke, 2, 3, 5–6, 49, 51, 294–95
Altmühl River, 2, 4, 294, 295
Ambrose, Stephen, 285–86
America (SS), 14, 70–71, 73
American citizenship: Shalikashvili and, 15, 93, 317
American success stories: Clinton's fascination with, 251–52; Shalikashvili's life, 14–19, 97, 292–93, 311–20, 321–22
American Wild West, 54–55
Ancona, 59, 98
Andrachio, Nick, 214
Anfal Campaign, 137
Ankara, 103
Ansbach, 54, 58
Antwerp, 157
Aristide, Jean-Bertrand, 299, 300
aristocratic values: Shalikashvili and, 17–18, 19, 63–69, 313–14
Arlington Cemetery, 301, 310
Armed Forces Examining Station (Chicago), 95

Armstrong, David, 203, 207
Army Air Defense Command Post and
    Missile Control Center, 161
Army Communities of Excellence Pro-
    gram, 184–86
Army War College, 212, 213
artillery logistics: Shalikashvili's mas-
    tery of, 158–59
Aspin, Les: Bosnian crisis and, 245;
    on the controversy over Dimitri
    Shalikashvili's war record, 268,
    269; defense budget cuts of 1993
    and, 246; Colin Powell and, 21,
    246; Shalikashvili's description
    of Operation Provide Comfort to
    the House Armed Services Com-
    mittee and, 227, 313; Shalikash-
    vili's selection for nomination
    as chairman of the Joint Chiefs
    of Staff and, 11, 241, 242, 244,
    249, 252–53; at Shalikashvili's
    White House nomination cer-
    emony for chairmanship of the
    Joint Chiefs of Staff, 10, 20, 240
assistant to the chairman of the Joint
    Chiefs of Staff, 13, 227, 250,
    293, 318
Australian warrant officers, 234–35
Aziz, Tariq, 191

Bagrationi, Prince Alexander, 101
Baird, Zoe, 270
Baker, James, 13
Baku, 100, 101
Balkans. See Bosnian crisis
Baltic Germans, 65
Bartsch, Gunhild, 178–80, 186–87, 212
Barzani, 198
Bavaria, 4, 39, 54, 59, 68, 165. See
    also Pappenheim (Germany)
Bechtold, Donna. See Kurtz, Donna
Belgium, 157
Berger, Sandy, 12, 253, 291

Berger, Susan, 292
Bialystok, 64, 65, 66
Bielaieff, Count Alexandre, 35, 66,
    67, 68–69
Bielaieff, Mikhael, 35, 68
Bingaman, Jeff, 269
"Black Hawk Down" incident, 298,
    315
Black Hawk helicopters, 191
Blair, Dennis, 301
Blondie. See Kurtz, Donna
Boeing Corporation, 304
Bolshevik revolution. See Russian
    Revolution
Boorda, Mike, 201
Bosnian crisis: Dayton Accords, 300;
    NATO airstrikes, 13; Powell
    Doctrine and, 245–46; Shalikash-
    vili and, 13, 248–49, 297, 300
Bradley, Omar, 13, 302
Bradley University, 90, 91, 92–93,
    112–13, 114, 280
Bremerhaven, 70, 157
Bricquebec, 263
British POW camps: Dimitri Sha-
    likashvili and, 59, 98, 107–10
Bronze Star, 235, 236
Brooks, Billy, 200
Brucker, Wilber M., 147, 148
Buckley, Paul, 144, 148
Burch, Harold, 194, 230
Burg, 1–2, 51
Bush, George H. W.: Kurdish refu-
    gee crisis and Operation Provide
    Comfort, 135, 151, 154, 190,
    191; Shalikashvili's appointment
    as Supreme Allied Commander
    Europe and, 243
Butler, George ("Lee"), 251
Bydgoszcz, 104

C-130 cargo aircraft, 152, 168, 170,
    172–73

Campbell, Donald, 173, *194,* 231
cannoneers, 159
CAPSTONE course, 206
Carroll, Susan, 196–97
Casinger, Roger, 164, 181–82
Castres, 263
Caucasian Cavalry Division, 264–65
Caucasian Native Division, 101
Cedat Fortuna Peritis, 158
Center for Disease Control, 173
Central Cavalry School (Poland),
    104–5
Central Illinois Light Company, 321
CH-47 Chinook helicopters, *152*
chairman of the Joint Chiefs of Staff:
    Omar Bradley as chairman, 13;
    Goldwater-Nichols Act and, 9,
    250; Colin Powell as chairman,
    10, 244–46; Shalikashvili and
    the Haitian refugee crisis, 315,
    316; Shalikashvili's confirmation
    as, 272; Shalikashvili's contribu-
    tions and achievements, 295–300;
    Shalikashvili's dedication to the
    military family, 301–3; Shalikash-
    vili's interview with Larry King,
    272, 273, 276–78; Shalikash-
    vili's media shyness, 272–73;
    Shalikashvili's public retirement
    ceremony, 291–92, 293–95, 296,
    298, 300–301, *302;* Shalikash-
    vili's selection for nomination
    as, 241–44, 246–54; Shalikash-
    vili's Senate confirmation hearing
    and the controversy over Dimi-
    tri's war record, 255–56, 267–71,
    319–20; Shalikashvili's swearing-
    in ceremony, 273; Shalikashvili's
    White House nomination cere-
    mony for, 9–21, *240, 255*
chamberlain of the Royal Georgian
    Court, 17–18, 100
Charles V, 1

chemical weapons: attack on the
    Kurdish town of Halabja, 136,
    137; Kurdish refugee crisis of
    1991 and, 137, 138; long-term
    effects of, 136–37; Shalikashvili
    and Operation Steel Box, 165–66
Cheremeteff, Kyra, 163
Chevau-Legers, 37, 39, 106
"Chiefs and CINCs" conference, 242,
    249
children: Shalikashvili's compassion
    for, 175–77, 189, 316, 321–22
Chodakiewicz, Marek Jan, 259
cholera, 173–74
Christopher, Warren, 12, 249
Cirillo, Roger, 201, 202, 203, 226
Civil Affairs Command, 171, *194,*
    230
civil-military relationship, 299–300
Clark, Mike, 309
Clark, Wesley, 297–98, 300
Clarke, Bruce, 142
Class 3-A deferment, 275
Clinton, Bill: Comprehensive Test
    Ban Treaty and, 304; credibility
    issues with the military, 249–50,
    299; fascination with American
    success stories, 251–52; Haiti
    and, 299–300; relationship with
    Colin Powell, 19–21, 251; the
    Resolute desk and, 254; on Sha-
    likashvili as an American suc-
    cess story, 14–16; Shalikashvili's
    achievements as chairman of the
    Joint Chiefs of Staff and, 296,
    298, 299–300; Shalikashvili's
    Joint Chiefs of Staff confirma-
    tion hearing and the controversy
    over Dimitri's war record, 256–
    57, 268; at Shalikashvili's public
    retirement ceremony, 291, 292,
    294, 295, 298, 299; Shalikashvi-
    li's selection for nomination

Clinton, Bill (*cont.*)
  as chairman of the Joint Chiefs of
    Staff and, 241, 242, 244, 249–50,
    251–54; White House nomina-
    tion ceremony for Shalikashvili
    as chairman of the Joint Chiefs of
    Staff, 9–11, 12–16, 19–21, *240,*
    255
Coggsdale, Bobby, 125
Cohen, Richard, 255, 256
Cohen, William, 291, 292, 294, 295,
  296, 298
Collins, Ruth, 184, 201, 202
Comeglians, 265
community commander, 182–86, 223
Community Family Force Forum, 185
competency: Shalikashvili and, 203–7
Comprehensive Test Ban Treaty, 304
Conegliano, 107
consensus-building: Shalikashvili's
  skills in, 200–203
Constantinople, 103–4
Crawford, Laurence, 123
Crimean War, 90
Croix de Guerre, 111
Cross of Saint George, 101
Crowe, William, 246, 304
Cua Viet, 236

Danzig, 261
Daschle, Tom, 301
Davis, Russell, 125, 126
Dayton Accords, 300
DCINC. *See* deputy commander in
  chief, US Army Europe
defense budget cuts: Colin Powell
  and, 26; Shalikashvili and, 247,
  298–99
Defense Daily, 255–56, 257–58,
  268–69
Defense Distinguished Service Medal,
  295
DEFSOL, 174

de Gaulle, Charles, 105
dementia, 309
Democratic National Convention,
  305–6
deputy commander in chief, US Army
  Europe (DCINC, USAREUR):
  reasons for Shalikashvili's
  appointment to, 221–26; Shalikashvili and the Kurdish refugee
  crisis, 133–35, 139–40 (*see also*
  Kurdish refugee crisis of 1991;
  Operation Provide Comfort);
  Shalikashvili's relationship with
  Butch Saint, 221–24
deputy director of the Strategy, Plans,
  and Policy Directorate, 206–7
Dickson, Caroll, 211
Dinkelsbuhl, 54, 57–58
diplomacy skills: Shalikashvili and,
  162–64, 165–66
Dirksen, Everett, 258
Disaster Assistance Response Team
  (DART), 196
Displaced Persons Program, 72
division artillery (DIVARTY) com-
  mander, 159, 177, 181–82, 204,
  208, 214
Diyarbakir airstrip, 151, *152,* 167,
  173
Doctors Without Borders, 171, 197
Dojlidy, 65–66, 69
"Don't Ask, Don't Tell" policy, 244,
  304
draft: Shalikashvili and, 93–95,
  275–76
Drug Abuse Resistance Education
  (DARE) program, 185
drug problems, 183, 185
Duhok, 137, 231, 232
Dunlop, Olga, 267

Eastern Legions, 262
Eielson Air Force Base, 140, 148

86th US Infantry Division, 6
emotional intelligence, 207, 208
empathy: John Shalikashvili and, 34,
    58, 128–29, 203, 232–33, 286,
    314–15; Missy Shalikashvili and,
    281–82
Erbil, 137
Errico, Bob, 126–27
EUCOM. See US European Command
European Union: Kurdish refugee cri-
    sis and, 153

Families Learn About Germany
    (FLAG) program, 185
family support groups, 185
Field Artillery Officer Candidate
    School (FA-OCS), 86; Artillery
    and Guided Missile School, 120;
    difficulty of the program and
    practices at, 116–17, 118–24;
    emotional trauma experienced by
    candidates, 123–24; harassment
    of candidates, 120–23; hierarchy
    of candidates, 117–18; history of,
    116; Jark Marches, 88, 118, 120–
    23, 124, 127–28; Roger O'Dwyer
    and, 116, 117, 124, 126, 127–30;
    Shalikashvili and the big brother/
    little brother relationship, 124–
    29; Shalikashvili's experiences at,
    87–90, 112, 115, 117, 124; Sha-
    likashvili's graduation from, 129;
    Shalikashvili's indecision about
    accepting Regular Army Commis-
    sion, 129–30; Shalikashvili's rea-
    sons for applying to, 95–97
Finland, 68
fire direction specialists, 159
1st Armored Division: Butch Saint
    and, 224; Shalikashvili as divi-
    sion artillery commander, 159,
    177, 181–82; Shalikashvili as
    the community commander of

Nuremberg, 183–84, 185–86;
    Shalikashvili's care for soldiers
    and their families, 177, 181–82
1st Battle Group, 9th Infantry Divi-
    sion ("Manchus"), 140–50. See
    also Alaska
1st Light Horse Regiment (Poland), 37
Fischer, David, 165
Fisher House Foundation, 304
Ford, Grover, 321–22
Fort Bliss: Shalikashvili and the soc-
    cer team, 215, 218; Shalikash-
    vili at the High Altitude Missiles
    Department, 160–62; Shalikash-
    vili's disillusionment with mili-
    tary life and, 178; Shalikashvili's
    worldly mystique and, 162, 163
Fort Bliss Air Defense School, 161
Fort Chaffee, 96
Fort Leonard Wood, 88
Fort Lewis, 162, 181. See also 9th
    Infantry Division
Fort Myer, 242, 291
Fort Sill, 87, 112, 122. See also Field
    Artillery Officer Candidate School
Fort Wainwright, 147–48, 162
forward observers, 158–59
Foster, Vince, 252
France: Kurdish refugee crisis and,
    153, 196
Francis II, 1
Frank, Barney, 244
Free Georgia: Dimitri Shalikashvili
    and, 47, 99, 102–3
French Foreign Legion, 103, 110–11
Frye, Larry, 123

Gabliani, Givi, 265, 267
Gallagher, Mike, 300
Galvin, John ("Jack"): Operation Pro-
    vide Comfort and, 151–52, 154,
    193, 194, 195, 200, 211; on Sha-
    likashvili and US Army Europe,

Galvin, John ("Jack") (*cont.*)
164–65; Shalikashvili's appointment as deputy commander in chief, US Army Europe and, 224; on Shalikashvili's movement of the VII Corps to the Persian Gulf, 158
Garner, Jay, 155, 194–95, 230
gays in the military: Clinton's credibility with the military and, 249; "Don't Ask, Don't Tell" policy, 244, 304; Joseph Hoar and, 252; Shalikashvili and, 304
Georgia: annexation by the Communist Russian government, 103; Germany and, 260; independence in 1918, 102; Shalikashvili family lineage, 17–18, 90, *91*, 100–101; Dimitri Shalikashvili's military service and diplomatic mission to Turkey, 47, 99, 102–3; Dimitri Shalikashvili's upbringing, 99–100; John Shalikashvili's visit to, *305*
Georgian 2nd Battalion, 263
Georgian Cavalry Regiment, 265–68
Georgian Colonies, 103. *See also* Warsaw Georgian Colony
Georgian Infantry Battalion 797, 263
Georgian Legion: General Koniashvili and aid to Missy Shalikashvili, 44; John Shalikashvili's knowledge of Dimitri's service with, 280–81, 285–86, 319–20; Missy Shalikashvili's reaction to Dimitri's joining, 281, 282; Dimitri Shalikashvili's service with during World War II, 43, 47, 54, 58–59, 99, 107, 260–68
Georgian Liaison Offices, 47, 264, 265, 279
Georgian POWs, 108–10
Gergen, David, 241, 252

German Federal Railway, 157
Germany: Georgia and, 260; Shalikashvili and deployment of the US VII Corps to the Persian Gulf, 157; Shalikashvili and Operation Steel Box, 165–66; Shalikashvili as a community commander, 183–86; Shalikashvili's diplomatic skills in Bavaria, 165; Shalikashvili's marriage to Joan Zimpelman, 188. *See also* Nazi Germany; Pappenheim
Geronimo, 122
Gestapo, 43–44
Getty, Ken: on army officers and conflict-aversion, 200; on Hayri Kozakcoglu, 167; Kurdish refugee crisis and Operation Provide Comfort, 172, 175, 194–95, 196, 197, 198, 199
Gettysburg, 315
Gia Dang, 237
Ginsburg, Ruth Bader, 252
Glenn, Charles, 140, 145
Goldwater-Nichols Act (1986), 9, 250, 299
Gore, Al, 10, 20, 291
Grand-Maitre de la Cour de Georgia. *See* chamberlain of the Royal Georgian Court
Grand Order of Nuts and Bolts, 292
Great Britain: Kurdish refugee crisis and Operation Provide Comfort, 153, 171, 195–96
Great War. *See* World War I
Grice, William Rudy, 142–44, 148, 187
Grubbs, William, 160
Grudziądz, 104
Guantanamo Bay Naval Base, 315
Gulf War, 156–64
Gulyas, Steve, 193, 195, 196, 202–3
Guramishvili, Princess Ekaterina, 101

Gures, Dougan, 138
Gurjaani, 99

Haig, Brian, 163, 180, 207, 300
Haiti, 299–300
Haitian refugee crisis, 315, 316
Halabja, 136, 137, 139
Halberstam, David, 158
Hamre, John, 291
Harbur, 190, 193
Harbur River, 190
Harrison, Steve, 280
Harrison, William, 216, 219, 220, 224
Haynes, John, 144, 149
heart disease and heart attacks, 306–7
Heidelberg, 184–86, 188
Helms, Jesse, 299
Herrling, John, 201, 213
Hershey, Lewis Blaine, 94
Hier, Rabbi Marvin, 257, 258, 259, 268
High Altitude Missiles Department, 160–62
Hilfswillige, 261
Hill, Rich, 308
Hitler, Adolf, 264, 282, 285
Hitler Youth, 5, 261, 262
Hoar, Joseph P., 242, 249, 252
Hobson, James, 194
Hofgarten, 60
Holbrooke, Richard, 250, 300
Holmes, Oliver Wendell, 295
Holt, Brian, 195
Home Army, 263
homosexuality. See gays in the military
Hoover, William, 161
Hoover Institution, 256, 259–60, 267
Hotel Krone, 5, 51
House Armed Services Committee: Shalikashvili's account of Operation Provide Comfort to, 227–31, 232; views of Shalikashvili in, 12

Howerton, William, 144, 149
Human Rights Campaign Fund, 252
Human Rights Watch, 137
Hummel, Ted, 145
humor: Shalikashvili and, 144–45, 146, 162
Hungary, 296
Hurley, Jack, 164
Hussein, Saddam, 135–36, 138, 211, 298
Hyster Lift Company, 94, 113, 115

Icenogle, Larry, 272
identity theft, 304
Imerteti, 90
Implementation Force, 297
Incirlik, 151, 155, 173
Incirlik Air Base, 133, 152, 167
Infantry Officer Candidate School, 92
Institute for International Studies, 304
intellectual intelligence, 207, 208
intelligence: of Shalikashvili as an officer, 207–9
International Refugee Organization, 72, 110, 258
Iran, 136
Iraq, 135–36, 137, 190–93, 211. See also Kurdish refugee crisis of 1991; Operation Provide Comfort
Iraq-Iran War, 136
Isikveren, 134–35, 139, 169–71, 172, 176
Iskenderun, 173
Italy: Dimitri Shalikashvili as a POW of the British, 59, 98, 107–10; Dimitri Shalikashvili's mission to during World War II, 58–59, 107, 264–68

Jaco, Tom, 163–64, 200, 208, 215
Jamerson, Jim: on the challenges faced in Operation Provide Comfort,

Jamerson, Jim (*cont.*)
196, 198–99; on creating and
sizing the security zone in northern Iraq, 194, 231, 232; on distributing relief supplies to the
Kurdish refugees, 170, 172;
importance to Operation Provide
Comfort, 167–68, 230; Kurdish
refugee relocation and, 175, 190;
levels of command held by in
Operation Provide Comfort, 152,
155, *194;* on the nonmilitary
components of Operation Provide
Comfort, 196, 197
Jaqeli dynasty, 90
Jark, Carl, 121
Jark March, 88, 118, 120–23, 124,
127–28
Jenks, Robert, 127
Jeremiah, David, 252
Jews: Missy Shalikashvili's attitude,
281–82; Shalikashvili's experi-
ences with, 283–84, 286, 319
Johnston Atoll, 165
"jointness," 204–6, 299
joint task forces (JTFs) in Opera-
tion Provide Comfort: Joint Task
Force-Alpha, 171–72, 230; Joint
Task Force-Bravo, 194–95, 196,
226, 230; overview, 152
Joint Vision 2010, 299, 305
Jones, Bob, 188
Jones, David, 304
Joulwan, George, 242–43, 272

Kaiserslautern, 161, 188
Kapaun Barracks, 161
Katyn Forest massacre, 41–42
Kelly, Thomas, 211
Kendall, Mike, 202, 220
Kennedy, John F., 254
Kerry, John, 305
Kessler, Jim, 203

King, Larry, 273, 276–78
Kirkuk, 137
Kobiashvili, Zurab, 95
Koniashvili (Georgian Legion gen-
eral), 44
Kozakcoglu, Hayri, 167, 168
Kraków, 40–41
Krumbhaar, George, 121
Krusen, Philippe de, 65
Krusenstern, Adam Johann Ritter von,
64, 65
Krusenstern, Baron Alexander, *65, 66*
Krusenstern, Evert-Phillippe, 65
Krusenstern, Sophie, 64–65
Krusenstern family, 64–65
Krushina, 260, 262–63
Kurdish Democratic Party, 137
Kurdish refugee crisis of 1991: cause
of, 135–36; concerns about vio-
lence and terrorists, 174; condi-
tion of the refugees in Isikveren,
169–71; disease concerns,
173–74; factors underlying the
decision to move the refugees,
172–77; flight of Kurds to the
Turkey-Iraq border, 137–39;
impact of the combined efforts of
Joint Task Force-Alpha on, 171–
72; Isikveren, 134–35, 139; mushrooming of the crisis and of the
international response, 152–54;
Norman Schwarzkopf and, 225;
Shalikashvili and the relocation of
the refugees, 188–89; Shalikashvili's first observation of, 133–35,
139–40; suffering of children,
175–76, 189; UN Security Council resolution regarding, 151. *See
also* Operation Provide Comfort
Kurds: chemical weapons attacks on,
136–37; failed rebellion against
the Saddam Hussein regime,
135–36

Kurtz, Donna (née Bechtold), 75; high school relationship with and insights into Shalikashvili, 27–31, 33–34, 74, 76–83, 278–79, 281, 282–85, 286–87; kidnapped child of, 276; personal early history of, 31–32; pregnancy and abortion, 274; Shalikashvili's interview with Larry King and, 272, 273, 276–78; Shalikashvili's lasting feelings for, 287–88; Shalikashvili's nomination ceremony for chairman of the Joint Chiefs of Staff and, 22–23; Shalikashvili's phone call from Alaska and proposal of marriage, 149–50, 276, 287; sudden departure from Shalikashvili and Peoria, 83, 113, 274–76

Kwieciak, Stan, 203, 217, 219

L-3 Communications, 304
Ladd Air Field, 140, 147, 148
La Haye-du-Puits, 263
Lake, Anthony, 11–12, 315
leadership and Shalikashvili: agile intelligence and, 207–9; appointment as commander of Operation Provide Comfort and, 156–66; care for soldiers and their families, 180–87; competency and holistic training in the US military, 203–7; consensus-building skills and, 200–203; development of leadership skills in Alaska, 142–45, 146–47; diplomatic skills and worldly mystique, 162–64, 314; qualities of compassionate leadership, 18–19; Three Pillars of Leadership, 187
Lee, John, 202, 219
Legion of Merit, 248
Levin, Carl, 269

Liaison Office, Department of Defense (Free Georgia), 102–3
Libby, I. Lewis ("Scooter"), 318
Lieberman, Joseph, 271
Lientz, 265
Lindsay, Robert, 123, 204
line drawings, 56–57
Litzmannstadt (Lodz), 36
Liu, Y. King, 92, 112, 280–81
Livingston, Steve, 187–88
Lodz (Litzmannstadt), 36
logistics: Shalikashvili and Operation Steel Box, 165–66; Shalikashvili's mastery of, 158–59
love of soldiers: Shalikashvili's Three Pillars of Leadership and, 187
Loy, James, 309
Luarsab of Georgia, 100
Lublin, 41, 42, 63–64, 66, 69
Luitwieler, Peter, 234
Luther, Martin, 1
Luthy, Ferdinand, 258
Luthy, George, 73, 90, 91, 94, 114, 258
Luthy, Winifred, 71–72, 73, 258, 313
Luthy family, 76, 258, 280
Luxembourg, 171

MACV. See Military Assistance Command, Vietnam
Madigan Army Medical Center, 306, 310
Majid, Ali Hassan al- ("Chemical Ali"), 137
Malloy, M. Shawn, 181
Manchus. See 1st Battle Group, 9th Infantry Division
Manteuffel, Baron Henry von, 40
Manteuffel, George, 261
Manteuffel, Hasso von, 40
Manteuffel, Sophie, 40
manual for military families, 182
Massoud, Barzani, 137

Matchabelli, Prince Georges V., 71
May, Karl, 54
McCaffrey, Barry, 249, 291
McCain, John, 269
McCarthy, J., 194, 195, 198
McGary, James, 89, 120
McLain, Rachel, 309
McMahon, Mike, 141–42, 148
McPeak, Merrill, 250–51
measles, 173
mechanical engineering degree, 94
Medal of Freedom, 295
Medal of St. George, 101
Mehar, Dave, 163, 185, 222
Meigs, Montgomery, 203, 207, 221
Mersin, 173
MH-53J Pave Low helicopter, 168
Michel, Robert, 291
Military Assistance Command, Vietnam (MACV), 234–37
Military Coordination Center, 194, 230
Military Personnel Center, 205–6
Miller, David Paul, 251
Miller, Joe, 163
Millie, David, 234–35
Mix, Tom, 54
Molino, Mike, 202, 222
Molino, Tom, 166, 222
Mooney, Harvey, 234, 235
Morris Minor automobile, 141–42
Mount McKinley, 141
Multinational Force and Observers in the Sinai, 248
mustard gas, 136

Naab, Richard, 194, 230
National Bureau of Asian Research, 304
National Press Club, 292
National Public Radio (NPR), 278, 279, 280
National Security Council, 246

National Training Center, 220
naturalization. See American citizenship
Nauman, Klaus, 291
Naval War College, 205, 208, 285
Nazi Germany: controversy over Dimitri's war record with, 255–60, 267–71, 319–20; Eastern Legions, 262; Dimitri Shalikashvili as a POW in, 39, 40–41, 107, 259; Shalikashvili family in Pappenheim (see Pappenheim); Dimitri Shalikashvili's military service in the Georgian Legion with, 43, 47, 54, 58–59, 99, 107, 260–68
Netherlands, 157
New Schloss (Neues Schloss), 51; Countess Julie Pappenheim and, 49; history of, 2; incident on the Altmühlbrücke and, 2–3, 4–5; influence on the adult Shalikashvili, 186; the refugee Shalikashvili family and, 52; Dimitri Shalikashvili's work in the library of, 60
news media: scrutiny of Shalikashvili during Operation Provide Comfort, 210, 211; Shalikashvili's attitude toward, 318; Shalikashvili's interview with Larry King, 273, 276–78; Shalikashvili's reluctance to address as chairman of the Joint Chiefs of Staff, 272
New York City, 14
New York Times, 246, 259
Ney, Ed, 183
Nicholas II, 66, 67
Nike guided missiles, 160, 161
Nim (Vietnamese major), 235
Nino, Saint, 38
9th Infantry Division: Joan Shalikashvili and, 188; Shalikashvili and the downsizing of, 218, 247; Sha-

likashvili's care for soldiers and their families, 176–77, 181, 182; Shalikashvili's challenges and performance as a commander, 216–20; Shalikashvili's experiences and lessons in Alaska, 140–50 (*see also* Alaska); Shalikashvili's promotion to lieutenant general, 221; J. B. Taylor on Shalikashvili, 166

nongovernmental organizations (NGOs): Kurdish refugee crisis and Operation Provide Comfort, 153, 171, 196, 197

Nordenham, 166

North Atlantic Treaty Organization (NATO): Allied Rapid Reaction Corps, 249; Operation Provide Comfort and, 193; Reforger exercise, 223; Shalikashvili and the Bosnian crisis, 13, 248–49, 297, 300; Shalikashvili and the Partnership for Peace initiative, 296; Shalikashvili as Supreme Allied Commander Europe, 11, 13, 242–43, 248–49, 293

North Italian partisans, 265–66

North Korea, 298

NPR. *See* National Public Radio

Nuclear Surety Program, 208

nuclear weapons: Comprehensive Test Ban Treaty, 304; North Korea and, 298; Shalikashvili's skills in understanding and communicating about, 159–62, 208

nuclear weapons control officer, 161

Nunn, Sam, 270, 271, 296

Nuremberg, 183–84, 185–86, 188

Nuremberg High School, 183

OCS. *See* Officer Candidate School

OCS Standard Operating Procedure, 87–88

O'Dwyer, Roger, 116, 117

Office of the Deputy Chief of Staff for Operations and Plans, 206

Officer Candidate School (OCS), 15. *See also* Field Artillery Officer Candidate School

Ohlstein, Allen, 183, 186, 188, 202, 211

Old Schloss *(Altes Schloss),* 2, 51, 52–53, 54, 63

Operation Desert Storm, 135

Operation Fisher, 237

Operation Proven Force, 167

Operation Provide Comfort: challenges integrating the international military components, 195–96; challenges integrating the nonmilitary components, 196–98; challenges posed by the Kurds, 198–99; challenges posed by Turkey, 198, 199; concerns about violence and terrorists, 174; condition of the refugees in Isikveren, 169–71; cost of, 175; creating and sizing a security zone in northern Iraq, 190–93, 211, 231–32; decision to move the refugees back into Iraq, 172–77, 188–89, 190; disease concerns, 173–74; establishment and mission of, 151–52; as a joint task force, 152; Joint Task Force-Alpha, 171–72, 230; Joint Task Force-Bravo, 194–95, 196, 226, 230; major challenges for Shalikashvili, 193–200; media scrutiny of Shalikashvili, *210,* 211; movement of the refugees back into northern Iraq, 226; mushrooming of the crisis and of the international response, 152–54; overall organizational structure, 193–95; problems with C-130

Operation Provide Comfort (*cont.*)
airdrops, 172–73; Eugene Ronsick and, 151, 167–68; Shalikashvili becomes a world figure, 211;
Shalikashvili's account of to the
House Armed Services Committee, 227–31, 232; Shalikashvili's
appointment as commander, 13,
151, 154–55, 156–66, 167–68;
Shalikashvili's aristocratic values and, 313; Shalikashvili's
career path and, 225–26, 293;
Shalikashvili's meeting with
Nashwan Thanoon, 191–93;
Shalikashvili's nomination as the
chairman of the Joint Chiefs of
Staff and, 247, 248; Shalikashvili's personal refugee experiences
and, 232–33; Sub-Task Force
Express Care, 153; suffering of
children, 175–76, 189; theater
of operations, *174;* upgraded to
a combined task force structure,
154; upgraded to a humanitarian
intervention, 154. *See also* Kurdish refugee crisis of 1991
Operation Steel Box, 165–66
Ostlegionen, 262
Osttruppen, 261

Palastra, Joseph, 220
Palm, Charles, 267
Pappenheim (Germany): description
and history of, 1–2; diminished
privileges of the Pappenheim family and, 49–50; flight of the Shalikashvili family to, 3, 47, 53–54,
259; gift packages from Winifred
Luthy to the Shalikashvili family in, 71–72; impact of World
War II on, 4–6, 51–52; Julie Pappenheim and, 49, 52; postwar
life of the Shalikashvili family,
52–53, 59–61; postwar occupation, 49; John Shalikashvili and
the 1945 *Altmühlbrücke* incident,
2–6, 294–95; Shalikashvili family
and Marie Rudiger-Bielaieff, 63;
Dimitri Shalikashvili's departure
for Italy in 1945, 58–59; wartime
childhood and education of John
Shalikashvili and siblings, 2–6,
54–58
Pappenheim, Countess Julie, *50;* flight
of the Shalikashvili family to Pappenheim and, 3, 47; influence on
John Shalikashvili's values and
abilities, 18, 19; in postwar Pappenheim, 49, 52; Dimitri Shalikashvili's status as a German
POW and, 39
Pappenheim, Count Gottfried Hein-
rich, 50
Pappenheim, Count Joachim-Ludwig,
51
Pappenheim, Count Ludwig Magnus
Heinrich Carl, 3
Pappenheim, Liutta, 52, 54
Pappenheim, Ludwig, 52
Pappenheim, Theodor Friedrich, 1
Pappenheim, Ulrich von, 1
Pappenheim, Ursula, 52
Pappenheim family: aid to the refugee
Shalikashvili family, 3, 52–53,
54; diminished privileges of,
49–50; history of Pappenheim
and, 1–2; impact of World War II
on, 4–5, 51, 52. *See also* Pappen-
heim, Countess Julie
Parade (magazine), 272
Parent, Ron, 308–9
Partisans of North Italy, 265–66
Partnership for Peace initiative, 296
patriotism: Shalikashvili and, 317–18
peacetime draft: Shalikashvili and,
93–95, 275–76

Peoria: Donna Bechtold's personal early history, 31–32; Donna Bechtold's relationship with and insights into Shalikashvili, 27–31, 33–34, 74, 76–83, 278–79, 282–85, 286–87; Donna Bechtold's sudden departure from, 83, 113, 274–76; Winifred Luthy and the Shalikashvili family's relocation to, 71, 73; the Shalikashvili brothers at Bradley University, 90, 91, 92–93; Shalikashvili's immigrant experience in, 317, 321–22; Shalikashvili's life as an American success story, 14–15

Peoria High School: Donna Bechtold's relationship with and insights into Shalikashvili, 27–31, 33–34, 74, 76–83, 278–79, 282–85, 286–87; Shalikashvili's character and personality during the years at, 74–83; Shalikashvili's graduation from, 34; Shalikashvili's reluctance to speak about his family history at, 280–81, 286–87

Peoria Journal Star, 287–88

Perry, William, 11, 291, 300, 304, 321

Pershing, John, 303

Persian Cossack Brigade, 101

Persian Gulf, 156–58

Personnel Reliability Program, 160–61

Peshmerga, 174

Phillips, Henry, 140

Pilsudski, Jozef, 37

PKK, 174

Poessinger, Peter, 162

Point Barrow, 146–47

Poland: flight of the Shalikashvili family from, 3, 35–36, 47, 259; Home Army, 263; Katyn Forest massacre, 41–42; Partnership for

Peace initiative and, 296; Marie Rudiger-Bielaieff's personal and family history, 63–64, 65–66, 68–69; Shalikashvili family in Warsaw (see Warsaw); Dimitri Shalikashvili's first encounter with Maria Rudiger-Bielaieff, 69, 106–7; Dimitri Shalikashvili's immigration to, 103–4; Dimitri Shalikashvili's military schooling in, 104–5; Dimitri Shalikashvili's military service with, 38, 99, 106, 107, 261; Dimitri Shalikashvili's views of, 260–61; Warsaw Uprising, 3, 35, 45–47, 259; World War II and, 38

Polish General Staff Academy, 105

Polish-Russian War (1919–21), 260–61

Polish Underground, 45–46, 47

Potter, Richard, 139, 194, 196, 197, 198, 230

Powell, Colin: as chairman of the Joint Chiefs of Staff, 10, 244–46; Comprehensive Test Ban Treaty and, 304; defense budget cuts of 1993 and, 246; gays in the military and the "Don't Ask, Don't Tell" policy, 244; relationship with Clinton and the Clinton administration, 19–21, 250–51; relationship with Shalikashvili when FORSCOM commander, 217, 221; Shalikashvili and deployment of the VII Corps to the Persian Gulf, 156, 158; Shalikashvili as assistant to when chairman of the Joint Chiefs of Staff, 13, 227, 250, 293, 318; Shalikashvili's appointment as Supreme Allied Commander Europe and, 242–43; Shalikashvili's selection for nomination

Powell, Colin (*cont.*)
    as chairman of the Joint Chiefs
        of Staff and, 242, 243, 252–53;
        at Shalikashvili's White House
        nomination ceremony as chair-
        man of the Joint Chiefs of Staff,
        10, 19–21; Vietnam War experi-
        ence, 244–45
Powell Doctrine, 245–46, 248
Poznań, 36, 47
press. *See* news media
Preventive Defense Project, 304, 321
prisoners of war (POWs): Dimitri Sha-
        likashvili as a POW of the British
        in Italy, 59, 98, 107–10; Dimi-
        tri Shalikashvili as a POW of the
        Germans, 39, 40–41, 107, 259
private volunteer organizations
        (PVOs): Kurdish refugee crisis
        and Operation Provide Comfort,
        153, 171, 196, 197
Pushkin, Alexander, 100
PVOs. *See* private volunteer
        organizations

Quang Tri, 234, 237

Rapp, Bill, 280
Rasputin, 66
Redbirds, 117–18, 123
Red Cross: Kurdish refugee crisis and,
        173; Liutta Pappenheim and, 52;
        Missy Shalikashvili and, 38–39, 40
Reforger exercise, 223
refugee relocation: Shalikashvili and
        Operation Fisher in Vietnam,
        237. *See also* Operation Provide
        Comfort
Refugees International, 171
Regiment of the Horse Guards,
        98–99, 101–2
Regular Army Commission, 129–30,
        145–46

Reichserbmarschall, 1
Reno, Janet, 251
Republican Guard (Iraq), 136
Reserve Forces Act (1955), 94
Reserve Officers' Training Corps
        (ROTC), 92–93, 94
Resolute desk, 254
Rimini, 107–8
Riscassi, Robert W., 208
Robinson Barracks, *86,* 87–90, 112,
        115. *See also* Field Artillery Offi-
        cer Candidate School
Romania, 296
Ronsick, Eugene J., 151, 167–68, 198
Roosevelt, Franklin Delano, 93
Ross, Tom, 163
ROTC. *See* Reserve Officers' Train-
        ing Corps
Rotterdam, 157
Rudiger, Count Johann Friedrich, 64
Rudiger, Helene, 65
Rudiger, Julie, 62, 63, 65, 66
Rudiger, Sophie, 62, 63, 65, 66
Rudiger, Theodor, 65
Rudiger-Bielaieff, Countess Maria,
        106–7. *See also* Shalikashvili,
        Maria
Rudiger-Bielaieff, Countess Marie:
        death of, 63; flight of the Sha-
        likashvili family from Warsaw in
        1944, 35–36, 47; impact of World
        War II on, 63; life with the Sha-
        likashvili family in Pappenheim,
        63; personal and family history
        of, 63–69; Shalikashvili family
        relocation to America and, 62–63,
        73; values transmitted to the Sha-
        likashvili children, 18, 19, 63, 69;
        wartime life and experiences in
        Warsaw, 41, 42, 44–45, 46
Ruoff, John, 123–24, 125
Russia: Partnership for Peace initiative
        and, 296

Russian Empire: Countess Marie Rudiger-Bielaieff's family and personal history in, 35, 63–68; Russian Revolution and, 68, 102; service of Dimitri Shalikashvili and siblings in World War I, 101–2; Dimitri Shalikashvili's military career with, 98–99; Dimitri Shalikashvili's upbringing in, 99–100
Russian Lyceum, 100, 102
Russian Revolution, 68, 102
Rwanda, 297–98

Sabre Air Command Squadron, 93
SACEUR. See Supreme Allied Commander Europe
Saint, Crosbie ("Butch"): Kurdish refugee crisis and Operation Provide Comfort, 154, 157, 194, 195, 200, 211, 226; relationship with Shalikashvili, 221–24; on Shalikashvili as a community commander in Nuremberg, 184–85; Shalikashvili as an assistant division commander under, 214; on Shalikashvili as commander of the 9th Infantry Division, 219; Shalikashvili nominated to replace as head of USAREUR, 242; on Shalikashvili's agile intelligence, 207; on Shalikashvili's consensus-building skills, 201; on Shalikashvili's work ethic, 215
Saint Nino's Cross, 38
Salzburg, 265, 282
Samtskhe, 90
San Antonio State Hospital, 149
Sandla, Robert, 127
Sarajevo, 13, 242, 245
Saudi Arabia, 156–58
Saunders, Larry, 181, 217
Schact, Bruno, 203
Schake, Kori, 207, 251

Schellenberg, Walter, 257, 262
Schiller, Friedrich, 50
Schreyach, Jon, 159, 208
Schwarzkopf, H. Norman, 156, 225, 293
Scowcroft, Brent, 242
Seigneur de Lublin, 66
Selective Service System, 94. See also peacetime draft
Self-Help U-Fix-It program, 185
Senate: confirmation of Shalikashvili as chairman of the Joint Chiefs of Staff, 272; support for Shalikashvili as chairman of the Joint Chiefs of Staff, 12
Senate Armed Services Committee: Shalikashvili's Joint Chiefs of Staff confirmation hearing and the controversy over Dimitri's war record, 255, 269–71, 319–20; views of Shalikashvili in, 12
Seneca, 156
Serbia, 245, 248–49. See also Bosnian crisis
SETAF. See US Army Southern European Task Force
Seventh Army Operations Center, 161
VII Corps, 156–58, 161
Shalikashvili, Alexandra ("Gale"): birth name, 36–37; childhood in wartime Pappenheim, 6, 54, 58, 59; childhood in wartime Warsaw, 43; Dimitri as a POW of the British and, 110; emigration of the Shalikashvili family to America, 62, 63, 73; on John and Gunhild Bartsch, 179; John's caring relationship with, 58; on John's childhood personality, 57, 58; at John's high school graduation, 34
Shalikashvili, Brant, 212, 225, 272, 309, 316
Shalikashvili, Christina-Maria, 179

Shalikashvili, David, 99, 101, 102, 103, 110–11, 306

Shalikashvili, Dimitri: children of, 36–37; concept of being a "gentleman" and, 279; cousin Dimitry Starosselsky, 71; emigration of the Shalikashvili family to America, 62, 63, 72–73, 257–58; emigration to Poland, 103–4; emotion versus reason in, 282; first encounter with Maria Rudiger-Bielaieff, 69, 106–7; Free Georgia and, 47, 99, 102–3; health issues, 73, 306, 308; immigrant experience in Peoria, 321; impact of World War II on mother and siblings of, 110–11; influence on John as a child, 57; influence on John's adult values and abilities, 18, 19, 279–80; John's conflicted feelings toward, 287, 314; John's reluctance as an adolescent to speak about the past of, 280–81, 286–87; John's similarity to as a military officer, 279, 321; Katyn Forest Massacre and, 41–42; lineage and family history, 100–101; memoirs of, 255–60, 285–86; military schooling in Poland, 104–5; military service with Germany in the Georgian Legion during World War II, 43, 47, 54, 58–59, 99, 107, 260–68; military service with Poland, 38, 99, 106, 107, 261; mission to Italy in 1945, 58–59, 107, 264–68; Missy's reaction to his joining the Georgian Legion, 281, 282; overview of the military career of, 98–99; personality of, 59–60; postwar life in Pappenheim, 59–61; as a POW of the British in World War II, 58–59, 98, 107–10; as a POW of the Germans in World War II, 39, 40–41, 107, 259; Regiment of the Horse Guards and, 98–99, 101–2; release from the British POW camp in Italy, 110, 111; service in World War I, 101–2; service with the Waffen-SS (see Waffen-SS); upbringing in Georgia, 99–100; views of Germany and the Germans, 260; views of the Poland and the Poles, 260–61; Warsaw Georgian Colony and, 42, 107, 261, 262

Shalikashvili, Gale. See Shalikashvili, Alexandra

Shalikashvili, Iossif, 99

Shalikashvili, Jean, 37

Shalikashvili, Joan (nèe Zimpelman), 187–88, 251, 291, 302

Shalikashvili, Joe. See Shalikashvili, Othar

Shalikashvili, John (Prince John Malchase David Shalikashvili): the 1945 Altmühlbrücke incident in Pappenheim, 2–6, 294–95; activities in retirement, 304–6; Air Force ROTC and, 92–93, 94; as an American success story, 14–19, 97, 292–93, 311–20, 321–22; aristocratic values, 17–18, 19, 63–69, 313–14; Army War College and, 212, 213; as assistant chief of staff for operations, US Army Southern European Task Force, 213, 214; as assistant to the chairman of the Joint Chiefs of Staff, 13, 227, 250, 293, 318; awards received by, 235, 236, 248, 295; Donna Bechtold and (see Kurtz, Donna); birth and christening in Warsaw, 37–38; birth status as a stateless person, 38; at Bradley University, 90, 92–93, 112–13, 114; on brother Othar's childhood personality, 57; care for soldiers and their families, 180–87; as chairman of the Joint Chiefs of Staff (*see* chairman of the Joint Chiefs of Staff); character and personality as an adolescent in Peoria, 74–83; childhood, developing personality, and education in Pappenheim, 1–6, 54–58; Clinton on the virtues of, 12–14; as a community commander, 182–86; compassion for children, 175–77, 189, 316, 321–22; competency and holistic training in the US military, 203–7; concept of being a "gentleman" and, 279; conflicted feelings toward father Dimitri, 287, 314; consensus-building skills, 200–203; creativity and childhood line drawings, 56–57; death of, 310; de facto life philosophy and the meaning of his life, 311–20; as deputy director of the Strategy, Plans, and Policy Directorate, 206–7; Dimitri's service with the Waffen-SS and (*see* Waffen-SS); diplomatic skills and worldly mystique, 162–64, 314; effects of childhood war experiences on, 78–81, 282–85, 286–87, 311–13, 315–16; emigration of the Shalikashvili family to America and, 62, 63, 69–73; empathy and, 34, 58, 128–29, 203, 232–33, 286, 314–15; on entering the US Army, 90; experiences in Alaska, 140–50 (*see also* Alaska); Field Artillery Officer Candidate School and (*see* Field Artillery Officer Candidate School); 1st Armored Division and (*see* 1st Armored Division); flight of the Shalikashvili family from Warsaw in 1944, 35–36; Rudy Grice and, 142–44; home improvement projects and, 212–13; humor and, 144–45, 146, 162; immigrant experience and, 317, 321–22; influence of Dimitri and Missy on, 18, 19, 278–80; intelligence as an officer, 207–9; Kurdish refugee crisis and (*see* Kurdish refugee crisis of 1991); leadership and (*see* leadership and Shalikashvili); Winifred Luthy and, 72; marriage to and death of Gunhild Bartsch, 178–80, 186–87, 212; marriage to Joan Zimpelman, 187–88; mastery of logistics, 158–59; mechanical engineering degree, 94; at the Military Personnel Center, 205–6; naturalized as an American citizen, 15, 93, 317; Naval War College and, 205, 208, 285; 9th Infantry Division and (*see* Alaska; 9th Infantry Division); Roger O'Dwyer and, 117, 124, 126, 127–30; Old World ancestors, 1–2, 3, 4, 17–18, 63–69; Operation Provide Comfort and (*see* Operation Provide Comfort); Operation Steel Box and, 165–66; overall assessment of the life and career of, 320–22; patriotism and, 317–18; peacetime draft and, 93–95, 275–76; Pentagon assignments from 1981–1989, 206–7, 215, 248; personality as a young man, 28–31; personal values, 314–15; physical features and presence of, 28, 29, 163; Colin Powell and (*see* Powell, Colin);

Shalikashvili, John (*cont.*)
  promotions, ambition, and career
    path, 211–26, 242–44, 292–93;
    public retirement ceremony, 291–
    92, 293–95; Regular Army Com-
    mission and, 129–30, 145–46;
    relationship with Butch Saint,
    221–24; reluctance as an ado-
    lescent to speak about his family
    history, 280–81, 286–87; reputa-
    tion as a polyglot, 164; VII Corps
    and, 156–58, 161; siblings of,
    36–37; similarity to Dimitri as a
    military officer, 279, 321; skills in
    understanding complexity, setting
    standards, and communicating
    clearly, 159–62; stroke and other
    late-life health issues, 306–10;
    as Supreme Allied Commander
    Europe, 11, 13, 242–43, 248–49,
    293; surname pronunciation, 11;
    as a team player, 218–19; uncer-
    tainty about life as a young man,
    112–15; at UN headquarters in
    Korea, 205; Vietnam War expe-
    riences, 233–37, 247, 318; visit
    to Georgia, *305;* wartime life
    and experiences in Warsaw, 45,
    46; Lester Wheeler and, 145–46,
    148; work ethic, 215–16; experi-
    ences with Jews, 283–84, 286,
    319; Anita Ziegler and, 113–14,
    115, 285
Shalikashvili, Maria ("Missy"): atti-
    tude toward Jews, 281–82; birth
    and childhood of, 66, 68–69;
    children of, 36–37; death of
    father, 41; Dimitri as a POW of
    the British and, 59, 109–10; Dim-
    itri's 1945 mission to Italy and,
    58, 59; Dimitri's unpublished
    memoirs and, 256, 286; emigra-

tion of the Shalikashvili family to
    America, 62–63, 73; emotion ver-
    sus reason in, 282; first encoun-
    ter with Dimitri, 69, 106–7; flight
    of the Shalikashvili family from
    Warsaw to Pappenheim, 35–36,
    47; influence on John's values
    and abilities, 18, 19, 278–80;
    John's capacity for empathy and,
    314–15; at John's high school
    graduation, 34; postwar life in
    Pappenheim, 52–53, 60–61; reac-
    tion to Dimitri's joining the Geor-
    gian Legion, 281, 282; stroke
    and, 306; Warsaw Georgian Col-
    ony and, 42–43; wartime life in
    Pappenheim, 53–54, 58, 59; war-
    time life in Warsaw and Skoli-
    mow, 38–47
Shalikashvili, Nina, 37, 99, 110, 111
Shalikashvili, Othar ("Joe"): birth
    name, 36; childhood in Pappen-
    heim, 4, 6, 54, 259; childhood in
    Warsaw, 36, 44, 45, 46, 47, *55,*
    259; controversy over Dimitri's
    war record and, 259; on Dimi-
    tri and the Katyn Forest massa-
    cre, 41; on Dimitri's and Missy's
    influence on John, 278–80; on
    Dimitri's service in the Georgian
    Legion, 263; emigration of the
    Shalikashvili family to Amer-
    ica, 62, 73; enlistment in the US
    Army, 90–92; on grandmother
    Marie Rudiger-Bielaieff, 63; hand
    grenade accident, 92; on John
    and Gunhild Bartsch, 179, 212;
    on John as a college student, 114;
    on John's childhood personal-
    ity, 57, 58; on John's command
    of the 9th Infantry Division,
    220; on John's lying to the Sen-

ate confirmation committee about knowledge of Dimitri's war service, 319; on John's most important career achievement, 311; on John's patriotism, 317; on John's promotions and ambitions, 215; on the Luthy family, 311
Shalikashvili, Prince Elisbar, 100
Shalikashvili, Prince Jean Osipovich, 90, *91*
Shalikashvili, Prince Jevanchir, 100
Shalikashvili, Prince Joatham, 100
Shalikashvili, Prince O'tar, 90
Shalikashvili, Prince Rostom Ier, 100
Shalikashvili, Tamara, 99, 101, 110, 111
Shalikashvili family: crest of, 100; emigration to America, 62, 63, 69–73; flight from Warsaw to Pappenheim, 3, 35–36, 47, 53–54, 259; impact of World War II on Dimitri's mother and siblings, 110–11; life in Pappenheim during World War II, 1–6, 52–59; lineage in Georgia, 17–18, 90, *91,* 100–101; Winifred Luthy and, 71–72, 73; naturalization as American citizens, 15, 93, 317; Old World aristocratic values and their influence on John, 17–18, 63–69, 313–14; postwar life in Pappenheim, 52–53, 59–61; as stateless refugees from World War II, 38
SHAPE. *See* Supreme Allied Headquarters Allied Powers Europe
Shelton, Hugh, 291, 299–300, 304, 314
Shelton, Sharon, 201
Shoffner, Wilson ("Dutch"), 160, 161, 218
Shook, Albert, 124–25

Short, Coy, 120, 124
Silopi, 173
Simon Wiesenthal Center, 255–56, 269
Sinai, 248
Sinnreich, Rick, 220
Sisiki, Norman, 232
ski patrols, 140, *141. See also* Alaska
Skolimow, 38–39, 40, 41
Slagle, Jim, 120
Slivinsky (Polish doctor), 37
Smith, Perry M., 208
Snow Hall, 120, 123
Somalia, 298, 315
Sorenson, Wilbert, 121
South Korea, 205
Soviet Union: escape of the Rudiger-Bielaieff family from, 68
Spain, 196
Specter, Arlen, 270
square meals, 119
SS Waffengruppe Georgien, 265–67
Staar, Richard, 285
Stalin, Joseph, 282
standards: Shalikashvili's skill in setting and communicating, 159–62
Stanford University, 304
Starosselsky, Dmitry, 71, 100–101
Starosselsky, Vesevold, 101
Starosselsky family, 100–101
Steilacoom, 304, 307
Stephanopoulos, George, 12
Stevenson, Adlai, II, 258
Stotler, Jim, 129
St. Petersburg, 64, 65, 71, 100, 101, 102
stroke, 306–10
Strykers, 218
St. Thomas, 71
Sub-Task Force Express Care, 153
Sullivan, Gordon, 247
Supreme Allied Commander Europe (SACEUR): John Galvin as, 193; George Joulwan replaces

Supreme Allied Commander Europe (*cont.*)
Shalikashvili as, 272; Shalikashvili as, 11, 13, 242–43, 248–49, 293
Supreme Allied Headquarters Allied Powers Europe (SHAPE), 254

Taiwan, 298
Talabani, Jalal, 198, 231
Tatar Regiment, 101
Taylor, J. B., 166, 201, 214, 216, 217
Tbilisi, 99, 100, 102, 103
Tenet, George, 291
10th Special Forces Group, 171, 230
Texas Western College, 178
Thanoon, Nashwan, 191–92, 211
Thatcher, Margaret, 245
Theta Chi fraternity, 92, 114
3rd Cavalry Regiment (Free Georgia), 102
3rd Marine Division, 237
Third US Air Force, 161
39th Special Operations Wing (USAF), 171
32nd Army Air Defense Command (AADCOM), 161, 162
Thirty Years' War, 50
Thompson, Gerald, 184, 188, 222, 223, 224
Three Pillars of Leadership, 187
Thresher, Colby, 148–49
Thurmond, Strom, 270
TRADOC. *See* training and operational doctrine
Tragedy Assistance Program for Survivors, 179–80, 304
training and operational doctrine (TRADOC), 217
Treuchtlingen, 54
Trieu Phong, 234, *236*
Truman, Harry S., 93

Tsulukidze, Michail Fridon, 265, 266, 267
tuberculosis, 73
Turkey: Kurdish refugee crisis of 1991 and, 135, 138–39 (*see also* Kurdish refugee crisis of 1991); Kurdish refugees of 1988 and, 137, 139; Operation Proven Force and, 167; Operation Provide Comfort and, 167–68, 173, 198, 199; Dimitri Shalikashvili's mission to, 103
Turkish Armed Forces, 198
Tym, Alice, 258, 313, 321
typhoid, 173

Udine, 107, 266
UH-60A Black Hawk helicopters, *152*
United Nations, 151, 196–98
United Nations Children's Fund (UNICEF), 173
United Nations High Commissioner for Refugees (UNHCR), 138, 196–97, 198, 229
UN Truce Supervisory Organization, 248
US Agency for International Development, 196
USAREUR. *See* US Army Europe
US Army Artillery and Guided Missile School, 120, 158
US Army Europe (USAREUR): Shalikashvili and movement of the VII Corps to the Persian Gulf, 156–64; Shalikashvili and Operation Steel Box, 165–66; Shalikashvili as a community commander, 183–86; Shalikashvili nominated to replace Butch Saint as head of, 242, 293; Shalikashvili's air defense operations center innovations, 161;

Shalikashvili's relationship with Butch Saint, 221–24; Shalikashvili's worldly mystique and, 164–65

US Army Southern European Task Force (SETAF), 213, 214

US Department of Defense: cost of Operation Provide Comfort, 175; Shalikashvili's Joint Chiefs of Staff confirmation hearing and the controversy over Dimitri's war record, 256; Shalikashvili's Pentagon assignments from 1981–1989, 206–7, 215, 248

US European Command (EUCOM), 151–52, 193, 194, 195

US military: Clinton and credibility issues, 249–50, 299; defense budget cuts of 1993, 246; downsizing under Shalikashvili as chairman of the Joint Chiefs of Staff, 298–99; homosexuals in (see gays in the military); nontraditional military missions under Shalikashvili as chairman of the Joint Chiefs of Staff, 297–98; Shalikashvili and "jointness," 204–6, 299; Shalikashvili and the civil-military relationship, 299–300; Shalikashvili's dedication to the military family, 301–3; Shalikashvili's development of competency through holistic training, 203–7; Joe Shalikashvili's enlistment in the army, 90–92

US Senate Foreign Relations Committee, 137

values: Shalikashvili and Old World aristocratic values, 17–18, 19, 63–69, 313–14; Shalikashvili's key personal values, 314–15

Van Brero, Gay, 181, 222

Vietnam War: Operation Fisher, 237; Colin Powell's experiences, 244–45; Shalikashvili's experiences, 233–37, 247, 318

visa regulations: Shalikashvili family entry into the US and, 72–73, 257–58

Volk, P. J., 317–18

Volkssturm, 5–6

Waffen-SS: the controversy over Dimitri Shalikashvili's war record with, 256, 264, 268–71; distinguished from the Allgemeine-SS, 264, 268; John's comments on and denials of knowing about Dimitri's service with, 269, 270–71, 277–78, 319–20; John's knowledge of Dimitri's service with, 280–81, 286, 319–20; Dimitri Shalikashvili's mission to Italy with, 264–68

Walker, Jack, 200, 203, 208

War College (Poland), 105

Warner, John, 271

Warsaw: flight of the Shalikashvili family from, 3, 35–36, 47, 259; impact of the early war experiences on John, 78–81, 312–13; John's birth and christening in, 37–38; Rudiger-Bielaieff family residence, 69; Missy Shalikashvili's attitude toward Jews, 281–82; wartime experiences of Missy Shalikashvili and family in, 38, 39–40, 41–47, 259

Warsaw Georgian Colony, 42–43, 107, 261, 262

Warsaw Ghetto, 281

Warsaw Uprising, 3, 35, 45–47, 259

Wayne, John, 15

Weaver, Rex, 182

Wehrersatzinspektion, 3, 4
Weinberger, Caspar, 309
Weisberg, Jacob, 255
Weissenberg, 54, 58
Wentburg Estate, 71
West Point, 92
Wheeler, Helen, 146, 148
Wheeler, Lester L., 145–46, 147, 148
White, John, 291
"Why Generals Get Nervous" (Powell), 246
Wilhelm, Guy, 121
Winter Palace, 66, 67
Wood, Kimba M., 256
Working Friendly campaign, 185
World War I, 66, 68, 71, 101–2
World War II: effects of childhood war experiences on Shalikashvili, 78–81, 282–85, 286–87, 311–13, 315–16; experiences of Missy Shalikashvili and family in Warsaw and Skolimow, 38–47, 259; flight of the Shalikashvili family from Warsaw to Pappenheim, 3, 35–36, 47, 53–54, 259; impact on Marie Rudiger-Bielaieff, 63; impact on Dimitri Shalikashvili's mother and siblings, 110–11; impact on the Pappenheim family

and village, 51–52; invasions of Poland in 1939, 38; Katyn Forest massacre, 41–42; Dimitri Shalikashvili as a POW of the British in Italy, 59, 98, 107–10; Dimitri Shalikashvili as a POW of the Germans, 39, 40–41, 107, 259; Shalikashvili family and life in Pappenheim during, 1–6; Dimitri Shalikashvili's military service with Germany in the Georgian Legion, 43, 47, 54, 58–59, 99, 107, 260–68 (*see also* Georgian Legion; Waffen-SS); Dimitri Shalikashvili's military service with Poland, 38, 99, 106, 107, 261; Warsaw Uprising, 3, 35, 45–47, 259
Wright, Stewart, 181, 201

Yakima training center, 163
Yukon Command, 145

Zakho, 137, 190, 191, 192, 195, 231
Ziegler, Anita, 113–14, 115, 285
Zimpelman, Joan, 187–88. *See also* Shalikashvili, Joan
Zinni, Anthony, 152, 155

www.ingramcontent.com/pod-product-compliance
Lightning Source LLC
Chambersburg PA
CBHW020336100426
42812CB00029B/3146/J